BTEC L2 First in IT

Second Edition

Orders: please contact Bookpoint Ltd, 130 Milton Park, Abingdon, Oxon OX14 4SB.
Telephone: (44) 01235 827720. Fax: (44) 01235 400454. Lines are open from 9.00 to 5.00,
Monday to Saturday, with a 24 hour message answering service. You can also order through
our website www.hoddereducation.co.uk

If you have any comments to make about this, or any of our other titles, please
send them to educationenquiries@hodder.co.uk

British Library Cataloguing in Publication Data
A catalogue record for this title is available from the British Library

ISBN: 978 1 444 110500

First Edition Published 2006
This Edition Published 2011
Impression number   10 9 8 7 6 5 4 3 2 1
Year   2015, 2014, 2013, 2012, 2011

Hachette UK's policy is to use papers that are natural, renewable and
recyclable products and made from wood grown in sustainable forests.
The logging and manufacturing processes are expected to conform to the
environmental regulations of the country of origin.

This material has been endorsed by Edexcel and offers high quality support for the delivery
of Edexcel qualifications.

Edexcel endorsement does not mean that this material is essential to achieve any Edexcel
qualification, nor does it mean that this is the only suitable material available to support any
Edexcel qualification. No endorsed material will be used verbatim in setting any Edexcel
examination and any resource lists produced by Edexcel shall include this and other appropriate
texts. While this material has been through an Edexcel quality assurance process, all
responsibility for the content remains with the publisher. Copies of official specifications
for all Edexcel qualifications may be found on the Edexcel website - www.edexcel.com

Cover photo © Johann Helgason/Alamy
Typeset by Pantek Arts
Printed in Italy for Hodder Education, an Hachette UK Company, 338 Euston Road, London NW1 3BH
by LEGO.

BTEC L2 First in IT

Second Edition

Mark Fishpool and Bernadette Fishpool

Contents

Acknowledgements

Mark- For students past, present *and future*.

Every effort has been made to trace and acknowledge ownership of copyright. The publishers will be glad to make suitable arrangements with any copyright holders whom it has not been possible to contact.

The authors and publishers would like to thank the following for the use of images in this volume. Screenshots of Microsoft products used with permission from Microsoft.

1.11 TTS Demo; **1.12** The Official Google Blog **http://googleblog.blogspot.com/**; **1.14 www.gametrailers.com**; **1.15 http://www.bbc.co.uk/iplayer**; **1.16 http://www. islington.org.uk/**; **1.17** © CEOP Child Exploitation and Online Protection Centre. All rights reserved 2006-11; **3.19, 3.20, 3.21, 3.29** Linux; **3.22** Google Chrome; **3.23** Piriform's Defraggler; **3.24** WinRAR; **3.30, 9.1** AVG Technologies CZ, s.r.o.; **4.7** Wikipedia.org **http:// upload.wikimedia.org/wikipedia/en/timeline/a048814763412f40be7c6773f81ad7e7. png**; **4.8** Google; **7.9** Gigabyte Technology; **9.14** ©2010 Amazon.com Inc. and its affiliates. All rights reserved; **17.3** Namesco Limited; **17.4 www.bloglines.com**; **17.6** © 2011 McDonald's; **17.7 www.bbc.co.uk/news**; **17.14** Mozilla firefox; **17.16 www.ebay. com**; **17.21** Streamline.net; **17.23** Adobe product screenshot(s) reprinted with permission from Adobe Systems Incorporated Adobe® Flash®; **17.24, 17.26, 17.27** Adobe® Dreamweaver®; **18.7** Visual Solutions; **23.4** Adobe® Photoshop®; **23.7, 23.11, 23.20 www.gimp.org**; **23.16** Corel Paint shop Pro.

Photo credits

1.4 John Birdsall/Press Association Images; **1.5** © iStockphoto.com/Steve Lucker; **1.6** paulo cruz – Fotolia; **1.13** AVAVA – Fotolia; **2.4** © yobidaba – Fotolia; **3.1** Alexey Stiop – Fotolia; **3.2** Norman Chan – Fotolia; **3.3** Vladimir Liverts – Fotolia; **3.4** dinostock – Fotolia; **3.5** Vladyslav Danilin – Fotolia; **3.6** Entropia – Fotolia; **3.7** © Roger Davies / Alamy; **3.8** Marc Dietrich – Fotolia; **3.12** Roman Milert – Fotolia; **3.13** alessandrozocc – Fotolia; **3.14** WuTtY – Fotolia; **3.15** pwillitts – Fotolia; **3.16** soilbedust – Fotolia; **4.2** Ron Jingling/ Spokane Community College; **7.1** © Jacob Hamblin/iStockphoto.com; **7.2** © Michael Ventura / Alamy; **7.4** Lusoimages – Fotolia; **7.5** Eray – Fotolia; **7.6** Bestshortstop – Fotolia; **7.7** © SAV / Alamy; **7.8** Norman Chan – Fotolia; **9.19a** by-studio – Fotolia; **9.19b** Vasilis Akoinoglou – Fotolia; **10.12** Marc Dietrich – Fotolia; **10.13** Sergii Shcherbakov – Fotolia; **10.14** Scanrail – Fotolia; **10.15** Leonid Smirnov – Fotolia; **10.16** Alex Vasilev – Fotolia; **10.17** MWiner – Fotolia; **10.19** Vladimir Liverts – Fotolia; **10.24** ZetaZeta – Fotolia; **10.25** airborne77 – Fotolia; **10.26** Vtls – Fotolia; **10.31** Fluke Corporation; **23.1** © Christopher Gould / Alamy; **23.13** © Lesley Pegrum / Alamy.

Introduction

Welcome to the BTEC First in IT!

Although BTEC First qualifications have been around since 1983, this **revised** version of the qualification is designed to fit into the new Qualifications and Credit Framework (QCF) so it is brand new for September 2010!

The BTEC First in IT is an example of a **level 2 qualification** and it is broadly equivalent to studying four GCSEs. For this reason you will often see the title of this course written as the Edexcel BTEC **Level 2** Diploma in IT. As most educational professionals and employers still call them BTEC Firsts we have decided to follow suit in this book.

BTEC First in IT are traditionally studied in school or at a Further Education (FE) college. They are designed to give you a robust and challenging introduction to the world of Information Technology – providing you with the **knowledge** and (most importantly) the **practical skills** necessary to enter the workplace or progress on to level 3 study.

About the qualification

To complete a BTEC First in IT you have to **successfully complete** a number of **credits**. Your course will be broken down into a number of different subjects called '**units**'. Successful completion of each unit will generate a number of credits (usually 5 or 10).

There are actually **three nested** qualifications within the BTEC First in IT family. The following diagram shows how the qualification grows as you achieve more credits:

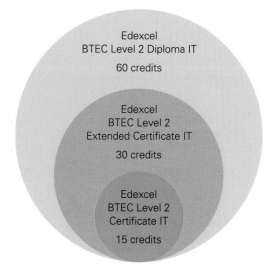

Edexcel
BTEC Level 2 Diploma IT
60 credits

Edexcel
BTEC Level 2
Extended Certificate IT
30 credits

Edexcel
BTEC Level 2
Certificate IT
15 credits

The structure of the BTEC First in IT

It is important to remember that the qualification **builds** as you study. This means that the 15 credits you earn for the Certificate will **contribute towards** the 30 credits you need for the Extended Certificate – you would **only** need to complete 15 more credits.

Units and coverage in this book

Although some units are **mandatory** – you have to study these – there is a wide menu of optional units from which your school or college can choose. At the time of publication there are 36 units listed in the BTEC First in IT specification but it would be impossible for this book to cover all of these!

What we have attempted to do is to provide coverage for **all** the **mandatory units** for the Certificate, Extended Certificate and Diploma and those which are the **most popular optional units** taught by schools and colleges across the country.

The grid below shows how this book supports the three nested qualifications by covering these 12 crucial units. Remember, even for a Diploma you only need 60 credits.

Unit number	Unit title	Credit value	Certificate	Extended Certificate	Diploma
1	Communicating in the IT Industry	5	M	M	M
2	Working in the IT Industry	5	O	M	M
3	Computer Systems	10	O	O	M
4	Business IT Skills	10	O	O	O
7	Installing Computer Hardware	10	O	O	O
9	Customising Software	10	O	O	O
10	Setting up an IT Network	10	O	O	O
16	Database Systems	10	O	O	O
17	Website Development	10	O	O	O
18	Software Design	10	O	O	O
23	Computer Graphics	10	O	O	O
27	Spreadsheet Modelling	10	X	OS	OS

Key: M = Mandatory, O = Optional, OS=Optional Special, X = not studied

Book coverage by unit.

An Introduction to Grading

Each unit has a number of **grading criteria** which will be used to assess you. It is likely that your teacher will give you an **assignment** which covers a number of criteria for a unit and that you may need to complete multiple assignments for each unit. These assignments will vary from unit to unit and this is very much the decision of your centre although Edexcel do provide guidance, examples and quality assurance to ensure that standards are similar nationally.

Criteria are designated **Pass** (P), **Merit** (M) or **Distinction** (D) and it is fair to say that Merits and Distinctions are much tougher to achieve than Passes. Units do not have the same number of grading criteria but generally each unit has more Passes than Merits and more Merits than Distinctions. Each criterion is numbered, for example the first Pass criterion is called **P1**, the second is called **P2** and so on. Each chapter in this book shows you all the grading criteria for the unit it covers so you should be in no doubt what is required!

In order to help you achieve, we have **linked** the criteria to the learning content throughout the book so you will always be able to use the '**Make the grade**' boxes to help you understand what you need to evidence to achieve each criterion.

How grading works

Step 1 – work out the **unit grade** for each unit.

In order to achieve a Pass for a unit you must achieve **all** Pass criteria.

In order to achieve a Merit for a unit you must achieve **all** Pass **and all** Merit criteria.

In order to achieve a Distinction for a unit you must achieve **all criteria listed** (Pass, Merit and Distinction).

Step 2 – work out the **points** for each unit.

Each unit has a **point value** calculated from its **credit value** (5 or 10) and the **grade** you achieve (Pass, Merit or Distinction).

The table below shows the number of points scored depending on the unit's credit value and grade:

Unit credit value	Pass	Merit	Distinction
5	25 points	30 points	35 points
10	50 points	60 points	70 points

Points per grade and unit credit value

Step 3 – work out the **overall grade**.

Each of the three nested qualifications can have an **overall grade** between Pass and Distinction*.

The following table illustrates these ranges.

Qualification	Points range			
	Pass	**Merit**	**Distinction**	**Distinction***
BTEC Level 2 Certificate	75-84	85–94	95–99	100 and above
BTEC Level 2 Extended Certificate	150-169	170–189	190–199	200 and above
BTEC Level 2 Diploma	300-339	340–379	380–399	400 and above

Overall grades and point ranges

In order to calculate the overall grade you will need to **add together** the points you have achieved on **each unit**.

Step 4 – a worked example

Aled completes a BTEC Level 2 Certificate in IT, studying Units 1 and 3 (15 credits in total).

He gets a **Merit** for Unit 1 and a **Pass** for Unit 3. This is how we work out his **overall grade**.

Unit number	Unit title	Credit value	Grade	Calculation
1	Communicating in the IT Industry	5	Merit	30 +
3	Computer Systems	10	Pass	50 +
			Total points	80 =
			Overall grade	**Pass**

Overall grades and point ranges

As you can see, Aled passes his qualification but doesn't **quite** get enough points to get a merit: He would have needed a minimum of 85.

For more information, please visit: http://www.edexcel.com/quals/firsts10/it/Pages/default.aspx

Unit 1
Communicating in the IT industry

Learning objectives

By the end of this unit you should:

1. Be able to communicate information to suit audience, purpose and content
2. Be able to use IT tools to communicate and exchange information
3. Understand the impact of IT on individuals, communities and society.

In order to pass this unit, the evidence you present for assessment needs to demonstrate that you can meet all of the above learning outcomes for this unit. The criteria below show the levels of achievement required to pass this unit.

To achieve a **pass** grade the evidence must show that the learner is able to:	To achieve a **merit** grade the evidence must show that, in addition to the pass criteria, the learner is able to:	To achieve a **distinction** the evidence must show that, in addition to the pass and merit criteria, the learner is able to:
P1 Demonstrate effective interpersonal skills in face-to-face communication		
P2 Communicate IT-related information to a technical audience		
P3 Communicate IT-related information to a non-technical audience		
P4 Use IT tools safely to effectively communicate and exchange information		
P5 Select, set up and use a specialist communication channel to communicate and exchange information	**M1** Justify why a specialist communication channel is effective for a given purpose	**D1** Explain how to ensure safe and secure use of a specialist communication channel
P6 Explain the social impacts of the use of IT	**M2** Discuss the potential threats which the use of IT has introduced	

Introduction

To succeed in the world of work it is very important that you demonstrate good communication skills and show that you can communicate with a range of different audiences, such as technical as well as non-technical staff.

In this unit you will learn some of the techniques that will help you to become a successful communicator. You will learn various methods of communication and have the chance to show that you can use a range of IT tools confidently to support communication.

You will be assessed through coursework which could be in the form of:

- Presentations
- Videos
- Witness statements and evidence log
- Role play
- Web pages
- User guides
- Proofs (before and after versions of documents)
- Blogs.

1.1 Communicate information to suit audience, purpose and content

This section will cover the following grading criteria: **P1** **P2** **P3**

1.1.1 General communication skills

Adapting content and style to audience

> ## Activity A
>
> #### Texting
>
> Think about the times when you use your mobile phone to text your family and friends. Do you always write words in full or do you sometimes use abbreviations or shortcuts like the examples shown below?
>
> CUL8R (See you later)
> DKDC (Don't know, don't care)
> TG2BT (Too good to be true)
> EOD (End of discussion)
> ILBL8 (I'll be late)
> WAM (Wait a minute)
>
> In small groups, discuss how you use text messages and think about the following questions:
>
> 1. Do you usually use full words or do you use abbreviations when you write a text?
>
> 2. Would you find any of the examples above in a formal letter? If not, why not?
>
> 3. When is it appropriate to use abbreviations and when would it not be?

Do you adapt the way you speak when communicating with different people?

With friends you might use slang words or abbreviations which your parents, grandparents or carers might not understand.

When presenting to your class about an IT-related subject, you might use technical terminology because you will be able to assume that the other students and teachers will be able to understand what you are saying.

If communicating on behalf of a business, however, you will require a more formal style: avoiding slang, expanding abbreviations and using subject-specific terminology only if the audience is able to understand it.

Communication skills are, therefore, split into two parts:

1. Being able to modulate your voice, use terminology appropriately and select the right format for the situation and audience.
2. Being able to recognise what a situation and audience requires in the first place!

Either way, you will need to make the way you communicate interesting to make sure that your audience listens to you. How you use your voice is a good place to start!

Using the right words and saying things in the right way can be learnt and will become easier with practice.

To communicate effectively, use this as a general checklist:

- Modulate your voice (it makes listening to you much more interesting)
- Choose the right terminology (do not use technical language or jargon unless you are sure that your audience will understand)
- Choose the right format (abbreviations are acceptable when texting; write words in full in a formal letter or email).

There are many websites that can provide practical help for those who need to improve their general communication skills. Some examples are given in Table 1.1.

Activity B

Did you know?

Say the following sentences out loud and listen carefully to the way in which you say them:

Can we go out now?
I said we would go out later.

What you should notice when you read these two sentences is that when you read the first one, the question, the pitch of your voice will rise when you say the last word. This is something you will have learned to do naturally and is a common way to stress to a listener that you have asked a question.

With the second sentence, a simple statement, your voice will go down when you say the last word because it is a statement and your voice pitching downwards will stress that the sentence has ended. Again you will have learned to do this naturally and it is perfectly normal.

Skill	Website
• Modulation: changing pitch and understanding why you do this • Using repetition • Making your voice interesting	http://changingminds.org/techniques/language/modifying_meaning/modulation.htm
How to use emphasis (and how using emphasis can change the meaning of what you say)	http://changingminds.org/techniques/language/modifying_meaning/emphasis.htm

Table 1.1

Providing accurate information

Activity C

How accurate are you?

Answer this question: How tall are you?

Did you answer the question accurately?

Let us say that you are 162.5 cm tall. Were you that specific when you answered the question?

Did you say you were 163 cm tall? (You would have rounded up the actual value to a whole number.)

Or did you say 'I am about 160 cm tall' (an understatement) or 'I am about 165 cm tall' (an overstatement)?

How accurately you provide the information will depend on how accurate the information needs to be.

When you are asked about your height, does it really matter how accurate you are? That will depend on what the information will be used for.

On the other hand, imagine you are selling an item on eBay®. If you advertise the item as being 'blue' then it must actually be blue, otherwise you are breaching the Trades Description Act 1968. This means that you are breaking the law because you are misleading potential buyers by making incorrect claims about the item.

Accuracy in information is not just about being precise, but is also about thinking about how you present the information to your audience. Look at Figure 1.1. What is it about?

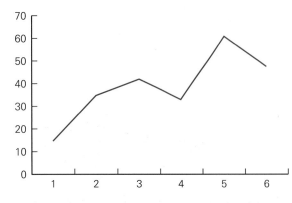

Figure 1.1

You probably have no idea! What about if we add some additional information (see Figure 1.2)?

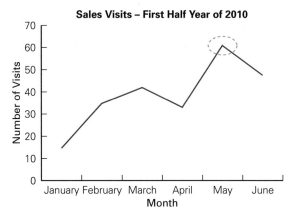

Figure 1.2

Now the data makes more sense. By adding a title (Sales Visits – First Half Year of 2010) it is clear what the data is about. The values on the y-axis are now clearly marked as being number of visits and the scale has been identified. In addition, x-axis values have been included so that each spike or dip on the graph can be connected with a particular month. If we now look at the highest peak on the graph (circled in green for clarity), what does this information tell us? It tells us that in May 2010 more than 60 visits were made in the month and that this was the highest peak over the six-month period. In a meeting situation, this may well have been the right level of detail as the exact amount over the 60 was probably less important than the fact that May was the best month.

As discussed previously, the skill you need to develop is being able to identify when you can be nearly accurate, when you must be totally precise and how to present the information in a meaningful way.

Techniques for engaging an audience

The best presentations are those that are done in an interesting way. This can be achieved by:

- Having different speakers for different parts of the presentation (so the audience hears different voices). This may not always be possible.
- Including a **brief** personal story (anecdote) to emphasise a point.
- Using handouts to provide extra information rather than trying to cover too much in the presentation itself.
- Having something visual to keep the audience interested – PowerPoint® slides, an animation or a moving image. Some presentation software packages have tools to spin words or images. This can add emphasis. Learn how to use the tools in your presentation software so you can bring your presentations to life. Be careful not to use too much of any one software tool as this too can become boring!

Activity D

Giving presentations

It can be daunting to give a presentation, so you might find it helpful to watch the following short clip entitled 'Presentation skills – How to improve your presentations'.

http://www.youtube.com/watch?v=bt8YFCveNpY

The clip contains a short presentation and some feedback from a specialist about what could have been done better.

Ensuring the message gets across

Check that your audience has understood the message you are trying to get across.

Have a question and answer (Q&A) session to give your audience an opportunity to interact with you. Allowing them to ask you questions or indeed you asking them questions can liven up a session.

1.1.2 Interpersonal skills

Communicating with other people is not just about what you say but is also about understanding other visible clues like body language – not just the body language *you* display, but the body language and other signs that the person you are talking to is displaying as well.

The next section explores some of these.

Methods for communicating interpersonally

Talking to another person is known as a verbal exchange and this is clearly easy for those of us who can hear. But what about those who are unable to hear at all, or who have limited hearing? For such people there are two main options – signing and lip reading.

Signing is based on a particular set of movements and hand positions. The discussion literally takes place with each person making the movements or positions to represent the words of a discussion.

Some words have to be spelled out letter by letter (using the finger alphabet), but other more common words can have a movement, series of movements or a specific position as you can see with the symbol for noon (midday) shown in Figure 1.3.

Figure 1.3 This position represents the sign language for 'noon'

Activity E

Sign language

Can you spell your name using the finger alphabet? Use the link below and teach yourself!

http://www.learnsignlanguage.co.uk/ uploaded_images/bsl-alphabet-761657. gif

If you would like to explore more words and sentences, the British Sign Language website is full of useful information:

http://www.britishsignlanguage.com/

Activity F

Lip reading

Stand in front of a mirror and make an 'ee' sound. You should notice that your own mouth position is the same as that shown in Figure 1.4. Make each of the vowel sounds (A, E, I, O, U) and see how your mouth position changes. Try to remember these positions.

Techniques and cues

Body language

Body language can tell its own story! Can you identify the emotions being displayed by the person in Figure 1.5?

Many people (both hearing and hearing impaired) can also lip read. To lip read, you need to teach yourself to recognise the shapes that are made by someone's mouth when they speak letters and vowels. Some people find this relatively easy to learn because everyone makes the same mouth shapes when they speak. In Figure 1.4, the person is making an 'ee' sound.

Figure 1.5 What is this person's body language telling you?

The person in the picture is unhappy and possibly even angry as they have their arms folded.

Figure 1.4 Signing and mouthing words

What about the person in Figure 1.6? If you were talking to this person, do you think they would be showing much interest in what you were saying?

Figure 1.6 How does this person feel?

Think about body language next time you are in class. It is often how your teacher knows whether you are taking part in your lesson or not.

Use of intonation
Similarly, as suggested earlier in this unit, your vocal intonation can give the person you are talking to clues about the way you are feeling. Changes in intonation are very difficult to describe in writing, but here are a few examples:

Speaking s-l-o-w-l-y and deliberately. If someone speaks to you in this way, it can often be a sign of their frustration. They are speaking in this way because they do not feel that you understand what they are saying.

If someone is SHOUTING, they are probably angry!

As previously mentioned, by raising your voice in pitch on the last word or syllable of a sentence, you are indicating to the other person that you are asking a question!

Use of emoticons
When communicating in writing, there are no visual cues or clues that you can observe, so in this situation there are other ways that you can make your point or share your emotions.

Emoticons are a representation of an emotion such as happy or sad that can be shared with someone in writing. Let us have a look at some examples. In each case, the key presses you need to make the emoticon are shown:

| : and) | (colon and right round bracket) | ☺ (happy) |
| : and (| (colon and left round bracket) | ☹ (sad) |

There are lots more examples on the internet and even some animated ones that you can send in emails. The link below has a range of emoticons with their meanings:

http://messenger.msn.com/Resource/Emoticons.aspx

In texting, you can also use the emoticon shortcut keys as abbreviations. You could say 'I am looking forward to seeing you' and end it with a :) – meaning that you are smiling as you write the text.

Capitalisation of text in emails
Sometimes, if we are trying to stress something in writing, particularly in an email, we could be tempted to put it in capital letters. For example: 'I am really ANGRY about this.'

Using capital letters in this way in an email is considered to be bad netiquette (internet etiquette – a way of behaving online) because the use of capitals can be interpreted as shouting!

Positive and negative language

Think about the words you use when you talk to other people. Try as much as possible to say things in a positive way. Even negative things can be said in a more positive and supportive way. Think about these sentences:

> 'Jane, you are obviously not very committed to this course.'

That statement is very critical. It could be softened by saying:

> 'At the moment, Jane, you are possibly not as committed to this course as I know you could be.'

It still conveys the same message – just not as harshly.

If you have to say something negative, try saying it a more positive way – you will find it very useful when dealing with difficult situations in the future.

Paying attention and active engagement

It is common courtesy to pay attention when someone is speaking to you. Trying to have a conversation (or teach) someone who is clearly not paying attention is both irritating and frustrating.

So how can you show a person you are talking to that you are interested in what they are saying?

- Give them eye contact.
- Nod occasionally if you are in agreement.
- Summarise what was said to you (repeat the main points of an exchange).
- Paraphrase (use your own words to explain what has been said to show you understand).

Using these techniques will help you to show the other person that you are interested in what they have to say. This is known as active engagement.

Make the grade

For this criterion you must show that you can communicate effectively in face-to-face situations. You will need to do this well at least three times for you to achieve P1. These communications might be videoed or your teacher(s) may complete a witness statement. Example communications could include an informal group discussion, a more formal role play or an individual tutorial where you are negotiating targets.

Make sure you apply the skills you have learned in the first part of this unit. Use the right terminology and language, make sure that any information you share is accurate, use technology or other aids where possible and make sure that you use positive and negative language with care. Show that you can be interested in any discussion.

1.1.3 Communicating in writing

Many of the techniques we have considered that form good practice in face-to-face communication also apply when you communicate in writing. But when communicating in writing there are some additional things to think about.

Following guidelines and procedures

When it comes to written documents that are designed for communication, such as letters and emails, there are many different styles and structures that you could use. Which one you choose for personal letters is certainly up to you. But an organisation is likely to have adopted a 'house style' – that is a particular way that letters or other business documents should be laid out. In the two examples that follow, the actual content is identical, it is merely the structure and layout that change between them.

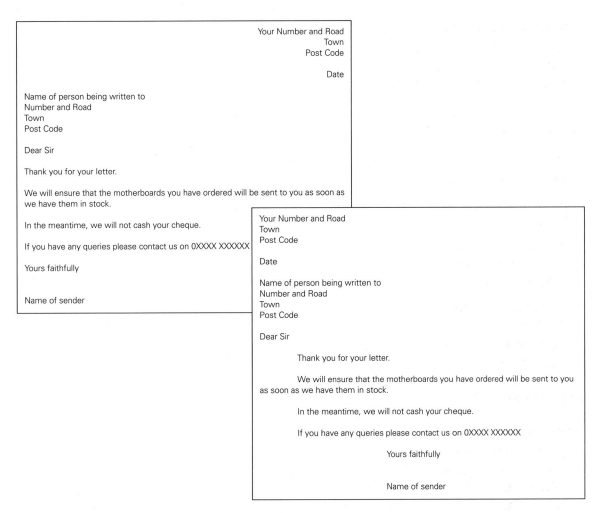

Your Number and Road
Town
Post Code

Date

Name of person being written to
Number and Road
Town
Post Code

Dear Sir

Thank you for your letter.

We will ensure that the motherboards you have ordered will be sent to you as soon as we have them in stock.

In the meantime, we will not cash your cheque.

If you have any queries please contact us on 0XXXX XXXXXX

Yours faithfully

Name of sender

Your Number and Road
Town
Post Code

Date

Name of person being written to
Number and Road
Town
Post Code

Dear Sir

Thank you for your letter.

We will ensure that the motherboards you have ordered will be sent to you as soon as we have them in stock.

In the meantime, we will not cash your cheque.

If you have any queries please contact us on 0XXXX XXXXXX

Yours faithfully

Name of sender

Figure 1.7

When working for an organisation, you should always investigate whether they have a house style for any business documentation and use this when communicating on their behalf. The range of possible styles is vast. There are template examples that can be downloaded from websites using the internet, in addition to templates that can be used inside software. The example shown in Figure 1.8 is just for the letter and fax templates available in Microsoft Word®.

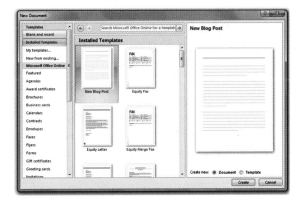

Figure 1.8 Letter and fax templates

Key term

A **template** is an example of a document where the layout is pre-set and all the user needs to do is to add text in the right places.

Identifying and conveying key messages in writing

In a busy world, it is important that when you communicate in writing, you get your message across as quickly and simply as possible and use the right type of document for the situation.

The main document types include:

- Letter – this is the most formal document type and it gets to its destination through the UK postal system.
- Fax – a letter or other document that needs to reach its destination quickly, but which is not available as an electronic version, can be sent via a fax machine. With this technology, the paper version of the document is fed through the machine where it is scanned and then the image is sent over a phone line to a receiving machine where the image is reassembled and printed out on paper. This can take a few minutes depending on the number of pages being transmitted.
- Email – increasingly the most common method of communication, this is usually received at its destination a few seconds after being sent. The main advantage of email is obviously its speed. If you send large attachments, however, it can take time to send and receive.

To make sure that you get your message across quickly and simply, here are a few tips:

1. Keep it simple! Avoid long written sentences and complex paragraphs as these can be difficult to read. Avoid technical words or other terminology that you are not certain the reader will understand.
2. Plan ahead! Decide in advance exactly what the main points are that you want to share with your reader. Decide on how you want to say it and the tone you want to use.

In these days of word processing, letters and emails are easy to correct. There is, therefore, no excuse for sending out a poorly worded or incorrect document. Always read your letter or email before you send it and correct it if necessary.

Using correct grammar and spelling

Most modern software (particularly word processing and presentation software) has spell-checking and grammar-checking facilities. Although the functions can be turned off, most people use them. Spelling errors are highlighted by the system in red:

Tomorrow I am going to fotoball practice.

Users can then either choose from suggested spellings or they can simply correct the word or words manually.

Grammatical errors are highlighted by the system in green:

Have you ever thought about having an weekend in the country?

Again, the system will make a suggestion on how this error can be corrected.

Bearing in mind that this functionality exists, there is no real excuse for sending out emails or letters containing spelling errors although some people find grammatical errors more difficult to deal with and such errors can slip through. This is also true of your coursework. If you are ever in doubt about spelling or grammar, ask someone else to check your work.

Reviewing and proofreading your own written work

One thing that spell checking and grammar checking may not be able to identify is errors in context. This is where you use another valid spelling of a word by mistake.

The incorrect word might sound the same, but it has a different meaning.

Reviewing and proofreading are very important to make sure that your written communications and your coursework look smart and professional.

Reviewing – checking that the facts in the communication are correct.

Proofreading – looking for errors in spelling, grammar and context.

Activity G

Identifying errors

Below are three versions of a question. Which is the right version?

　Ware are you going?
　Where are you going?
　Wear are you going?

Having identified the correct version, can you explain why the other two are wrong?

Using the wrong version of a word is a common error that proofreading should pick up. Here are some examples of other word pairings where the meaning of the words is quite different.

Word	Meaning
There	In that place
Their	Belonging to them
Where	In what place? – used in a question
Wear	To be dressed in, to erode
Pair	Two identical items
Pear	Fruit
Whether	Often used to introduce a number of alternatives, for example, 'whether it works or it doesn't, we still need to proceed with this idea'
Weather	Sunshine, rain etc.
Fair	A place you go with dodgems and rides
Fare	The cost of getting from A to B

Reviewing and editing documents created by others

Sometimes you will be asked to review and edit documents that have been created by other people. This could be a colleague in the workplace or even a member of your family.

When you review documents in these circumstances you should read them through and check that you understand the content fully. If you do not, ask the person who wrote the original what they meant. It might just be the case that a few words need to be changed to improve the text.

What is really important is that when you edit the document and make changes, you do not change the sense of what the other person is trying to say! Checking with them will help.

Note taking

Throughout your life you will find yourself taking notes in a variety of situations. Here are some likely situations:

- Taking information over the telephone
- Wanting to record a thought or idea
- Recording things you have learned in class.

There will also be more formal situations like recording what was said at a meeting.

The most important aspect of successful note taking is to make sure that you record the key points, even if that means that you miss recording some of the less important information.

Very few people would ever be able to write fast enough to get down every word spoken when a person is speaking at normal speed. As a result, where a job requires lots of note taking, employees usually learn some sort of note-taking language (known as shorthand) such as Pitman® or Teeline® or Speedwriting®. These systems use symbols to represent letters, words and phrases in a shortened form.

In Pitman® shorthand the term 'we have' is written as shown in Figure 1.9.

Figure 1.9 'We have' in shorthand

The advantage of these shorthand languages is that all you need to carry with you is a pad and a pen or pencil.

Whichever system you use, you should always make sure that you write up your notes as soon as possible, otherwise you might forget what you actually meant, especially if you made mistakes when you wrote them!

Modern technology makes the task of note taking a little easier, particularly with the development of dictaphones. A dictaphone is a voice-recording device where the recording is stored on small tapes or in an electronic memory. Most modern mobile phones even have voice recording facilities!

1.1.4 Audience

As you become more experienced with IT, you will find that you use technical terminology more easily. You will talk about URLs, database relationships, ISPs and use other technical terms and abbreviations with confidence because you understand what they mean. What is important, though, is that you learn when it is appropriate to use such language in conversations or communications with other people and when it is not.

So, when *is* it right?

Technical

People who use IT a lot, or who work as engineers or technicians, will obviously be familiar with many or most technical terms – but most importantly, if they are not familiar with a particular word or abbreviation they will be happy to ask.

Non-technical

Non-technical people, who will often be occasional computer users or those who do not use computers at all, will be less likely to understand complex computing and IT terminology. Using this language when you are speaking to them is likely to be unhelpful.

If you do need to use these terms when communicating with non-technical people, you will need to be prepared to explain the terms using simple language.

You should also only explain as much as the other person needs to know without complicating the situation by providing information that really is not relevant.

Make the grade   P2   P3

To achieve these pass (P) grading criteria, you must show that you have developed the skills to communicate with people who may have different levels of understanding in terms of IT.

For P2 you must show that you can communicate with a technical audience. You should use technical language and terminology confidently. This could be achieved through a presentation to your classmates (because they would have a similar technical understanding).

For P3 the audience should be non-technical, so you will need to be much more careful how you use language. You could present ideas for a computer-based solution to a local business customer who may not have any technical understanding.

When you create your evidence, remember to say whether your evidence is for the technical or non-technical audience to show you fully understand the difference.

1.2 Use IT tools to communicate and exchange information

This section will cover the following grading criteria: P4 P5 M1 D1

To make sure that you can use IT tools to communicate safely, it is vital that you understand some of the different IT communication channels that are available to you. This means that you can identify them, you can explain their use and you can give an advantage and disadvantage for using each one.

1.2.1 Communicating and exchanging information

Word-processed documents

A word-processed document could be a letter (usually used to communicate with customers), report (often to record some sort of investigation), leaflet or poster (used for advertising and marketing) and it is likely that you will already have used word-processing software to create one of more of them. These documents are used to exchange a variety of information.

To help inexperienced users with document layout, many of the document types are available as templates. Word-processing software contains grammar- and spell-checking facilities that users should employ to make their documents look more professional.

Channel	Benefit	Disadvantage
Word-processed documents	As they are stored electronically they can provide a permanent record of a communication that can be easily edited and reused. If stored on a computer's hard drive, they do not take up any physical space.	Users do need reasonable word-processing skills otherwise creating the documents can be time consuming, particularly if they do not type very fast!

Table 1.2

Activity H

Poster

Create an A4 poster about your course that your teacher could use to advertise the course to the students in the year below you.

Try to make it eye-catching and interesting by using a combination of text and images.

Presentations

Presentations are used to communicate information to a number of people at the same time.

The presenter speaks to the audience using presentation slides (individual pages containing text, numbers and images) to support what he or she is saying.

It is likely that you will create a presentation slide show as part of your coursework.

Web pages

The internet is made up of millions of web pages. These pages can be static, dynamic or interactive.

The content of a static web page is prewritten into the page and each time the page opens, the content is the same (unless of course it is changed by the website's staff).

A dynamic web page is a little different because the content of the page can be different each time the page is opened. For example, a web page that draws its information from a database could potentially change if stock levels go up or down.

With an interactive web site, the content can change based on the choices and key presses made by the user. Google™ is an interactive web page as the next page you view will be based on the item or items you choose to search for.

Channel	Benefit	Disadvantage
Presentations	An interactive way of presenting information to a large number of individuals simultaneously.	They can be quite scary for those who are shy or who are not used to giving them.

Table 1.3

The type you choose to use as a communication channel will depend on what the user needs it to do.

Web pages can be created and uploaded using the world wide web (the internet) or they can be included on an organisation's own internal website, usually called an intranet.

Channel	Benefit	Disadvantage
Web pages	Can be interesting and interactive, and can reach many people across the whole world.	Might need to be updated regularly and checked for accuracy.

Table 1.4

Email

Email is now the main method of communication, particularly inside organisations where you do not need to be quite as formal.

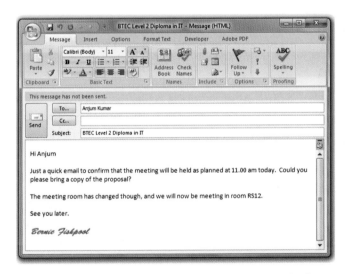

Figure 1.10 Emails are now the main method of communication

Channel	Benefit	Disadvantage
Email	Cheap and quick (more or less instant) to send.	They can be irritating, particularly if you start receiving SPAM email (email from companies trying to sell you things).

Table 1.5

1.2.2 IT tools

Software

Word processing

If you have ever used a computer to type out and print a letter, poster, newsletter or even just blocks of text, you will probably have used a word-processing software package.

The most common word-processing packages that make use of the Windows® platform include Microsoft Word®, Microsoft Works® or Corel WordPerfect®. For Linux-based systems, AbiWord® has become one of the most commonly used packages. Whichever product you use, it will contain a range of tools and templates that will help less able users to create professional documents with little effort.

OpenOffice.org® also offers an open-source software suite for word processing, spreadsheets, presentations, graphics and database functions (see http://www.openoffice.org/).

Presentation

Microsoft PowerPoint® is an important software package as it allows you to create slide shows to support presentations.

Each slide will usually contain text, images, charts and graphs (or a combination of these). Inexperienced users can create a competent and professional presentation quickly using any one of a range of styles and formats, while experienced users can create their own.

Once the presentation is over, the presenter can give the audience a printed set of presentation slides in the form of a handout that can be taken away as a permanent record of the presentation.

Other types of software

Just as there are a range of products for word processing or presentation generation, there is a variety of software for email. The most common is Microsoft Outlook®, but many ISPs (internet service providers such as Blueyonder®, Yahoo®, AOL®) have their own software interface for email.

Some organisations have their own messaging software built in to their intranet system to reduce the number of phone calls that are made between people in different departments.

You can also buy software for visually impaired people. This software uses speech recognition to enable users to create documents. Users speak into a microphone and the software turns the speech into text on the page. This is obviously useful for blind people or those with physical disabilities.

There are a number of Braille software products available for the visually impaired, such as Braille n' Speak® and Braille Lite®. In addition, there is a Braille email package available called Pine® that was developed by the Computing and Communications Group at the University of Washington, USA. For more information see http://www.washington.edu/pine/tutorial/index.html.

Proofing tools

Spell checkers check the spelling of individual words. They are able to identify if letters in a word are missing or if they have been transposed (switched around).

However, this tool is unable to understand the sense of a word so there is no substitute for reading the document through yourself. A spell checker cannot tell the difference between words that sound the same but have different spellings. In addition, the spell checker must be compatible with the language in which you are writing.

While this may sound silly, it would not be very helpful to use a spell checker that has been set on American spelling if you are writing documents in the UK for UK recipients. This is because some common words are simply spelt differently in the USA. For example:

colour is color (the u can thus be omitted with some words)

organisation is organization (the s is substituted with a z in the USA).

A thesaurus is a very useful tool if you are unable to think of an alternative word. By keying in a word, highlighting it and activating the thesaurus, you will be offered a number of alternatives from which you can choose. Most have the same or very similar meaning to the word you highlighted. You should be cautious, however, that your choice of a substitute word does not change the sense of what you are trying to say.

Other

Inside some packages there are additional converters. For example, some word-processing software will take a table that

Make the grade   **P4**

For P4 you must show that you can use various software tools to help you check your communications so that you can exchange information effectively.
As the basis for this you could use an email, poster, report or presentation slides. Your evidence should include proof that you have used at least two proofing tools and one other tool type (for example spell check, grammar check and a text reader).

contains numbers and allow you to create a chart or graph from it so that it becomes more visually accessible.

Some packages allow you to print to a file. This means that instead of printing the document using a conventional printer, the tool converts the content of your word-processing file into a different file format (for example, making a .pdf file which stands for portable document format) that cannot be altered by a reader.

There is also software available which can convert typed text into speech. Go to

http://www.naturalreaders.com/ to try it for yourself. Notice in Figure 1.11 that hyphens have been included in the terms B-TEC and I-T. When you use the software, remove the hyphens and you will see why they were added in order to have the sentence read in a meaningful way. Obviously you would take this out in a formal written piece of text!

Figure 1.11 An example of text-to-speech software

Quite often it is simply useful to experiment with software to find out what it does. Alternatively, you can read the manual, and most software packages have online help systems.

Activity J

Software

Pick a typical computer room at your school, college or institution and identify the following:

1. Types of common software installed (excluding the operating system)

2. Types of specialist software installed

Using this information, copy and complete the following grid:

Software name (e.g. Microsoft Word®)	Function (e.g. word processing)

1.2.3 Specialist communication channels

Blog is an abbreviation for weblog. This is usually a newsletter-style information website (it may also contain a diary).

In the example taken from the official Google® blog in Figure 1.12, you will find a combination of recent news and archived information (news items and stories from the past – stored in case you might want to go back and look at them).

Figure 1.12 The official Google® blog

Many modern software websites have blogs where developers share information about the product and advise about any known problems, patches or updates. Users too can ask for answers to questions. No user manual can cover every question!

Activity K

Blogs

Think about software that you are using as part of your course that you are not particularly familiar with.

Check out the web and see if there is a blog for this product. If so, save it into your favourites or make a note of the address – you never know when this might be useful.

A **wiki** is a website containing inter-linked web pages that are easily created and edited. As contributions can be made by anyone, wiki users should always carefully consider the validity and accuracy of information and they should check information with other sources before they use it.

A **vlog** is principally the same as a blog, but uses video as part of its format. As with the blog, it will often also contain archived information.

A **podcast** is a media file that can be downloaded to your own computer or to a mobile device so that you can play the file back at any time. Podcasts may be free, or you might need to pay some sort of subscription.

The BBC, for example, releases some of its radio programmes as podcasts (see the BBC podcast directory):

http://www.bbc.co.uk/podcasts/

The BBC's podcast directory contains listings of all programmes that can be downloaded and these are available across a variety of genre including comedy, children's programmes, news programmes and music.

The term podcast has been created from two other words – the 'pod' comes from the Apple® iPod and the 'cast' from the word broadcast.

Channel	Benefit	Disadvantage
Blogs/vlogs/podcasts	These tools have ensured that there is now information on more or less anything on the net! They are easy to use, access and create (see http://www.weebly.com/).	Some content might not be suitable for some age groups and, as they are difficult to police, some might cause offence or they might have material that is considered unsuitable.

Table 1.6

Figure 1.13 Video conferencing

Video conferencing has brought the way in which businesses communicate up to date!

As you can see in Figure 1.13, not all of the people attending the meeting are in the room – the other person is somewhere else.

Using simple webcams and TV or computer screens, or even fully integrated systems, users can see each other during the discussion. They can also see demonstrations of products and drawings.

Channel	Benefit	Disadvantage
Video conferencing	Being able to communicate visually with others without having to travel.	Unlike using the phone where it really does not matter, you will need to look smart and professional when you take part in a video conference, particularly if one or more of the other participants are customers!

Table 1.7

1.2.4 Safety

Personal information

> **Activity L**
>
> **Personal information**
>
> When you are asked to provide personal information, which of the following would you give freely? (List all that apply.)
>
> ✓ Name
> ✓ Home address
> ✓ Telephone number
> ✓ Email address
> ✓ Date of birth
> ✓ Gender
> ✓ Photograph
> ✓ School or college details
> ✓ Bank account details
> ✓ Passwords
> ✓ Names of your parents or guardians
>
> Discuss your list with a group of other students. Are your answers the same? Why would you give some information and not other information?

Sharing personal information can lead to individuals being targeted for **identify theft**. This is when someone else uses your personal information and pretends to be you. In more serious cases this could lead to fraud with your details being used to get credit.

As a general rule, **do not** give out any personal information to people you do not know, whether this is over the phone or the internet.

The safest way to use the internet is to use a nickname (that you tell your friends) and do not provide any further information.

> **Activity M**
>
> **Securing Facebook**
>
> Having studied this topic, if you think you might have given too much personal information on websites like Facebook, read the following news item from the BBC website and change your settings.
>
> Securing Facebook: http://www.bbc.co.uk/news/10117106
>
> For additional information on being safe on the internet see:
>
> http://www.teach-ict.com/ks3/internet_safety/staying_safe/stayingsafe1.htm

Viewing digital content

One of the most common ways your computer can become infected is through viruses that you have activated accidently by opening attachments in an email. Similarly content downloaded from the web can also be hiding viruses and other threats. For this reason you should have effective anti-virus software installed and you should not open attachments unless you are confident they are safe.

Video content held on the internet can be rated in terms of suitability for particular age groups. In the example shown in Figure 1.14 you need to input your date of birth before it will allow you to access the content.

Figure 1.14

Even BBC iPlayer content can be locked and may require the user to confirm their age. In the case of the BBC example shown in Figure 1.15, the lock explains the nature of the possibly inappropriate content.

Figure 1.15

Uploading digital content

Users must consider carefully any content that they upload. There have been a number of cases in the last few years of individuals who truly regret uploading content that then becomes freely accessible to others.

You should never upload any content that you would not be happy for the whole world to see! Once images in particular are in the public domain, it is almost impossible to remove them.

Respect towards others

When communicating via the internet, most of us would show the same level of respect to others as we would wish for ourselves and even if we did find personal information about others, most of us would not use that information to ridicule or disadvantage someone else.

There are some people, however, who set out to hurt or damage the reputation of others using the internet as their tool. Here are some examples:

28 July 2010 – 'Law student dubbed 'paedophile' by former friend who posted child porn on his Facebook page wins £10,000 libel damages'

http://www.dailymail.co.uk/news/article-1298010/Facebook-libel-Law-student-dubbed-paedophile-wins-10-000-libel-damages.html

In this case a student's Facebook pages had been accessed by an ex-friend and indecent photographs of children had been uploaded. This allegedly happened because of an unpaid debt and it almost destroyed the student's future.

20 March 2010 – 'Twitter in trouble after setting Sarkozy rumour mill whirring'

http://technology.timesonline.co.uk/tol/news/tech_and_web/the_web/article7069210.ece

A tweet on the social networking site Twitter started a rumour about the French President's wife. This information was picked up and passed on by journalists and became a media frenzy. How this occurred is described in the article.

These issues have affected individuals – but what about the wider issue? Should our privacy and integrity receive the respect of others? In July and August 2010 two important news items brought new issues into the public domain:

3 August 2010 – 'Web attack knows where you live'

http://www.bbc.co.uk/news/technology-10850875

This article explored how websites could be booby-trapped to pass on information that would identify someone's physical address.

29 July 2010 – 'Details of 100m Facebook users collected and published'
http://www.bbc.co.uk/news/technology-10796584

This article details how a computer program has been written to scan Facebook accounts and collect information from personal profiles. This information was then collated and published.

Most of us consider these issues relatively serious and this has triggered extensive debate about the vulnerability of individuals and groups.

Activity N

Personal safety on the internet

Working as a small group, make a short video about personal safety on the internet aimed at young people aged 10 to 15.

Show your video to your class.

Data protection regulations

Data Protection Act 1998

The Data Protection Act sets out guidelines on how data about us must be stored and how it can be used. If these guidelines are broken by organisations, they can be prosecuted by both individuals and other organisations.

Computer Misuse Act 1990

This legislation is designed to prevent users from using computers for criminal activities such as theft, pornography and terrorism.

Freedom of Information Act 2000

As a result of this act, individuals are now entitled to see the information that is being stored about them. This is an important step forward, particularly if you find you are one of those unfortunate individuals who are affected by data that may not be correct.

Securing data

Encryption

Data that is **encrypted** is scrambled so that even if it is accessed or stolen, the data itself is useless without the decryption software needed to unscramble it.

Firewalls

Firewalls are programs that watch a computer's **traffic** (data that is incoming and outgoing when we communicate online). The software is configured to allow or deny communication with remote websites, as chosen by the user.

Backups

If the only copy of a file is on the hard drive inside your computer and your computer breaks down (becomes infected by a virus or suffers some sort of hardware failure), you are in danger of losing your data. To prevent this, you should make a **backup** copy of your file or files. The file copies should be kept on an alternative device – a USB device such as an external hard drive is one example, although there are others.

If backup files are made they should be stored off-site or in a secure medium such as a fire-proof safe, otherwise there will be little point in having the backup (it could potentially be destroyed along with the original). Backups should be made regularly!

Secure sites

When making payments via the internet you must be sure that the website you are using is secure to reduce the risk of your financial details being stolen. The best way to reduce the risk is to use an intermediary payment service like PayPal® or NoChex®.

This service protects both the buyer and the seller:

- The buyer's information is not passed on.
- The seller has confirmation that the buyer is genuine because he knows the funds are available.

PayPal® and NoChex® take a small payment from the buyer for this service.

Make the grade   D1

For D1 you must expand on the poster you created to support P5 and discuss the wider issues of safety when using IT tools to communicate and exchange information. A few PowerPoint® slides will help you to focus your evidence. You must consider personal safety as well as how to ensure that the data being transferred is kept secure.

1.3 Understand the impact of IT on individuals, communities and society

This section will cover the following grading criteria: P6 M2

Make the grade   P6

For P6 you will need to explain some of the ways that IT has impacted on society. You do not need to go into great depth, but you should be able to explain a range of issues. You could talk about the way we now manage our finances or how it has affected the way we work.

Think about some of the advances in technology over the last few years and how they have affected the way we do things.

Cash machines mean we can now withdraw cash from our bank accounts even when the banks are closed. This was not possible until the first cash machine became operational in 1967.

Modern cash machines provide many more services. This technology has changed how we manage our finances and our lives.

1.3.1 Impacts

Over the last 40 years or so, IT has been responsible for changing the way that many things are done. Let us have a look at some examples and look at a positive and a negative impact in each case.

Social

How has IT affected society as a whole?

Effects on local communities

Positive impact – communities have access to much more local information that is likely to be up-to-date and they may be more likely to become more actively involved in local issues.

Negative impact – local printed publications and newsletters may have gone out of business (these were often funded by advertising income from local businesses).

People do not need to chat with other local people as much as previously because they can get the information on the web. This means they can become more isolated.

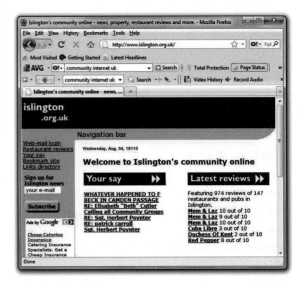

Figure 1.16 A local community website

Economic

What about working and environmental issues? What impact has IT had?

Employment structure

Positive impact – in some jobs it is now possible for workers to work from home for some or all of their working day. This reduces time spent travelling to and from the office and also means that some people who would not normally have been able to have a job now can (for example carers or people who have conditions which mean they cannot leave the house).

Negative impact – if you work at home you can become isolated and you might not feel part of the business because you rarely, if ever, see other staff. Also some people who work from home say that they often work longer hours because the job can intrude on their home lives.

Activity ⭕

Working from home

Working with a partner, use the following website to find out about more positive and negative impacts related to working from home:

http://theworkpad.com/making-the-move/upsides-and-downsides-of-working-from-home/

Write down two more positives and two more negatives.

Working practices

Positive impact – because communicating in the office is easier (with the availability of email and office intranet chat software like MessagePal® – see http://www.messagepal.com) most organisations have become much more efficient and customer responsive. This means that they can react quicker to customer requests because they can get the answers faster.

Negative impact – sometimes employees get caught up in chats and emails which are not really about work. Obviously, this is wasting the company's time.

Sustainability

Negative impact – computers use consumables such as ink cartridges and paper for printing, and they generate technical waste such as old components like motherboards and memory from machines that have been upgraded. These have to be disposed of safely without causing a negative impact on the environment.

Positive impact – businesses have been launched that aim to recycle some of the waste products from IT use (such as companies that refill ink cartridges). This means new employment opportunities as well as people becoming generally more thoughtful about how they dispose of their rubbish.

Legal

What are some of the legal issues in relation to IT?

Ownership

Some aspects of computer use are hard to trace which has meant that some activities have been difficult to stop, such as the illegal downloading of music and movies. The statistics might surprise you:

18 March 2010 – '82% of people admit downloading content illegally'

http://www.computerweekly.com/Articles/2010/03/18/240655/82-of-people-admit-downloading-content-illegally.htm

Most people agree that if we illegally download music, for example, then the owners of the music, such as the artists and the record companies, will have less income and in some cases they may not survive. For this reason the government has been trying to find ways of stamping out illegal downloading. One of the more recent articles explains new powers for record companies made possible by the introduction of the Digital Economy Act 2010.

28 May 2010 – 'UK illegal downloaders' details to be stored on official list'

http://www.nme.com/news/various-artists/51284

This article suggests that the larger ISPs (internet service providers) have agreed to a code of conduct whereby they will provide the 'evidence' that will allow record companies to take individuals to court if they breach the regulations. This may well see individuals who have been found guilty placed on a database.

Activity P

Digital Economy Act

This Act came into force in April 2010. Use the following article to find out the main principles of the Act and note down three key points.

9 April 2010 – 'Digital Economy Act 2010 becomes law'

http://www.webuser.co.uk/news/top-stories/450077/digital-economy-act-2010-becomes-law

Copyright

Most materials published officially are subject to copyright. This material could include music, documents, graphics and images. The rules mean that material cannot be republished or used without the permission of the copyright owner. This could be the person who created the material or the organisation that paid for its creation.

Plagiarism

Have you ever wondered how teachers know when you have copied from a web page? You might think that they have read every web page on a topic, but in fact they just know how to use Google® to their advantage.

Activity Q

Plagiarism

Open a web browser and activate Google®.

Into the search bar key in: 'These measures include the disconnection of broadband customers who are deemed to be infringing copyright laws'

You must do this exactly as written and include speech marks at the beginning and end of the text. Click on Search. What is the first article identified? Have you seen this article before?

It is illegal to use someone else's written word and claim it as your own.

If you do copy and paste information from the web, you should always say where you got the information from. This is easy to do. Simply type in 'Source:' and then copy and paste the web address!

Ethical

What impact is there in terms of the ethical use of IT?

Privacy of information

With so much information now in the **public domain** (freely accessible to all) it is becoming increasingly difficult to keep information private. But do we have a right to privacy? Many people think that the line is drawn at 'information that should be shared in the public interest'.

What do you think?

1.3.2 Unequal access

Implications

What are the implications of different areas, people, organisations and groups, for example, not having equal access to IT?

Locally

Have you ever felt left out?

This could be because someone forgot to invite you to a party, or because a group of your friends do not include you in a conversation. It could be because your family cannot afford the latest designer trainers or clothes.

The developments in technology have now added another aspect to this – those who do not have access to technology and/or computers and the internet.

This could be because you and your family cannot afford the technology or the costs of internet connectivity, but it could also occur because there is no high-speed broadband access to the area in which you live. In such cases, homes often find themselves relying on satellite or low speed dial-up connections.

Activity R

Who has the technology?

Collaborate with your class to create a list of all the IT-related technologies you can think of (include technologies like mobile phones, portable games machines etc).

Make enough copies of this list for the whole class and ask each person in the class to tick what he or she has access to.

Collate the information and then use it to create a pie chart or bar chart.

Nationally

Prior to the general election (election for the prime minister of the UK) in 2010, the Labour government made a pledge to the residents of the UK that everyone in the country would have access to broadband by 2012.

Activity S

Broadband for 2012?

Working with a small group access the following online article:

16 July 2010 – 'Coalition dumps Labour pledge of broadband for all of Britain by 2012'
http://www.independent.co.uk/news/business/news/coalition-dumps-labour-pledge-of-broadband-for-all-of-britain-by-2012-2027679.html

Discuss the article with your group and answer the following questions:

1. Does it matter if all of Britain does not have access to broadband by 2012?

2. Why?

Globally

In the UK and Europe we enjoy being able to access websites like Facebook® and YouTube® and we contribute to the millions of users globally. However, there are parts of the world that have little or no access to the internet.

To address this, organisations have been set up to refurbish old computer equipment so that it can be taken to those parts of the world where this technology is not freely available.

Activity **T**

Computers 4 Africa

Find out about the work of this organisation: http://computers4africa.org.uk/

Watch the video, read the web pages and see if you can answer the following questions:

What do they do?
How does it work?
What could you do to help?

Consider setting up a voluntary group of students to help.

1.3.3 Abuse of IT

There are many ways in which IT can be abused, however for this topic we will focus on four main threats:

- Cyber bullying
- Spam
- Phishing
- Denial of service attacks

Cyber bullying

Cyber bullying is when the internet or mobile phones are used to send vicious and unpleasant messages (often anonymously) to others with the direct intention of upsetting them.

Activity **U**

Cyber bullying

Watch the following video with a group of your colleagues:

Childnet International – Cyber Bullying

http://www.youtube.com/watch?v=fNumIY9D7uY

Create a storyboard for your own cyber bullying video.

Activity **V**

e-safeguarding

The 'panic' button in Figure 1.17 now appears on many of the social networking sites used by young people. What is it all about?

Figure 1.17 'Panic' button

Find out and create an A5 leaflet.

The following link might be helpful:

http://www.thinkuknow.co.uk/

Spam

Spam is a general name given to junk email. This is email that you have not signed up for that is sent to you from a variety of sources. To prevent spam, you can adjust your spam filter in your email client or web browser. This is usually found in the options menu (see Figure 1.18 on the next page).

Make the grade

M2 requires you to discuss some examples of potential threats with using IT. You should be able to identify that some threats are more serious than others and suggest possible ways of minimising some of these threats. You could, for example, look at spam and how you could change the settings in your email to filter it (which is a relatively low threat) or you could investigate cyber bullying and how the effects of this can be reduced (which is a more serious threat).

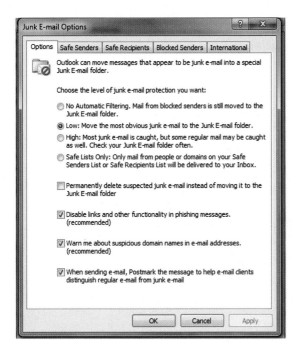

Figure 1.18 Preventing spam

Phishing

One of the most recent online crimes involves fraudsters trying to get an individual's personal information by sending them an email asking for a response.

The poor spelling and grammar in the example shown in Figure 1.19 should immediately flag that something is not as it should be, even if the fraudster has attempted to make the email appear genuine by copying the actual Alliance & Leicester® logo.

This activity is known as **phishing**.

What was most interesting about this particular email was that the person who received it did not have an Alliance & Leicester account. The same email, almost word for word, has been sent to millions of UK account holders with the bank details changed!

Figure 1.19 A hoax letter 'phishing' for information

Denial of service attacks

In a **denial of service** (DoS) attack the communication between computers is sabotaged. This is done by bombarding networks with activity to slow down processing and reducing the user's quality of service.

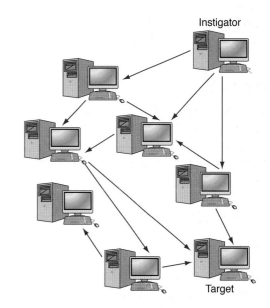

Figure 1.20 A denial of service attack

This essentially is an irritant rather than a criminal or fraudulent activity.

Achieving Success

In order to achieve each unit, you will complete a series of coursework activities. Each time you hand in work, your tutor will return this to you with a record of your achievement.

This particular unit has 9 criteria to meet: 6 Pass, 2 Merit and 1 Distinction.

For a **Pass** you must achieve **all 6** Pass criteria.

For a **Merit** you must achieve **all 6** Pass **and both** Merit criteria.

For a **Distinction** you must achieve **all 6** Pass, **both** Merit criteria **and the single** Distinction criterion.

Help with assessment

Your tutor will give you one or more assignments that you will complete as coursework. This could consist of:

- Presentations
- Videos
- Witness statements and/or an evidence log

- Role play
- Web pages
- User guides
- Proofs (before and after versions of documents)
- Blogs.

You should read the guidance given for each of the criteria (shown across the unit) carefully and remember to check your work.

r Further reading

Textbooks

Maggio, R. *The Art of Talking to Anyone: Essential People Skills for Success in Any Situation.* (McGraw Hill Higher Education, 2005) ISBN 007145229X

Websites

www.btplc.com/Responsiblebusiness/ Supportingourcommunities/ Learningandskills

www.mindtools.com/CommSkll/ CommunicationIntro.htm

Unit 2
Working in the IT industry

Learning objectives

By the end of this unit you should:

1. Be able to know the characteristics that are valued by employers in the IT industry

2. Be able to know the common job roles undertaken by people working in the IT industry.

In order to pass this unit, the evidence you present for assessment needs to demonstrate that you can meet all of the above learning outcomes for this unit. The criteria below show the levels of achievement required to pass this unit.

To achieve a **pass** grade the evidence must show that the learner is able to:	To achieve a **merit** grade the evidence must show that, in addition to the pass criteria, the learner is able to:	To achieve a **distinction** the evidence must show that, in addition to the pass and merit criteria, the learner is able to:
P1 Describe the characteristics valued by employers in the IT industry		
P2 Describe common IT industry job roles		
P3 Explain the characteristics required for a specific job role in the IT industry	**M1** Explain why certain characteristics are important for a specific job role	**D1** Justify a choice of an appropriate job role for a given set of employee characteristics

Introduction

With the rapid change in the IT industry, new technologies developed, new jobs created and new skills needed, employers are always looking for staff who have specialised knowledge, but who are also able to function effectively because they have good 'soft skills'. These skills include the way you behave, interact with others, solve problems and so on.

In this unit you will learn some of the characteristics that employers look for in new employees and you will investigate a range of job roles that you might aim for when you have finished your studies.

You will be assessed through coursework which could be in the form of:

- Presentations
- Newsletters or leaflets
- Videos
- Witness statements and/or an evidence log
- Web pages
- Blogs

2.1 Know the characteristics that are valued by employers in the IT industry

This section will cover the following grading criterion: **P1**

When you read job advertisements and person specifications/job descriptions, you will see four key words. These words are used to group together things about us in a meaningful way. The examples below show these categories:

Attributes and **abilities** – most people think these are hard to identify, but they are actually quite easy. Attributes and abilities are personal characteristics that employers expect you to have, such as:

- Being able to solve problems
- Being able to work in a team
- Being creative.

Skills – most skills can be measured. For example, do you have IT skills at a particular level? If you complete the course you will have a qualification at Level 2. In general, skills can be demonstrated through certificates that you have earned or through a job-related test

Attitudes – these describe the way you behave at work, such as being confident, being interested in your work, having pride in your personal appearance and being polite and respectful to others.

We will now explore some of these characteristics in a little more detail and think about why they are valued by employers.

2.1.1 Industry specific characteristics

These are directly related to the job you are doing and they are usually specified in the job advertisement.

Activity A

What are the key requirements?

Read the following extract from a job advertisement and make a note of the key words that are used to identify the attributes and skills an employee must demonstrate:

'We are seeking to appoint a Trainee IT Technician to work in a very busy college environment. If you are interested in this role you will need to show that you are flexible, that you can show initiative in your work and that you are able to work closely with the other IT technicians and the college's staff to maintain workstations and systems. You will also need to show that you can work independently as some unsupervised work will be required.

You will need to demonstrate an understanding of installing and configuring Microsoft Windows XP® Pro Workstation and Microsoft Office® Applications and show that you have an understanding of Microsoft Server®. You must also have good ICT skills and show that you have a sound knowledge of hardware and network configuration. Good communication skills at all levels are essential. Candidates with no experience will be considered.'

Using a **job specification** and **person specification** is the best way for employers to find out about candidates. In most organisations, before they even choose which candidates to interview, they begin by scanning the applications and finding those candidates who have all or most of the characteristics they require.

If you apply for a job and you only have one or two of a list of ten required skills and attributes, you will probably not even be considered for an interview in the first place. It is very important that you are realistic about your applications to avoid disappointment.

The employer will be looking for an ideal candidate who can demonstrate most of the requirements.

In Figure 2.1, we can see that Candidate A clearly has a range of relevant qualifications, training and experience in addition to skills and abilities. When starting out, most candidates will be similar to Candidate B (Figure 2.2) with no experience or job specific training, limited qualifications but some good skills and abilities.

Technical knowledge

What is **technical knowledge**? Technical knowledge in an IT environment will be defined by the job you are applying for and it could include:

- Practical knowledge and understanding of specific **application packages**
- Practical knowledge and understanding of **operating systems**
- Practical knowledge and understanding of **programming software**
- Understanding of **networks**
- Understanding of **communications technologies**
- Understanding of **hardware**
- Understanding of **installation**.

Figure 2.1 Candidate A

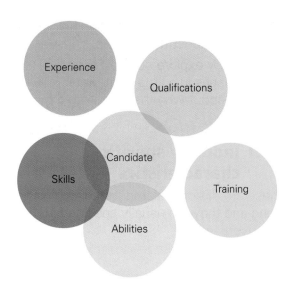

Figure 2.2 Candidate B

Some of this understanding will be demonstrated through qualifications such as your BTEC Level 2 Certificate, Extended Certificate or Diploma in Information Technology. In an interview situation you should not only be able to name your qualifications, but you should be able to list the units you have studied.

As your career progresses, you will also be developing your technical experience which will give you further evidence of your technical knowledge.

Working procedures

Some jobs allow employees to work the hours they choose within boundaries (this is known as **flexi-time** or **flexible working**); other jobs have set times and working patterns.

In certain jobs you might need to clock in and out (this means you insert your **time card** into a machine that stamps your start and finish times (see Figure 2.3)). This information is used to work out how much you should be paid. In other jobs you might be asked to complete a **time sheet** where you simply record your start and finish times in writing.

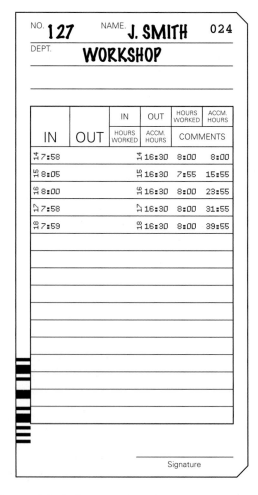

Figure 2.3 A time card

The organisations may well have their own way of doing things which you will have to learn. They will set **boundaries** and **expectations** and they will help you in the first days of your employment with training where they will introduce and explain their **procedures** to you. During your training you should always make sure that you:

- ask for clarification if you are not sure about something
- ask if you can observe another member of staff doing something you think you should know.

Activity **B**

Working procedures

Using the internet, find three IT-related jobs and compare their working hours. Put the information into a simple table. Answer the following questions:

1. How many days a week will the employee work?

2. How many hours a week will the employee work?

3. Are the hours fixed or flexible?

4. Is the job all in one place, or does the job require the employee to work in different places?

Health and safety knowledge

In school or at college, in a job situation and at home you have the same responsibility as everyone else to make sure that your classmates, work colleagues and family are healthy and safe. You should always be prepared to point out **hazards** or any other issues that make a situation unsafe and the older you get, the more you will be expected to take responsibility for **your own health** and safety as well as that of **those around you**.

In a working situation, however, there are **laws** and **regulations** that set expected standards that employers should meet. Examples of these laws and regulations are the **Health & Safety at Work Act 1974** and **The Management of Health and Safety at Work Regulations 1999**.

Figure 2.4

While these Acts set out the responsibilities for employers and employees, you will be expected to have a basic knowledge and understanding of health and safety issues in relation to the job you are applying for (for example, wearing wrist straps when working with the insides of computers). In addition, there are more general responsibilities which are detailed below.

In the workplace you should:

- Be observant and identify any obvious hazards or dangers.
- Report any hazards or dangers you have identified to your manager or supervisor.
- Anticipate any situations that might be hazardous – in other words think about what you are doing before you do it, and if you think there could be dangers you should not ignore them!

Employers also have basic responsibilities including providing you with any health and safety equipment you need in your job, and providing you with the necessary tools or circumstances to ensure you have a safe working environment.

Activity C

Health and safety

What about health and safety in your classroom?

Have a look around you to see if you can identify any immediate health and safety issues. These could include:

- Cables trailing on the floor
- Loose floor tiles
- Students leaving bags in places where others walk
- Drinks and/or food around computer equipment
- Damaged cables or loose plugs.

Make a list of any issues you find and give it to your teacher or tutor.

2.1.2 General characteristics

These are characteristics you have just because of who you are and who you choose to be. For example, you see someone fall in the street. Do you choose to be helpful or do you just walk away? The decision you make is a personal choice. Employers look for positive personal characteristics and skills in their employees that they know will help the organisation function. Here are some examples.

Interpersonal skills

Your **interpersonal skills** are how you interact with those around you and how you relate to others. This includes:

- The way you **speak** to other people, the words you use and how you say them.
- How well you **listen** and whether you seem interested in what others say.
- How **tactful** you are.

These skills definitely improve as you get older and as you begin to appreciate how the way you behave impacts on others.

Planning skills

If you have learned to plan effectively, you will know how to break problems down into smaller tasks. For example, if the goal is to make a cup of tea, you will be able to identify what resources you need and the steps you need to go through to make the tea (a bit like trying to do a jigsaw and deciding what goes where). In addition, if the tea is supposed to be ready at a particular time, you will be able to work out when you need to start the process to meet the deadline.

There are a number of tools you can use to help you with planning, including **Gantt charts** and **mind maps** and there are **software tools** available, like Microsoft Project®, to help you tackle bigger projects.

Organisational skills

These are the skills that show you can plan your time effectively, organise your work and respond to priorities that could suddenly change. This can occur when an additional task comes along that is considered more important than what you are doing and needs to be done first.

To test a potential employee's organisational skills and his or her ability to prioritise work-related activities, some organisations use an **in-tray exercise** as part of the interview process. In this exercise the candidate has to rank the problems or tasks in **priority order**, saying which should be done first and which can be done last.

The final consideration is a simple one. How tidy are you in your work? Do you leave paperwork unfiled or tasks incomplete? This would be classed as an employee having poor organisational skills.

Time management skills

Time management is not just about your ability to meet deadlines; in the more general sense it also means that you show that you can arrive at work on time. This does not mean that you arrive at one minute *past* your start time; it means you arrive at one minute *to* your start time, or earlier if you want to show your employer that you are keen.

Team working skills

Most organisations rely on employees being able to work as a team. This means that employees should be able to work together and co-operate, to communicate effectively, to share ideas and to have a common sense of purpose.

All team members should be equally committed to the task and be prepared to put in the same amount of work as the other team members.

Numeric skills

Some jobs require numeric or number skills. This does not necessarily mean that you have to be confident in doing mental maths as in most cases you would be allowed to use a calculator. As part of the course you may also be asked to take a Functional Skills Maths exam to test your maths skills. This is an important skill to have even if it is just showing that you can calculate how much to charge a customer!

Activity D

Calculating the bill!

A customer has bought some items from your company and you now need to calculate the bill. Here is the information you need:

10 black printer ink cartridges at £18.50 each
5 boxes of paper at £11.90 each
1 box of red pens at £1.95 each
2 boxes of blue pens at £2.50 each

You need to charge 20% VAT on the pre-VAT bill.

Work out how much you will charge the customer and show how you worked out the answer. Look at the Answer section at the back of the book to see if you were right.

Creativity

Some people find it very easy to be creative and to come up with new ideas all the time. Other people struggle. Part of it is down to confidence – believing in your own idea – and not being worried what others will think.

In whatever you do you should always be thinking:

* Is there an easier way of doing this?
* Is there a quicker way of doing this?
* Can I do this better?

If something occurs to you and you are not confident about implementing your ideas, always talk your ideas over with someone you trust like your manager or a colleague.

You should never be worried about sharing ideas even if you think others might laugh at you.

Problem solving

Problem solving is about being able to **analyse problems** and then **suggest** and **find solutions**.

Once the solution needed is known, the steps needed to implement the solution need to be identified and put into action so that the problem can be solved.

As with many of the other skills, this skill improves with experience.

2.1.3 Attitudes

Attitudes are generally thought to be a combination of the way you behave and the personal approach you take, such as being tolerant of others, being determined, or showing that you are a leader. Here are a range of attitudes that employers may look for, with an explanation of what they are.

Determination

Your **determination** is your desire to achieve or succeed in a given situation or to complete something like a project, or even your Diploma, Extended Certificate or Certificate. You will be able to focus on the goal and find ways of achieving it, even if things do not always go according to plan!

Independence

If you are working with **independence** it means that your teacher, tutor or manager can give you a task to do and know that you will carry it out with little or no supervision. The main skill needed to be able to work independently is that you do not allow yourself to get distracted. Being able to get on and do what you have been asked to do will be invaluable to an employer.

Integrity

Your **integrity** is your honesty, respect and sense of duty. Your employer will need to be able to trust you. He or she will want to know that you arrive at work on time, do not steal from the organisation, that you will be considerate and respect your colleagues and that you will try at all times to do your best.

Tolerance

Working with other people can be difficult at times. You might be asked to work with someone you do not like, or who treats you with less respect than you feel you would treat them.

At these times you will need to be **tolerant**. You will need to show that you respect other people's views, practices and opinions, even if you do not always agree with them. It is a lack of tolerance that can often lead to conflict and arguments.

Dependability

Being reliable and consistent in your attitudes and approach makes you a **dependable** employee. The quality of your work will always be good, you will work hard to consistently meet deadlines and you will show that you are willing to help the organisation meet its objectives.

Leadership

A leader is not someone who simply takes charge of a situation and makes all the decisions. In fact if you are bossy and controlling, you will probably be a bad leader!

Good leaders know how to support the people in their team and how to get the best out of them.

Confidence

Confidence is simply about believing in yourself and your abilities. Doing tasks well and being praised for your achievements will help your confidence to grow.

Practising speaking to an audience will help you to prepare for giving presentations. Think about running through your presentation in front of some of your classmates or even in front of a mirror. This will make you feel better about standing in front of others.

Self-motivation

When you are **self-motivated** it means that you are able to keep focused on your goals without needing to be constantly kept on track by others.

You will have control of your work, you will have the confidence to complete tasks, your work will always be of high quality and you will find that you enjoy meeting deadlines.

You will be able to do all this just because you want to.

Make the grade   P1

For P1 you will need to be able to describe some of the characteristics that are valued by employers in the IT industry. Investigate the sorts of characteristics employers look for by reading a range of job advertisements for IT jobs. You can use the internet as well as local newspapers. Remember to write about industry-specific attributes and skills as well as general skills and attitudes.

Later in the unit you will link these skills, attributes and attitudes to a specific job and explain why these are important in the context of that particular job.

Activity E

How do people see you?

Below is a table of various attitudes and skills. Copy and complete the table and then use it during a tutorial as the basis for a discussion.

Skill or attitude	How do you see yourself ?
What are your interpersonal skills like? How do you talk to others? Do you listen to them?	
Are you good at planning?	
How organised are you?	
Do you usually get to school or college on time?	
How effective are you when working in a team?	
How creative are you?	
How good are you at problem solving?	
Are you a determined person?	
Can you work independently?	
How honest and trustworthy are you?	
Are you always tolerant of others?	
Are you reliable?	

2.2 Know the common job roles undertaken by people working in the IT industry

This section will cover the following grading criteria: **P2** **P3** **M1** **D1**

2.2.1 General IT job opportunities

To explore the job market we will look at a number of job categories, both general IT roles and more specific technical roles.

Job roles

Solutions architecture

A **solutions architect** is an IT expert who usually has a wide range of technical knowledge and experience. This knowledge and experience is used to design a range of possible solutions to real business problems for clients. This could be designing networks or computer systems, designing user interfaces or even working with applications to design a customised solution.

Solutions development and implementation

In this role, employees take a design and carry out the actual development of the solution. They know what the solution should do, and they decide what software and/or hardware is needed. They then build and test the solution to make sure that the system works as it should.

Network management

With so many business functions relying on computer technology in today's business world, this is a very important job. It involves supervising the whole internal network including email, servers, any security and the actual network itself (including cabling and connectivity).

Information security

Those working in **information security** have to stay up to date with the advances in technology as new viruses and other information security threats surface. They design solutions and strategies to prevent data loss and ensure that the organisation's information is safe and secure. This can also include designing backup plans and data recovery strategies.

Technical writers

Technical writers have the ability to make complex technical information sound relatively easy to understand. They interpret technology or applications and use this information to design and write a range of documentation from user guides to technical manuals.

Using a range of visual media in addition to more tradition written materials, technical writers might also develop software demos and interactive demos using web technology, video and Microsoft PowerPoint® in addition to other graphical tools and illustrations.

Data administrators

Data held by organisations must be carefully managed to make sure that it complies with regulations like the Data Protection Act 1998 (often referred to as the DPA). Administrators design how the data will be organised and stored in a system and once the data is in the system they manage the data's integrity. For example:

- Data needs to be checked to make sure that there is no duplicated data (this just takes up data storage space).
- Any data that is no longer needed must be deleted to comply with the DPA.
- Data administrators ensure that data is secure, is regularly backed up and can be recovered in the event of a disaster.

IT service management and delivery

A **service manager** oversees the delivery of IT services to employees within an organisation. He or she will manage the IT technicians, deal with suppliers and manufacturers of hardware and/or software, oversee the replacement of system components and schedule upgrades.

Hardware-specific roles

Manufacturing

The simple act of building a computer by placing all the components into the case in the correct order and in the right way does not really require any skill. What does require some skill though is testing the computer, running any diagnostics and making sure the computer works before it is despatched to the store where it will be sold.

Repair

Repairing computers requires significantly more skill as the technician often has to diagnose the problem as well as identifying and implementing the solution.

These technicians must always be vigilant about their own safety, wearing the necessary wrist straps and using the right tools on an isolated computer.

Activity G

Talk to your technician

Your school or college will have one or more people employed as an IT technician. These staff will look after the computers and networks in your classrooms.

Ask your teacher if you can interview one of the technicians and find out what they do on an average day.

Make an A4 poster about the role of the IT technician.

Supply

Most computers are sold through stores like Currys and PC World, or through online sources like e-Buyer®.

Members of the sales staff usually have a wide knowledge of computers and peripherals and they can give you advice and guidance.

Activity H

Retail jobs

Use the following link to investigate the range of jobs available at PC World. What sort of job could you get with good technical knowledge? What would the job involve and what would you do each day?

http://www.jobvacanciesadvice.co.uk/pc-world-job-vacancies.html

Installation

Employees who install computer systems will be familiar with computers and their components. They will be able to build machines from an empty case to a full working system. They will also install the relevant operating system and any software that the user will need.

These people need to be good problem solvers.

Networks

Working with networks requires a good understanding of network communication and protocols. Cables will need to be installed or wireless technology configured to enable computers to connect.

Those working with networks need to be logical and good at problem solving.

Software-specific roles

Applications programmer

An **applications programmer** uses generic software like the components of the Microsoft Office® suite to create solutions for users.

They may use the **VBA (Visual Basic for Applications)** programming language to automate processes or actions to carry out a range of functions that are needed by the user.

Systems programmer

A **systems programmer** uses programming languages such as **Visual Basic net®**, **C#®** or **Java™** to write solutions to business problems. Unlike applications programming, they generally do not start with a pre-written application, they start with a blank screen and they write code that makes things happen.

To work as a programmer it helps if you can visualise what you are aiming for!

Website developer

Web developers are usually creative and artistic people who also like the challenge of working with technology. They design web pages for organisations.

Once websites are up and running, **website managers** then take over, carrying out maintenance, fixing any problems and making sure that the website is working for the customer.

Activity ▮

Investigate a web page

Find your school or college's web pages on the internet. What do you think of the page or pages?

Are they interesting to look at?
Are they easy to navigate?
Is the information up to date?
Do you think there is information that is not included that could or should be?

Write down three things about these pages and share them with another classmate or your tutor.

2.2.2 Jobs in investigation and design

Analysts

Analysts need to be methodical people with good investigation skills. They must have good communication skills and be able to talk to system users to find out what they do.

They will look at existing systems and problems in those systems and document their findings so that designers can understand the problems they are trying to resolve.

Their activities could include interviewing users, observing activities, reading existing documents about policies and procedures, looking at transactional documents (invoices, delivery notes and orders, for example) and investigating how records are kept.

This is an important job as if anything is left out, the solution that is implemented might not work!

Designers

Designers take the investigation done by an analyst and decide how the problems can be solved.

Drawing on their experience of similar successful projects, they come up with a design for the solution. They might select software and/or hardware, they will decide how any data in the system will be stored and may well make some suggestions to the client about changes in policies or processes.

You should always remember that a computerised solution is not always the only option. In some cases, improving an existing manual system might be just as valid an option!

Project managers

A **project manager** is usually someone who is good at leading a team.

He or she will be confident and will take control of the project, will be well organised and will have a good understanding of what needs to be done to complete the project.

A project manager should support the team and should be good at getting the best out of staff.

Make the grade

P2
P3
M1
D1

For P2 you need to describe a variety of common IT job roles. Your tutor might select jobs for you to describe or might give you the opportunity to choose your own. Either way, you simply need to describe what the employee does when they work in that role. You do not need to explain why they do it. To complete the assessment for this unit you will select a particular job role to explore.

To evidence P3 you will look back at the first section of this unit and for M1 you will explain which characteristics would be needed by someone working in this role. You will then need to explain why these characteristics would be important. Why, for example, is it important for a web developer to be creative? Why does a network technician need qualifications? Why is it important for a project manager to be well organised?

For the final criterion (D1) you will be given a set of employee characteristics and asked to state which job would be the most appropriate for a candidate with those characteristics. You will need to be able to justify your reason – so be prepared to explain why you have made a particular choice.

Achieving Success

In order to achieve each unit, you will complete a series of coursework activities. Each time you hand in work, your tutor will return this to you with a record of your achievement.

This particular unit has 5 criteria to meet: 3 Pass, 1 Merit and 1 Distinction.

For a **Pass** you must achieve **all 3** Pass criteria.

For a **Merit** you must achieve **all 3** Pass and **the single** Merit criterion.

For a **Distinction** you must achieve **all 3** Pass, **the single** Merit criterion **and the single** Distinction criterion.

Help with assessment

Your tutor will give you one or more assignments that you will complete as coursework. This could consist of:

- Presentations
- Newsletters or leaflets
- Videos
- Witness statements and/or an evidence log
- Web pages
- Blogs.

You should read the guidance given for each of the criteria (shown across the unit) carefully and remember to check your work.

Further reading

Textbooks

NCCER. *Employability Skills: Trainee Guide 00108-04*. (Prentice Hall, 2005) ISBN 0131600125

Websites

www.bcs.org/server.php?show=nav.5677

www.computingcareers.co.uk/

www.mindtools.com

Unit 3
Computer systems

Learning objectives

By the end of this unit you should:

1. Know the common components of computer systems
2. Know the different uses of computer systems
3. Be able to connect computer hardware
4. Be able to configure computer systems.

In order to pass this unit, the evidence you present for assessment needs to demonstrate that you can meet all of the above learning outcomes for this unit. The criteria below show the levels of achievement required to pass this unit.

To achieve a **pass** grade the evidence must show that the learner is able to:	To achieve a **merit** grade the evidence must show that, in addition to the pass criteria, the learner is able to:	To achieve a **distinction** the evidence must show that, in addition to the pass and merit criteria, the learner is able to:
P1 Identify the common components of a computer system	**M1** Describe different ways to connect to a computer network	
P2 Describe the purpose of different types of computer systems		
P3 Represent how data flows around a computer system		
P4 Specify suitable components to meet user requirements	**M2** Give reasons for the choice of components to meet a given business need	**D1** Suggest alternative setups based on user feedback
P5 Safely connect hardware to a computer system, testing for functionality	**M3** Explain working practices and health and safety procedures when connecting hardware devices	
P6 Configure software for a given user requirement		**D2** Discuss how the configuration of software will help a given user perform their tasks
P7 Identify potential security risks		

Introduction

It is likely that you will set up a computer system at some stage in your life. It may be yours or belong to the company you may work for. It might be a desktop PC, a laptop, PDA (Personal Data Assistant) or a games console such as a Nintendo® Wii or a Microsoft® Xbox360. To get this right, it helps to know about the different elements of the computer system and how hardware and software must work together to make it function correctly.

Computer systems and their components are built by many manufacturers and they all have different specifications. It is very important that you understand every bit of computer 'jargon' that you read as part of a computer system's technical specification.

When you think about the specifications needed for a new computer system, you cannot decide which components to select unless you have considered the typical tasks it may be used for. Once you have selected the appropriate components, you will need to be able to connect hardware devices safely and configure the different types of software correctly so that they meet the needs of the intended users. This unit is designed to help you make these decisions.

You will be assessed through coursework which could be in the form of:

• Presentations
• Practical sessions which may be photographed, videoed or witnessed
• Web pages and wikis
• Screen captures
• Blogs
• Podcasts.

In this chapter you will encounter a number of different units that are used in IT to measure time, frequency, memory and storage capacities. You will find these useful when comparing the specification of different computer systems' components.

The most commonly used units are shown in Table 3.1.

Used in	Term	Abbreviation	Meaning	Example
Memory and storage capacity	Bit		Smallest unit of computer memory (short for binary digit) – a bit can only store either a 0 or a 1	
	Byte		A byte is a collection of eight bits	A single character can be stored in 1 byte
	Kilobyte	KB	1024 (2^{10} bytes)	An image file size is 64 KB
	Megabyte	MB	1024 kilobytes	A CD can store up to 700 MB of data
	Gigabyte	GB	1024 megabytes	A user's computer has 4 GB of RAM
	Terabyte	TB	1024 gigabytes	A user's hard disk has 1 TB of free space
Frequency	Hertz	Hz	Unit of frequency, how many times 'something' happens per second	
	Megahertz	MHz	Million cycles per second	A computer's RAM
	Gigahertz	GHz	Billion cycles per second	A computer's CPU
Time	Millisecond	ms	1/1000th of a second	The time taken to access data on a hard disk is 5.6 ms

Table 3.1 Common computer system units

3.1 Know the common components of computer systems

This section will cover the following grading criteria:

P1 P2 P3 P7 M1

You will encounter many different types of computer system which are used both at home and at work. It is important to appreciate the different types available.

3.1.1 Computer systems

By the end of this section you should have developed a knowledge and understanding of which types of computer system are available in the home and workplace and be able to give short descriptions of them confidently.

Types of computer system

PCs

Usually found on a desktop, a **PC (personal computer)** consists of a **base unit**, a **monitor**, a **keyboard** and a **mouse**.

The base unit contains all the major hardware components, such as the motherboard, the central processing unit (CPU) and the memory. The monitor is used to display images from the PC's video card and may be CRT-based (cathode ray tube) or the increasingly popular TFT-based (thin-film transistor). The PC uses a keyboard and mouse as its input devices and these can be wired or wireless.

PCs are relatively easy to repair and upgrade and this makes them highly popular in both the home and at work. PCs can be programmed to do many different types of job and are the main tool used in the modern business office.

Laptops

A **laptop** or **notebook** is similar to a PC but is designed to be portable with an integrated screen and keyboard. Laptops are typically less powerful than their desktop counterparts. What they lack in raw power, however, they make up in convenience and portability. Laptops usually have a built-in touch-sensitive pad that is used instead of a mouse.

Netbooks

A **netbook** is very similar to a laptop but is much smaller and is designed to be used for simple tasks such as word processing, email and browsing the world wide web (WWW). They are ideal for home use or when travelling.

They are designed with power-efficient components that have good energy consumption but this limits its processing capabilities. They often do not use a Microsoft® Windows Operating System.

PDAs

A **PDA** or **Personal Digital Assistant** is a hand-held device which is often used instead of a traditional notebook, calendar or diary, especially in the workplace. Being hand-held they are typically very portable and are used with a stylus. They can also process emails and have support for web browsing and simple tasks such as word processing and spreadsheets.

PDAs are often synchronised to desktop PCs in order to keep a user's diary (or 'schedule') up to date.

Figure 3.1 A typical PDA

Mobile phones

A **mobile cellular telephone** is a cheap portable device which gives its user access to a cell network in order to communicate with others across the world. Modern mobile phones allow the user to make voice calls, video calls, send **SMS** (short message service) **messages**, **MMS** (multimedia message service) **messages**, emails and browse the World Wide Web.

More capable handsets (**'3G' or 3rd generation**) have more complex functions including playing audio and video and running downloaded applications.

Games consoles

Games consoles are used for home entertainment to play video games, audio CDs (compact discs) and DVDs (digital versatile discs). Games consoles may be **hand-held** or **static**. Some manufacturers (such as Sony and Nintendo) have both types and they can be connected together. (For example, a Sony PSP™ can be connected to a PlayStation®3 to share and play a downloaded game.)

Hand-held consoles can be used outside of the home, especially while on a journey. Due to the complexity of modern-day video games, the processing power of a games console is very good and compares favourably with high-end PCs.

Tablets

A **tablet** is a common management tool resembling a larger PDA; the tablet often has the same level of processing power as a laptop. Although some tablets have a keyboard, they often allow their users to use a stylus instead of a mouse. Tablets use **character recognition software** to convert handwritten writing into typed text and many have touch sensitive screens (for example, Apple's® iPad). Some laptops can be converted into a tablet by rotating their screen and 'hiding' the keyboard.

Embedded devices

Many household devices are controlled by computer systems. In these cases, the computer system is said to be '**embedded**'. Common examples include: telephones, televisions, DVD players, washing machines, microwave ovens and a car's **global positioning system** (**GPS**).

Most embedded systems have limited processing capabilities but are likely to have very **user-friendly** interfaces (for example, a microwave keypad). Unlike most computer systems, embedded systems are **dedicated** to performing a specific function.

Activity A

Types of computer system

You need to be able to identify different types of computer system and say what they are and where they may be used.

Select five different types of computer system and write down:

- Who the user is.
- When it might be used.
- What it might be used for.

For example, if you chose a games console, your answer might look something like the table below.

Who might use one?	When might it be used?	What might it be used for?
A member of the family	To relax or entertain the family. This could be at home or in transit (such as on a train or bus) if the device is portable.	To play a game, watch a video or listen to some music.

3.1.2 Hardware components

Any type of computer system is created from a combination of different components. Some components are **hardware**, some are software.

Key term

Hardware is any physical component in a computer system; something which is tangible and can therefore be 'seen' and 'touched'.

Computer system hardware comes in a variety of different component types. Although there can be some differences between manufacturers, they all adopt similar standards in order for their hardware to be used interchangeably.

The following section will show you the most common types of hardware used. You should learn from this what **job** each component **does** and **how** they are connected.

Figure 3.2 shows a typical PC system **motherboard**. The motherboard is the largest component inside the base unit. All of the other components are plugged into or connected to the motherboard. All computer systems, no matter what size, have a 'main' board of some kind.

Figure 3.2 A modern PC system motherboard

The popular type of motherboard shown in Figure 3.2 is called ATX (advanced technology extended) compatible.

The following components are connected directly to the motherboard:

1. the CPU
2. the RAM
3. the chipset.

The **CPU** (central processing unit or 'processor' for short) is the brain of the computer. Its job is to control the operation of the system. The frequency of the processor's internal clock is measured in hertz (Hz). CPUs are usually 32-bit or 64-bit. This describes the **size** of data and instructions it can process. In addition, some CPUs have **multiple 'cores'** which can work independently or can combine to process data faster. CPU performance is measured by a combination of its bit size, number of cores and frequency: bigger is usually better! CPUs are usually the most expensive component of a system, manufactured by either Intel or AMD (Advanced Micro Devices).

The job of **RAM** (random access memory) is to store data and instructions temporarily when a program is being run by a CPU. When the power is removed the data is lost – this is what we call volatile storage.

Figure 3.3 Modern RAM

RAM is a key factor in good computer system performance (more is better). RAM is a relatively inexpensive system component so is an obvious choice to upgrade to improve system performance. There are many different types, sizes and speeds of RAM, with DIMMs (Dual Inline Memory Module) and DDR (Double Data Rate) being the most common.

Motherboards make use of many specialist **microchips** ('chips' for short). The common ones are:

- **Northbridge** – which manages data traffic between faster motherboard components (RAM, CPU and video card).
- **Southbridge** – which manages traffic between slower motherboard components.

In addition the motherboard may have chips dedicated to:

- video
- sound
- network connectivity.

Alternatively, these could be **separate cards** which are plugged into the motherboard through its **expansion slots**.

Internal hard disks (or disk drives) are connected to the motherboard by either a PATA (Parallel Advance Technology Attachment) or the newer SATA (Serial ATA) connection.

Figure 3.4 Modern SATA hard drive

These are magnetic data storage units and they store vast amounts of data and spin at speeds of around 7200 rpm (revolutions per minute). Although hard disks are typically stored inside the base unit (or laptop) they can also be purchased as an external device, usually connected by USB (universal serial bus) or eSATA cables. Most new computer systems are using SATA drives and often have at least 500 GB of storage.

Optical drives use a laser to read data from a CD, DVD or a BD (Blu-ray disc). Most drives can use either read-only discs, such as CD-ROMs and DVD-ROMs, or can be used to record data on recordable or rewriteable discs. Drives are usually marked to indicate what type of discs they will accept. The typical data **capacity** of these discs is as given below:

- CD: 650–700 MB
- DVD: 4.7–16 GB
- BD: 25–128 GB

Flash drives use a special type of electronic memory which can be rewritten very quickly and remains intact even when the device is removed from the computer system's power. This makes them ideal for medium- and long-term data storage.

Figure 3.5 Flash drives

Relatively inexpensive and easy to use, flash drives connect to modern computer systems via a USB port. These devices are very popular, primarily due to their highly portable nature. A typical flash drive can store anything between 16 MB and 250 GB depending on the age of the technology. The increased use of flash drives is certainly a major factor in the demise of the floppy disk drive whose ageing technology could only store up to 1.44 MB. This soon became impractical for modern data usage such as music, video and presentations. Although the flash drive is normally connected externally, the USB hub which it connects to is built into the motherboard.

The following components are connected to the motherboard via external ports (usually on the '**backplane**' of the motherboard which is visible on the back of the base unit). These components are **peripheral** (connected outside the base unit) and are classified as input devices.

Touch screen technology is not new – it has been around since the 1970s. However, recent advances and a reduction in costs have made it popular in mobile telephones, GPS devices, public access points, bank ATMs (automatic teller machines) and hand-held games consoles. Touch screens are easy to use because they require no special equipment other than the user's hand. Combined with a simple icon-based interface, even non-technical users can interact with a computer system quite quickly. The Surface project from Microsoft® is a good showcase for this technology (see http://www.microsoft.com/surface/en/us/default.aspx).

Beloved by digital artists, the **graphics tablet** is an alternative to using a mouse when greater precision for drawing is required.

Figure 3.6 A graphics tablet

A professional digital artist will use a tool like this when using graphical applications software such as Adobe Photoshop®. Graphic tablets come complete with a stylus and often come in A5, A4 and A3 sizes. They are usually connected to a computer system via USB.

Although some **game controllers** can be used with a PC or Apple® Mac, most are specific to a chosen games console. Most game controllers contain force-feedback technology which 'rumbles' the controller in the user's hand to reflect on-screen events. While some controllers use a proprietary connection (i.e. specific to a particular console) most modern devices use either USB or wireless connections.

A **microphone** is used to convert sound waves made by human speech into electrical signals which can be used to control a computer system or talk to other users via internet telephone services such as Skype.

The **keyboard** is the most basic form of input device and is also the most commonly used in a computer system. Although the traditional QWERTY keyboard (named after the arrangement of top row letter keys) is the one most commonly seen, there are other variations. Most PC keyboards are either wireless or use USB or PS/2 connections.

A **mouse** uses either a mechanical roller ball or optical light-emitting diodes and sensors to move a pointer on the screen. A mouse is a key component of modern GUI (graphical user interfaces) and helped to popularise Microsoft® Windows and the Apple® Mac. Most PC mice are either wireless or use USB or PS/2 connections.

Other types of peripherals are classified as **output devices**.

A **printer** is a device which produces monochrome (black and white), grey scale or colour prints containing text and/or images. Two major types of printer are common in homes and businesses: ink-jet and laser. Ink-jet printers use wet cartridge ink to form images on a page. Laser printers work in a process similar to photocopiers by using dry toner which is heat-bonded to certain points of the page. Most printers use wireless, USB or (much older) parallel port connections.

Although still popular, older **CRT** (cathode ray tube) **monitors** are diminishing in use due to their bulky nature and higher power consumption. Sleeker, flatter **LCD** (liquid crystal display) screens have become the standard for new computer systems. Connections to a computer system are usually by the older 15-pin (or VGA) connector or a newer (typically) 29-pin DVI (digital visual interface). The type of connection used must be compatible with the computer system's video card.

Speakers connect to the sound card of a computer system. The speaker's job is to convert electrical signals into sound waves (basically the opposite of the microphone). Two speakers are common, offering the user stereo sound. More complex speaker systems are possible, depending on the sound card, where a set-up like 5.1 indicates five speakers (front right, front left, back left, back right, centre) plus a sub-woofer for lower frequency 'bass' sounds.

In addition to input and output devices, computer systems can be connected together. Any device which helps to achieve this comes under the classification of **network connectivity**.

3G®, or 3rd generation mobile telephone technology, can be used to transmit data over a cellular network between two different computer systems. Although the technology is built into 3G telephones, traditional computer systems such as a desktop PC or notebook can make use of USB **3G dongles** to access the same network.

Figure 3.7 A 3G dongle

Wi-Fi networks can be accessed by an appropriate wireless network controller and many devices have these built-in (for example, Apple iPhone, Nintendo Wii®, Sony PlayStation®3 and most netbooks). Where Wi-Fi connectivity is not built into the device, it is possible to connect a **USB wireless dongle** that will do the same job.

Although not as fast, flexible or powerful as a Wi-Fi network, **Bluetooth** connectivity can be a useful tool when transmitting data between a mobile telephone and a computer system. Inexpensive USB Bluetooth dongles enable a user to back up mobile telephone data (such as pictures, SMS texts) to their computer system or upload music to them. Most Bluetooth devices are effective within 10 metres.

A **network interface card** (**NIC**) usually plugs into the motherboard of a computer system. Many different types (and speeds)

exist and it is not uncommon to find its circuitry built into the motherboards of most desktop PCs, laptops and netbooks. Although some NICs use a wired (ethernet) connection, others use wireless connectivity and often have a visible antenna.

Figure 3.8 A network interface card

Make the grade   M1

For this criterion you must show that you can describe different ways to connect to a network.
Read through the network connectivity entries in section 3.1.2 as they describe the most common hardware components used to join a computer system to a network. You may find the RJ45 details in section 3.3.1 useful too!

Activity B

Common components of a computer system

You need to be able to identify the different components of a computer system, specifying whether they are typically internal or external and whether they are input, output or connectivity devices.

Copy and complete the following table, placing each component into its appropriate location: (to get you started, 'Printer', 'Optical Drive' and 'Keyboard' have already been completed!)

Component	Internal (connects to the motherboard)	External (an input device)	External (an output device)	Provides network connectivity
RAM				
NIC				
Printer			Yes	
Hard disk drive				
Mouse				
CPU				
3G				
Chipset				
Microphone				
Optical drive	Yes			
USB drive				
Touch screen				
Bluetooth				
Wireless				
Monitor				
Keyboard		Yes		
Graphics tablet				
Game controller				

Make the grade

For this criterion you must show that you can identify the common components of a computer system.

Read through the entries in section 3.1.2 as they describe the most common components in a typical computer system and give a short description of their key features.

Completing Activity B will provide a good way of remembering how the component is connected to the computer system (for example, internally or externally) and what its job actually is (such as input or output device).

3.1.3 Software components

Key term

Software is a set of instructions which tell the computer what to do, such as Microsoft Windows®, Microsoft Word®, Mozilla Firefox®.

Software can be broken down into three different categories: systems software, application software and software utilities. These are described in more detail below.

1. **Systems software**:
   - Operates and controls the basic computer hardware.
   - Provides a way for users to input data.
   - Provides a platform for application software to run.
   - Manages resources such as the RAM.
   - The most important example of systems software is the **operating system** (OS).
   - Common operating systems include Microsoft Windows®, Linux® and Mac OS X.

2. **Application software**:
   - Performs specific tasks for the user.
   - Requires a compatible operating system to work.
   - Common applications software includes office productivity suites (such as Microsoft Office®), communication suites (such as Mozilla Firefox®, Microsoft Outlook® etc.), educational software, industry software such as CAD (computer aided design), games and simulators.

3. **Software utilities**:
   - Often treated as a type of system software.
   - Helps user to manage their computer system.
   - Requires more advanced skills in order to use.
   - Common utilities include: disk defragmenters, disk repair, anti-virus, file managers, data compression, data backup, data encryption and software development suites.
   - Most operating systems come with free utilities.

Activity C

Software components

Research the following software components and decide whether they are:

- Systems software
- Application software
- Software utilities.

Media Player®	Activision®	Call of Duty®: Black Ops
Google Chrome	Microsoft Access®	Lavasoft
Ad-aware	Piriform® Defraggler	Microsoft Excel®
Microsoft Visual	C#®	Microsoft Windows 7®
AVG Technologies	Microsoft Word®	Apple iTunes
Adobe® Dreamweaver®	Notepad	Apple IOS 4

3.1.4 Security

The security of modern computer systems is threatened by a number of common risks. Some of these risks are detailed below.

Phishing

> ### Key term
>
> **Phishing** is a common online fraud technique which relies on a criminal attempting to get a user's personal details by pretending to be a legitimate business.

The most common examples of phishing occur through bogus emails sent to users, typically from what looks like, genuine banks and companies, which ask them to log onto a website to update their personal details, often under the pretence that their account is vulnerable if they do not. Unfortunately many users unwittingly fall for this type of scam! A typical phishing email might read like this:

> ### *Message Alert:*
>
> This is to inform you that your Hsbc Internet Banking Secure Message Centre has2 New Internet Banking ALERT.
>
> To access and view your Hsbc Internet Banking personalized Secure Massages Centre, Click on the link: **Read** to logon page.
>
> Hsbc Bank Internet Banking Customer Services & Security Team 2010

A closer look at this email reveals poor formatting, odd grammar and incorrect branding (HSBC rarely use anything other than capital letters when writing their name). If this were not suspicious enough, hovering the cursor over the 'Read' hyperlink shows the following shortcut: http://www.biosesang.com/bioshop/session/verify-v1.php.

Clearly that is not linking to a recognisable HSBC website; in all likelihood this is a phishing attack.

Malware

> ### Key term
>
> **Malware** is an abbreviation of **mal**icious soft**ware**. This type of software is designed to gain access to a user's computer system without their knowledge or permission. Malware is an umbrella title covering other terms such as viruses, worms, spyware and Trojan horses.

Viruses

Key term

A **virus** is a type of malicious software that infects a computer and can copy itself in order to spread its infection. Virus behaviour varies greatly from mild irritation to destruction of data depending on its actual payload.

Viruses are transmitted by the use of removable backing storage media (such as flash drives, floppy disks, CDs, DVDs etc.) and infected email attachments.

The installation of an anti-virus utility can usually protect the user from new infection and can either **heal** (remove the virus), **quarantine** (move the infected file to a safe folder) or **delete** an existing infected file. Thousands of different computer viruses exist and the number increases daily.

Spyware

Key term

Spyware is a type of malware that is installed on a user's computer system secretly. It sends information about the user (accounts, passwords etc.) and their web browsing habits to other computers without their knowledge or permission.

Spam

Key term

Spam is unsolicited email, that is to say, email that you have not requested from people or organisations you do not know. Spam is estimated to represent over 90 per cent of all email received and many businesses attempt to filter it from their systems before its users can see it.

Activity D

Security

Visit an online news site such as news.bbc.co.uk to find names of recent viruses which have made the headlines and any phishing, spyware or spam attacks which were newsworthy. The following links provide some examples to get you started.

http://www.bbc.co.uk/news/world-us-canada-11917471

http://www.bbc.co.uk/news/business-10952604

http://www.telegraph.co.uk/technology/internet/8159442/Stuxnet-computer-virus-in-hands-of-criminal-gangs.html

Make the grade   P7

For this criterion you must show that you can identify potential security risks. Most of the obvious security risks are listed in section 3.1.4. Read through these and familiarise yourself with them. A number of security measures are discussed in section 3.4.6 which help to combat these.

3.1.5 Data flow

The core components of a computer system can be represented by a simple block diagram. If we then add arrows to this diagram, we can show how the data flows around the computer system (see Figure 3.9). The dotted line shows the typical 'base unit'.

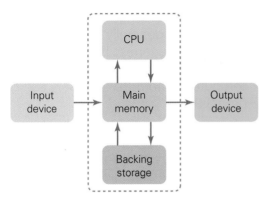

Figure 3.9 A simple block diagram of a computer system

Input device – allows the user to enter data manually (e.g. a keyboard).

Main memory – temporarily stores data entered by the user (i.e. the RAM).

CPU – processes data transferred from main memory and returns the results it calculates back to main memory.

Output device – displays results of the processed data as information (e.g. on a monitor).

Backing storage – more permanently loads and saves data (e.g. hard disk drive).

3.2 Know the different uses of computer systems

This section will cover the following grading criteria: P4 M2 D1

In order to be able to specify a new computer system for a particular user or business need, you must first know what is actually required!

3.2.1 Components

Whether they are hardware or software, all components in a computer system perform a basic job. Your task is to know what type of job they do! Let us look at the most familiar types of component and describe their basic uses:

Activity E

How data flows in a computer system

It helps to be able to link the logical block model to the hardware components you have already read about in section 3.1.2.

If you took the hardware components from section 3.1.2 and used them as labels for the logical block model seen in Figure 3.9, what would it look like?

Try updating the logical block model with these hardware component labels.

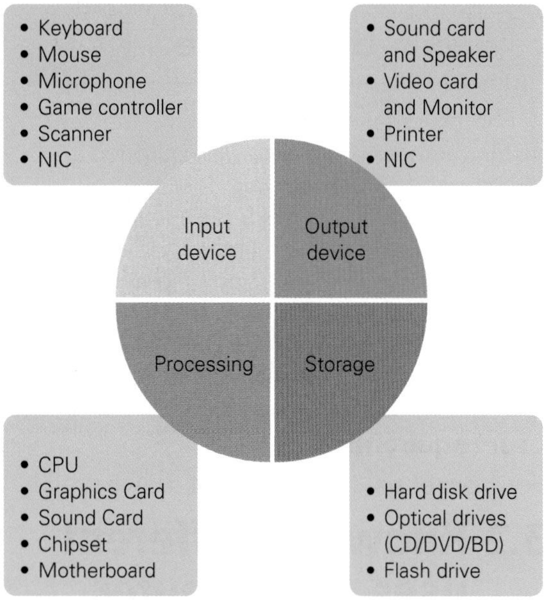
• Keyboard
• Mouse
• Microphone
• Game controller
• Scanner
• NIC
• Sound card and Speaker
• Video card and Monitor
• Printer
• NIC
Input device
Output device
Processing
Storage
• CPU
• Graphics Card
• Sound Card
• Chipset
• Motherboard
• Hard disk drive
• Optical drives (CD/DVD/BD)
• Flash drive

Figure 3.10 Hardware components

As you can see from Figure 3.10, hardware components can generally be grouped into four different categories. These categories have a strong link to the block diagram of the computer system that you saw earlier in Figure 3.9.

This diagram is useful because it helps you to think about which aspect of a computer system's hardware that a user's priorities will influence. For example, if the user is concerned about having good processing power, then you would need to concentrate on the CPU, graphics card, sound card, motherboard and chipset.

We can group **software components** by the **functionality** they provide for users. This is shown in Table 3.2 but it is not meant to be an exhaustive list.

Uses for software component	Software components that may be involved	Type of software component
Basic control of computer system	Operating system	Systems software
Internet and web access	Operating system, web browser	Systems software/Application software
Web browser	Systems software	Application software
Email client	Web browser	Application software
Basic budgeting	Spreadsheet	Application software
Accounting	Spreadsheet/accounting package	Application software
Records keeping and reporting	Database	Application software
Graphic design	Computer graphic package	Application software
Entertainment	Video games	Application software
Providing security for computer system	Anti-virus, firewall, spam filter	Utility software
Fixing hard disk drive	Disk scan, fragmenter, backup	Utility software

Table 3.2 Sample software uses

3.2.2 User

Users want different things from a computer system and these differences will greatly alter the way you select hardware and software components for them.

The common types of user are shown in Figure 3.11.

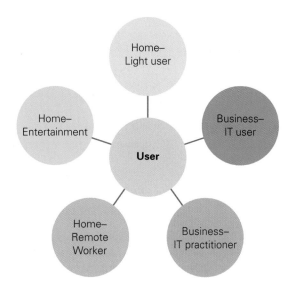

Figure 3.11 Types of user

- A **light user at home** may just want to use basic application software (this would mean low demands on the hardware and software components).
- A **business IT user** would also want to use basic application software but may in addition need to use software that is specialised for their industry (such as bookkeeping software for an accounts manager).
- An **IT practitioner** in the workplace would want to use specialist utilities that enable them to fix networks, program, administer a network and create complex databases.
- A **home worker** would have similar needs to a business IT user but would want connectivity for email and company intranet access (over the internet via a VPN – virtual private network).

- A **home user** with **entertainment needs** would want media players for video and music and possibly mastering software for CDs and DVDs.

As you can see, different types of users have different needs; this will shape the computer system required.

3.2.3 User requirement

Although computer systems are used both in the home and in business, their uses are very different. We can call this the **user requirement**.

For **home**, user requirement may be:

- Simple word processing for letters or homework.
- Basic spreadsheets for home budgeting.
- Internet connectivity for browsing the web, online shopping or gaming.
- Media player for watching films and listening to music.
- A fast graphics card and processor for playing new video games.
- A portable system that can be used around the home or even in the garden.

For **business**, the user requirements may be more challenging:

- A business dealing in finance needs specialist accounting software.
- A manufacturing firm may want high-end graphics hardware and expensive CAD (computer aided design) software.
- A graphic design firm would want high-quality monitors, video cards, powerful CPU and expensive colour laser printing.

In addition, any solution should take into account the **accessibility features** that a user with **learning difficulties** or **physical challenges** may require. This might include:

- Modified keyboards and pointing devices
- Speech recognition and narration of onscreen events and content
- High contrast visual displays with zoom facilities.

3.2.4 Performance requirements

As discussed in section 3.1.1, the performance of a computer system is largely measured by the power, size and speed of its components. This is particularly true for the CPU, RAM, video card and hard disk drive. Table 3.3 shows which aspects are desirable for each component.

Hardware component	What is important in terms of performance?
CPU	Frequency (measured in GHz) – faster is better Number of processing cores – more is better 32-bit or 64-bit – 64 is better but needs compatible software
RAM	Size – more RAM is always better Frequency (measured in MHz) – faster is better Manufacturer reputation – some produce more reliable memory than others
Video card	Frequency of GPU (graphic processing unit) – faster is better Number of processing cores – more is better Size – more video RAM is always better Maximum resolution (in pixels) – higher values are better Maximum number of colours – higher values are better
Motherboard	Support for processors – which type of processor does it support? Chipset – some are considered to be more stable than others Expansion – what scope is there to add new components RAM – how much memory expansion can it accept Features – does it have a rich mix of attractive components Manufacturer reputation – some produce more reliable motherboards than others
Hard disk drive	SATA or PATA – SATA is the new standard Storage capacity (measured in GB) – bigger is better Rotational speed (measured in RPM, revolutions per minute) – faster is better Data access time (measured in milliseconds) – faster is better Data transfer rate (measured in MB/second) – higher/quicker is better Manufacturer reputation – some produce more reliable drives than others
Network interface card	Data transfer rate (measured in Mb/second or Gb/second) – higher/quicker is better Type of motherboard connection – wireless or wired Manufacturer reputation – some produce more reliable NICs than others
Battery (for portable computer systems)	Battery life (measured in hours and minutes) – longer is better Battery recharge time (measured in hours and minutes) – shorter is better

Table 3.3 Performance requirements for different components

Activity F

Performance requirements

Understanding performance requirements relies on your reading through technical specifications for computer systems – you have to become familiar with the jargon.

Explore hardware components on the following websites and see if you can start to work out:

- Which components are bigger?
- Which components are faster?
- Which components are better value for money?

PC World: http://www.pcworld.co.uk/gbuk/index.html

Ebuyer: http://www.ebuyer.com/

Make the grade   P4 M2 D1

Criteria P4 and M2 are linked. P4 asks that you can specify suitable components to meet user requirements and M2 asks that you can give reasons for your choice of components to meet the user's given need. Reading through sections 3.2.1, 3.2.2, 3.2.3 and 3.2.4 will help you prepare for this task. It is likely that you will either be given a scenario by your teacher or investigate a real user's needs. These needs could be in the home or within a business
Try the following set of steps:

1. Find out what the user wants to achieve with the computer system.
2. Find out which software components are required to achieve these user goals.

3. The application software needed will have recommended hardware requirements (and system software). Match these hardware components.
4. Put together a document containing the user's needs and the software and hardware requirements. This should generate P4.
5. You will then have to justify your choices – *why* did you pick these components? If you have made the links between (a) what the user wants to achieve, (b) the software and (c) the hardware, it should be easy to do this. This should generate M2.

D1 follows on from P4 and M2 and asks you to suggest alternative set ups based on user feedback. Completing P4 and M2 will provide you with a computer system set up for a user. If the user says, 'this is too expensive' or 'I would prefer to use an Apple® Mac' then you will need to revise your set up. This will undoubtedly have an effect on the hardware and software components you have selected. D1 is asking you to provide *at least* two different alternatives.

3.3 Be able to connect computer hardware

This section will cover the following grading criteria: P5 M3

3.3.1 Connections

As computer systems have developed, the process of connecting computer hardware has become easier due to the use of **colour coding**.

Peripheral devices – those connected outside of the base unit – use specific connections (often called '**interfaces**' or '**ports**') which you have to be familiar with.

Most of these connections are found on the **motherboard's backplane**. If you take a look at Table 3.4 you will see the most common types you might encounter.

Connection	What it is	What to connect it to
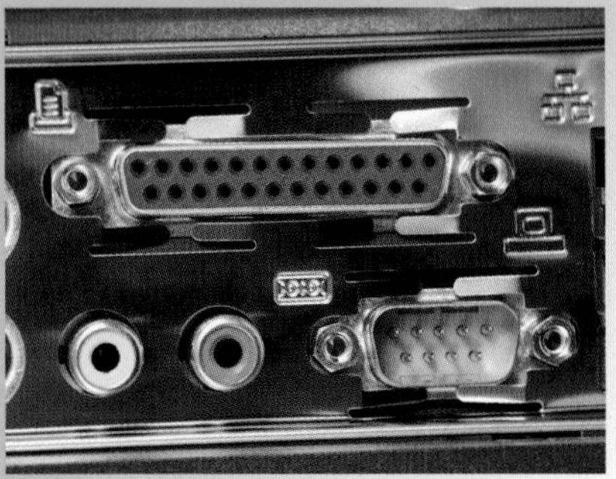 **Figure 3.12** A parallel printer port	A DB-25 or Centronics parallel port. An older port, often referred to as a **legacy connection**. Mostly replaced by USB. Usually pink or black.	Printer Scanner
 **Figure 3.13** A USB port	USB stands for universal serial bus. This is probably the most popular interface in modern computer systems. There are three distinct versions (1.0, 2.0 and 3.0) which vary data transfer rates. USB ports are usually marked with the distinctive **trident logo**.	Keyboard Mouse Printer Scanner Digital camera Webcam Barcode reader Graphics tablet Wireless/Bluetooth dongle Flash drive Fingerprint reader

Table 3.4 Common connections (continues on next page)

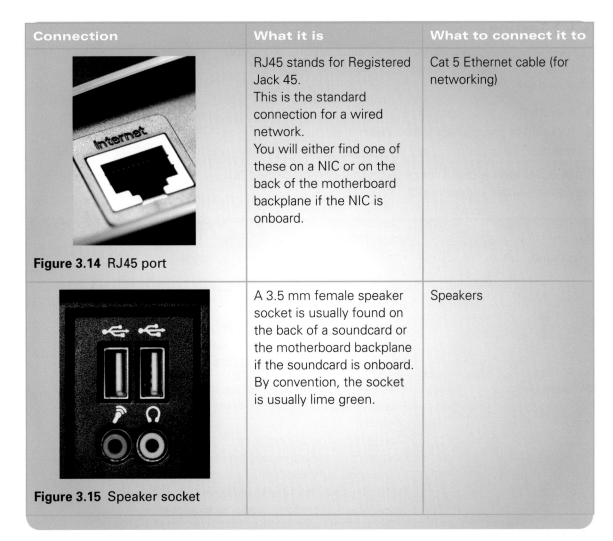

Connection	What it is	What to connect it to
Figure 3.14 RJ45 port	RJ45 stands for Registered Jack 45. This is the standard connection for a wired network. You will either find one of these on a NIC or on the back of the motherboard backplane if the NIC is onboard.	Cat 5 Ethernet cable (for networking)
Figure 3.15 Speaker socket	A 3.5 mm female speaker socket is usually found on the back of a soundcard or the motherboard backplane if the soundcard is onboard. By convention, the socket is usually lime green.	Speakers

Table 3.4 Continued

Activity G

Hardware connections

Locate a computer system that you can safely examine; if the computer system is not yours, you should ask for permission first!

Which hardware components are connected externally?

What type of connections do they use?

Using information supplied in sections 3.1.2 and 3.3.1 create a list of the hardware components and connections used by your selected computer system.

3.3.2 Testing

Testing is an important aspect of connecting any computer hardware components. Hardware should be tested to ensure that:

1. It works!

2. It provides the correct functionality that the user requires.

Table 3.5 shows a checklist of tests that can be carried out on some sample components.

Hardware	Sample tests
Keyboard	• If wireless, that keyboard is recognised and works • Standard key presses work • Caps lock key (LED should light) • Shift keys work • Number lock key works (LED should light) • Scroll lock key works (LED should light) • Shift + 2 key produces a quotation mark (") for UK
Mouse	If wireless, that mouse is recognised and works Mouse responds to normal movement as pointer moves correctly Mouse movement is smooth Pointer does not move when mouse is idle Left mouse button works as expected Right mouse button works as expected Scroll wheel (if present) works as expected
Printer	If wireless, that printer is recognised and works Printer switches on Printer prints a test page from the connected computer system Paper is not jamming Print quality produced is acceptable
Network interface card	Network interface card is recognised by the operating system Computing system has an IP address A simple ping to test connectivity is successful (see Unit 10) If the system is connected to the internet, that a sample web page can be downloaded by a web browser

Table 3.5 Checklist of sample tests for components

Clearly the more complex a hardware component is, the more difficult it is to test effectively and the more things that can go wrong!

3.3.3 Health and safety

It is always worth reminding ourselves of the most common hazards which can risk the health and safety of an individual.

When installing new hardware you should:

- Use an **anti-static wrist strap** when installing components.
- Only use the correct tools.
- Be careful when using tools.
- Be careful of sharp edges inside computer cases when installing network cards.
- Switch off mains sockets before plugging in mains cables.
- Only switch on a mains socket when *all* mains cables are in place and firmly plugged in.
- Ensure that there are no trailing cables that can be tripped over.

Figure 3.16 An anti-static wrist strap with grounding wire

Other factors which could pose problems include **manual handling** of equipment. The UK's **HSE** (Health and Safety Executive) provides details of recommended maximum safe loads and recommended postures for lifting, lowering, pushing and pulling heavy equipment.

Health and safety issues also apply to any computer system users, particularly with regard to:

- **DSE** (display screen equipment) – for workstation ergonomics, users' posture and reduction/prevention of eye strain.
- **RSI** (repetitive strain injury) – a soft tissue injury typically resulting from poor posture, bad ergonomics, stress and repetitive motion.

Most organisations would have a **risk assessment** procedure and a local Health and Safety Officer who would ensure compliance with any relevant legislation.

3.3.4 Working practices

For an IT technician, the task of installing new hardware or software components follows standard procedures that are typically laid down by their organisation as **best practice**.

This would typically include:

- Assessing and minimising risks – observing health and safety regulations (see 3.3.3)
- Obtaining resources – having the hardware, software or paperwork required
- Backing up important data before starting
- Recording relevant information – logging actions as they are performed
- Communicating progress – keeping interested parties informed on how the job is progressing, any problems encountered or changes of plan
- Communicating outcomes – telling interested parties what impact the installation has on the system (good or bad).

In theory, having good working practices should reduce errors being made which cause damage to new hardware, existing computer systems or loss of user data.

Make the grade **P5**

M3

For P5 you must show that
you can connect hardware to a
computer system, testing for functionality.
Reading through sections 3.3.1, 3.3.2 and
3.3.3 will help you prepare for this task.
This is a practical task and it is likely that
it will be evidenced through photographs,
videos, witness statements (from your
teacher) and a short written account
describing your actions.
For M3 you must show that you can
explain working practices and health
and safety procedures when connecting
hardware devices. This is clearly
connected to criterion P5 and is likely to
be completed at the same time. Reading
through sections 3.3.3 and 3.3.4 will help
you prepare. This task could be evidenced
through a short written account, a wiki, a
podcast, a presentation or a viva (a verbal
examination by your tutor).

3.4 Be able to configure computer systems

This section will cover the following grading criteria: **P6** **D2**

3.4.1 Requirements

As we have already seen, users in the
office or at home will have different
requirements in terms of both the software
they use and the tasks they perform with
it. For this reason, although there may be
some similarities, the configurations will be
quite different.

For example, for home users you may need
to configure data recording, photo editing
or media playback settings – you are likely
to encounter few of these requests in a
company's administration offices!

3.4.2 Systems software

On traditional PCs and Apple® Mac
computer systems, the configurations you
can perform on the systems software may
be limited by your school or college, as
making such changes can seriously affect
the way a computer system works!

Given below are some common
configuration examples for the most
common type of system software – the
operating system. These examples use
a mixture of different computer systems
to highlight the fact that while system
software is a critical component in each,
they all have similar configuration needs.

Configuring date and time

In Microsoft Windows® Vista and 7, the
taskbar has a system tray or 'notification
area' in the bottom right-hand corner of the
screen. If the time is clicked, the following
window will occur (Figure 3.17):

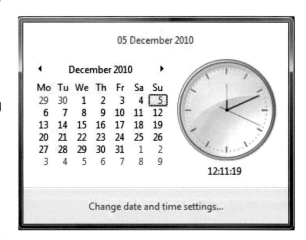

Figure 3.17 Date and time

An option is present to change the date
and time settings. Clicking this will open a
new dialogue window (Figure 3.18).

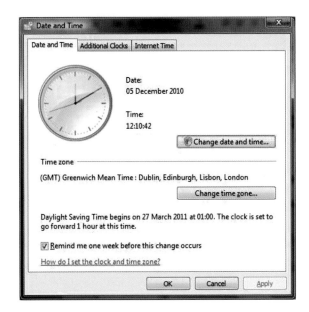

Figure 3.18 Date and time dialogue

From here it is possible to configure the date and time of the computer system, even specifying which time zone the machine is in.

Turning Wi-Fi on

Apple®'s iPhone IOS4 has the ability to use a wireless connection to access internet services. Using this feature can make the battery drain faster so many users have this switched off by default. Turning the wireless connection on is very easy. First, you must touch the Settings 'cogs' icon on the main menu – doing so will display the Settings page. You can then use your finger to slide the Wi-Fi option from OFF to ON.

The iPhone will then start to scan for available wireless networks in range. Depending on the security of the network you choose, you may have to provide a username, password or both before you can use it – so have these details ready!

Changing a user's password

Most computer systems permit **multi-user access**. To do this the systems software must be able to login separate users with a **password**. Changing a user's password is a common configuration issue.

In Linux Fedora™, passwords can be configured by accessing the Administration → Users and Groups menu option (see Figure 3.19).

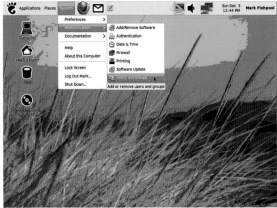

Figure 3.19 Changing a user's password in Linux – Step 1

Then selecting the user (Figure 3.20).

Figure 3.20 Changing a user's password in Linux – Step 2

The next step is to click the Properties menu option (Figure 3.21).

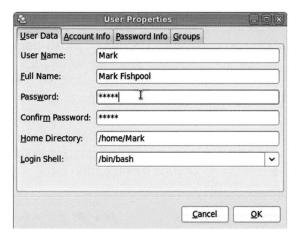

Figure 3.21 Changing a user's password in Linux – Step 3

Figure 3.22 Google Chrome®'s Options menu

The last step is to type in a new password and confirm it. Pressing the OK button will then make the change permanent. Be warned that some systems software has strict rules for password strength – you can read about this in section 3.4.6.

3.4.3 Applications software

Almost all applications software has a **menu** listing 'Options' (see Figure 3.22).

Inevitably, clicking this menu option will reveal a feast of available settings which you can configure. Each setting will change the way that the application behaves for its user.

Unfortunately it would require a separate book to list all the configuration options for even a limited number of applications! Table 3.6 lists some sample applications and shows a few of the common settings that you may want to configure.

Type of applications software	Common options to configure
Word processing e.g. Microsoft Office®	Whether spaces are shown as ".". Which country's dictionary is used (e.g. US or UK) for spell check How often a document is auto-saved (e.g. every 10 minutes) If spelling errors are corrected as a user types How many recently opened documents it should list
Spreadsheets e.g. Microsoft Excel®	What the default font and font size is for a new worksheet The number of worksheets in a new workbook Whether to recalculate values automatically Whether to show a zero or not Whether to auto complete a recognised cell entry

Table 3.6 Common configuration options in popular applications (continues on next page)

Type of applications software	Common options to configure
Web browser e.g. Mozilla Firefox®	The address of the home page The folder to use for saving all downloads Whether it will block pop-up windows Whether it will display images on a web page Whether it will remember passwords Whether it will warn the user if a web page attempts to install an add-on

Table 3.6 Continued

3.4.4 Utilities

Utilities are generally complex tools and require some thought before they are configured as mistakes could destabilise the computer system! Common utilities which can be configured simply could include:

- compression tools
- defragmentation tools
- drive formatting tools
- internet clean-up tools (for cookies, browsing history etc.)
- disk drive clean-up tools.

Let us take a look at some simple but effective configurations for two common utilities.

Piriform® Defraggler

When a file is saved on a hard disk drive, it is broken into pieces and each piece (or fragment) is fitted into a free gap. When a disk's files become too fragmented (10 per cent is too much), the computer system slows down. Piriform®'s Defraggler is a third-party tool to defragment the contents of a Windows'® hard disk drive (it puts the pieces back together).

Figure 3.23 Configuring Defraggler

In Figure 3.23 we can see that it is possible to configure Defraggler to run as a scheduled task at 11 p.m. each day. Defraggler is freely downloadable from: http://www.piriform.com/defraggler.

RARLAB's WinRAR

This is a utility which can be used to compress and decompress files. Although .ZIP support has long since been integrated into many operating systems, many other types of compression exist and WinRAR is a good utility for dealing with them.

WinRAR has many options; one in particular is to configure which types of compressed file it is associated with.

Figure 3.24 WinRAR configuration

WinRAR is downloadable from: http://www.rarlab.com/.

Activity H

Configuring utilities

Many third-party utilities are freely available for download from websites using the internet and every operating system has a number of utilities already built in (Microsoft Windows® usually calls these Accessories).

The following list suggests some types of utilities you may want to try and configure.

For getting **system information**:

Speccy – http://www.piriform.com/speccy
Belarc Advisor – http://www.belarc.com/free_download.html

For **disk clean-up** tools:

CCleaner – http://www.piriform.com/ccleaner
RedButton – http://pothos.ru/eng/index.php?mod=redbutton

3.4.5 Configure

For many users, the appearance of the desktop in a GUI-based (Graphical User Interface) operating system is a very important personal choice.

We can configure many different aspects of this quite easily in Microsoft Windows®. Detailed below are some aspects of the desktop that you could consider configuring to meet a target user's needs. Most other types of computer systems (such as mobile telephones) have similar features but they are accessed differently.

Colour scheme

This is accessible through Microsoft Windows'® Control Panel. It is relatively simple to set a different colour scheme (or create a new one).

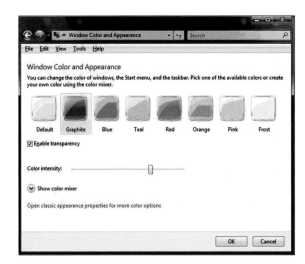

Figure 3.25 Windows® colour and appearance

The older style Windows® Appearance dialogue is also available (see Figure 3.26).

Figure 3.26 Setting a high contrast colour scheme

Each colour scheme change is specific to the user. This permits a personalised approach to the user interface.

Screen resolution and colour depth

The **screen resolution** and **colour depth** of the screen display can be changed in most operating systems. The actual upper limits of both the screen resolution and colour depth are limited by the graphic card component – if this is too low for user needs, a replacement may be required.

In Windows®, these settings can be configured through the Display Settings in the Control Panel.

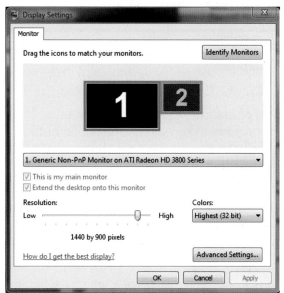

Figure 3.27 Display settings in Windows®

Setting higher resolutions and colour depths produces more detailed and realistic images – something particularly important to users working with graphics. A higher resolution also creates more desktop 'space' to work on.

Background (wallpaper)

The background or wallpaper is a simple configuration and is again accessed via Windows'® Control Panel (see Figure 3.28).

Figure 3.28 Desktop background selection in Windows®

Figure 3.29 The icon configuration in Linux Fedora™

The operating system often comes installed with sample backgrounds but users can download or create their own images to use instead.

In a business environment wallpapers are often **corporate** in design, for example they may use the **company logo**.

Changing icons

Icons are the small images which represent objects and actions in a modern operating system. Most icons have a **default appearance** (in other words, what they look like at the beginning) but this can be configured for the user. In Microsoft Windows®, this is again accessed via the Control Panel but similar functions exist in other computer systems. Figure 3.29 shows icons being changed in Linux Fedora™.

Many operating systems allow the configuration of the icons to be changed stylistically (for example, to become high contrast) or to change a specific icon for a particular object (such as change what the recycle bin looks like).

In addition, it is possible to configure other aspects of the operating system:

- **Creating start-up options** (for example whether a user needs a password to log in or which processes and applications start automatically).
- **Creating and reconfiguring application toolbars** (for example new toolbars containing new options and macros or modified toolbars which reorder, add or remove buttons).
- **Changing folder management options** (for example, whether hidden files are visible, which files a user can access (user rights) and how files are displayed (in a detailed list, file names only, thumbnails etc.)).

3.4.6 Security

Although it is not possible to protect a computer system against every possible threat, the most common ones can be stopped in their tracks by some **basic software** and **physical security** measures.

Virus protection

The most effective method of protecting against viruses is to use an **anti-virus utility** – there are many to choose from and some basic editions are free to download and use. Modern anti-virus suites can protect against malware, viruses and some website phishing attacks.

Figure 3.30 AVG Technologies anti-virus overview panel

A basic configuration checklist for anti-virus software is:

- Ensure anti-virus is automatically started at log in.
- Ensure anti-virus signatures are regularly updated.
- Ensure a full anti-virus scan is made regularly (e.g. once a week).
- Ensure that emails are being scanned (especially attachments).
- Ensure that the resident shield is enabled (this will scan a file when you attempt to open it).

Firewall

Although third-party **firewall** utilities are available which have more features, Microsoft Windows® comes pre-installed with a basic firewall which will handle most problems.

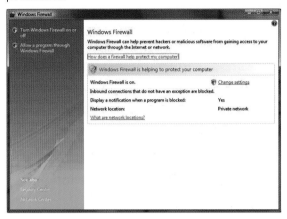

Figure 3.31 Windows® firewall overview

Windows®' firewall permits the following configuration options:

- Turn firewall on or off.
- Choose which programs to block.
- Choose which network connection to firewall.

Figure 3.32 Windows®' firewall exceptions tab

Although these options seem limited, there is enough scope to fully customise the network traffic which can enter and leave your computer system.

Password protection

The configuration of a **password** may not seem obvious at first, but Microsoft® itself has recommendations which help users create passwords which are harder for a determined hacker to crack.

The general configuration advice for passwords is that they should:

1. Use a mixture of alphabetic (upper and lower case), digits and punctuation.
2. Comprise a minimum of six characters (but 14 is recommended).
3. Be changed regularly (e.g. monthly).
4. Not be a word found in the dictionary.

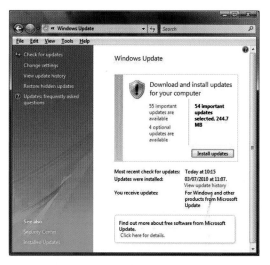

Figure 3.33 Windows® update

You can configure a Windows® operating system to download regular system updates by changing the settings in the Control Panel (see Figure 3.33).

Activity I

Configuring passwords

Microsoft® has a handy web page which can help you create strong passwords:

https://www.microsoft.com/protect/fraud/passwords/checker.aspx

Visit this website and try to create some strong passwords that you can use to reset a Windows® user account's password.

Activity J

Configuring software

As you will see from looking at this section, you must be able to configure the three basic types of software component – systems software, applications software and utilities.

Usually you configure this type of software for yourself and your own preferences – this makes the task a little easier. It is much more difficult to configure settings to meet other users' requirements.

Ask a teacher, friend or family member to suggest a computer system and some configurations they would like you to attempt for them. If you are unfamiliar with the software, you may need to read a user guide, FAQ (frequently asked questions) list or ask for help before achieving your goal. This will be good experience for the P6 and D2 assessment criteria in this unit.

Regular system updates

Many attacks on computer systems are made by exploiting weaknesses in the system software. Most operating systems have the ability to be '**patched**'. In this process, files downloaded from websites using the internet can be used to fix the faulty program code. This should be done regularly.

Make the grade `P6` `D2`

These criteria are linked. For P6 you will be asked to configure software for a given user requirement. In D2 you need to be able to discuss how the software configuration will help the target user to perform their tasks.

P6 is clearly a practical task and is likely to be set by your teacher as part of a case study or by a real-life user. Document your configuration through video or screen captures – remembering to label clearly what you have done. For D2 you need to be able to discuss how these configuration changes help the same user perform their daily tasks.

For example, you may be asked to configure the desktop for a partially-sighted user. This may require using a high-contrast colour scheme. After you have successfully configured this (P6), you can explain how having this scheme makes fonts, windows and buttons appear more distinct for the user and helps them to use traditional software more easily (D2).

Achieving Success

In order to achieve each unit, you will complete a series of coursework activities. Each time you hand in work, your tutor will return this to you with a record of your achievement.

This particular unit has 12 criteria to meet: 7 Pass, 3 Merit and 2 Distinction.

For a **Pass** you must achieve **all 7** Pass criteria.

For a **Merit** you must achieve **all 7** Pass **and all 3** Merit criteria.

For a **Distinction** you must achieve **all 7** Pass, **all 3** Merit criteria **and both** Distinction criteria.

Help with assessment

Your tutor will give you one or more assignments that you will complete as coursework. This could consist of:

- Presentations
- Videos
- Photographs
- Witness statements and/or an evidence log
- Web pages or wikis
- User guides
- Podcasts
- Blogs.

You should read the guidance given for each of the criteria (shown across the unit) carefully and remember to check your work.

(r) Further reading

Textbooks

Fulton, J. *Complete Idiot's Guide to Upgrading and Repairing PCs*. (Que, 3rd Edition) ISBN 0789716429

White, R. and **Downs**, T. *How Computers Work*. (Que, 2003) ISBN 0789730332

Journals

Which? Computer
Computer Weekly

Websites

www.bized.co.uk
www.computerweekly.com

Unit 4
Business IT skills

Learning objectives

By the end of this unit you should:

1. Be able to understand the requirements for solving business problems
2. Be able to know how to find information to support business solutions
3. Be able to use spreadsheet models to support business solutions
4. Be able to present business solutions
5. Be able to evaluate business solutions

In order to pass this unit, the evidence you present for assessment needs to demonstrate that you can meet all of the above learning outcomes for this unit. The criteria below show the levels of achievement required to pass this unit.

To achieve a **pass** grade the evidence must show that the learner is able to:	To achieve a **merit** grade the evidence must show that, in addition to the pass criteria, the learner is able to:	To achieve a **distinction** the evidence must show that, in addition to the pass and merit criteria, the learner is able to:
P1 Explain information requirements for solving a business problem		
P2 Prepare a business plan	**M1** Justify choices made in the business plan	
P3 Identify and select data from appropriate sources to solve a business problem	**M2** Validate sources and acknowledge copyright	**D1** Evaluate sources for accuracy, completeness and reliability
P4 Set up and test a spreadsheet model including automated features to solve a business problem	**M3** Explore possibilities by answering 'What if?' questions	
P5 Develop the model based on user feedback		
P6 Present a business solution using a range of software tools to suit the audience	**M4** Justify the use of software tools	
P7 Carry out an evaluation of a business solution		

Introduction

This unit is designed to teach you the skills you will need to enable you to solve business problems. This will involve finding information, developing and presenting ideas and finally evaluating the business solution.

You will carry out some simple spreadsheet modelling using the information gathered from the spreadsheet to help you inform decisions.

Finally you will present your solution and, using feedback, you will evaluate the effectiveness of your solution.

You will be assessed through coursework which could be in the form of:

- Posters
- Research tasks
- Presentations
- Spreadsheet model(s)
- Screen shots and printouts
- Test plans and results
- Written evaluations
- Informal report(s)

4.1 Understand the requirements for solving business problems

This section will cover the following grading criterion: **P1**

4.1.1 Information requirements

Making successful business decisions becomes easier if you have investigated your options and analysed available information. For example, the decision about which supplier to use may depend on their prices or how quickly they can meet your needs. The decision about the location for a new shop, though, will depend on what products will be sold and the target market (the people you want to sell your products to). There would be little point opening a shop where there will be no customers.

Investigating

To investigate business problems, there are a range of methods we can use. Each method has advantages and disadvantages and you will need to learn how to make sure you use the right one at the right time. Here are some examples:

Talking to users

You can learn a lot about a business problem by talking to the people who are experiencing it. With an IT-related problem this would be the users of a system.

Making a record of the discussion is essential so that you have something to refer back to later.

You should plan the questions you are going to ask in advance and try to use the same questions as the basis for each discussion. This does not mean that you cannot ask other questions if they occur to you, but using a prompt will make sure that the information you gather is more reliable.

Talking to users is a really good way of investigating the problem when you only have a small number of users. You will probably think of other questions to ask as you go along, but you should be careful that you do not get sidetracked into talking about things that are not relevant.

Interviewing users can be quite time consuming. You would be less likely to carry out interviews if you had hundreds of users!

Activity A

Talking to users

In any formal situation it is always best if you have thought carefully about what you want to say or the questions you want to ask. In other words, you should prepare in advance.

Working with a partner, create a questionnaire that gathers information about computer use. For example, what sorts of programs people use or what they use the internet for. You should create a list of about ten questions.

Try your questionnaire out on at least three people and look at your results. How successful was the questionnaire at gathering information? Decide what three things you might you do differently if you created another one.

Observing activities

Another way of investigating a business problem is to observe the activities associated with that problem. This literally means watching what the users do and making notes.

One example could be to observe what happens to an invoice from the moment it comes into the company to the point where it becomes filed as having been paid. This could involve:

- Matching the invoice with any delivery notes and checking the values.
- Placing the invoice in an unpaid invoice file.
- Checking the calendar.

- Completing the payment release form and getting it signed when payment is due.
- Organising the bank transfer of funds.
- Marking the invoice as paid and filing it in the invoices paid file.

As with observation, this method is a little time consuming and is not practical for a large number of users. Some staff might also feel uncomfortable if they know they are being watched. It is, however, very good at helping you understand exactly what is going on in the process.

Activity B

Observing activities

Use the website below and watch the video on being a receptionist. In a real-world scenario you could well find yourself observing a receptionist as part of the information-gathering process to solve a business problem that includes a receptionist's duties. You are going to watch the video and take notes as if you were observing the receptionist in a work situation. You must watch the video continuously – you may not stop and start it as you take notes.

http://www.youtube.com/watch?v=3SBQCpCdDl4

Once you have taken your notes, play the video again from the beginning and check your notes. Did you have to make any adjustments or add any information? The answer will probably be yes! How could you have improved the information you gathered the first time around? Talk to your teacher about some possible options.

Checking existing documents

You should also remember that the organisation will have lots of documents that record what it does, such as accounting books or ledgers that record what money is received by the organisation and what is paid out.

In addition, there will be customer records, supplier records, employee records, wages records and health and safety documents. All of these will give you clues about what information the organisation needs to manage.

In reality, you would probably use all of the methods explained here to make sure you have gathered all the information and you might well also hold meetings with groups of people to discuss the problem. If you have a large number of users, you might create, distribute, collect and analyse the results of a questionnaire.

As the information you will be gathering will have to be analysed and judgements and/or decisions made as a result, it is usually helpful if you think about how you will present your findings or expected outcomes before you do the information gathering to ensure you get the right information to share.

Expected outcomes

It is just as important to understand what should come out of a system as what goes into it! As an IT professional you will need to ask the right questions to ensure that the outputs from the system are what is needed. Some examples of outputs are given below.

Management reports

This is where information in a business is analysed and conclusions are drawn. This information will enable managers to make better decisions. An example of a management report could be an outstanding invoices list – that would give managers an overview about how much money is owed to the business. Decisions could then be made about which customers to chase with a letter or a phone call.

Graphs and charts

These are very useful, especially for interpreting numbers or values. In the following example, we have some data that shows the value of sales over a number of months, the costs for the same period and how much profit was made by the organisation. Have a look at the data in Table 4.1 – imagine you are a manager. What trends can you see in this data? Is there anything that really stands out?

What about if you saw this information represented as a chart (Figure 4.1)? What can you see now?

Gadgets for U Financial Statement			
	Sales	Costs	Profits
December 2009	£24,256.00	£13,098.24	£11,157.76
January 2010	£26,075.20	£14,080.61	£11,994.59
February 2010	£28,030.84	£15,136.65	£12,894.19
March 2010	£30,133.15	£18,381.22	£11,751.93
April 2010	£32,393.14	£19,759.82	£12,633.32
May 2010	£34,822.62	£21,241.80	£13,580.82
June 2010	£35,867.30	£21,879.06	£13,988.25
July 2010	£36,943.32	£27,707.49	£9,235.83
August 2010	£38,051.62	£28,538.72	£9,512.91
September 2010	£39,193.17	£29,394.88	£9,798.29

Table 4.1 Data table

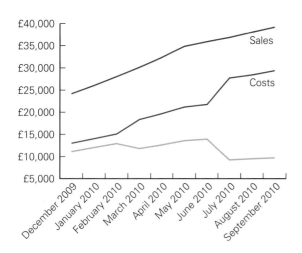

Figure 4.1 Line graph

It is very obvious from the chart that sales in general are rising steadily. But in June 2010 the company's costs suddenly increased and its profits went down. Was it as easy to see the same trends in the columns of numbers?

Simulations

This can mean all sorts of different things! One example could be where components designed on a computer could be simulated by printing them on a 3D-printer (see Figure 4.2). This can be useful for developing engineering components.

Figure 4.2 A simulation of engineering components

Another simulation could be a financial one, possibly a cash flow forecast. This simulation is usually created in a spreadsheet where you can change numbers (called **variables**) to see how changing one or two of the numbers would affect the overall project.

Steve Hodder skateboards

Steve Hodder runs a small skateboard company selling off-the-shelf skateboards that are pre-built and custom-built ones that are made to the customer's specific requirements. Steve employees three staff including Rebekah, who designs the custom-built boards.

Rebekah has just handed in her notice and she is due to leave the company at the end of December. Because of the recession, sales of boards have reduced, particularly sales of the higher-priced customised boards. Steve now has three options:

1. Recruit a replacement for Rebekah immediately.
2. Outsource the work on custom-built boards to another company.
3. Outsource the work for the anticipated quiet months of January, February and March and recruit a replacement to start in April 2011.

Steve creates a spreadsheet model (this is very basic and does not reflect all of Steve's costs realistically, but it does give you an idea of how it works by simply changing some of the values).

Model A – In this model, Steve has projected his sales for the next year and he has included the costs of sales where he buys the pre-built boards for about 40 per cent of the resale cost. He has included wages for all three staff, so in this scenario he is replacing Rebekah. Notice the loss made in February 2011.

	A	B	C	D	E	F	G	H	I	J	K	L	M
1		Jan-11	Feb-11	Mar-11	Apr-11	May-11	Jun-11	Jul-11	Aug-11	Sep-11	Oct-11	Nov-11	Dec-11
2	SALES												
3	Projected sales (pre-built)	£2,309	£2,979	£2,572	£2,447	£2,797	£2,971	£3,234	£3,266	£3,543	£3,290	£3,868	£4,759
4	Projected sales (custom-built)	£1,688	£1,341	£1,617	£2,236	£2,465	£2,777	£2,246	£2,560	£2,012	£1,997	£2,651	£4,043
5	Total Sales	£3,997	£4,320	£4,189	£4,683	£5,262	£5,748	£5,480	£5,826	£5,555	£5,287	£6,519	£8,802
6													
7	EXPENSES												
8	Cost of pre-built boards (40% of resale)	£923	£1,912	£1,029	£979	£1,119	£1,188	£1,234	£1,304	£1,417	£1,316	£1,547	£1,904
9	Wages for Admin and Sales staff	£1,200	£1,200	£1,200	£1,200	£1,200	£1,200	£1,200	£1,200	£1,200	£1,200	£1,200	£1,200
10	Wages for Custom-built staff	£1,000	£1,000	£1,000	£1,000	£1,000	£1,000	£1,000	£1,000	£1,000	£1,000	£1,000	£1,000
11	Cost of buying in custom-built boards (60% of resale)												
12	Overheads (heat, light, rent etc)	£550	£550	£550	£550	£550	£550	£550	£550	£550	£550	£550	£550
13	Total Expenditure	£3,673	£4,662	£3,779	£3,729	£3,869	£3,938	£3,984	£4,054	£4,167	£4,066	£4,297	£4,654
14													
15	Profit/Loss	£324	-£342	£410	£954	£1,393	£1,810	£1,496	£1,772	£1,388	£1,221	£2,222	£4,148

Figure 4.3 Model A

Total profit/loss over the year would be: £16,436 profit (by adding monthly figures together).

Model B – In this model, Steve has the same projected sales and costs of sales, but the wages for Rebekah's job have been removed and the cost of buying in the boards has been calculated instead. Notice he still makes a loss in February 2011, but it is smaller than if he had recruited a new member of staff.

Continues on next page

Continued

	A	B	C	D	E	F	G	H	I	J	K	L	M
1		Jan-11	Feb-11	Mar-11	Apr-11	May-11	Jun-11	Jul-11	Aug-11	Sep-11	Oct-11	Nov-11	Dec-11
2	SALES												
3	Projected sales (pre-built)	£2,309	£2,979	£2,572	£2,447	£2,797	£2,971	£3,234	£3,266	£3,543	£3,290	£3,868	£4,759
4	Projected sales (custom-built)	£1,688	£1,341	£1,617	£2,236	£2,465	£2,777	£2,246	£2,560	£2,012	£1,997	£2,651	£4,043
5	Total Sales	£3,997	£4,320	£4,189	£4,683	£5,262	£5,748	£5,480	£5,826	£5,555	£5,287	£6,519	£8,802
6													
7	EXPENSES												
8	Cost of pre-built boards (40% of resale)	£923	£1,912	£1,029	£979	£1,119	£1,188	£1,234	£1,304	£1,417	£1,316	£1,547	£1,904
9	Wages for Admin and Sales staff	£1,200	£1,200	£1,200	£1,200	£1,200	£1,200	£1,200	£1,200	£1,200	£1,200	£1,200	£1,200
10	Wages for Custom-built staff												
11	Cost of buying in custom-built boards (60% of resale)	£1,013	£805	£970	£1,342	£1,479	£1,666	£1,347	£1,536	£1,207	£1,198	£1,590	£2,426
12	Overheads (heat, light, rent etc)	£550	£550	£550	£550	£550	£550	£550	£550	£550	£550	£550	£550
13	Total Expenditure	£3,686	£4,467	£3,749	£4,071	£4,348	£4,604	£4,331	£4,590	£4,374	£4,264	£4,887	£6,080
14													
15	Profit/Loss	£311	-£147	£440	£612	£914	£1,144	£1,149	£1,236	£1,181	£1,023	£1,632	£2,722

Figure 4.4 Model B

Total profit/loss over the year would be: £12,217 profit.

Model C – In the final model, Steve has the same projected sales and costs of sales, but he has outsourced the custom-built boards for the first three months of the year before recruiting a replacement for Rebekah to start in April 2011. Notice that he is still carrying a loss in February 2011, but later in the year when he sells more boards, the profit is much higher.

	A	B	C	D	E	F	G	H	I	J	K	L	M
1		Jan-11	Feb-11	Mar-11	Apr-11	May-11	Jun-11	Jul-11	Aug-11	Sep-11	Oct-11	Nov-11	Dec-11
2	SALES												
3	Projected sales (pre-built)	£2,309	£2,979	£2,572	£2,447	£2,797	£2,971	£3,234	£3,266	£3,543	£3,290	£3,868	£4,759
4	Projected sales (custom-built)	£1,688	£1,341	£1,617	£2,236	£2,465	£2,777	£2,246	£2,560	£2,012	£1,997	£2,651	£4,043
5	Total Sales	£3,997	£4,320	£4,189	£4,683	£5,262	£5,748	£5,480	£5,826	£5,555	£5,287	£6,519	£8,802
6													
7	EXPENSES												
8	Cost of pre-built boards (40% of resale)	£923	£1,912	£1,029	£979	£1,119	£1,188	£1,234	£1,304	£1,417	£1,316	£1,547	£1,904
9	Wages for Admin and Sales staff	£1,200	£1,200	£1,200	£1,200	£1,200	£1,200	£1,200	£1,200	£1,200	£1,200	£1,200	£1,200
10	Wages for Custom-built staff				£1,000	£1,000	£1,000	£1,000	£1,000	£1,000	£1,000	£1,000	£1,000
11	Cost of buying in custom-built boards (60% of resale)	£1,013	£805	£970									
12	Overheads (heat, light, rent etc)	£550	£550	£550	£550	£550	£550	£550	£550	£550	£550	£550	£550
13	Total Expenditure	£3,686	£4,467	£3,749	£3,729	£3,869	£3,938	£3,984	£4,054	£4,167	£4,066	£4,297	£4,654
14													
15	Profit/Loss	£311	-£147	£440	£954	£1,393	£1,810	£1,496	£1,772	£1,388	£1,221	£2,222	£4,148

Figure 4.5 Model C

Total profit/loss over the year would be: £17,008 profit.

If you were Steve, what decision would you make?

What are the benefits of gathering information?

To inform management decisions

Managers need to make decisions that are right for all the stakeholders of the organisation.

> **Key term**
>
> A **stakeholder** is someone who has an interest in an organisation's activities. For example, employees want to be sure that the organisation has enough money to pay them. Suppliers also want to know that they will be paid for the goods and services they have provided. Customers want to know that the company has the resources to produce and provide the goods and services they buy.
>
> But there are other stakeholders too, such as HM Revenue and Customs, who gather taxes on behalf of the government, or the local council, who will want to be sure that the organisation is disposing of its waste in a suitable way.

Having good quality information that is accurate and up-to-date will help the managers of the organisation to make quality decisions.

Cost effective solution

The organisation or business must weigh up the initial costs of a solution against the benefits it will bring to the company in terms of reduced costs, greater efficiency or better customer service. Any solution that does not bring more benefits than it actually costs is not a good solution!

Are there any constraints?

When solving any business problem you will have to work within boundaries. These boundaries are known as **constraints**. Some examples of these are explored below.

Budget

The **budget** is the amount of money you have to spend on the problem. In some situations the budget can be 'open'. This means that any reasonable amount of money can be used to find a solution. It is more likely, however, that the budget will be set and all of the investigative, design, implementation and review work will need to be completed within that set amount.

Activity C

Budget

You will probably find that you have to work to a budget! This could be what you are given by your parents or carers as pocket money, or it could be money you earn through a part-time job. But, do you really know how much you spend and what you spend the money on?

For one week write down everything you spend. Keep the receipts as evidence. At the end of the week, think about your spending and what you could have done without.

Try saving 5 per cent of your budget the following week by making some basic changes in your buying habits.

Existing systems

Sometimes existing systems need to be included in the solution to the problem. This could be because they are specialist systems that cannot be replaced or it could be because replacing them would just be too expensive.

Resources

Most businesses would expect that as many of the existing resources as possible could be used as part of the solution to reduce the expense. Desks, chairs, computers, filing cabinets, telephone systems, among others, will need to be considered and replaced only where it is necessary to do so.

Business preferences

Is your school or college part of a Sustainability programme? Does your school or college have the Investors in People award?

There are a number of awards that organisations can work towards that say something about them as an institution. For example, being part of the Sustainable Schools programme means that your school does everything it can to make the best use of resources, dispose of its waste and reduce its carbon footprint (the impact that our existence has on the planet based on the things we do and the choices we make).

For more information on Sustainable Schools use the following link: http://www.suschool.org.uk/

From a business perspective, having an award can add to an organisation's credibility and in some cases it can lead to more customers. This is because customers will start to feel that the organisation is responsible, honest and has integrity.

Activity D

Preferences

Find out about your school or college. What awards does it have? (You might find these awards displayed in the school or college reception.)

If it has received awards, find out about them and what they actually mean.

Supplier contracts

When resolving any business problem with a new solution, you will have to take into account any existing contracts you might have with suppliers. For example, if you have a 2-year contract for IT support that is provided by an external company, you will probably not be able to simply tell them that you do not want them anymore. You will either have to include the contract in your solution until it ends, or you will have to pay the contractor a penalty for ending the contract early, which could be as high as the full cost of the remaining months of the contract!

You might also have an agreement to only use particular suppliers because of discount arrangements or other special considerations like a quick delivery on all orders. You may therefore need to discuss your proposed solution with the supplier or suppliers to make sure that they can still meet your needs.

4.1.2 Business problems

Understanding the problem

Although a business problem could be about almost anything, there are some typical problems that are faced by most organisations at some point. Here are a few typical examples.

Networking an office

It might surprise you to know that some offices are still not **networked**! This means that the members of staff are carrying out their activities on stand-alone machines that are not connected to each other.

Most modern offices are networked as it enables all users to share the system resources and the organisational information and data. Many organisations, however, are now moving to wireless networking to take advantage of the greater flexibility it provides.

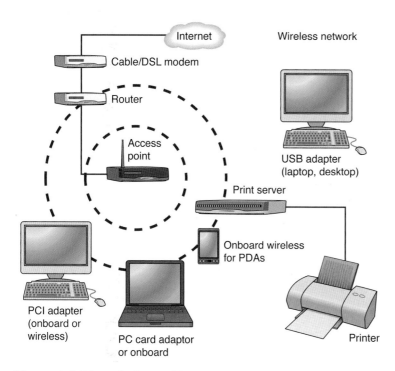

Figure 4.6 The wireless office

As an IT professional you could find yourself involved in installing a new network, expanding an existing network or converting a network from a cabled to a wireless solution.

Setting up a company website

No one would argue the benefits of a company website, whether it is to support e-commerce (selling goods and services directly to customers online) or just to provide information to encourage customers to visit a store or other business location.

When making decisions about websites, the company needs to be very sure what they want to achieve and how they want users to use their site.

Once the decisions have been made, the organisation will work with the website designer and developer (this could be the same person or different people or groups) to create the right solution for the company.

Launching a new product or service

It is possible that a business will need to change internally in order to facilitate the launch of a new product or service. For example, Tesco®, Asda® and Sainsbury's® all provide customers with opportunities to visit a store, or buy their products online (including delivering purchases to the customer's door).

In contrast, Morrisons® has a website, but this currently provides information only and does not offer customers the opportunity to purchase items online (see http://www.morrisons.co.uk/).

In order for Tesco®, Asda® and Sainsbury's® to be in a position to offer this service, they had to make major changes to their internal systems. This would have included the development of a website, ordering system and communications system to distribute orders to the nearest store or distribution point. They will also have had to invest in delivery vans and staff to drive them.

For this reason all three organisations will have thought very carefully about the investment and the possible benefits.

Upgrading an existing IT system

When you upgrade an existing IT system you usually audit (check out) the existing system and identify which components or whole workstations would benefit from being renewed. For example, if you suddenly need your computer to cope with lots of animation or image manipulation, you might have to replace a graphics card. This might be preferable to buying an entire, more powerful new machine!

Equally, many organisations have a replacement policy. This could, for example, be the decision to replace every computer when it reaches a particular age.

As an IT professional you may well have to respond to different types of business problems and help in the identification and implementation of a solution. This does get easier with experience!

Make the grade

For P1 you must be able to explain the information that would be required to solve a given business problem.

You will need to explain the following:

- What the problem is.
- How you will research the information to help you towards a solution.
- What the outcomes of the solution should be.
- The benefits of the right solution.
- The constraints on the project.

This will probably be presented as a report, as a presentation or as a series of documents as instructed by your teacher.

4.1.3 Business plan

This section will cover the following grading criteria: **P2** **M1**

To formalise the chosen solution, a business plan is developed that sets out the whole solution as a document so that it can be referred to as the resolution to the business problem is being developed. The plan will cover the following elements.

Inputs

In this section you will reflect the resources that are needed to make the solution possible. It could include answers to these questions:

- Will the solution require new computers?
- Will the solution need new software or a new operating system?
- How will the company's data be manipulated to become part of the new

system (will, for example, the data need to be converted to a different format)?

- Will new network cabling be needed?
- Will new peripherals be required (for example printers, wireless routers etc.)?

Outputs

You now reflect on the **outputs** that the system will be designed to produce. For example:

- What reports will the system be able to generate?
- What format will the outputs be in?
- What charts and graphs can the system produce?

Processes

This is the slightly more complex part of the business plan because in this section you will need to show your real understanding of the outputs of the system by being able to talk about the technical IT aspects of the solution. You will need to be able to identify and show the calculations the system will need to do (for example, what **calculations** are needed to work out the total of an invoice and the addition of 20 per cent VAT on the invoice total).

Sometimes the system will need to be able to do something different depending on a particular input or situation. For example, if a discount is going to be applied, the invoice total might need to be checked and then compared with a range of discount values. The relevant value would then need to be applied to the invoice. This is known as a **logical operation**. Another logical operation could be setting up a password on a file or area of the system and could include a decision on how many attempts the user will have to access the file or area before they are locked out.

Macros are like mini programs that are often activated by a button press. For

example, if a spreadsheet always needs to be printed three times, the user would have two options:

1. Click on 'print' three times every time the prints are needed.
2. Go into the print setup and change the default value of 'print 1' to 'print 3' and do this every time the prints are needed.

With a macro, a mini program could be written that prints the spreadsheet three times automatically. The macro would be triggered by a button press.

Macros are generally used to speed up user activity and to make the use of a solution more efficient because they require the user to do less than they would otherwise have to.

The system may also contain a number of **models**, for example a spreadsheet model that can be used to work out the resale price of items based on the costs of raw materials, a proportion of the overheads and the percentage profit that the business wants to make on the items. The user would simply input some numbers and the answer would be calculated automatically.

The design for these models would be included in the business plan and in the long term the IT professional would set up the models and test that they output the right answers.

Timelines

A **timeline** can be created to show what will happen when. If any of the activities can happen at the same time, the timeline will reflect that. It will also show what has to be finished before another part can be started.

The timeline can be drawn as a diagram or it can be a list of activities and completion dates. Figure 4.7 shows the development of the iPod® and gives a rough timeline for the development and approximate release dates for the different iPod® products.

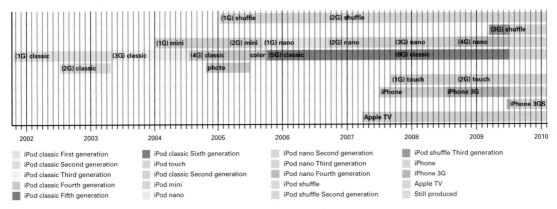

Figure 4.7 Timeline for the development of the iPod® (source: http://upload.wikimedia.org/wikipedia/en/timeline/a048814763412f40be7c6773f81ad7e7.png)

Research

The final part of the business plan provides information about the sources of information. It will reflect any that have been used so far, but will also suggest others that might prove useful during the development of the solution.

You should remember when carrying out any research that the internet is not the only source of information! You should also use newspapers, magazines, journals and books.

Activity E

Research

There will be a number of situations during this course where you will need to carry out and record evidence of research.

Work with a partner to create a simple recording mechanism for your research. This could be a spreadsheet or a word-processed form that allows you to collect information about your research.

Example headings could include:

Source (for example, internet or newspaper)
Name of book, journal or URL of website
Information obtained
Comments

This document could then be used regularly to record this activity.

Make the grade P2

Make the grade

P2

M1

When you prepare and write your business plan to meet the requirements for P2 you should make sure that you include all the elements included in section 4.1.3.

M1 is an extension of P2 and to achieve M1 you will explain why you have chosen the inputs, outputs, processes, and so on, that you have outlined in the plan. You will also include some possible alternatives and explain briefly why you have chosen one particular solution and rejected another.

4.2 Know how to find information to support business solutions

This section will cover the following grading criteria: **P3** **M2** **D1**

There are so many possible sources of information to support decision making that at times the sheer volume can feel a little overwhelming. Here are some tips on ways to approach your research.

4.2.1 Data

Carrying out research

Developing a solution to a business problem will require you to research products, technologies and even manufacturers and suppliers to ensure that you get the best products or technologies for the money you can afford to spend. With products, for example, you will need to compare their specifications including features and functions. You will then be able to answer the question 'which one is best?'. This could involve comparing two products from the same manufacturer, similar products from different manufacturers or a range of products across a wide price range.

Activity F

Researching products

Use the website http://www.pricerunner.co.uk to compare the prices for the following products:

Acer Aspire Laptop
HP LaserJet P2055DN printer
Belkin N+ Wireless ADSL modem router

In each case write down the best price you can find and the name of the retailer.

When researching technologies you may well have to compare two completely different solutions. For example you might need to answer the question 'cable or wireless?'. It will help if you understand the difference when you start your research!

Activity G

Researching technologies

What is the difference between infrared and Bluetooth®?

Find out and create a poster that demonstrates the differences and gives examples of some of the products that use each technology.

You might find the following website useful:

http://www.sharpened.net/helpcenter/answer.php?101

It might also be a valid research approach if you investigate all the products and technologies offered by a single manufacturer. There is some argument for buying products in this way as it can eliminate some of the compatibility problems that can be experienced, although modern operating systems like Windows 7® are getting better and better at managing conflict.

As organisations frequently choose to use the same suppliers to take advantage of discounts or credit agreements, you might be limited to researching the products and technologies provided by a single supplier. You should, however, never be afraid to ask a supplier for something new or different. Many of them will do everything they can to meet your needs, even if that means stocking products they have not stocked before.

In reality it is likely that some or all of these different research approaches will be used in developing the solution to business problems!

Looking at alternatives

It is likely that you will have to compare products or technologies to find the most suitable one to help you solve the business problem. For example, is the best personal communications technology a Blackberry® or a PDA (Personal Digital Assistant) (see Figure 3.1)?

You would most probably compare these devices by considering their **price** (initial outlay and ongoing service charges), **functionality** (availability of applications such as email) and **performance** (such as the number of hours it maintains power when in use and/or on standby).

Investigating costs

When investigating the costs of a solution, there are many additional or ongoing expenses that you should think about. These may be less obvious than the costs of buying the technology initially. Here are some examples:

- **Set-up costs** – these are the costs of getting the solution up and running. They will be 'one-off' costs, which means that they will only be experienced at the implementation of the solution and will not be experienced again. An example of a set-up cost could be the expense of having another organisation convert the business data from the format needed in the existing system to the format existing in the new system.
- **Ongoing costs** – how often do you think about the price of consumables when you buy a product?

Key term

A **consumable** is something about a product that needs to be replenished from time to time. The most obvious example is the ink cartridges you need in a printer.

Is it better to buy an inexpensive printer that uses expensive replacement cartridges or to buy an expensive printer that uses low-cost replacement cartridges?

A printer may well appear to be low-priced, but if the replacement ink cartridges are very expensive, it can be a **false economy**. For this reason, both the cost of the printer and the ongoing cost of the cartridges should be considered.

- **Staffing costs** – when implementing a solution you will need to consider the costs of staffing. Does the organisation have staff members who can work the new system or will it have to recruit them? If so, will they be paid the same rates as existing staff or will the costs be higher because the staff have better or different skills?

  You might also need to consider whether you will need all of the existing staff, particularly if their jobs are now being done by the system. You might need to make them redundant or you might be in a position to suggest that the staff are retrained to take another role within the organisation.

- **Training costs** – you should always remember that when staff are being trained, you have the obvious training costs, but have you considered the actual costs of not having that member of staff available for their usual job while the training takes place? If you ask someone else to do their work for them, then that person will be doing the job of two people (which will be more stressful).

  If you employ someone else to do the work (for example someone from a temporary staff agency) then you will need to pay them in addition to paying your staff member who is on training. If no one does the work at all, then customers could be let down or other colleagues may not be able to work efficiently.

  You should always try to make sure that you have identified any hidden costs, as well as the more obvious ones!

4.2.2 Sources

Good research means being confident enough to use a **variety** of information sources rather than just relying on a single source like the internet. This way,

your solution to the business problem is likely to be more **reliable** and **robust** (of a good quality).

Range

Let us explore some of the options, although you should bear in mind that this is not a full list, just some examples.

Internet

The most effective way to use the internet is to use a search engine to find articles, web pages, videos and images for you.

> ## Key term
>
> A **search engine** is essentially a website where information about other websites, web pages and web content is stored. It contains a program that will sift through all the information when the user keys in a word or phrase that he or she wants to search on.
>
> The results are displayed and the user can then choose which of the results to look at. These results are known as **hits**.

There are many search engines available on the web, with the most commonly used site being Google®.

Figure 4.8 Google®

Activity H

Search engines

Not all search engines have the same functionality. Working with a partner, investigate ten search engines and create a short PowerPoint® presentation that explains what each one does.

You should make sure that you have at least one example from each of the following categories: shopping, business, games, international, jobs, multimedia and news.

You may find the following website useful: http://www.thesearchenginelist.com/

Trade magazines

These are printed (published) sources that are very useful at providing a range of information about a particular area of interest or a specific trade sector (like computing, cars or music, for example). They also carry the most recent news. Some are published weekly, others monthly, bi-monthly (every two months), quarterly (every three months) or annually (once a year). Some trade magazines also have a web presence (like Computer Weekly®).

Retail outlets

As part of your information gathering, you might also choose to visit retail outlets. These could be large stores like PC World® or Curry's®, or they could be smaller, local shops.

The advantage of visiting a store is that you can usually see the product first hand and can ask questions if you need to.

The alternative is to buy your products online. Some businesses give discounts to customers who purchase in this way.

Activity I

Trade magazines

Working with a partner, use the following website to identify at least eight computer-related trade magazines.

http://www.world-newspapers.com/business.html

Of the eight you identify, find out how many of these are stored as published copies in your school, college library or local public library. Identify how many of them also have websites and note down the web addresses.

Copy and complete the following table with your findings.

Magazine	Available in library?	Website presence? If so, what is the web address?

Activity J

Retail

Identify two major retailers and two local businesses that sell computer products. Identify two retailers who *only* trade online (this means that they do not have a store).

Create an information sheet about these six organisations and share it with your teacher or classmates.

Advertisements

Businesses carry out a lot of research to find the best places to advertise. They do this to make sure that they use their advertising budget most effectively and that they reach the maximum number of potential customers each time they advertise.

Activity K

Advertisements

Use a copy of a local newspaper to find an advertisement for computers and/or peripherals.

Tips for good quality, effective research

The most important aspect of research is that you must be sure that your research facts are **valid** and **accurate**. It is good practice to check your facts with **more** than one source. This is particularly true with internet sources as the internet is harder to police for inaccuracies than a book.

Copyright

Key term

Anything that has a **copyright** cannot be used or reproduced without the permission of the original owner. For example, computer games cannot be copied and shared if they are subject to copyright.

There are strict rules around copyright. Data or information that has been copyrighted cannot be used or quoted by anyone else without permission.

Unless classified as freeware or shareware (where there is a small charge), software cannot be copied to multiple machines. This could mean that you will need to buy a site licence that allows multiple installations from a single CD.

When quoting from books, for example in coursework or maybe in a report, you need to **acknowledge** the source. This means that you must explain fully where the quotation was taken from.

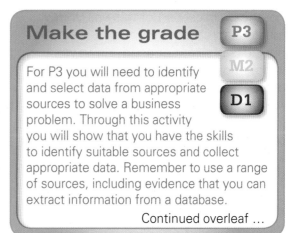

Make the grade   P3   M2   D1

For P3 you will need to identify and select data from appropriate sources to solve a business problem. Through this activity you will show that you have the skills to identify suitable sources and collect appropriate data. Remember to use a range of sources, including evidence that you can extract information from a database.

Continued overleaf ...

continued...

To evidence M2 you will show that you have **checked** your sources (to validate your information) and you will acknowledge any copyright. All sources should be acknowledged.

For D1 you will need to carry out an evaluation of the sources you have used. For each source you **evaluate** you will need to comment on its accuracy (is the data valid?), **currency** (is the data up to date?), **completeness** (is anything missing?) and **reliability** (are there regular updates, and is the source well-known?).

4.3 Be able to use spreadsheet models to support business solutions

This section will cover the following grading criteria: **P4** **M3** **P5**

For the practical part of this unit you will create a spreadsheet model to resolve a business problem or need. However, there is not enough space in this unit to include guidance on using spreadsheet software. As there is a whole unit on spreadsheets in this book (Unit 27), you will need to read the unit first if you think you need to improve your spreadsheet skills before tackling a spreadsheet model.

4.3.1 Spreadsheet models

Purpose

The spreadsheet model you will create for this unit will need to solve a business problem. Below are a range of possible models that you could develop.

Estimate costs

To estimate costs you may need a range of information to help you. For example, if you need to calculate how much you will spend on raw materials for a new product, you will first need to calculate how much you might sell over a future period and then you will be able to calculate the relevant costs as a proportion of what you will sell.

Remember an estimate is just an informed guess!

Let us look at an example of estimating costs.

Activity **L**

Estimating costs

A company has decided to run a health and safety training programme for eight of its newest staff. The course will run over three days and the managers of the company have decided that it should be held at an external venue, with accommodation provided for all staff attending the training.

Here are the overall costs:

Cost of trainer – £750 for the whole course

Cost of meeting room at venue – £200 per day

Cost of overnight accommodation – £80 per delegate per night

Total meal allowance – £60 per delegate per day

Total travel allowance to and from venue – £30 per delegate

Create a spreadsheet model that calculates the overall cost of the training and the cost per delegate (this is so that the costs of the training can be allocated to the relevant departmental training budgets).

Print the results and the formulae used. Check your answers at the back of the book.

Estimate returns

Spreadsheet models are useful for helping businesses predict the returns (money they earn) on the investments they make or on goods and services that they sell.

Activity M

Estimating returns

A small marketing company uses students and young people (known as canvassers) working door-to-door to sign up householders to make monthly payments to charities by standing order.

The company intends to send a group of canvassers to a new housing estate and they are trying to estimate how much money will be earned. This is what they know:

> The housing estate has 700 homes. One person can knock on 25 doors in an hour.
> The plan is to be on the estate for 4 hours.

How many staff do they need to take to make sure that every house is visited in the time allowed? Print the results and the formulae used.

They also know that statistically:

> 18% of homeowners approached sign up for £5 per month.
> 15% of homeowners approached sign up for £10 per month.
> 9% of homeowners approached sign up for £25 per month.

What is the total value of a month's sign up expected to be? Print the results and the formulae used.

As an expansion task, calculate how much of the money will be passed to the charity after the canvassers have been paid and the marketing company has taken its share. You will need the following information:

The canvassers earn 30 per cent of the monthly value they manage to secure as a one-off payment – so for every £5 per month committed, they earn £1.50 in commission.

In addition, the marketing company receive 20 per cent of the monthly value as a single payment – so for every £5 per month committed, they receive £1.

Print the results and the formulae used. Check your answers at the back of the book.

Explore alternatives

When considering alternatives, most people will write a list of positives and negatives (or pros and cons) about different aspects. Spreadsheets can be used as part of this investigation for calculating costs and comparing the costs of different solutions.

Predict business impact

Organisations that rely on importing raw materials from other countries to be used as part of their manufacturing process worry about the foreign currency exchange rates and how changes in these rates will impact on their business.

When interest rates go up, they have to pay more; when they go down, they have to pay less. Either way, this has an impact on their financial situation.

Another example is the interest that companies have to pay on money that they borrow.

Identify breakeven points

A **breakeven point** is the point at which a company begins to make a profit on selling an item because it has covered its costs fully. On a graph it would look something like Figure 4.9.

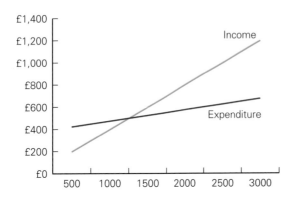

Figure 4.9 The breakeven point

The breakeven point is where the two lines cross and the income starts to be more than the amount spent. This graph shows that the company would need to sell something like 1250 items to break even.

Answer 'what if?' questions

Spreadsheets are extremely useful for answering 'what if?' questions. For example:

If we put up the resale price, would we lose customers?

What would happen to our profits if our suppliers put up their prices?

What would happen to our cash reserves if interest rates on the loans we have went up?

The most beneficial part of using a spreadsheet model is that once the model has been created, the user only needs to change one or more values to see the difference it makes to the overall picture.

Activity N

Breakeven

A company has decided to manufacture a new product. They know that the materials cost for each item will be 10p and they can resell the items for 50p each. This means that the materials cost for each item is 20 per cent of the resale value.

Their overheads are £750 per day and this includes a proportion of rent, light, heat, staffing etc.

In the first instance you might create a spreadsheet that reflects the figures above, with some random quantities to see roughly where the breakeven point might be:

Number of items	100	500	1,000	2,500	5,000	10,000
Raw materials	£ 20	£100	£200	£ 500	£1,000	£2,000
Resale value	£ 50	£250	£500	£1,250	£2,500	£5,000
Overheads	£750	£750	£750	£ 750	£ 750	£ 750
Profit/loss	–£720	–£600	–£450	£ 0	£ 750	£2,250

You can see from the table of information that breakeven point is when 2,500 items have been sold.

Use the information (you will need to adapt the data to have more even 'number of items' values) to create a spreadsheet and from the information, make a chart that shows where the breakeven point occurs. Check your answer at the back of the book.

'What if?'

In this example we ask a very simple question.

A company uses five ingredients to make a product. We will call it Product X. Each mix of the product makes ten items that can be resold individually. The company needs to make 23.5 per cent profit on each batch of ten.

Create a spreadsheet using the prices:

> Ingredient A – 3.47
> Ingredient B – 6.21
> Ingredient C – 2.22
> Ingredient D – 4.69
> Ingredient E – 6.97

> Calculate the cost of 10.
> Calculate the resale value for 10.
> Calculate the resale price for each item.

Now adjust the spreadsheet because the company has been advised that the cost of Ingredient A may go up 13 per cent and the cost of Ingredient D may go up 40 per cent.

If that happens, what should the resale price be?

You can continue to change values to reflect other scenarios! Check your answers at the back of the book.

4.3.2 Automated features

Generating graphs or charts

You will already be aware that graphs and charts can be created from tables of numeric data. Do you realise, though, that the graph or chart and its data are linked

and, if you change the numbers or headings, the graph or chart will change as well.

Have a look at the example in Figure 4.10 (both the data and the pie chart are visible).

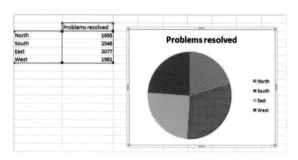

Figure 4.10

We now change the title and the values for the East and West regions. See how the chart has changed (Figure 4.11).

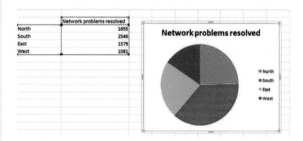

Figure 4.11

It was not necessary to create the pie chart from scratch.

Other features

Macros and script

There are other ways of making spreadsheets more efficient for users, for example, using macros or a scripting language to carry out a repeated series of actions.

A macro is a sequence of written commands that carries out one or more actions when it has been activated. Macros can either be written using a scripting language or can be recorded. To record a macro you have to start the recording, carry out the actions and then stop the macro (see Figure 4.12).

Figure 4.12 Recording a macro

The macro is given a name and that macro can then be activated either by double clicking on it in the macros menu or by attaching it to a button. Once complete, macros can also be edited. So what can a macro do? Here is an example of some macro code (Figure 4.13).

```
(General)                                              Macro1

   Sub Macro1()
   '
   ' Macro1 Macro
   '


   '
       ActiveSheet.ChartObjects("Chart 1").Activate
       ExecuteExcel4Macro "PRINT(1,,(5),,,,,,,2,,,TRUE,,FALSE)"
   End Sub
```

Figure 4.13 Macro code

All macros start with the word Sub and end with End Sub. This is immediately followed by the macro's name.

The code begins at ActiveSheet.

The first line identifies the part of the spreadsheet that needs to be printed. In this case, that is the chart.

The second line then activates the Print dialogue box. Each of the values in the brackets following PRINT show the choices made in the dialogue box. The number of prints selected was 5 (as shown by the blue circle). If the user now wanted to increase or decrease the print number, they could simply change the value in the code rather than re-recording the macro.

User interface

There are other settings that can be activated to improve the user interface and make the spreadsheet easier to use. For example, the spreadsheet can be **locked** to prevent users from changing values (this is known as protection). But to make it easier for the user to navigate the spreadsheet, some cells can be **unlocked** so that they can still be accessed by a user even when the rest of the cells are locked.

To unlock cells they need to be highlighted and then the properties need to be unlocked on the Protection tab. To unlock cells simply remove the tick from the Locked checkbox (Figure 4.14).

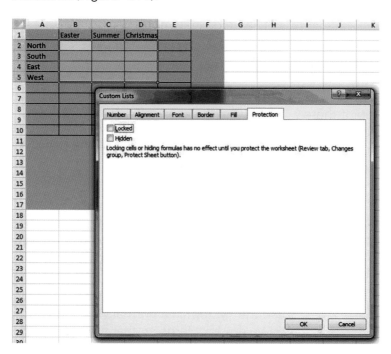

Figure 4.14 Unlocking cells

The locked cells can now be accessed by moving the mouse into the cell using the cursor keys or the tab button (Figure 4.15).

	A	B	C	D	E
1		Easter	Summer	Christmas	
2	North				
3	South				
4	East				
5	West				
6					
7					

Figure 4.15 Accessing locked cells

4.3.3 Developing mode

Seeking feedback from users

When developing a spreadsheet solution, you should check your progress with your user regularly. This will ensure that the solution you create is what the user wants.

Once the solution is fully complete and has been implemented, you should ask the user for feedback. You can do this by talking to them directly or using a questionnaire that the user could complete (this is very useful if you have multiple users).

Assessing fitness for purpose

When you assess the solution to check how fit for purpose it is, you and the user(s) will be making decisions about how well the solution works and does its job. If there is anything that does not work properly, that could have been done better, or if there is something extra that could be added to improve the system, then it will be put on a list.

Obviously, if the system does not work, it needs to be fixed immediately. Things that could be improved or any extras will be done at some time in the future, depending on how urgent and important they are judged to be.

Making improvements

Very few systems are implemented without any problems surfacing or requests for improvements being made. You should not take these requests as criticisms – quite often they are simply just new ideas!

4.3.4 Test

There are a number of tests that can be carried out to check that a solution meets the user's needs and is technically complete and correct. Here are some examples:

Functionality

When the original plan was put together that defined what the solution should be and what it should do, a list will have been made of all the functionality that would be developed. This could have included:

- Create customer record
- Create sales invoice
- Create account statements for customers
- Record invoices in sales ledger
- Create supplier record
- Create delivery note
- Create purchase invoice
- Record purchase ledger.

To test for functionality, the first thing would be to check that all the expected activities have been developed and then to check that the solution is working fully.

User testing

Just because the developer thinks something is good or is working does not mean that the user will too! As suggested in the previous section, it is essential that the user is involved in testing the final solution.

Often this testing will require the user to use the system in a normal way and write down any problems so that these can be fed back to the developer. If possible, all aspects of the system should be tested.

Activity P

Testing computer games

It is obviously in the best interest of a games development company to get computer games tested by potential end users.

Use the following websites to research the role of the tester:

Continued on next page

www.gamestester.com
http://www.kaspersky.com/beta
http://betatestgamers.com/

Create an A4 poster that explains what a beta tester does and how problems are reported.

Fitness for purpose

A product, a program or other business solution may well work perfectly, but it still might not be **fit for purpose**. Fit for purpose also means that the user interface would have been checked for errors. For example – what would you think of a system if you saw this prompt:

Plase inpet nimber

Do you think that this is very professional?

What about an invoice where the final total looks like this:

Grand Total   ############

The customer would not be able to read the amount due!

To be considered fit for purpose a business solution has to work and it has to look professional!

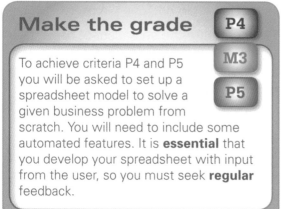

Make the grade   P4

M3

P5

To achieve criteria P4 and P5 you will be asked to set up a spreadsheet model to solve a given business problem from scratch. You will need to include some automated features. It is **essential** that you develop your spreadsheet with input from the user, so you must seek **regular** feedback.

To evidence the criteria you will be able to show your spreadsheet model and you might also produce printouts, screenshots and witness statements. You will also produce a formula print.

Your user will provide feedback which could be collected as a completed questionnaire or even a video or audio recording. To show that your user feedback has been incorporated into the development, you will provide screenshots of before and after views of your system. Do not forget that you can also ask other classmates in addition to your user.

To achieve M3, you will have answered 'What if?' questions. Again, screenshots and printouts can be used as evidence, but you will need to make sure you annotate the screenshots to show what changes in values were made.

Make sure you regularly save your spreadsheet and that you have a backup copy.

4.4 Be able to present business solutions

This section will cover the following grading criteria: P6   M4

When it comes to sharing your solution for a business problem, it is essential that you can present your ideas with confidence, otherwise the user will not have much faith in the system.

4.4.1 Present

Software tools

You will be able to use a range of software tools to present the information. The contents of the presentation slides below suggest some useful approaches:

Presentation – title page (do not forget to name your solution and give your name).

Figure 4.16 Title page of presentation

Word processing

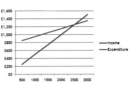

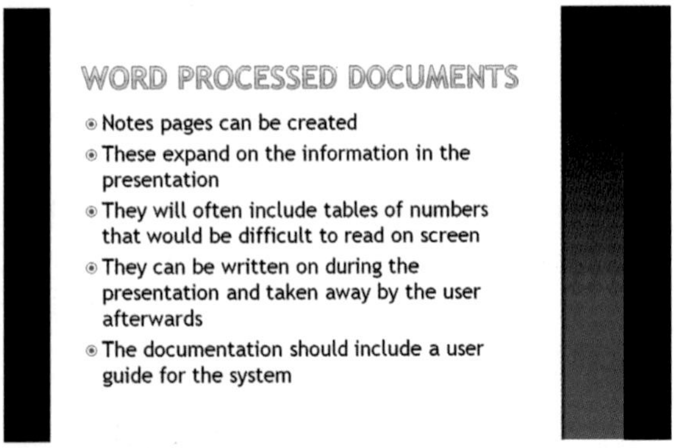

Figure 4.17

Spreadsheet

Figure 4.18

Graphics

Figure 4.19

Make your presentation interesting and use a range of other tools to help you to share the information.

Activity Q

PowerPoint®

Working with a partner, carry out some research with your classmates.

What mobile phones do they own and use (for example, Motorola®, LG®, Nokia®)?

What service providers do they use (such as 3®, Orange®, Vodaphone®)?

Create a spreadsheet to analyse the data and create at least one bar or column chart and one pie chart.

Incorporate the spreadsheet data and the chart and graph into a PowerPoint® presentation that you can share with your tutor or other members of your class.

4.4.2 Business solution

Recommended solution with justification

In the professional world of IT, it is not enough just to identify a possible solution to a problem; you will need to justify it. You may well be asked to offer two or three different ways of solving the problem, but you will then choose a single one to recommend. Non-technical staff in particular will trust you to make the right decisions because you have the knowledge and expertise.

You will need to:

1. Explain the possible solutions (you may well have more than one for the user to choose from).
2. Say how they would solve the problem.

Make the grade P6 M4

For P6, you will use a range of software tools to present your spreadsheet model. For example, you will create a PowerPoint® presentation showing screenshots of the solution and graphics demonstrating some of the charts and graphs that the system generates. In addition, you will have developed a user guide (this could be paper-based or electronic).

As it is essential that you use software tools confidently to present your ideas, for M4 you will need to justify the software tools that you have used to present your solutions. You will need to say why each method you used to present your idea is suitable for the audience and purpose.

4.5 Be able to evaluate business solutions

This section will cover the following grading criterion: **P7**

4.5.1 Evaluate

It is common to evaluate IT software, hardware, products and solutions from a number of perspectives.

Key term

When you **evaluate** something, you make judgements about it. For example, if you are evaluating a new flavour of ice cream, you might make judgements about its colour, texture and taste.

In an IT environment it is essential that you learn to evaluate across a range of products, software, and so on. For example, when you evaluate a new mobile phone you might make judgements about:

- The number of functions
- Battery life on standby
- Size of keyboard
- Ease of use.

When evaluating, you will always make judgements against pre-defined criteria.

Solution against original requirement

Using the list of user needs defined at the beginning as part of the problem, you will check to see that the solution does in fact solve the problems it was intended to solve.

Activity R

Evaluation

Working with a partner, create ten criteria that you would look for in a new laptop computer.

List the criteria and then find five examples of laptops on the internet or in trade magazines.

Judge each of the laptops against the ten criteria you listed and identify which laptop meets the most criteria.

Use of IT tools

You will evaluate the IT tools you used to create the solution and to support the process.

Development of the model

Evaluating the spreadsheet model is the most important aspect. Does it meet the user's needs? Is it fit for purpose?

Suggesting improvements

Can you really say that you have ever used a computer program, computer game or even a piece of technology and not thought about something that could have been done better?

Activity S

Suggesting improvements

Using the research you did for Activity R, identify the laptop that met the fewest criteria and suggest what could have been done to improve the laptop (for example, load a more up-to-date operating system or provide a better battery).

Make the grade

For P7, you must evaluate your solution. You will need to evaluate it against the original requirements and evaluate your use of IT tools. You must evaluate the development of the model and suggest some improvements that could be made.

Achieving Success

In order to achieve each unit, you will complete a series of coursework activities. Each time you hand in work, your tutor will return this to you with a record of your achievement.

This particular unit has 12 criteria to meet: 7 Pass, 4 Merit and 1 Distinction.

For a **Pass** you must achieve **all 7** Pass criteria.

For a **Merit** you must achieve **all 7** Pass **and all 4** Merit criteria.

For a **Distinction** you must achieve **all 7** Pass, **all 4** Merit criteria **and the single** Distinction criterion.

Help with assessment

Your tutor will give you one or more assignments that you will complete as coursework. This could consist of:

- Posters
- Research tasks
- Presentations
- Spreadsheet model(s)
- Screen shots and printouts
- Test plans and results
- Written evaluations
- Informal report(s)

You should read the guidance given for each of the criteria (shown across the unit) carefully and remember to check your work.

Further reading

Textbooks

Beattie, V. and **Pratt**, K. *Business Reporting: Harnessing the Power of the Internet for Users.* (Institute of Chartered Accountants of Scotland, 2001) ISBN-10: 1871250900

Harvey, G. *Excel 2007 for Dummies.* (John Wiley & Sons, 2006) ISBN-10: 0470037377

Tapscott, D. *Digital Capital: Harnessing the Power of Business Webs.* (Nicholas Brealey Publishing, 31 May 2000) ISBN-10: 1857882091

Waller, D. *Basic Projects in Excel 2007.* (Payne-Gallway, 2008) ISBN 978 1905 29242 4

Websites

www.businesslink.gov.uk/

www.forrester.com/

www.gartner.com/technology/home.jsp

www.ovumkc.com/

Unit 7
Installing computer hardware

Learning objectives

By the end of this unit you should:

1. Be able to know the reasons for and implications of installing hardware components
2. Be able to understand risks involved and precautions needed when installing hardware components
3. Be able to install and test hardware components
4. Be able to document an installation or upgrade.

In order to pass this unit, the evidence you present for assessment needs to demonstrate that you can meet all of the above learning outcomes for this unit. The criteria below show the levels of achievement required to pass this unit.

To achieve a **pass** grade the evidence must show that the learner is able to:	To achieve a **merit** grade the evidence must show that, in addition to the pass criteria, the learner is able to:	To achieve a **distinction** the evidence must show that, in addition to the pass and merit criteria, the learner is able to:
P1 Describe the reasons for and implications of installing hardware components		
P2 Explain potential risks to consider when installing hardware components	**M1** Discuss precautions that can be taken to avoid problems	
P3 Prepare a computer system for a specified hardware installation or upgrade		**D1** Justify the resources chosen for an installation
P4 Install or upgrade hardware components safely, configuring associated software		
P5 Test the computer system for functionality	**M2** Suggest possible solutions to resolve hardware functionality issues	
P6 Produce updated documentation for the modifications	**M3** Explain the benefits of registering with the hardware provider	

Computer systems will go wrong from time to time. When they do, it is the IT support technician that an organisation relies on to get the fault fixed in the most timely and cost-effective manner.

Doing this relies on knowledge of hardware, software and the procedures needed to carry out this task confidently and safely. This unit will give you the grounding to do just that.

You will be assessed through coursework which could be in the form of:

- Presentations
- Practical sessions which may be photographed, videoed or witnessed
- Printed reports and manuals
- Websites and wikis
- Screen captures
- Blogs
- Podcasts.

7.1 Know the reasons for and implications of installing hardware components

This section will cover the following grading criterion: **P1**

This section looks at the reasons for installing hardware components and the implications of doing so.

7.1.1 Reasons

There are a number of reasons for installing hardware components. These include:

- routine maintenance
- fault repair
- upgrades.

Routine maintenance

You may have heard the expression, 'prevention is better than cure'. Well, routine maintenance occurs when work is carried out on hardware which may *not* actually be broken. Performing this type of maintenance can ensure that further problems are avoided by keeping the equipment in good working order. It is the same reason why cars are serviced on a regular basis.

The actual maintenance carried out may not be complex – it could be as simple as cleaning the equipment. For example computer systems build up a lot of dust around their fans and heatsinks inside the case. Removing this will prevent the hardware from overheating and becoming damaged.

Fault repair

When a fault is discovered in a piece of IT equipment, the technician has two basic choices: **replace** or **repair**.

Purchasing replacement hardware components is a common fix but in tight financial times, repairing the fault may be preferred. It really depends on how complex the repair is.

Scorecard

Repairing components

− It often takes longer (and costs more) to repair than to replace.

− Modern hardware uses very small components, making repairs difficult.

− Repairing often introduces other faults.

− Repaired components will need to be tested before use.

+ The component may be expensive to replace (a financial concern).

+ The component is now rare and replacements are difficult to locate quickly.

+ The skills to repair the hardware component already exist with the organisation.

Upgrades

Upgrades occur when part or all of the hardware in a computer system is replaced with better and/or newer components. Upgrading can be used to resolve faults but is more commonly performed in order to increase the speed of a computer system or enable it to run new software.

A popular reason for upgrading is the release of a new operating system, such as Microsoft Windows®. New versions of Windows® (for example, Windows Vista® and Windows 7®) often require more powerful hardware than their predecessors required as they often need more CPU speed, RAM and hard disk drive capacity.

While a slow computer system is not the same as a faulty system, users often feel frustrated when using equipment that does not function as quickly as they would like it to.

Apart from running newer operating systems, there are many other reasons to upgrade!

Some of these can be found in Table 7.1.

User requirements	The needs of the user have changed and the current computer system no longer meets these demands (for example, it is too slow, it does not run the right software, it cannot store enough data etc.)
Compatibility	The hardware currently being used is not compatible with either a new software application, a new operating system or another piece of hardware that has been purchased.
Increased capacity	The hardware cannot store enough data – this is typically either the amount of RAM or space on the hard disk drive.
Increased speed	The hardware is no longer quick enough to meet the demands of the user (for example, a CPU cannot process data quickly enough for a game).
Increased reliability	The hardware has been unreliable and cannot be guaranteed to work properly every time it is used (for example, the computer system will not work every time it is switched on).
Software requirements	New software has been purchased which has requirements which exceed the hardware specification of the current computer system.

Table 7.1 Reasons to upgrade

7.1.2 Implications

Installing new equipment has implications for any organisation. Common concerns include:

- **Training** – employees will need to be trained to use the new equipment.
- **Compatibility** – upgrades may create unexpected problems with compatibility (for example, applications no longer working as expected, other hardware components starting to cause problems).
- **Costs** – upgrading will cost the organisation money.

7.1.3 Decommissioning

Key term

The term **decommissioning** means taking something out of use. Obsolete or faulty equipment generally has very little value to an organisation and they may have to pay another company to dispose of it safely.

Old hardware has to be disposed of safely. Concern must be paid to health and safety issues, the environment and sustainability.

Obsolete hardware may still have some marginal value as it may not have completely depreciated in worth before it is decommissioned. Some organisations may donate their equipment to charity or attempt to sell it through auction. Doing so may incur extra costs, however, for administration and transport.

If an organisation chooses to dispose of its equipment, it will need to be done responsibly and legally; many IT hardware items contain toxic substances (such as nickel, cadmium and lead) that can damage the environment. Disposing of equipment in an environmentally friendly and sustainable manner will undoubtedly cost

the organisation more money, but there are plenty of recycling companies which will help (for a fee!).

Service level agreements

New hardware could mean changes to an existing **service level agreement** (SLA) as the new hardware may not be covered by it.

Key term

A **service level agreement** is an agreement between departments inside the same organisation which defines what standard of service and cooperation they should expect from each other.

SLAs are often linked to an organisation's IT helpdesk and will typically state how long it will take to resolve simple problems or how often an employee will be updated on the status of their reported fault.

Buying and installing new hardware can cause problems for an IT helpdesk as they may have little experience of using the hardware or solving problems it may create.

Activity A

Disposing of obsolete or faulty IT equipment

You are working in an organisation's IT support section and have been asked to find out what the local options are for disposing of broken or obsolete computer systems (and components) in a responsible and environmentally friendly manner.

Carry out some research to find out what options are available for your area.

Make the grade

P1 asks you to describe the reasons for installing hardware components and the implications of doing so. These issues are dealt with in sections 7.1.1, 7.1.2 and 7.1.3. You must remember to cover both aspects in your answer. A presentation is the ideal method for submitting this kind of information.

- By forgetting to turn electricity supply off when installing or removing equipment.
- By damaging components in the immediate area when installing or removing components.
- By damaging the equipment through **electrostatic discharge (ESD)** – see section 7.2.2.

Figure 7.1 The CPU has a bent pin as a result of poor installation

7.2 Understand risks involved and precautions needed when installing hardware components

This section will cover the following grading criteria: P2   M1

7.2.1 Risks to systems

Whether new or repaired hardware is installed, there is always a risk to the computer system. There are three main risks that you should consider:

Equipment damage

Physical damage can occur to equipment in a number of ways:

- When removing new components from packaging.
- When installing or removing components.
- By installing incompatible hardware, particularly in terms of voltage.
- By using incorrect tools to install or remove components.
- By forcing new components to fit into incorrect slots and sockets.

Loss of or corruptions of data

Although you may not believe it, data is the most valuable component of any computer system!

Data takes considerable time to collect, enter and process and this makes it a costly commodity for any organisation to lose. Many companies rely on their data as it may contain their customers' addresses, transactions, balances or bank details.

Poor hardware replacement can cause damage to the hardware components that store this data, typically the hard disk drive.

Loss of service

Any disruption to a computer system due to damage to its hardware, software or data can make the service it provides to the employee unavailable.

This loss of service, if critical to an organisation, could be very costly as it may inconvenience the customer to such an extent that they might want to take their business elsewhere.

Longer term there is also the issue of customer confidence; there is an expectation that a company's systems are robust and reliable. Any loss of service will dent the customer's confidence in using the company to process their orders in the future.

7.2.2 Electrostatic damage

Key term

Electricity comes in two basic forms: current and static. Current electricity is the type that flows from your electricity mains or a battery. Static electricity occurs when little charges build up on a surface – your body is very good at storing this and you will have seen the effect if you have ever seen the 'balloon, jumper and hair' trick at a party! Static electricity builds up slowly and it is possible that you may build up a charge of thousands of volts which need to be released. This electricity is released when the charges find a route to earth. If this happens quickly it is called **electrostatic discharge**. You may have experienced this 'electric shock' before when touching the bare metal of a car door or a shelf in the supermarket.

Hardware components such as motherboards, graphics cards and RAM are particularly sensitive to electrostatic discharge and will become damaged beyond repair if they are exposed. For this reason it is important that static electricity is kept to the minimum and safely discharged before work is started.

Figure 7.2 The boy's hair sticks up because of static electricity

7.2.3 Precautions

Once you know the risks, you should take appropriate precautions!

Checking health and safety regulations

If you are going to work with equipment, you must understand the risks which are involved and the precautions you need to take. Any failure to understand these risks could result in personal injury or injury to colleagues or customers. In the worst scenario, it could prove fatal, for example, electrocution.

Health and safety

As an IT practitioner, you need to understand how the law relates to health and safety as well as knowing the organisation's guidelines for safe working practices. These are usually available as part of an organisational policy or are printed in the staff handbook. Be aware that you have a legal responsibility to work safely and protect the health of both yourself and other people inside the organisation.

Some common risks and their precautions are discussed below.

To prevent damage to equipment, use the correct tools for the job.

Screwdrivers are used to remove and replace screws in the case and motherboard and can also be used to connect components firmly.

Different types and sizes of screwdriver exist (slot head and cross-head – or 'Phillips' – are the most common). You should always use the correct size and type otherwise you risk shredding the head of the screw.

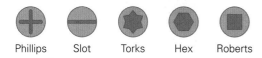

Phillips   Slot   Torks   Hex   Roberts

Figure 7.3 Different types of screw head

Multi-meters are used to check that electrical connections with a device or cable are OK and that voltages are in the correct range.

Pliers are used for holding or squeezing components together. They can also be used to pick up screws that have fallen out of computer system cases.

Mains-testers are used to determine whether or not mains power is present before starting to work on a device. Once power is restored, they can also be used to check that mains power is getting to the components that need it.

To prevent Electro static discharge, use the corrct tools for the job.

Electrostatic discharge can be reduced by keeping hardware components in **anti-static bags** until they are needed.

Those working with electronic equipment should use an **anti-static wrist strap** (see Figure 3.16) and place hardware components on an **anti-static mat** to reduce the chances of damage by static electricity.

Figure 7.4 Anti-static bags

To prevent loss or corruption of data use the correct tools for the job.

Loss or corruption of data – ensure all sensitive and important data is backed up to another computer system or removable medium (such as CD, DVD or USB pen drive) before starting to install new hardware. Making multiple copies is a good idea. You should also make sure that the backup data is complete and can be safely recovered (if needed).

Activity B

Quiz

Test your knowledge by answering the following questions. The answers are given at the back of the book.

1. Give two reasons why you would repair a component.

2. Give three valid reasons for upgrading a hardware component.

3. Explain ESD.

4. Name three risks that might occur during hardware installation.

5. Name two precautions against ESD.

6. If a screw had a Phillips head, what shape would the screwdriver tip be?

7. Name one implication of installing new equipment.

8. What is the main precaution against data loss?

type of slot or connector is being used in order to replace the component correctly. Forcing a hardware component into the incorrect slot or connector will damage both the motherboard and the component.

Table 7.2 shows some of the most common types of motherboard slot and connector in a standard PC. You will need to become familiar with them.

Make the grade P2 M1

P2 asks you to explain potential risks that you need to consider when installing hardware components. Most of the obvious risks are covered in sections 7.2.1 and 7.2.2 and you will need to detail these in your own words.
M1 follows on from P2 and asks you to think about the precautions you can take to avoid these types of problems. Section 7.2.3 examines simple precautions you can follow to reduce risks to the equipment, data and yourself.

Activity C

Slots and connectors

The following abbreviations refer to type of slot or connector. But what are they? Check your answers at the back of the book.

1. USB

2. PCI and PCIe

3. SATA and IDE

4. DDR DIMM

5. AGP

7.3 Be able to install and test hardware components

This section will cover the following grading criteria:

7.3.1 Hardware

Each component in a computer system is installed into a different connector or slot. One of the main skills in being an IT technician is being able to recognise what

7.3.2 Preparation

Undertaking proper preparation before an installation will prevent a lot of potential problems!

Test selection

You will need to ensure that the equipment works properly when you have completed your installation. Prepare for this by selecting suitable tests to use. Some of these are given below.

- A workstation may have had some new USB ports installed. Some tests may be needed to check that devices such as USB pen drives are recognised and can be accessed at the correct speeds from these ports – this may involve some large file transfers.

Name of slot/connector	Image
RAM slots	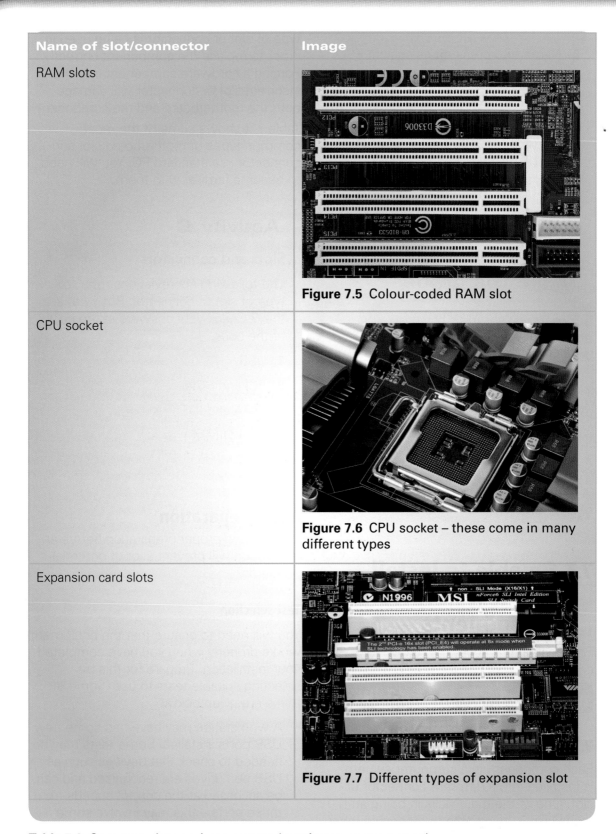 **Figure 7.5** Colour-coded RAM slot
CPU socket	**Figure 7.6** CPU socket – these come in many different types
Expansion card slots	**Figure 7.7** Different types of expansion slot

Table 7.2 Common slots and connectors (continues on next page)

Name of slot/connector	Image
Hard disk drive connector (SATA or IDE)	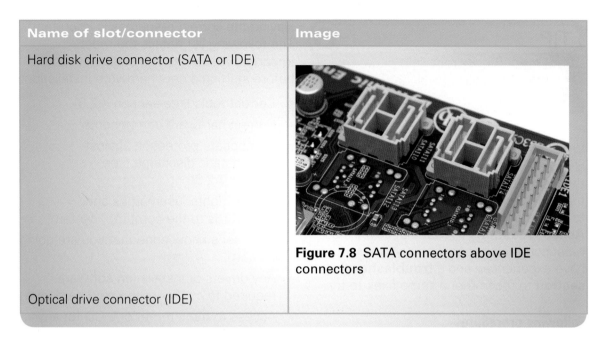 **Figure 7.8** SATA connectors above IDE connectors
Optical drive connector (IDE)	

Table 7.2 Continued

- A workstation which has had a faster CPU installed may have its performance measured by benchmarking software, for example SiSoftware's Sandra (http://www.sisoftware.co.uk/).
- A workstation may have had a new DVD rewriteable drive installed to replace a faulty unit. Tests will be needed to ensure that disks mastered on the old drive are readable on the new drive and that disks mastered on the new drive are readable in other computer systems.

Test configuration

Depending on the test you have selected, you may need to configure things exactly so that the new component is tested properly. For example, in the case where a new DVD rewriteable drive is installed, it would be necessary to ensure that the existing mastering software will work with the new drive and that the program's settings match those use by the original device (for example, in terms of writing speed) so that a direct comparison can be made.

Reading instructions

Most new hardware components come with installation instructions but increasingly, this is not in the form of a printed manual or leaflet. Modern hardware often comes with a CD containing an Adobe® PDF document or a simple 'readme' text file. Some manufacturers put the instructions onto their website and ask technicians to download them.

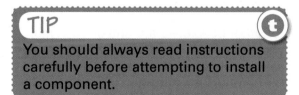

TIP

You should always read instructions carefully before attempting to install a component.

It is worth remembering that these instructions have been written by the designers of the components so they are likely to provide the most straightforward and reliable way of installing the component in order to ensure it works as intended.

TIP

Bookmark the correct web page on the manufacturer's website for your component.

Visiting a manufacturer's website is always useful to gain extra support if the installation does not go well. Many manufacturers have support pages devoted to each product which include **Frequently Asked Questions** (FAQs) that cover the most common issues that customers have experienced and a **troubleshooting section** to recommend some fixes to try.

Following procedures

Most organisations have published procedures which are designed to protect their employees' health and safety, their own data, their customers' loyalty and their reputation.

Although you are likely to have been trained correctly before you start the installation, it is still considered to be your responsibility to discover what these procedures are and to ensure that you follow them correctly.

Safety check

You should make sure you work safely and do not leave a dangerous situation for other people. At the end of each job, you should look back and see if there any safety issues which might need attention. Remember, you have a responsibility under Health and Safety at Work legislation to make sure the workplace is safe for yourself and for other people.

Obtaining resources

TIP

Never start an installation unless you have all the appropriate resources ready.

Having the correct resources is important! The following list details the most important resources you should assemble before starting a new hardware installation:

- Correct tools (see section 7.2.3)
- Correct hardware components
- Appropriate protection against electrostatic discharge (see section 7.2.3)
- Access rights, usernames and passwords to the computer system
- The user's knowledge that you are going to start!
- Any drivers or installation software required to configure the new hardware
- Access to the internet or a CD for any necessary software updates
- Access to correct instructions
- Sufficient time so that the task does not have to be rushed!
- Awareness of organisational procedures and health and safety responsibilities.

Check equipment is undamaged

New components are usually quite small, and so are likely to arrive via the postal service. It is important that you check that the component is undamaged when you first open the package. If the component is damaged, do *not* attempt to install it as it may needlessly damage other systems. The component will still be under the manufacturer's warranty so should be returned to the supplier for a replacement.

Associated installation software

Most hardware components need **installation software** before they will work properly with the rest of the computer system. The most common type of installation software is the **driver**.

Key term

Drivers are small programs which let the hardware component 'talk' to the operating system. Without the correct driver, the operating system is unable to communicate with the hardware and it will not work correctly. Drivers are specific to different operating systems. For example, a Linux® driver will not work in Microsoft Windows® and different versions of Microsoft Windows® often need particular drivers.

Other types of software may also come with the hardware. These are generally called 'help programs' and they help the users to operate the hardware effectively.

Examples of associated software include:

- Mastering software for use with a CD-RW or DVD-RW drive
- Control centre for a video card
- A configuration program for a broadband router
- Recording software with a CD-RW or DVD-RW drive
- Media players for a sound card.

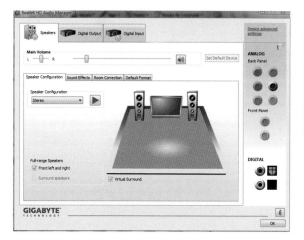

Figure 7.9 Associated installation software for a sound card

Backing up data

We have already discussed the importance of making a backup of the computer system's valuable data in section 7.2.3. Performing a backup is an important part of the preparation for a hardware installation. Ideally the data which is backed up will be stored elsewhere so that even in the worst possible circumstances, valuable data can be recovered.

> **TIP**
>
> Do not forget to ask the user where they have data stored on the local computer system.
>
> Unless the system is networked, you should also remember to export their emails, address book and website bookmarks.

Recording serial numbers

Most organisations have **manifests** which store details of the hardware and software they have purchased. Each hardware component will come with its own **serial number** and this is often found printed on a sticker applied somewhere to the component (often on the back).

> **TIP**
>
> Write down the serial number of the component before it is installed. It should be added into the installation record you create (see 7.4.1).

Be aware that the serial number for your component should be unique, but all components of this exact same type will have an **identical product code**.

Figure 7.10 The serial number on a hardware component

Make the grade   P3   D1

It is likely that your teacher will ask you to explore a particular fault in a computer system and ask you to implement a possible fix. Accordingly, P3 asks you to prepare a computer system for a specified hardware installation or upgrade. Sections 7.3.1 and 7.3.2 should help you think about the hardware and preparations details.

D1 is connected to P3 and asks you to justify the resources you chose for an installation. These resources can refer not only to the selected components used in the installation but also the resources you used in preparation for and during the installation.

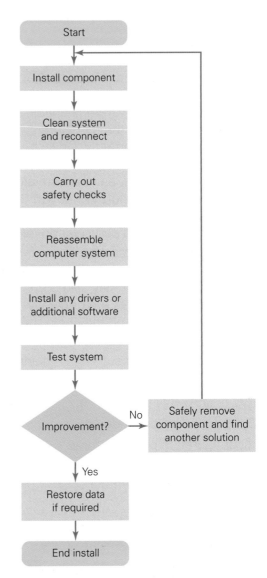

Figure 7.11 A flowchart of the installation process

7.3.3 Install

We can show the installation process as a simple flowchart of actions (see Figure 7.11).

Make the grade   P4

P4 is the key practical criterion of the unit. It is where you install or upgrade the hardware components safely and configure any associated software. This follows the work you completed for P3 and D1 and is most easily evidenced by photographs or videos of you actually performing the task.

7.3.4 Test

Testing must occur every time a new (or repaired) component is installed. It is important to discover whether the component is working properly and to its correct specification.

Section 7.3.2 discussed the need for a test plan to determine which kinds of tests are needed to confirm whether (or not) the components are working correctly.

Tools

The IT practitioner is generally spoiled for choice when it comes to testing and monitoring the running of computer hardware. Many utilities come free with the operating system and these can be used to find out how well newly installed hardware is working inside the computer and what impact it has had on the computer system as a whole.

> ### Key term
>
> A **runtime analyser** is a software utility which is able to display the impact of using software on the computer system's hardware resources. Analysis is possible by comparing results before and after new hardware components are installed.

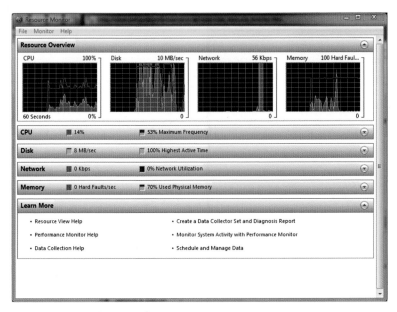

Figure 7.12 Windows® Resource Monitor

Tools such as the Resource Monitor in Microsoft Windows® can be used to monitor the computer system's drain on resources such as the CPU, hard disk drive, network interface card and RAM.

System information

Other useful utilities found in Microsoft Windows® include System Information, Device Manager, Performance Monitor and Event Viewer. These are shown in Figures 7.13–7.16.

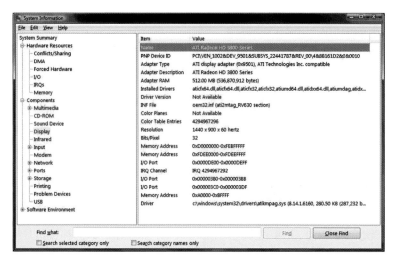

Figure 7.13 Windows® System Information

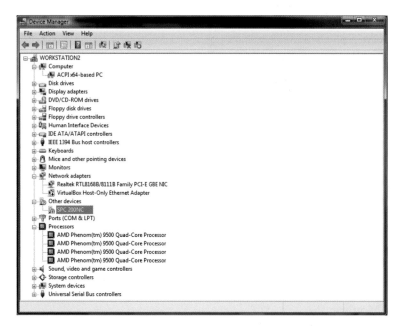

Figure 7.14 A problematic component highlighted in Windows® Device Manager

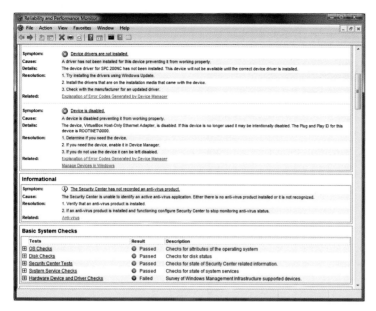

Figure 7.15 Windows® Reliability and Performance Monitor's report

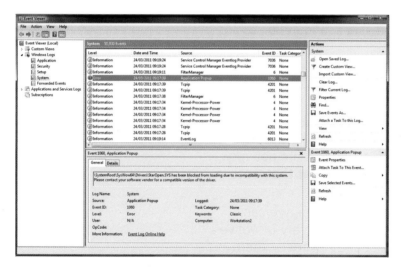

Figure 7.16 Windows® Event Viewer showing a critical error

Test procedures

It is important that you gather information when you test the system in order to discover the outcome. Common techniques for gathering information include:

- Creating a text file which contains a log of all events
- Collecting output through a series of screen captures
- Video recording the computer system's output on screen.

A log file is particularly useful as it can be analysed at a later date in a spreadsheet application.

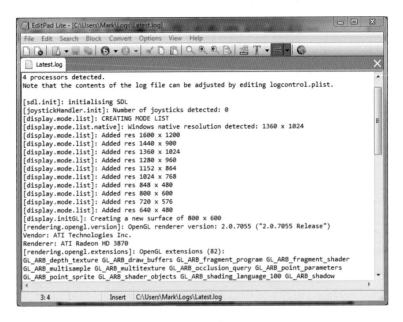

Figure 7.17 Log file detailing hardware configuration as an application is started

Validating information

After information has been gathered it is a good idea to **validate** it. This means checking that the information is sensible. As the results from one single test are not very conclusive, it is usually a good idea to **repeat the same test** several times.

If the tests show different results each time, we can only conclude that the selected test is not very effective on its own; we will need to select another test – there is absolutely no sense in believing results which are clearly invalid.

Responding to test information

The results from tests often contain complex **error codes** and messages which may need to be interpreted before any conclusion can be reached.

Most error codes can be found in the troubleshooting guides which come with new products and, optionally, by searching the world wide web. It is very likely that the error you have discovered has already been posted to a newsgroup or message board by another frustrated technician!

Figure 7.18 Windows® System Error Codes

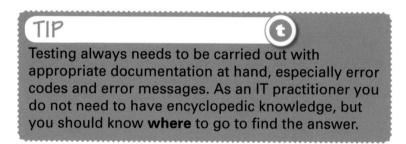

Testing always needs to be carried out with appropriate documentation at hand, especially error codes and error messages. As an IT practitioner you do not need to have encyclopedic knowledge, but you should know **where** to go to find the answer.

Once the testing results are understood, it should be possible to work out whether they have been successful or have failed. According to Figure 7.18, an error code of 0×0 means 'success' whereas a code of 0×3 does not!

What to do if the testing shows failure

You cannot ignore a valid set of test results. If the newly installed component has repeatedly failed the test, you will need to resolve the problem.

You could try:

- Re-running the tests to confirm failure.
- Fixing the problem and re-running the tests.
- **Escalating** the problem to a specialist for resolution.
- Reporting the issue to the component's manufacture for resolution.

If no resolution is found, the problem may be due to an unknown incompatibility or the fact that the component may have been damaged (without any obvious physical signs). In this case the component will need to be returned as faulty.

Checking the specification

Sometimes testing requires checking the performance of the component against its specification. This is to ensure that components are working at the levels they were advertised by the manufacturer. Common examples might include:

- Measuring the clock frequency of a CPU.
- Measuring the bandwidth of a network card.
- Measuring the range of a wireless network card.
- Finding the true capacity of a hard disk drive.

In most cases this is a mere formality but sometimes a technician does get a nasty surprise with a component performing well below the advertised levels!

7.3.5 Troubleshooting

Key term

Troubleshooting is the act of discovering the nature of faults and fixing them. In computer systems these faults are inevitably connected to hardware failure or poorly configured software.

Troubleshooting a computer system often involves finding:

- Loose connections (for example, CPU, RAM, PSU cables, data cables, poorly inserted expansion cards)
- Jumper settings incorrectly configured on a motherboard, hard disk drive or optical drive
- Incorrectly connected power supply
- Incorrect motherboard configuration
- Components not connected to their proper slots or sockets.

One of the most useful troubleshooting tools is a computer system's **Power On Self Test** (**POST**).

Key terms

Power On Self Test is a utility program which is part of the computer system's **Basic Input Output System** (**BIOS**). As the name suggests, it checks for basic faults when it is first switched on.

Some POST errors are fatal and will halt the booting up process, preventing the operating system from being loaded.

POST often checks:

- Power supply issues
- CPU issues
- RAM issues
- Graphics card issues
- Sound card issues
- Network card issues

- Hard disk drive issues (these have their own SMART – Self-Monitoring, Analysis and Reporting Technology)
- Date and time
- Keyboard issues
- Motherboard issues

Figure 7.19 A POST screen on a PC computer system

Various forms of third-party diagnostic software may also be used to isolate specific problems with hardware.

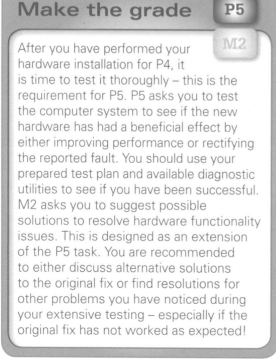

Make the grade P5 M2

After you have performed your hardware installation for P4, it is time to test it thoroughly – this is the requirement for P5. P5 asks you to test the computer system to see if the new hardware has had a beneficial effect by either improving performance or rectifying the reported fault. You should use your prepared test plan and available diagnostic utilities to see if you have been successful. M2 asks you to suggest possible solutions to resolve hardware functionality issues. This is designed as an extension of the P5 task. You are recommended to either discuss alternative solutions to the original fix or find resolutions for other problems you have noticed during your extensive testing – especially if the original fix has not worked as expected!

7.4 Be able to document an installation or upgrade

This section will cover the following grading criteria: P6 M3

7.4.1 Documentation

Keeping accurate documentation on an installation or upgrade is absolutely vital. The term 'documentation' means any printed or electronic material which is kept by the organisation.

Installation records

Any installation should record:

- Who the end user is.
- Who the IT support technician tasked with solving the problem is.
- When the problem was logged.
- What the fault was reported as.
- What the fault actually is.
- What solution has been tried … and whether it was successful after testing.
- Details of the new/repaired hardware (including serial numbers of the computer systems and the components involved).
- Details of the tests that were performed.
- Details of any resources (such as drivers) that were needed.
- What the cost of the repair or upgrade was.
- Whether the end user has accepted the solution (the 'sign off').
- When the helpdesk fault was closed.

This type of information is mainly recorded in specialised helpdesk database systems which can help track IT support performance for measuring against a SLA (see section 7.1.3).

Technical manual update

It is not uncommon for an IT support section to keep technical manuals which detail **common faults** and **solutions**. Guidance on how to install particular hardware components is always a useful resource, especially for new staff who may not have encountered the problem before.

These manuals are only useful if they are kept **regularly updated**; any new types of problem should be appended to the manual automatically (along with any proven solutions).

User manual update

The change of a hardware component may change the way a user must use their computer system. As a user manual acts as a guide for how to use the system, any significant changes caused by installing new hardware should be reflected. After all, incorrect use of a computer system's hardware can be one of the key causes of faults and breakdowns!

Make the grade   P6

P6 asks you to produce updated documentation for the modifications you have made to the computer system. This should include updated entries suitable for inserting into both the technical and user manual.

7.4.2 Product registration

Although it is not a mandatory procedure, **registering** a product is very useful as it helps to **validate the warranty** and will enable the customer (you) to access greater support from the manufacturer.

Product registration methods

There are three main methods of registering a new product:

- online (via the world wide web) or through an installation setup program
- by telephone
- by post.

The online option is the quickest and will usually provide instant acknowledgement in the form of a receipt email.

Postal registration involves mailing a special card back to the manufacturer. The card is usually found inside the product's box when it is received (so check carefully).

Organisations benefit from registration as it normally provides them with:

- Information about the component
- Notification about updated products, drivers or services
- Access to additional services at discounted rates
- Access to registration-only deals on new products
- Access to product support
- Free entry into product promotions.

Storing receipts

Your receipt is **proof of legal purchase** and it is important that you keep this safe.

A **warranty** for a product commences on the date of purchase but the actual **duration** period the warranty covers will vary from manufacturer to manufacturer.

A manufacturer may want to see both items in order to honour a claim on a faulty product.

Make the grade M3

M3 asks you to explain the benefits of registering with the manufacturer of the hardware. These advantages are detailed throughout section 7.4.2. As you are asked to 'explain' rather than 'identify', please ensure you have definitely thought (and said) why you think these registration perks are good for the organisation.

Achieving Success

In order to achieve each unit, you will complete a series of coursework activities. Each time you hand in work, your tutor will return this to you with a record of your achievement.

This particular unit has 10 criteria to meet: 6 Pass, 3 Merit and 1 Distinction.

For a **Pass** you must achieve **all 6** Pass criteria.

For a **Merit** you must achieve **all 6** Pass **and all 3** Merit criteria.

For a **Distinction** you must achieve **all 6** Pass, **all 3** Merit criteria **and the single** Distinction criterion.

Help with assessment

Your tutor will give you one or more assignments that you will complete as coursework. This could consist of:

* Presentations
* Videos and screen captures of installations

* Witness statements and/or an evidence log
* Websites, pages or wikis
* Leaflets or reports
* Posters.

You should read the guidance given for each of the criteria (shown across the unit) carefully and remember to check your work.

r Further reading

MacRae, K. *The Computer Manual: The Step-by-step Guide to Upgrading and Repairing a PC.* (Haynes Group, 2010) ISBN 1844259285

MacRae, K. and **Marshall**, G. *Computer Troubleshooting: The Complete Step-by-step Guide to Diagnosing and Fixing Common PC Problems.* (J.H. Haynes & Co. Ltd, 2008) ISBN 1844255174

Websites

www.computerhope.com/issues/chadd.htm

www.pcstats.com

Unit 9
Customising software

Learning objectives
By the end of this unit you should:

1. Understand why application software is customised
2. Be able to customise application software
3. Be able to create templates in application software
4. Be able to create macros and shortcuts in application software.

In order to pass this unit, the evidence you present for assessment needs to demonstrate that you can meet all of the above learning outcomes for this unit. The criteria below show the levels of achievement required to pass this unit.

To achieve a **pass** grade the evidence must show that the learner is able to:	To achieve a **merit** grade the evidence must show that, in addition to the pass criteria, the learner is able to:	To achieve a **distinction** grade the evidence must show that, in addition to the pass and merit criteria, the learner is able to:
P1 Explain why software may be customised to meet user requirements		**D1** Discuss the benefits and drawbacks of customisation
P2 Customise application software to meet user requirements		
P3 Test customised software to ensure it meets user requirements		
P4 Create templates to meet user requirements in different applications packages	**M1** Evaluate how effectively the templates meet user requirements	
P5 Record and test a macro to meet a given requirement	**M2** Explain the benefits of using macros	
P6 Assign and test shortcuts		

Introduction

Applications packages like Microsoft Office® are known as **generic** software. This means that they have a whole range of functionality that might be useful in a customised solution.

This unit will help you learn some basic skills that will help you to adapt applications packages and customise them to suit individuals or situations.

You will be assessed through coursework which could be in the form of:

- Presentations
- Witness statements
- Web pages
- Screenshots
- Electronic evidence of customised software
- Templates
- Macro code.

9.1 Understand why software is customised

This section will cover the following grading criteria: **P1** **D1**

9.1.1 Software

Application software

Application software has a range of inbuilt functionality like printing options, mail merge (creating customised letters where the letter itself is merged with an address list to create individual letters each with a separate name and address), functionality to make charts and graphs from tables of data, or the ability to store and manipulate records to help managers understand aspects of an organisation.

The applications will be used by both experienced users and novices (those with little or no experience) and making it easier for novices by customising the application can help them to be more efficient in their use of IT.

Utilities

Anti-virus software such as AVG® or Norton® has settings that determine how the software behaves. For example, you can work with the **scan options** and have different settings for different components.

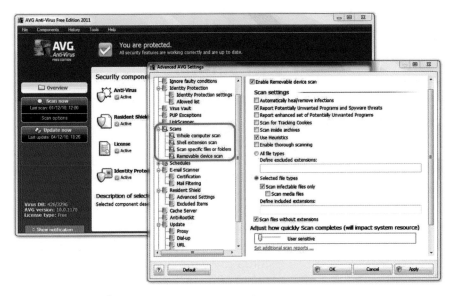

Figure 9.1 AVG® Technologies scan settings

You could, for example, scan the whole computer once a day, you could scan every removable device when it is attached to the system and you could scan specific files or folders hourly.

Systems

A firewall is a program that controls the way that your computer communicates with the internet. ZoneAlarm® is one such example. This software will scan the traffic that goes in and out of the system. It can be set to prevent access to specific websites or to prevent searches on specific words. Some firewalls are free, some have to be purchased and some programs have firewall functionality even though they are not specialist firewall products.

Activity A

Firewalls

Use the following website to investigate ten top firewall applications.

http://personal-firewall-software-review.toptenreviews.com

1. Identify two that have Wi-Fi security features.
2. Identify two with parental controls.
3. Identify two that have online chat help and support.
4. Name one that has all three.

Suitable packages

Unless an organisation needs bespoke software (that is software that is written with specific functionality to meet a specific need or needs), the likelihood is that they will be using generic applications packages like word-processing software (for example Microsoft Word®), spreadsheet software (like Microsoft Excel®) or database software (like Microsoft Access®).

In a truly customised solution (one which has functions for all areas of the organisation including accounting functions, word processing, data storage etc.), it is possible to use functionality from all of the products to create what appears to be a single customised solution.

To develop a solution like this will require you to have gained a range of skills and a good understanding of the software applications you will use. But what other applications are available?

Activity B

Alternative applications?

Use the internet to investigate software applications. You may NOT include any examples from the Microsoft® Office suite!

Find an example of:

1. A spreadsheet application
2. A word-processing application
3. A database application
4. An email application.

Types of customisation

So how can applications be customised?

Changing default settings

Default settings have been set as a basic standard and they are set as the most likely or common choices that a user might make. In Word®, for example, the default page setup settings control (among other things) how the margins are set when a new document is created and whether the document will be created in portrait or landscape orientation.

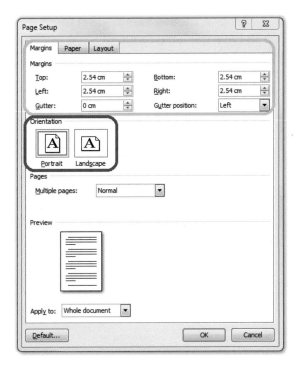

Figure 9.2 Word® page setup

The font settings control the type, style and size of font. All these settings can be changed so that whenever the user creates a new Word® file, the settings will be the same. To do this you select your choices from the options and then click on Default.

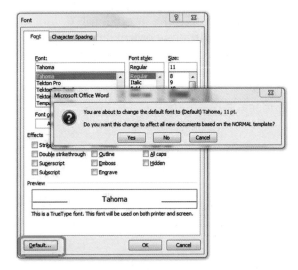

Figure 9.3 Fonts default

Menus and toolbars

Almost all applications software has menus and toolbars and each application will be different in terms of how these menus and toolbars can be activated, changed or hidden (depending on the user's needs).

To help an inexperienced user you might choose to hide menus and toolbars, particularly those you think the user will not need, to make the software appear simpler and less overwhelming.

Take Microsoft Word 2007® as an example. The menus are highlighted in blue, while the toolbars are shown in red.

Figure 9.4 Menus and toolbars

In Microsoft Office 2007®, the menus and toolbars have been replaced with a new term. They are now included as part of the **ribbon**. Above the main ribbon is the Quick Access Toolbar.

Ribbon

Although the ribbon itself is relatively fixed (you cannot add commands or rearrange the commands on it), you have complete control over the Quick Access Toolbar and if you automate processes, you can add buttons to this toolbar to activate the processes.

You will find out how to do this later in the unit.

Templates

Most applications software contains templates that can be chosen and used by users. Each template contains the structure for a document which the user can adapt. If we take the example of an invoice template, by adding the company's information and saving the template as your own version, it can then be used as the basis for all future invoices.

When an invoice is then created, the user would simply add the name and address of the customer, the date, the items bought, all amounts and totals. The invoice could then be printed and posted, or saved and attached to an email and sent.

Most software has built-in templates that a company can use. In spreadsheet software, the options would include templates for invoices, orders or budgets.

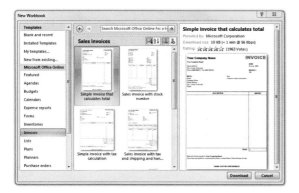

Figure 9.5 Invoice templates

In presentation software, however, you have quiz shows, photo albums and options for widescreen presentations.

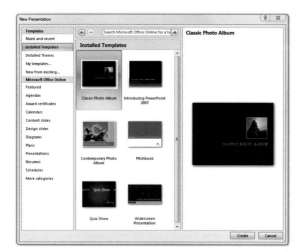

Figure 9.6 Presentation templates

Although many templates are free, users also have the option of downloading other templates for which they then have to pay.

Activity C

Templates

Identify four different types of applications software you use either at college, school or at home. For each application, find at least two templates and investigate what they do. Copy and complete the following table with your findings.

Application	Template 1	Template 2

Forms

While changing settings might make a difference to functionality, the most obvious customisation for any software is the creation of forms. This could be forms to **input data** into a database or maybe even a **switchboard** (a form with buttons) to activate different functions.

These can be created in almost all of the Microsoft Office® applications. The most common one will be forms created in Microsoft Access® to help the user input data into tables.

Booking_ID	Customer_Nam	Telephone_	Room_Num	Check_in_da	Check_out_
3	Mr & Mrs Smith	05555 558954	6	22/11/2010	26/11/2010
4	Helga Watzke	06666 687987	2	24/11/2010	29/11/2010
5	Miss Johnson	06666 412434	1	21/11/2010	23/11/2010
(New)					

Figure 9.7 Room bookings table

But to help the user work with the data, a form would be used to input the data and to display the records one at a time. This makes editing easier.

Figure 9.8 Access® input form

By using an input form you control the way that the user enters data. For example, the data is entered in a **specific order** (the user moving between the boxes with the tab key). In addition the input boxes can have **validation** on them to check that the data is reasonable.

Macros

Macros are mini programs that are often activated by a button press. For example, if a spreadsheet always needs to be printed three times the user would have two options:

1. Click on 'print' three times every time the prints are needed.
2. Go into the print setup and change the default value of 'print 1' to 'print 3' and do this every time the prints are needed.

With a macro, a mini program could be written that automatically prints the spreadsheet three times. The macro would be triggered by a button press. The print macro described above would look like Figure 9.9.

Figure 9.9 A print macro

In this example, most of the code has been inserted into the macro automatically during the recording process. We just changed one value – the number of copies to be printed. The default value would have been one. While recording the macro we chose three. Now, each time the macro is run, three copies will be printed automatically.

Macros are generally used to speed up user activity and to make the use of a solution more efficient because they require the user to do less than they would otherwise have to.

Scorecard

Macros

+ Macros can combine many complex actions into a single key press or mouse click.

+ Macros can be used repeatedly.

+ Macros can be recorded based on performing the task manually the first time.

+ Macros can be used to do the boring, repetitive jobs.

+ Macros are found in most office productivity suites.

− Macros can be complex to write.

− Macros can be difficult to debug when they are not working properly.

− To get the best out of macros requires a higher degree of technical skill.

Activity **D**

Keyboard shortcuts

The best way to understand keyboard shortcuts is to experiment and the first two obvious (and easy) shortcuts to learn are: CTRL + C and CTRL + V.

To use these, open Microsoft Word® or Excel® and highlight some text with the mouse. Then hold down the CTRL key and press C. Move the cursor to another position in the document or worksheet and hold down the CTRL key and press V.

What do they do?

Shortcuts

Buttons that activate macros are an obvious example of a **shortcut**. A very flexible alternative to having lots of buttons in your customised solution is the use of keyboard shortcuts. What this means is pressing a series of keys to trigger an action.

Activity **E**

Keyboard shortcuts in Microsoft Office 2007®

There are many pre-programmed keyboard shortcuts in the Microsoft Office® suite. To find out what some of them are and what they do, watch the following videos.

Begin with the video on the following link:

http://office.microsoft.com/en-gb/access-help/carry-out-commands-by-using-key-combinations-RZ010156267.aspx?CTT=1&section=17

Then click on Next and watch the video on the next page.

Write down three more keyboard shortcuts that you did not already know and describe what they do.

Scorecard

Shortcuts

+ Shortcuts can be used to perform more directly actions that may require several mouse clicks and navigation of many different menus and dialogues.

+ Shortcuts may be easier to remember than complex menu options.

+ Shortcuts could be standardised across different applications.

− Keyboard shortcuts may require combinations of key presses which are difficult for some users to perform.

9.1.2 Benefits

Speed

If you customise applications it can make using a computer much quicker by:

- Reducing the number of keys that need to be pressed when typing.
- Reducing the number of choices that have to be made in menus and toolbars, getting quickly to the action needed.
- Moving the cursor to the right place in a document or spreadsheet.
- Carrying out a series of tasks triggered by a keypress, button or shortcut that activates a macro.

Accuracy

Controlling the way that data is entered will help to make it more accurate because it makes it much more difficult to enter incorrect or bad data.

If data is more accurate, any information that is created from it through the functions in the application will be better and more reliable. Figure 9.10 is a chart that shows sales over a period of months, plus costs and profits in relation to those sales.

Managers would use this information to make judgements about the way the organisation is operating. What can you see from this chart?

You should notice that while sales have continued to go up, profits have gone down. Why? Because costs have gone up!

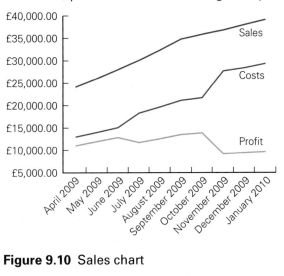

Figure 9.10 Sales chart

The managers would now investigate to see if they can reduce costs to improve the profits.

If this information was inaccurate, they might make judgements and decisions that were bad for the organisation. **Validation** is also essential to make sure that data is as accurate as it can be.

Key term

Validation means ensuring that data is 'reliable' and 'of good quality'. For example, a user might input a date of 45 October 2011! Is this valid? No, because it does not exist. Setting up a validation rule to check that dates are correct and in the right range will help to make sure that blatantly incorrect data is not accepted. Bad data should always be rejected!

Ease of use

How can customisation make applications easier to use? One example would be to open documents with formatting and some content already in place.

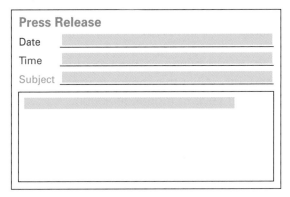

Figure 9.11 A press release

The document would only allow users to key in where indicated in yellow.

Using buttons and macros to navigate between screens and using keyboard shortcuts to select complex settings automatically also makes applications easier to use.

Style consistency

Most organisations like to have a consistent style across the documentation they use. This is often known as the **house style**.

The style may also be based on standard templates modified to suit the organisation's needs and may make use of **themes**. A theme is a series of settings (usually colours and/or fonts).

In addition, many organisations add a logo (image) to their document templates that represents the organisation.

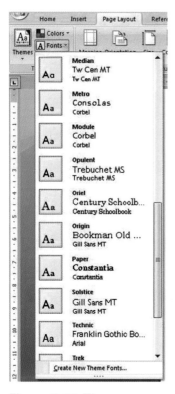

Figure 9.12 Themes

http://www.epsvectorlogosoncd.com/graphics/color_company_logos_on_dvd.jpg

There are many shown here – can you identify ten of them? In each case name the organisation and explain what they are well known for. Copy and complete the table below (one has been completed for you):

Organisation	What they do
Kodak	Manufacture cameras

Improved productivity

When software has been customised and made easier to use, it will have an immediate impact on user productivity.

Users will be less stressed because using the system is more straightforward, which also means they carry out their tasks more quickly.

9.1.3 Drawbacks

We have already identified some of the benefits of customising applications software, but there can be some drawbacks. These can include the need for users to have further training, the increased complexity of applications and the need for increased support for users. These will be analysed in greater detail below.

Training required

Users may need to be trained to use the software properly to produce the expected results. But training has several costs:

- While the user is being trained they are not doing their job!
- Their job might need to be done by another employee or by someone that the company has to hire on a temporary basis.

- If the job is not done, then customers could be let down and this could result in a loss of business.
- There will be a charge for the training.

Increased complexity of applications

Sometimes customising applications software can make the software more complicated. This is because for some customisation, programmers will need to write program code. Remember the example of the ribbon in section 9.1.1?

We suggested that the ribbon itself is relatively fixed (you cannot add commands or rearrange the commands on it). What you can do, however, is add custom tabs – but you can only do this if you can write XML and programming code.

This means that the application will contain programming code that will need to be written and then managed and adapted if necessary. Clearly someone within the organisation will need to have the skills to do this, otherwise the expertise will need to be brought in from outside, which could be expensive.

Support needs

Did you know that before applications software is released for the public to buy it is tested and tested and tested again? This is done so that any problems found when using the application can be resolved before the software is put on the market.

Even though testing has been carried out thoroughly, when the software is used by end users, problems can be expected. Some of these problems and difficulties will occur because the user is a novice (someone with limited or no experience and skill).

So whether it is bespoke (specially written) software, generic applications software or customised software there will be a need for different kinds of support. This support

could comprise user training videos, online training or face-to-face training.

There may also be a need to fix any bugs that give errors when the software is run. The fix might require changes to the code.

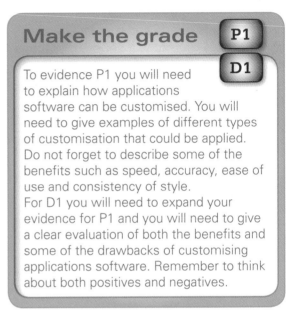

Make the grade P1 D1

To evidence P1 you will need to explain how applications software can be customised. You will need to give examples of different types of customisation that could be applied. Do not forget to describe some of the benefits such as speed, accuracy, ease of use and consistency of style.
For D1 you will need to expand your evidence for P1 and you will need to give a clear evaluation of both the benefits and some of the drawbacks of customising applications software. Remember to think about both positives and negatives.

9.2 Be able to customise application software

This section will cover the following grading criteria: P2 P3 P4 M1

To be able to customise applications software competently you will need to make use of a range of resources. This is because it is unlikely that you will have the technical skills and expertise to know exactly how to make the changes to every software application you could work with!

9.2.1 Resources

Help facility

Most software applications have a **help facility**. In Microsoft Office 2007® the help can be accessed through the question mark icon in the top right-hand corner of the ribbon. Clicking this icon automatically activates the internet and accesses the Microsoft Office 2007® help system (Figure 9.13).

Users can browse a particular category or they can search for help using the search engine at the top of the image.

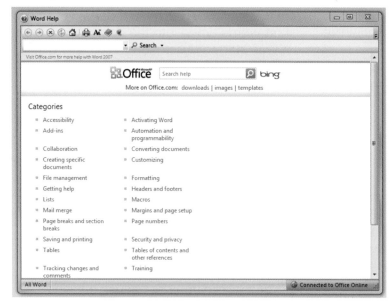

Figure 9.13 The Microsoft Office 2007® help page

Software manuals

Some software applications come with a manual. This could be a book, a CD or both. Alternatively, users and developers can buy manuals for software. These manuals range from really simple publications for novice users, to technical, complex publications for developers.

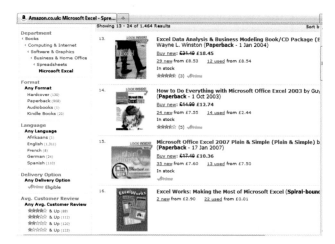

Figure 9.14 Software manuals © 2010 Amazon.com Inc. and its affiliates. All rights reserved.

Website FAQs

As publications, once printed, may not be reprinted for some time, the internet is full of FAQs (Frequently Asked Questions) websites where users and developers can go for help.

One such example is: http://accessjunkie.com/faq2007.aspx

This website specifically supports Access 2007®, although there is now a menu option on the website for the more recent Access 2010®.

Activity G

Getting help

Have a look in your school or college library, your classroom and on the internet, and see how many resources you can find that will help you when you carry out the practical activity for this unit.

Make a note of some of the resources and where you found them so that you can find them when you need them.

9.2.2 Default settings

Files

Most Microsoft® applications have a default file save location. This is usually the computer's **C drive**, in the User directory, for the named person using the system, in the Documents directory (see Figure 9.15).

Blank Database

Create a Microsoft Office Access database that does not contain any existing data or objects.

File Name:

Database1

C:\Users\Beanie\Documents\

[Create]   [Cancel]

Figure 9.15 Default save location

In addition the system software will suggest a file name. In Figure 9.15 it suggests Database1 for a new database file. This unit is being written in Microsoft Word® and the first time the unit was saved, the software suggested a file name of 'Credit Value' because those were the first words typed into the document when it was started! Microsoft Excel® always offers a file name of Book1.

But the default save location for any software can be changed. To make this change in Word® and send all your documents to an alternative default location, you will need to make the following changes in the Word® options.

1. Click on the Microsoft Office button.
2. Click on the Word Options button at the bottom of the dialogue box.
3. Click on the Save option in the list and it will take you to a new dialogue box where you can choose a series of settings: the format in which you want your documents to be saved, the **AutoRecover** intervals and the default file location for both AutoRecover files and general file storage.

Key term

The **AutoRecover** function exists in most software. It saves your open document at pre-set intervals (in our example that is every 10 minutes). This interval can be increased or decreased. In the event that the system fails (for example due to a power fault) then the most recently saved version of the file will be offered to the user.

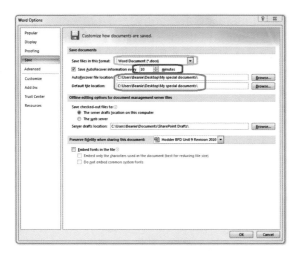

Figure 9.16 Default save options

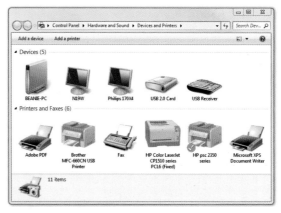

Figure 9.17 Default printers

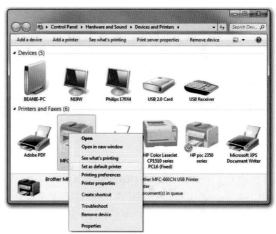

Figure 9.18 Set new default printer

To change the default in Microsoft Excel®, you access the options in the same way as for Word®. In Access®, however, you will find the default database folder on the Popular tab.

Hardware

If a computer is only attached to a single printer, then there is clearly no point in trying to change the default printer options! If, however, it is attached to a network, there may well be more than one option that the user can choose from.

To change the hardware options for a printer, for example, you would:

1. Click on the Windows button
2. Select Devices and Printers from the menu
3. Look at the options for Printers and Faxes and find the printer with the green circle and tick (Figure 9.17). This is the default printer on this machine, although other printers can be used.
4. To change the default printer, simply click on the printer you are choosing as the default, then right click and click on Set as default printer. (Figure 9.18)
5. The default symbol will have moved from the previous printer to the new one.

Others, for example language

During the installation of software you are usually asked your language preference. This is because your choice of language may alter the keyboard layout and will change the dictionaries that are used by the spell-checking function. In the UK we use UK-standard keyboards laid out in a particular way. In Germany some of the keys are in different places. Keyboards are designed with the most commonly used keys in particular places to make the keyboard easier to use. So because some letters are used less in English than they are in other languages, you will find different keyboard layouts to reflect the languages in different parts of the world.

Activity **H**

Language settings

Compare the following images and circle the keys that are in different positions:

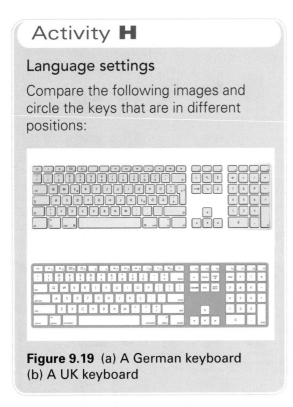

Figure 9.19 (a) A German keyboard (b) A UK keyboard

Changing the language preferences in Microsoft Office® might mean that you will need to add additional language packs and for some there will be a charge.

Once the relevant pack is loaded it can be activated through Microsoft Office Tools, in the Microsoft Office folder on the Windows Start menu.

Figure 9.20 Microsoft Office® Tools

Once installed and activated it affects all Microsoft Office® programs. In the example shown in Figure 9.21, where the Japanese pack has been installed and activated, the Japanese dictionaries have been loaded and the ribbon is now viewed in Japanese. The keyboard would also be in a Japanese layout.

Figure 9.21 Japanese

9.2.3 Interfaces

Toolbars

As explained earlier in the unit, when working with Microsoft Office 2007® you are not able to customise the ribbon easily. You do, however, have complete control over the Quick Access Toolbar which is in the very top left-hand corner of the screen for each of the Microsoft® applications.

The main benefit of customising the Quick Access Toolbar is that you can include all the programs and actions that you use regularly. Currently the toolbar being used to support the writing of this unit looks like Figure 9.22.

Figure 9.22 Quick Access toolbar

To add options you simply need to click on the Microsoft® Office button and then on Word Options. You can now choose the Customize menu (Figure 9.23).

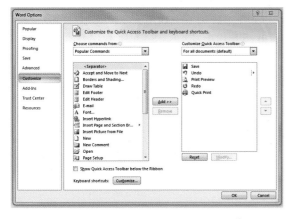

Figure 9.23 Customize menu in Word®

You will notice that the list of options in the panel on the right reflects what is currently in the menu (as shown). To add options, simply click on them in the left panel and click Add. When all options have been chosen, you click on OK and they will appear in the menu at the top of the screen. This toolbar can be viewed above or below the main ribbon. To make the change simply click on the dropdown box beside the toolbar and choose Show below the Ribbon.

Figure 9.24 Customised Quick Access

Menus

Although it is only really possible to add to the menus on the ribbon through programming, there are other menus you can customise. For example, you can customise the main Start menu.

To do this you right click on the Start Menu button, and then choose the Start Menu tab. When you choose the Customize button it presents you with a range of options that you can choose from simply by checking the relevant box or activating the appropriate radio button.

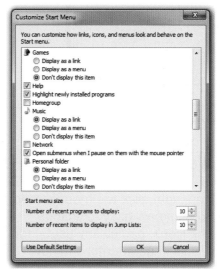

Figure 9.25 Customize Start Menu

Desktops

When working with desktops you have lots of aspects that can be customised. To change most of the desktop settings you simply right click on the desktop and click Personalize. You can then change the **wallpaper** (click on Desktop Background) to one of the preset options or an imported image of your own (see Figure 9.26).

Figure 9.26 Control Panel

You can change the icon type by clicking on Change Desktop Icons and then choosing from the selection (Figure 9.27).

Figure 9.27 Change icons

You can also change how the desktop icons are arranged. To do this, find an empty area of the desktop, right click the mouse, then click on View. It is now easy to change the size of the icons (particularly useful for those with visual impairments) and how they are organised (Figure 9.28).

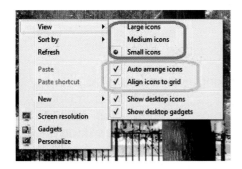

Figure 9.28 Arrange icons

Clicking on the option 'Align icons to grid' will ensure that the icons are set out with equal spacing. Removing this option would allow the user to overlap icons (Figure 9.29).

Figure 9.29 Non-aligned grid

Most operating systems also contain a screen clock. In Windows 7® this is one of the features known as a **gadget**. To access the gadgets you simply right click on any empty area of the screen and click on Gadgets in the options. Figure 9.30 shows some choices (although more can be downloaded).

Figure 9.30 Gadgets

Once you have added the clock gadget to your desktop, you can then change the clock's settings. Simply hover the mouse over the clock and then click on the wrench symbol (Figure 9.31).

Figure 9.31 Clock

You can now choose from eight different clock faces, you can opt to show or remove the second hand and you can select a time zone. This might be useful if you always need to see two different time zones as you could add two clock gadgets to your desktop and have them displaying different times (Figure 9.32).

Figure 9.32 Clock settings

Others (for example, colour schemes and mouse settings)

Other customisable options include the window colour scheme (this adjusts all the borders, the start menu and the task bar). To access these options right click on an empty area of the desktop and click Personalize then Window Color (note the American spelling of colour).

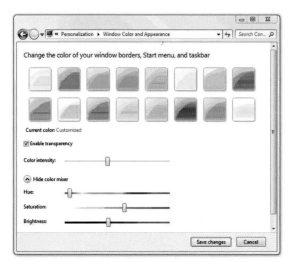

Figure 9.33 Window colour options

From the same dialogue box as you used to access the Window Color options, you can also personalise the mouse pointers. For example, those who are left-handed can change the configuration of the mouse buttons. It is possible to adjust the double click responsiveness, the speed of the pointer and how visible it is. Settings can also be adjusted for those working with mouse wheels. The best way to find out what these options do is to experiment with them.

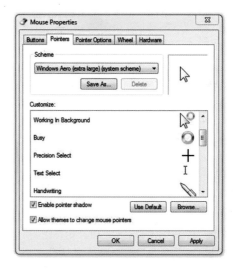

Figure 9.34 Mouse pointer options

Activity

Customisation

If you are not a Windows 7® user, find out how to implement three of the customisation options listed in this section for your operating system. If you are a Windows 7® user, choose three of the customisation options listed so far.

Implement these three changes for your operating system.

9.2.4 Specific tools

Tools

Software contains a range of tools that can be activated or deactivated and can be configured. Some examples of these tools are given below. You might find, however, that the software you are using might have additional options.

Microsoft Word® has a dictionary that is set when the software is installed. This does not mean that you cannot change the settings though. You can see the settings of your dictionary by looking at the very bottom of the software window (Figure 9.35).

Figure 9.35 Dictionary settings

Activity J

Dictionary

What is the difference between the English (United Kingdom) dictionary and the English (United States) dictionary? Carry out some research to find out. Give three examples of words that will be different in the two dictionaries.

Users also have the option to create a **custom dictionary**. A custom dictionary is a dictionary of the user's own words – those that would normally be highlighted as incorrect by the main dictionary. This is really useful for specialist situations or for storing names.

The **AutoCorrect** function is activated and customised by clicking on Office and then on the Word Options buttons. You will need to choose Proofing from the menu.

Once the dialogue box opens, you will see the AutoCorrect options at the top. When you click on AutoCorrect options, a second dialogue box opens. This is where you will make your choices.

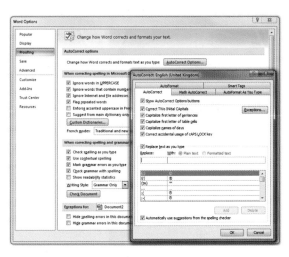

Figure 9.36 AutoCorrect options

If the settings are active, AutoCorrect will correct various common input errors, such as correcting two initial capitals (for example 'ANother' is automatically changed to 'Another') or capitalising the first letter after a full stop (the start of a new sentence) if the user has not started the sentence with a capital letter.

The AutoCorrect can also be used to create the ® (registered trademark) symbol. If you type (then R then), it will automatically be replaced with the correct symbol. In the bottom of the AutoCorrect dialogue box you can see a range of options including : (which becomes ☹ and :) which becomes ☺. Here you can also add some options of your own!

The **AutoSummarize** function automatically creates a summary of the chosen document. You will notice that you can choose how the summary is created and saved (i.e. in a new file) and how long the summary should be in relation to the original size of the document. In the example shown in Figure 9.37, the value is 25 per cent.

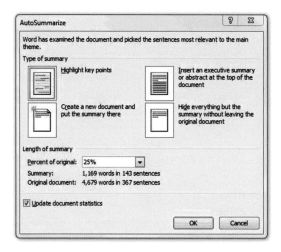

Figure 9.37 AutoSummarize

The **AutoSave** is probably the most essential of the tools because it automatically saves the open document at regular intervals. This means that if you are typing for a long time and you forget to save, the software will do it for you so you lose less of your document if your system fails. The default setting in the software is to save every 10 minutes. This can be adjusted up or down to suit the user's needs.

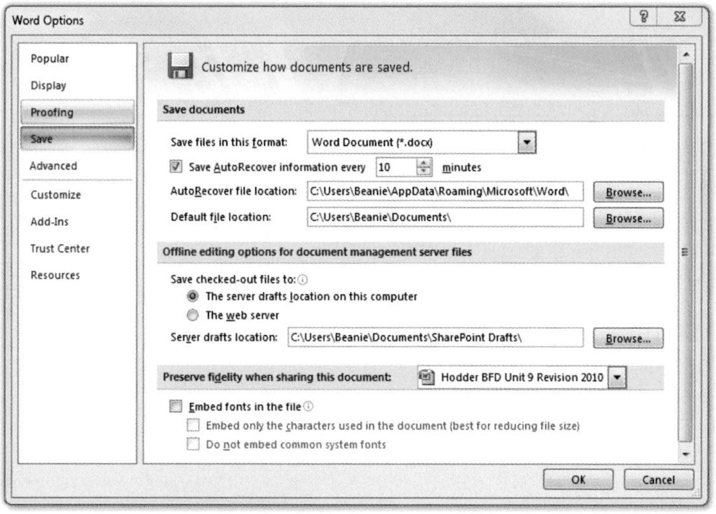

Figure 9.38 AutoSave options

Activity **K**

AutoSave

Check the AutoSave settings on the software you use. Is the setting the right one for you? If not, change it to something more suitable.

Format

Some of the formatting options can be used to customise documents. For example, paragraph and style options can both be chosen from the Home tab in the Paragraph and Styles options.

Figure 9.39 Format

Both of these can be adapted and saved as user defaults. In each case you would need to click on the expansion arrow at the bottom right of the relevant menu. Options can then be chosen and saved as defaults.

Paragraph styles include justification options such as left, right and centred:

This text has been left justified which means that each line will start at the left margin.

This text has been right justified which means that each line will start at the right margin.

This text has been centred which means that each line will be placed equally distant from both margins.

It is also possible to adjust line spacing such as:

Single

Single – where each line is immediately below the one above

And

Double

Double – where there is always a clear line between the current line and the
one above

Using Styles sets the fonts for headings for example. Be careful when applying styles, though, because you will find that when the style is applied, it will affect the whole document!

9.2.5 Testing

Test functionality

Once you have decided on the functionality your user needs and you have carried out the customisation, it needs to be tested, just as you would test any other IT solution (hardware, software, website, network etc.) that you had developed to make sure it is working fully.

Each time you carry out testing, you will create a test plan that tests the solution properly.

For a database, for example, we would need to make sure that we check all of the forms, queries and reports. We will also need to test any validation in the database tables.

If we have created Word® templates, we would do the same.

Essentially, we will create mini test plans to test every part of the system, one object at a time.

Test plan

To record the planned tests, a test plan is completed. This comprises a table with the following headings: test number, what is being tested, a test description (how the test will be carried out and any data that will be used in the test, if applicable), actual test results and actions required to fix any problems found.

TEST PLAN TEMPLATE

Test subject (e.g. database table) ....

Date of test ....

Test Number	What is being tested	Test Description	Actual results of test	Actions required

Figure 9.40 Test plan template

Check against defined requirement

After you have checked that any developments or customisations are functioning correctly, you should also go back and check that the solution does actually meet the original requirements identified by the user. Sometimes it is as simple as just asking them to confirm!

9.3 Be able to create templates in application software

9.3.1 Application packages

Document production

When you create the structure for a document that you will need to use again and again, the first thing you should always do is look in the Templates panel on the left-hand side of the New Document dialogue box.

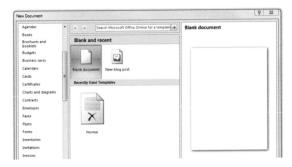

Figure 9.41 Templates

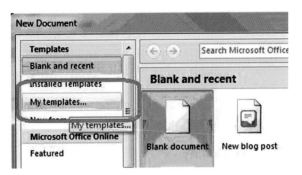

Figure 9.43 My templates

If the type of document does not exist, you could choose the nearest version to your needs and adapt it, or you could simply create your own.

If you choose to create your own template from scratch, it is just as easy to start with a blank document, create your structure and then save it as a Word Template.

In Microsoft Publisher® you have similar options and you could create your own template in the same way as you would in Word®.

Figure 9.44 Publisher® templates

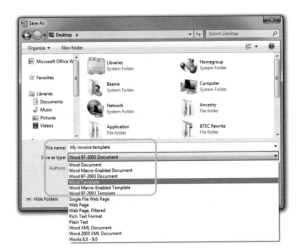

Figure 9.42 Saving as a Word Template

The templates available in Word® and Publisher® are essentially just structures which you can use to create documents of your own.

Data manipulation

Templates in Excel® and Access® are slightly different because they generally also 'do' things.

Once you have created and saved your document as a template, it will appear in the My templates option in the Templates panel on New Document.

Take the example of the Personal Monthly Budget template shown in Figure 9.45.

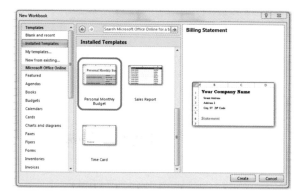

Figure 9.45 Excel® templates

In Figure 9.46 not only is the structure for the document set, but the necessary calculations are also already in place.

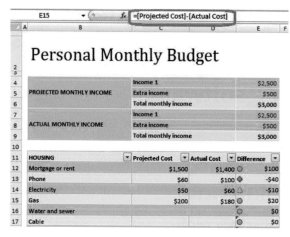

Figure 9.46 Personal monthly budget

Similarly, and as seen in Unit 16 (Database Systems), Access® templates also have some prewritten code, calculations or functionality in them to reduce the work for the user.

Other (for example, PowerPoint®)

Just as with the other Office® applications, PowerPoint® has a range of installed templates and an option for the user to create their own. The Quiz Show Template, for example, has preset animation to reveal the answers to the questions as the presentation is shown. You must make sure, however, that you fill in the right information in the right places! Do not forget to test it thoroughly.

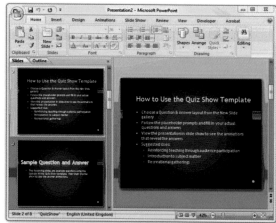

Figure 9.47 The Quiz Show Template in PowerPoint®

9.3.2 Templates

User need

When you use pre-existing templates, you will probably want to adapt their design rather than use them exactly as they appear because it is unlikely that the template chosen will meet the user's needs perfectly.

As part of your design you will probably want to limit the way the user enters data using form fields (see next section), or you may choose to add some validation to make it more likely that the information input will be correct.

You could introduce some dropdown boxes or list boxes to force the user to choose from preset options.

Whatever you choose to include in your template, it should be there for a reason – and that reason should be because it is needed by the user.

Other features, such as use of logos

To give documentation a **corporate identity** (this means to make all documents have something in common that represents the organisation), many organisations add a logo to their documents and marketing materials. By doing this, the organisation will be identified easily by existing customers and potential new customers.

Activity L

Logos

Use the internet to look up the following logos:

Google®, Microsoft®, Burger King®, The Body Shop®, BTEC, ICI®, Crown Paints®, your school/college.

Create an A4 poster displaying these logos. Explain which one you think is best and why.

Testing

This has already been covered in Section 2.5. You must make very sure that any templates you create are fully functional before they become standard use by an organisation.

Do not forget to create a test plan and carry out the relevant testing. You should fix any errors fully!

Make the grade   P2 P3 P4 M1

For P2 you will customise a software application to meet a defined user need. Your tutor might give you a scenario to work to or you might have a real client. Your customisation should include changes to default settings, an interface, a tool and a function. You will need to demonstrate that you can carry out the customisation required and your evidence will probably include screen shots.

For P3 you will need to test the customisations you implemented for P2. You will produce an evidence log and your teacher may also observe you carrying out some of the testing activities.
For P4 you will create and test two templates – one for each of two different applications packages.
Your testing should check that the templates meet the requirements.
To evidence M1 you will evaluate how effectively your templates meet the user requirements.

9.4 Be able to create macros and shortcuts in application software

This section will cover the following grading criteria: **P5** **P6** **M2**

9.4.1 Macros

Define user need

Firstly you must get the user to identify his or her needs. They must be very specific as creating macros needs specific actions to be carried out.

There is a very detailed section on how to record macros in Unit 27 Spreadsheet modelling, Section 27.2.6.

How to create macros in Microsoft Access® is included as part of Unit 16.

Assign

You have already seen how it is possible to customise the Quick Access toolbar, and just as with pre-written functions, you can record a macro and have it activated by a button on the Quick Access toolbar.

In the example shown in Figure 9.48, we are creating a macro that will print a section of a document when activated. In fact, it will print just the current page.

When setting up to record the macro we can specify that we want the macro **assigned** (made to be triggered by) a button or keyboard presses (a **key combination**).

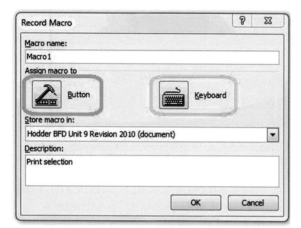

Figure 9.48 Assigning a macro

The actual macro code that has been recorded looks like this (Figure 9.49):

Figure 9.49 Word macro code

This macro basically says that the current file (shown by FileName:="") should be printed. The remaining code reflects the print settings chosen.

Once you are experienced at working with macros you will have the skills to be able to change the code when you need to.

Storage

As already suggested, macros are mini programs that automate chosen actions in a spreadsheet, word-processed document or database. They can be stored within the workbook, document or database or they can be stored so that they can be accessed by all files within the software.

When you store the macro inside a particular document or database, it is known as 'locally stored'.

When you store the macro within the software so that it is accessible to all files that are created within that software it is known as 'globally stored'.

It is also possible to include one or more macros in a template to automate processes and actions each time the template is used.

Activity M

Macros

Create a basic spreadsheet template to help a wages clerk process the wages.

You must be able to input:

> Employee name
> Week commencing (so the week being paid)
> Hours worked by the employee (e.g. 37.75)
> Hourly rate he or she earns (e.g. £5.59 per hour)

The system should then calculate gross wage, National Insurance, tax and net salary.

Wage Slip

Employee name ....

Week commencing ....

Hours worked	
Hourly rate	
Gross wage	
National Insurance (10% of gross)	
Tax (25% of gross)	
Net Salary (gross – NI – Tax)	

Figure 9.50

continued overleaf

continued...

Add a macro that prints out only the area needed for the wage slip. Add a button on the slip to activate the macro.

Create a test plan (shown earlier in the unit) to test your solution fully (including the macros).

Carry out the tests and make any necessary changes to the system. Share the solution with your teacher.

9.4.2 Shortcuts

Types

As the shortcut possibilities are extensive, what follows now is an example of each of the types suggested.

Keyboard

Did you know that you can copy and paste with keys rather than menus? You will need to use the cursor (arrow) keys on your keyboard:

- Use the cursor (arrow) keys to move the cursor to the start of some text.
- Hold down the Shift key and press the right cursor to highlight all the text you wish to copy and paste.
- Once this is highlighted, hold down the CTRL key and press C.
- Move the cursor to another part of the document.
- Hold down the CTRL key and press V.

This process works in most software!

Hyperlink

Sometimes you might want to use a live link to a website as part of an electronic document or a presentation.

It is particularly useful in a presentation as if you include the link and then click on it while presenting, it will take you to the relevant pages on the web.

To make a hyperlink, simply copy the URL into the document and press enter. The URL will change colour and appear underscored. This means it is a **hyperlink**.

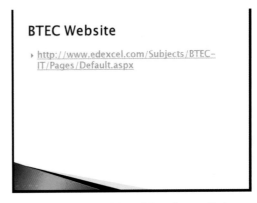

Figure 9.51 A slide with a hyperlink

To activate a hyperlink in PowerPoint® you simply need to click on it. To activate a hyperlink in an electronic document, you need to hold down the CTRL key and then click on the URL.

Drive mapping

If you have multiple hard drives in your computer, you might like to put a shortcut on your desktop to open the drive or drives without having to go through Computer. To create a shortcut, move to an unused area of your desktop, right click, then select New and Shortcut.

Figure 9.52 Desktop shortcut

In the next dialogue box enter the drive to map (in Figure 9.53 that is e:\).

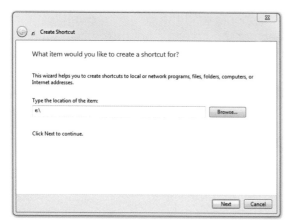

Figure 9.53 Drive shortcut

Click Next and give the shortcut a name (for example Local Disk (E)). Click Finish. The shortcut will appear on the desktop (Figure 9.54).

Figure 9.54 Drive shortcut for e:\

Make the grade   P5   P6   M2

For P5 you will need to demonstrate that you can record and test a macro. As you will need to show that you have gone through a logical process to create the macro, it might help if you make a plan of the steps you will go through. You can also create screen grabs.

You will show that you have tested your macro to ensure that it functions correctly (a log might be useful here).

For P6 you must develop at least three keyboard shortcuts and test them to ensure that they function correctly. Screenshots and a log would again provide useful evidence.

M2 will be awarded when you have explained the benefits of using macros. Your explanation must be detailed, clear and logical.

Activity N

End of unit crossword

Test your understanding of this unit by completing the following crossword (photocopy the page first!). The answers can be found in a separate Answers section at the end of the book.

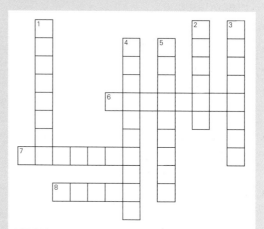

ACROSS

6 An application that controls the way that your computer communicates with the internet

7 Basic settings set when the software was installed or as chosen by the user

8 A mini program recorded by a user that is activiated by a button press

DOWN

1 When a computer automatically saves the open document

2 A macro that is available to all files

3 A structure for a document or spreadsheet set up in advance

4 A routine that checks data and makes sure it is relaible and of good quality

5 A URL pasted into a document or presentation that opens to the internet when clicked

Achieving Success

In order to achieve each unit, you will complete a series of coursework activities. Each time you hand in work, your tutor will return this to you with a record of your achievement.

This particular unit has 9 criteria to meet: 6 Pass, 2 Merit and one Distinction.

For a **Pass** you must achieve **all 6** Pass criteria.

For a **Merit** you must achieve **all 6** Pass **and both** Merit criteria.

For a **Distinction** you must achieve **all 6** Pass, **both** Merit criteria **and the single** Distinction criterion.

Help with assessment

Your tutor will give you one or more assignments that you will complete as coursework. This could consist of:

- Presentations
- Witness statements
- Web pages
- Screenshots
- Electronic evidence of customised software
- Templates
- Macro code.

You should read the guidance given for each of the criteria (shown across the unit) carefully and remember to check your work.

Further reading

Textbooks

CB Learning/Microsoft. *Collection 5347: Installing and Configuring Windows Vista.* (CB Learning/Microsoft, 2008) ASIN 1905707711

Maraia, V. *The Build Master: Microsoft's Software Configuration Management Best Practices.* (Addison Wesley, 2005) ISBN 0321332059

IBM Redbooks (editor). *Enterprise Software Configuration Management Solutions for Distributed and System Z.* (Vervante, 2008) ISBN 0738431885

Websites

http://documentation.openoffice.org/

http://office.microsoft.com/en-us/help/default.aspx

Unit 10
Setting up an IT network

Learning objectives

By the end of this unit you should:

1. Know the current use of computer networks
2. Know the features and services of local and wide area network technologies
3. Understand how network hardware and software components are connected

4. Be able to set up a simple local area network.

In order to pass this unit, the evidence you present for assessment needs to demonstrate that you can meet all of the above learning outcomes for this unit. The criteria below show the levels of achievement required to pass this unit.

To achieve a **pass** grade the evidence must show that the learner is able to:	To achieve a **merit** grade the evidence must show that, in addition to the pass criteria, the learner is able to:	To achieve a **distinction** grade the evidence must show that, in addition to the pass and merit criteria, the learner is able to:
P1 Describe how the use of computer networks can improve communications for individuals and organisations	**M1** Explain how networks may improve productivity for individuals and organisations	
P2 Describe how a network is used by an organisation to manage its resources		
P3 Describe potential issues with computer networks	**M2** Suggest possible solutions to resolve connectivity problems	
P4 Describe the features and services of local and wide area network technologies		**D1** Evaluate the features and services provided by a local and a wide area network
P5 Explain how hardware, software and addressing combine to support network communications		
P6 Set up and test a simple local area network	**M3** Set up and configure security on a local area network.	**D2** Explain how security issues can be minimised.

Introduction

Most organisations use modern computer networks to communicate and share resources. In this unit you will become familiar with the hardware components, software and configuration settings that are required to create a basic working network.

After introducing these concepts, the unit's strong practical focus will ask you to use this knowledge to build and test a simple local area network (LAN).

You will be assessed through course-work which could be in the form of:

- Presentations
- Practical sessions which may be photographed, videoed or witnessed
- Designs (written or graphical) such as flowcharts or storyboards
- Screen captures
- Viva
- Blogs
- Podcasts.

10.1 Know the current use of computer networks

This section will cover the following grading criteria: **P1** **P2** **P3** **M1**

Computer networks are everywhere and whether we are at home, at work, at college or at school, it is likely that we will be accessing one at some point each day.

Perhaps the most obvious use of computer networks is to help us communicate.

10.1.1 Communication

Communication can occur between individuals, within an organisation or between people working collaboratively. The rise of the computer network has created new ways to talk.

A computer network supports the following forms of communication tool:

As an individual

Blog

Accessed via a web browser, a **blog** or 'web log' contains entries (usually chronological) which contains a user's thoughts, feelings and personal interests. It may also contain images, music, videos and links to other websites of interest.

Email

Electronic mail or **email** is used to transmit messages between users on the same (or different networks). It permits rapid global communication.

Forums

A **forum** is an electronic message board system where threads of conversations are grouped under particular topic headings. Users can post new messages to extend the conversation or simply read what others have posted. Forums exist on all types of subjects.

Instant messaging

Instant messaging is a method for transmitting messages between users in real-time – this permits live conversations between a pair of users or party chat.

In an organisation

- **Email** – for business purposes, for example contacting customers
- **Wikis** – for creating user content online or on the company intranet

- **File storage** – to store shared spreadsheets, databases, documents etc.
- **Data centres** – also called a 'server farm', a data centre contains servers, networked devices and large data storage. The centres have back up power supplies to ensure that the business is not disrupted in a power cut.

Collaborating between individuals

- **Social networking** – to communicate and share ideas
- **Conferencing**
  - By using desktop sharing
  - By communicating by video
  - By communication through audio
  - By sharing files.

But how do computer networks improve communication? Well, apart from increasing options for communication by adding these new types of activity, let us look at some of the most obvious advantages:

- Communication can be worldwide.
- Communication can be almost instantaneous (it is quicker than traditional 'snail' mail).
- Publishing can be exceptionally cheap when compared with traditional print methods.
- Both parties need not be 'online' at the same time.
- Electronic communication can include media (for example pictures) or data (such as documents).
- Communication can be visual, auditory or textual.

- Remote assistance is possible through online collaboration.
- Data and information can be shared easily and quickly across large organisations.

Make the grade   P1

This criterion asks you describe how the use of computer networks can improve communications between individuals and organisations.
This could be assessed in many different ways (for example, presentation, wiki, viva) and in order to achieve it you must identify (a) how the communication occurs, (b) who the communication is between and (c) what the advantage is.
A simple example of this would be: 'Email provides a way for friends or work colleagues to communicate almost instantly and has the advantage of being able to include file attachments. The receiver does not need to be online when the message is sent and can reply at their leisure. Most importantly the email system is global so the two people could be anywhere in the world.'
You should include a few examples.

10.1.2 Resource management

Another advantage that networking brings is the ability to **share resources**. Although the costs of information technology have decreased over recent years, it is still relatively expensive so any possibility of reducing the purchase costs of equipment (and getting better value for money) is generally welcomed.

Common resources that can be shared over a network include:

Expertise

The skills of an organisation's employees can be shared over the network by:

- Use of an intranet
- Collaborative working and document management (for example, Microsoft SharePoint®)
- Remote desktop assistance (to solve technical support issues with computer systems)
- Email and forums.

Data

It may seem odd but data has a value as a commodity – both to an individual and an organisation. For example, customer names and addresses are very valuable for marketing purposes.

Sharing data which is stored safely in one place is a fundamental benefit of computer networks. If the data that is stored centrally is updated by one user, everyone in the organisation will instantly benefit and see the changes.

Hardware

Networks encourage the sharing of resources whether it is a networked printer or photocopier or an external hard disk drive used for backing up important data. Reducing the quantity of hardware saves money, maintenance costs and makes equipment easier to manage.

Software

Software is an expensive component of any computer system. The ability to network software can mean that:

- Software is shared between users – downloaded to the client system as and when needed.
- Software is always up to date and is at less risk of crashing (see section 10.1.3 on security).
- Software is legally registered and can be easily monitored.
- Software can be used collaboratively between users, reducing the need for them to meet in person.
- Anti-virus suites can be updated easily to ensure they can recognise the most current malware threats.
- Software can be deployed remotely to a computer system without the technician needing to be present.

10.1.3 Issues

As with any technology, a computer network will have problems from time to time!

Common issues which concern network users include:

- Speed – the network is slow; this often affects downloading, file transfer and log-in. One common cause is **narrow bandwidth** (see data rates, section 10.2.1) which causes **congestion** and **contention** (when multiple devices try to send data at exactly the same time). This often causes users a great deal of frustration!
- Staff skills – employees have to be trained in order to use the network effectively.
- Downtime – these are the periods when the network and its services are unavailable due to a system software fault or hardware failure. When individuals or organisations become very reliant on their networks, this can be a very big (and expensive) problem if the downtime is extensive: businesses will lose money.

In addition, any network is at risk from several key security risks:

- Unauthorised access – people gaining access to the network (its data and services) without proper permission.

- Loss of data – valuable data being lost through malicious or accidental damage.
- Malware – malicious software that may damage applications and/or important data.

Protecting against any of these security risks will involve:

- Virus protection – protection against malware invading the network.
- Backup and recovery – software and procedures to ensure valuable data is copied regularly.
- Anti-hacking measures – software to detect intrusions on the network.
- Firewalls – software to filter dangerous data entering and leaving the computer network.

Make the grade   **P2**

P3

M1

P2 asks you describe how a network is used by an organisation to manage its resources. If you read through section 10.1.2 you should gain an insight into this – remember that in order to answer this correctly, you should include examples across the range (for example, expertise, data, hardware, software etc.) and attempt to identify the advantages the network brings.

P3 asks you to describe potential issues with computer networks. Issues are covered throughout section 10.1.3. Good coverage of most of these should award you the criterion but do not forget to include security concerns.

M1 asks you to explain how networks can improve productivity for individuals and organisations. The key to this is explaining the benefits that a network can bring, for example how communication is improved (both in speed and range of options) and how resources are more effectively shared.

10.2 Know the features and services of local and wide area network technologies

This section will cover the following grading criteria:

10.2.1 Features

All computer networks have a set of features that help us describe them to others.

Network size

Computer networks can be classified by their size.

○ *PAN (or Piconet)*

A **Piconet** or **PAN (personal area network)** is a network of computing devices that use **Bluetooth technology** protocols to allow one master device to interconnect with up to seven **slave devices** (see IEEE 802.15).

○ *LAN*

Key term

A **LAN** or **local area network** is a computer network that covers a local area, typically like a home, connecting nearby offices or small clusters of buildings such as a college. These typically use wired Ethernet (IEEE 802.3) or wireless Radio Frequency (RF) technology (IEEE 802.11).

MAN

A **MAN** or **metropolitan area network** is a computer network that covers a town or city. This type of solution often relies on **fibre-optic** solutions.

Wireless MANs (WMANs using microwave technology) are becoming increasingly popular (see IEEE 802.16).

WAN

> **Key term**
>
> A **WAN** or **wide area network** is a computer network (public or privately owned) that uses high-speed, long-distance communications technology (for example telephone lines and satellite links) to connect computers over long distances.
>
> WANs can be used to connect LANs together, such as geographically distant branches of the same organisation.

Figure 10.1

This unit is mostly concerned with LANs and WANs.

Topologies

> **Key term**
> A **topology** is the technical word used to describe the network's shape or form.

In simple terms, this is how the **nodes** (servers, workstations etc.) are **physically** or **logically** connected. This is another way of classifying networks. Common topologies include:

Star

One central node with outlying nodes.

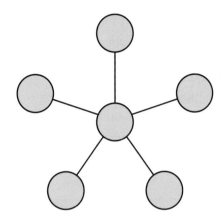

Figure 10.2 Star

Ring

A series of nodes connected daisy-chain style.

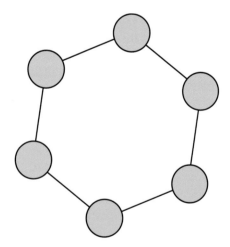

Figure 10.3 Ring

Mesh

Each node interconnected with others.

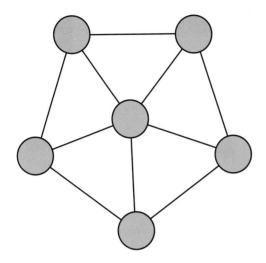

Figure 10.4 Mesh

Tree

Nodes are linked in a hierarchical structure.

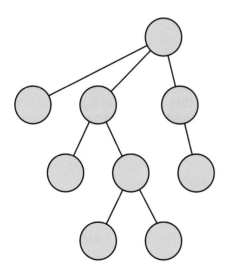

Figure 10.5 Tree

Bus

Different devices connected from a common backbone (a single run of cable).

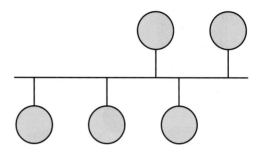

Figure 10.6 Bus

Types

The type of network can also be used to classify. The network type is decided depending on how the network is controlled.

There are two basic possibilities:

Key terms

In a **peer-to-peer network** no device has overall control of the network.

Each computer has equal rights and responsibilities, regarding each other as a peer (hence the name).

Networks like this are used when security issues are not a real concern, for example in the home. They are not really suitable for larger business use.

In a **client/server network** one computer system is more powerful (CPU, RAM, disk capacity etc.) and is given the role of the **server** – typically using a special version of the operating system.

The server controls the network resources and can limit a user's access to each client computer system and the data that is shared between them.

Most business networks operate in this way.

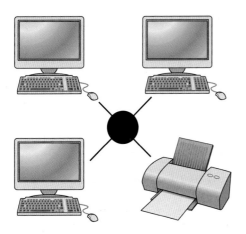

Figure 10.7 Peer-to-peer

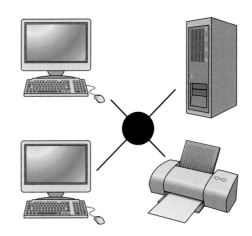

Figure 10.8 Client/server

Data rates

> ### Key term
>
> Often called the **data transfer rate**, this is a measurement which tells us how quickly data can move across a computer network. It is often measured in megabits per second (Mbps). Some professionals also call this the **network bandwidth**.

For example, 1Mbps means that 1 million bits are transmitted in one second.

Common network data rates are shown in Table 10.1.

Technology	Data transfer rate
Ethernet	10 Mbps
Wi-Fi (802.11g)	54 Mbps
Fast Ethernet	100 Mbps
Wi-Fi (802.11n)	300 Mbps
Gigabit Ethernet	1,000 Mbps

Table 10.1 Common network data rates

Faster transfer rates should provide more bandwidth for data transmission which should reduce network congestion and provide a better network experience for users. Data transfer rates should ideally support the type of services that users want, for example live video requires faster transfer rates than an email (there is much more data and it needs to be transmitted quicker).

Addressing

On a TCP/IP network (see section 10.2.3) each node on a network has to be **contactable** – this is achieved by given them an **address**. In order to transmit a message to a node we usually need two types of address.

MAC address

> ### Key term
>
> The **media access control (MAC) address** is a special hexadecimal (base 16) number which is assigned to a networkable device when it is originally manufactured. MAC addresses should be unique.
>
> If you have a mobile telephone that can access the internet, it will have a MAC address too, using one of the 281,474,976,710,656 possible addresses available worldwide!

Activity **A**

Who made my networking device?

A typical Mac address may be
00:26 : 08:94 : D9:99.

The first six digits usually represent
the organisation that manufactured
the networking device. If you have the
MAC address of a device, therefore,
you can find out who manufactured it!

1. Visit http://www.coffer.com/mac_
   find/

2. Key the MAC address of the device
   into the search box.

3. Click Search button.

IP address

Key term

The **internet protocol (IP)**
address is another number which is
assigned to a network device and it
looks like four whole numbers which
have been separated by dots, for
example 1.2.3.4.

An IP is not fixed to a device (they are
leased for a period of time) and so may
change; they are not unique either
as the same IP may exist on many
different computer networks.

Every web server on the internet has an
IP address although you usually access
these via a **DNS (domain name
server)** 'look up', for example:

www.bbc.co.uk/news/ is really
212.58.246.80

www.google.com is really
173.194.36.104

Currently there are two versions of IP
addressing in use – **IPv4** (version 4 – which
is what most people are still using) and
IPv6 – version 6, which was standardised
in 1998 and permits many more possible IP
addresses worldwide.

Activity **B**

Find out my IP address

Depending on your computer system's
operating system, there are many
different ways to find your own IP
address.

On a Windows® PC it is possible to
access the command prompt like so:

1. Click the Start or Windows button
   on the taskbar.

2. Click Run and type CMD into the
   dialogue box or CMD into the
   Search box.

3. At the command prompt type:
   IPCONFIG and press the enter key.

The computer should display your
IP address (assuming your PC is
networked!). Figure 10.09 shows a
typical example.

Figure 10.9 Windows® PC shows its
IP address

Tip: If you use ipconfig /all you will also
be able to see the MAC address.

10.2.2 Services

A number of services lie at the heart of the computer network.

As discussed in section 10.1.1, a network provides many services to its users. The most common services are detailed in this section along with some examples you may find useful.

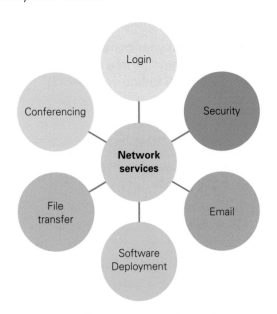

Figure 10.10 Sample network services

Login

Login services are provided by client/ server networks. The server will be used to **authenticate** a username and password for a user account which is stored on the central server.

If the user cannot login they will be unable to access the local client computer system and will be prevented from using any network services.

The server will control aspects such as:

- How often the password needs changing
- The user's environment (such as desktop appearance)
- Applications that can be launched

- Settings which can be changed
- Folders which can be accessed.

Security

Security services protect:

- Access to the computer system (login authentication)
- Access to resources (for example shared folders, printers etc.)
- Access to system configuration and utilities
- Encryption for secure data transfer.

Email

Email software such as Microsoft® Outlook allows users to send messages to each other at any time of day. A handy feature is the address book where the email addresses of people the user regularly communicates with are stored. This makes it much easier to use email as the address book shows these people by their names rather than their email addresses.

Address books also allow groups, so an email can be sent to several people at the same time – this is particularly useful in business when information has to be circulated quickly.

Software deployment

Networks can be used to deploy software onto multiple connected computer systems. This job is usually performed by a server in a client/server type network.

The process is often automated and, in a business, can be set to run automatically. It reduces the need for the technician to sit in front of every computer system that needs updating.

File transfer

Networks can permit the transfer of files from one networked computer system to another. The files are broken down into small packets of data, transmitted over the network and reassembled back into files on the target computer system. All the user has to be able to do is drag and drop the file icon from one computer icon to another.

Conferencing

Businesses with multiple branches often use **video conferencing** as it enables meetings to take place between employees who may be many miles apart – possibly in another country.

Conferencing uses a combination of **web cams** and **microphones** so that everyone can see and hear each other.

The advantages are clear:

- It connects people who may be unable to meet in person.
- You can see *and* hear the person you are talking to (unlike a traditional telephone conference call).
- It reduces travel costs (and is good for the environment).

But there are also some disadvantages:

- It can be expensive to set up.
- A fast (broadband) network connection is required.
- It can be difficult to keep eye contact and observe body language.

10.2.3 Protocols

Key term

A **protocol** is a way of laying down rules for how different networking devices can talk to each other. A number of different network protocols exist but the most popular by far is TCP/IP – Transmission Control Protocol/Internet Protocol. Your computer system will use this when talking to the internet.

TCP/IP

The TCP/IP protocol has two main parts: TCP and IP.

TCP (Transmission Control Protocol)

TCP's purpose is to verify that data has been delivered correctly from sender to receiver. It can also detect errors, missing or duplicated data and can request retransmission.

These are **transport functions**.

IP (Internet Protocol)

IP's function is to move data packets from one network node to the next network node (see section 10.2.1). Source and destination addresses use the (already seen) IP address.

This is a network function.

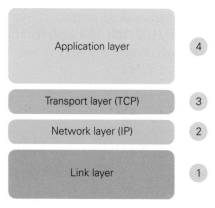

4 This layer deals with TCP/IP applications such as **Telnet**, **FTP**, **SMTP**, **Traceroute** etc.

3 This layer segments data into packets for transporting over the network. Both TCP and **UDP** (**User Datagram Protocol**) work at this layer. UDP is similar to TCP but less reliable; it does not acknowledge or guarantee safe delivery of data.

2 This layer handles basic communication, addressing and routing. Protocols seen here include IP (as discussed), **ARP** (**Address Resolution Protocol**), **ICMP** (**Internet Control Message Protocol**) and **IGMP** (**Internet Group Management Protocol**).

1 Defines the device driver and network hardware (**NIC** – network interface card).

Figure 10.11 Purposes of each layer

How IP works

TCP/IP networks work by breaking data down into small electronic **data packets**. These data packets are then transmitted between nodes on the network. Although this is a highly simplified view, a data packet will typically contain the following:

| Source IP address | Destination IP address | Data | Error detection |

IP forwards each data packet based on their destination address. The following are typical IP addresses:

Source IP	192.168.123.**11**
Destination IP	192.168.123.**22**
Gateway IP	192.168.123.**254**

In this example, host '11' wants to send data to host '22'. This is easy if both machines are on the same network (192.168.123.0), in other words in the same LAN.

However, if a different destination IP (such as 64.233.183.99) had been encountered, it would have been forwarded to the **Gateway** IP (192.168.123.254) for routing out to another network – which will probably move the data packet out onto its connected WAN.

Activity C

What does my network 'look' like?

Networks come in all shape and sizes and can range dramatically in complexity.

Ultimately they all have a topology and can be classified as a LAN or WAN. Using a familiar network (at home, school or college), work out:

1. What type of network it is (for example, LAN or WAN).

2. What topology it uses.

3. Whether it is a client/server or peer-to-peer network.

4. The IP address of your connected computer system.

Make the grade   P4   D1

P4 asks you to describe the services and features of LANs and WANs. These are covered in sections 10.2.1, 10.2.2 and 10.2.3. You will need to list the most important services and provide a short description of each – do not just list them as this will not be sufficient.

This criterion may be evidenced through a report, wiki, presentation, podcast or viva. D1 is an extension of P4 and asks you to evaluate these services and features. How important are they? What advantages do they bring to an organisation or an individual?

10.3 Understand how network hardware and software components are connected

This section will cover the following grading criterion: **P5**

A computer network uses many different hardware and software components. Generally we can divide these into:

- **Hardware** – physical devices used to transmit or receive network data.
- **Communication** – physical media used to carry transmitted data and how it gets there.
- **Software** – system, application and utility software used by the user to communicate over the network.

Let us examine each in turn:

10.3.1 Hardware

Network cards

> **Key term**
>
> A **network card** is more correctly known as a **network interface card (NIC)** or a **network adaptor**. This is a device which takes computer data and transmits it over a physical media. It can also reassemble a transmitted signal back into data at the target node.
>
> Many different types of network card exist. The most obvious difference between them is what type of physical media they use.

Ethernet

This is a **wired card** using an **RJ45 connection**. They usually use either **PCI (Peripheral Component Interconnect)** or **PCIe (PCI-express)** slots on a motherboard. Like any other device, drivers for the operating system installed will be required before the card will work properly.

Figure 10.12 PCI network interface card

Most modern computer system motherboards have an **onboard LAN** – this is where the Ethernet technology is built into the motherboard during manufacture.

Figure 10.13 An onboard Ethernet (RJ45) port (shown left)

Ethernet uses UTP or STP copper cables (see section 10.3.2).

Wireless

Using radio waves rather than wires, wireless connectivity ('Wi-Fi') can often be found built into modern portable devices such as PDAs, notebooks and hand-held games consoles.

When onboard connectivity is not available, wireless NIC adaptors of various types are available; USB is probably the most commonly found.

Figure 10.14 Wireless NIC USB adaptor

Server hardware is well specified with powerful CPU(s), a good quantity of RAM and a large hard disk drive capacity. Servers also use **Uninterruptible Power Supplies (UPS)** for use in power cuts.

Mail server

A computer system dedicated to processing **email** (**electronic mail**) requests.

Web server

A computer system processing **HTTP (Hypertext Transfer Protocol)** requests for **HTML(Hypertext Markup Language) files** and associated **assets** (images, video, sound etc.).

File server

A computer system managing access to shared network drives and folders.

Print server

A computer system managing print queues to shared network printers.

Workstation

> **Key term**
>
> A **workstation** is a common name for a computer system, particularly one operating within a business environment and connected to a network.

Servers

> **Key term**
>
> A **server** is a powerful computer system that provides a processing service for other networked computers, servers or devices. Servers usually require special system and application software in order to provide these services.

Hub

> **Key term**
>
> A **hub** is also known as a **multiport repeater** and it is used to connect networking devices together. A hub is not intelligent so simply boosts and repeats an incoming transmission signal to all its ports indiscriminately – it does not care which networking device the transmission is aimed at!

Figure 10.15 A 4-port hub

Switch

> **Key term**
>
> Although it might look like a hub, a *switch* is a much more intelligent type of hardware device. Most switches can filter network traffic based on target MAC addresses (i.e. which network device the network data wants to reach).

Each physical network port is associated with a particular MAC address. When network traffic is received, the switch will peek at the target MAC address and *only* forward it to the correct port.

This helps a computer network by preventing unnecessary traffic and thus reducing congestion.

Router

> **Key term**
>
> A *router* is a complex device, making decisions about which of several possible paths should be used to relay network data (see mesh topology in section 10.2.1).

Routers use a **routing protocol** to learn about their network and have special **algorithms** which help them to pick the best route based on several criteria (these are called **routing metrics**).

Sometimes the metric may be **time-based** (in other words, which route is quicker); sometimes the metric may be **reliability-based**. Uniquely, routes are regularly updated and, as part of a packet-switching solution, two consecutive packets could travel completely different routes.

Most network operating systems have a **traceroute** command or utility which provides information about the route being taken by a sample test packet, hop by hop.

Figure 10.16 An 8-port switch

Figure 10.17 A router showing its ports

```
C:\Windows\system32\cmd.exe

C:\Users\Mark>tracert www.google.com

Tracing route to www.l.google.com [173.194.36.104]
over a maximum of 30 hops:

  1    <1 ms    <1 ms    <1 ms  192.168.123.254
  2    11 ms    10 ms    11 ms  cpc2-stav14-2-0-gw.aztw.cable.virginmedia.com [92.238.98.1]
  3     9 ms    11 ms    11 ms  stav-gean-1a-ge210.network.virginmedia.net [80.1.243.121]
  4    10 ms    10 ms    12 ms  aztw-gean-1a-tenge71.network.virginmedia.net [195.188.230.49]
  5    15 ms    12 ms    11 ms  aztw-core-1a-ae0-0.network.virginmedia.net [80.1.241.9]
  6    13 ms    10 ms    11 ms  winn-bb-1a-as0-0.network.virginmedia.net [213.105.175.157]
  7    18 ms    19 ms    19 ms  manc-bb-1b-as7-0.network.virginmedia.net [212.43.163.189]
  8    23 ms    23 ms    22 ms  tele-ic-3-ae0-0.network.virginmedia.net [212.43.163.70]
  9    24 ms    22 ms    23 ms  158-14-250-212.static.virginmedia.com [212.250.14.158]
 10    28 ms    29 ms    25 ms  209.85.255.175
 11    26 ms    26 ms    25 ms  209.85.251.62
 12    24 ms    17 ms    28 ms  lhr14s01-in-f104.1e100.net [173.194.36.104]

Trace complete.

C:\Users\Mark>
```

Figure 10.18 Traceroute showing the routed hops to Google®!

Wireless access point

> ### Key term
> A **wireless access point (WAP)** is used to connect wirelessly connected computer systems to a wired network. A WAP can create a hotspot for public Wi-Fi access if it is not properly secured.

Figure 10.19 A WAP showing external antenna and RJ45 socket

A WAP is normally wired into a switch or router so that its wirelessly connected devices can gain access to a larger wired network. WAPs work by broadcasting an **SSID (Service Set Identifier)** signal – this is the name it uses to identify itself to wireless devices.

In order to prevent unauthorised connections, secured wireless access points should use **MAC filtering** and **encryption** (**WEP**, **WPA** and **WPA2** are common).

10.3.2 Communication

Computer networks communicate through the use of:

- network cabling
- connectors
- addressing.

Let us first take a look at **network cabling**. Cabling tends to rely either on sending electrical signals along a copper wire or by converting data to pulses of light which travel down optical fibres.

Coaxial cable

You may recognise **coaxial cable** from television aerials and cable equipment. It is used to connect telecommunication devices which use high-frequency, broadband connections.

A typical coaxial cable looks like Figure 10.19.

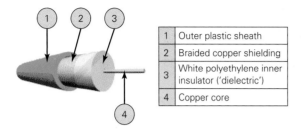

Figure 10.20 Inside a coaxial cable

1	Outer plastic sheath
2	Braided copper shielding
3	White polyethylene inner insulator ('dielectric')
4	Copper core

1 = Outer plastic sheath

2 = Braided copper shielding

3 = White plastic insulator

4 = Copper core

A braided copper shield (also known as a screen) surrounds the white plastic insulator. This shield provides a barrier from electromagnetic interference. At the centre of the cable is a single copper core. Coaxial cable can be quite hard to work with because it is inflexible.

Unshielded twisted pair and shielded twisted pair

Like a coaxial cable, **unshielded twisted pair (UTP)** and **shielded twisted pair (STP)** both use copper wires.

STP – with shielding

UTP – no shielding

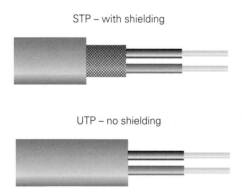

Figure 10.21 STP and UTP cables

STP has a metallic-coated plastic foil within the plastic sheath that is used to screen out electromagnetic interference. Because of this, STP is generally more expensive than its UTP counterpart and more difficult to work with.

Cross-talk can occur between two wires which run in parallel. In both UTP and STP cables, the individual wires are twisted in order to cancel out this form of interference (see Figure 10.23).

Figure 10.22 Wires are twisted to cancel out cross-talk

The core of STP and UTP wires is copper. Copper is an excellent conductor (having low electrical resistance), is an easy material to work with and is very flexible (which makes cabling simple in narrow spaces). **Cat 5** is a common type of UTP cable used to build LANs.

Optical fibre

> ### Key term
> **Optical fibre** uses light from **LEDs (light emitting diodes)** or a **laser (light amplification by stimulated emission radiation)** to transmit data through a very thin strand of glass. Each glass fibre is about 2 microns in diameter – which is roughly 15 times thinner than a single human hair.

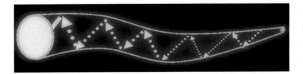

Figure 10.23 Optical fibres

Fibre optic cables can transmit data over 50 miles or more before the signal needs boosting; this makes them very useful in public network systems such as those operated by telecommunications companies like Virgin and BT.

Because they use light, optical fibres are not affected by stray electromagnetic interference (unlike copper cables). In addition, they are capable of sustaining high transmission rates – ideal for broadband applications such as voice, music and streamed video.

Two types are common: **single mode** (longer distances, single signal) and **multimode** (shorter distances, multiple signals).

Connectors

Many different types of connectors are used to connect network cables to networking hardware. The most common types are shown in Table 10.2.

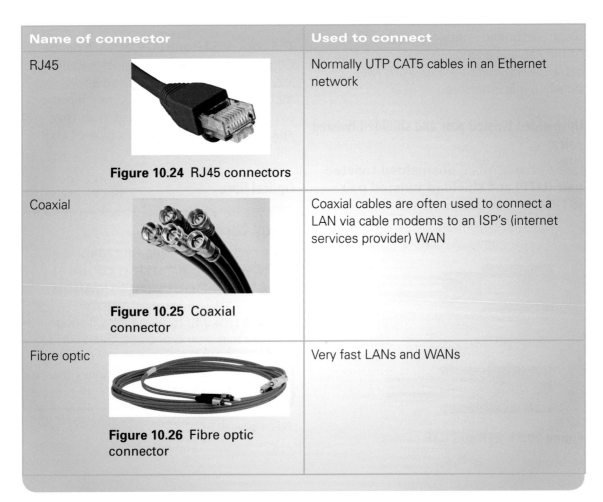

Name of connector	Used to connect
RJ45 **Figure 10.24** RJ45 connectors	Normally UTP CAT5 cables in an Ethernet network
Coaxial **Figure 10.25** Coaxial connector	Coaxial cables are often used to connect a LAN via cable modems to an ISP's (internet services provider) WAN
Fibre optic **Figure 10.26** Fibre optic connector	Very fast LANs and WANs

Table 10.2 Common network connectors

WAN Connectivity

WANs rely on high-speed data links to connect smaller LANs together. The most common technologies for forming a WAN are detailed below.

ISDN

ISDN (integrated services digital network) uses ordinary copper telephone wire.

ISDN represented a welcome upgrade from dial-up narrowband services (which relied on slow modems). In the mid- to late 1990s, any home or business customers wanting to use this early broadband service needed to install an ISDN adapter. It gave a bandwidth of about 128 kbps which was much faster than the traditional modems of the time (about 28.8 kbps).

ISDN has largely been replaced in the UK through the mass availability of relatively inexpensive DSL and cable services.

Broadband

Traditional telephone lines that usually carry our voices do not make full use of the transmission media's available bandwidth. Digital-signal based **DSL (digital subscriber line)** uses the unused frequencies available on the copper wire to transmit data traffic in addition to voice traffic. This means that DSL allows voice and high-speed data to be sent simultaneously over the same connection.

10.3.3 Software

All network software tends to be broken up into three different categories (see Figure 10.27).

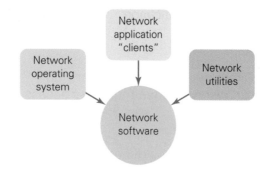

Figure 10.27 Network software categories

Network application clients

A **network application 'client'** is a program that uses a network connection to provide the user with a specific facility. Common application clients include:

- Internet world wide web (WWW) browser for visiting websites, for example Microsoft Internet Explorer®, Mozilla Firefox®, Google Chrome®, Apple Safari®.
- Email, for example Microsoft Outlook®, Mozilla Thunderbird®.
- Firewalls for blocking undesirable network traffic, for example Windows Firewall®, Smoothwall®, Check Point's ZoneAlarm®.
- File transfer protocol (FTP) for fast and reliable transfer of files between computer systems, for example SmartSoft SmartFTP®, FileZilla®.

Network operating systems

A **network operating System (NOS)** is an operating system which supports network protocols and client/server or peer-to-peer networking (or both).

A NOS supplies and controls the following network services:

- Log-in authentication
- File sharing
- Print sharing
- Directory services (particularly on client/server when multi-user access is required and users are placed in different groups).

Common examples of network operating systems include Microsoft Windows®, Apple® Mac OS X® and Linux®.

Network utilities

Common network utilities include:

- **Ping** – to test network connectivity (see section 10.4.8)
- **Traceroute** – to show network traffic routing from node to node (see section 10.3.1)
- **IPconfig** – to show current network configuration, including IP address (see section 10.2.1)
- **ARP** – to show a table containing a node's knowledge of other devices' IPs and their MAC addresses.

Make the grade **P5**

P5 asks you to explain how hardware, software and addressing combine to support network communications. This is detailed in sections 10.3.1, 10.3.2 and 10.3.3.

Ideally you will need to present an answer (possibly in a report, presentation, poster or leaflet) which describes examples in each category (hardware, software, address) and explains how they work together to make a network function.

10.4 Be able to set up a simple local area network

This section will cover the following grading criteria: **P6** **M2** **M3** **D2**

The stages of building a new LAN can be shown visually (see Figure 10.28).

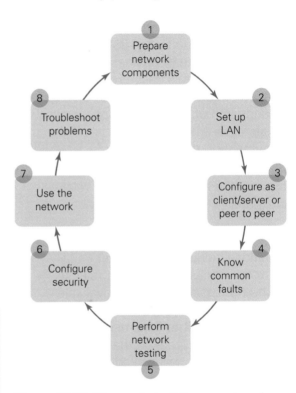

Figure 10.28 Stages in building a network

We will now explore these eight stages through sections 10.4.1 to 10.4.8.

10.4.1 Preparation

Before you start building your network, you must have made suitable preparations. This involves obtaining all the necessary components you need – a bit like a shopping list!

Network components I will need!

Cables (with connectors), for example CAT5 UTP

Network devices, such as switches, computer systems etc.

NICs (installed or built into selected computer systems)

Software, such as operating systems, application clients and utilities.

It is important that you ensure all of these components are compatible with each other.

Activity D

Planning a LAN in a SOHO (small office/home office)

A local business is planning to network its current premises and has asked you to purchase the equipment necessary to complete the task.

The building has a main office (ten PCs plus one printer), a reception (one PC), the manager's office (one PC) and a storeroom (two PCs).

Draw up a 'shopping list' for this network, selecting appropriate cables, network devices, NICs and software needed.

Note: The manager has indicated that their ability to safely run cables from room to room is limited.

10.4.2 Set up

Once you have successfully prepared and have your shopping list of components, it is time to set up the network.

It is obviously impossible to discuss every possible type of network that you might be asked to assemble so perhaps the best approach is to give you a simple flowchart (see Unit 18) which will help you perform the set up in the correct order.

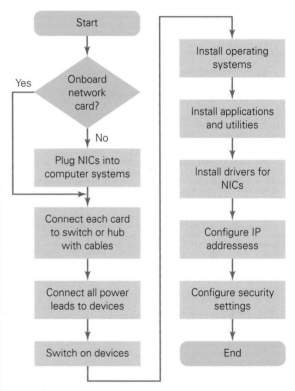

Figure 10.29 Set up a network

Health and safety

Your health is important so health and safety issues need to be understood. The following precautions should *always* be taken when working on computer hardware.

- Use an anti-static wrist strap when installing components to prevent electrostatic discharge.
- Use the correct tools for the job (ask your teacher if you are not sure) and always be careful when using them (especially screwdrivers).
- If fitting a new NIC, avoid the sharp metal edges inside the computer case.

- Always switch off the electricity at the mains before plugging in power cables.
- Only switch on the electricity at the mains after all cables are firmly plugged in.
- Be careful with trailing cables – you do not want to trip people over!

Activity E

Building a simple wireless LAN

Use the following network plan to build a small peer-to-peer LAN in a computer lab.

Shopping list:

- 2 x PC workstations with network operating systems (for example Microsoft Windows®)
- 1 x switch (minimum four port)
- 1 x WAP
- 1 x wired network card (PCI or PCIe) or onboard NIC
- 1 x wireless network card (PCI or PCIe), onboard Wi-Fi or USB adaptor
- 2 x Cat 5 UTP cables.

The best way of checking your LAN is to assign each PC an IP address in the range 192.168.123.X where X can be any value between 5 and 10. No IP must be duplicated. Use a ping command to check connectivity (see section 10.4.8).

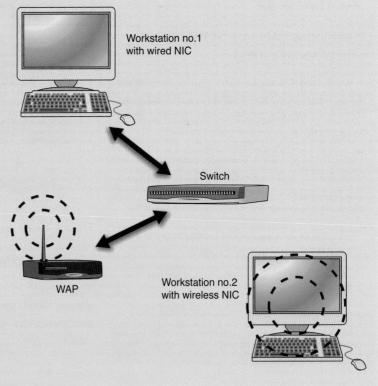

Workstation no.1 with wired NIC

Switch

WAP

Workstation no.2 with wireless NIC

Figure 10.30

10.4.3 Simple LAN

You will need to configure how your LAN will be managed. Look back at section 10.2.1 at the differences between peer-to-peer and client/server network configurations. You must choose which one to use.

In a Microsoft Windows® solution you will need to install a **Server edition** of Microsoft Windows® on one of the workstations if you want to configure the network to work as client/server network.

At the time of publication the current version is Windows Server 2008®. A 180-day evaluation version can be downloaded from:

http://www.microsoft.com/windows server2008/en/us/trial-software.aspx

The other workstations may be installed with a standard version of Microsoft Windows®, such as Windows XP®, Windows Vista® or Windows 7®.

The actual physical connections for the network are not changed.

10.4.4 Faults

When you are setting up your network you may encounter many common faults. Unfortunately, some are easier to diagnose than others!

Table 10.3 shows some common faults and the symptoms that might help you successfully diagnose them.

Suspect fault	Symptoms	Solution
Address conflict	IP addresses on a LAN must be unique in order for it to work correctly. If two devices have the same IP address, the network will be unable to determine which device it must send data to. On a Microsoft Windows® network a warning message usually appears to indicate an address conflict. ⚠ **Windows – System Error** ☒ There is an IP address conflict with another system on the network **Figure 10.30** Windows® IP conflict warning	See section 10.4.8 for resolving a conflicting or incorrect IP address.
Network card failure	A network card failure can be hard to diagnose because the symptoms may be varied. Common problems include: • Computer system may not load operating system. • Network card may not be listed in operating system's list of hardware (e.g. Device Manager in Microsoft Windows®). • Cannot install the driver for the network card. • Any attempt to use networking crashes the computer system. • Cannot assign an IP address successfully. • Ping (see section 10.4.8) shows data packets being lost when transmitted.	1 Try a different network card. 2 If the network card can be removed, try it in a different (but compatible) computer system. 3 Try reinstalling the drivers.

Table 10.3 Common networking faults and their solutions (continues on next page)

Faulty cable	A faulty cable will usually be obvious because the computer system will show 'no' or 'limited' connectivity (see section 10.4.8) or there will be no 'blinking' light on the switch for the port it is connected to. Breaks, crushing or poor 'crimping' into the cable connector are common problems.	1 Try a different cable! 2 A **ping** (see section 10.4.8) is a good way of testing connectivity along a cable. 3 Electronic **cable testers** are commercially available but can be very expensive. These will be able to identify any problems in the cable. 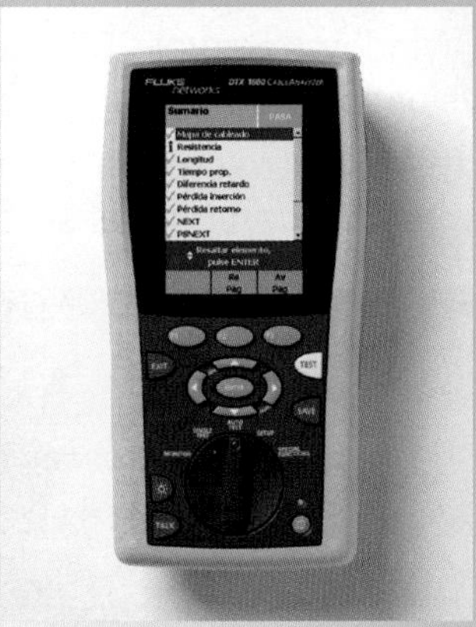 **Figure 10.31** Fluke cable tester
Loss of service	Common loss of service problems include: • Being unable to print • Being unable to share or access files on other networked computers • Being unable to email successfully.	Because it is a consequence of network faults, loss of service is resolved by fixing one or more of the previous issues.

Table 10.3 Continued

10.4.5 Testing

Testing your network is critical. In order to test you must know about common faults (see section 10.4.4). You must also be able to troubleshoot (see section 10.4.8).

Testing can be broken down into three main categories:

• **Functionality** – can you access shared resources? Can you communicate? Do network application 'clients' and utility work correctly?

• **Connectivity** – is the computer system talking to other computer systems on the network? Does the computer system talk to the networked printer?

• **Addressing** – do all networked devices have appropriate IP addresses? Are there any conflicts appearing?

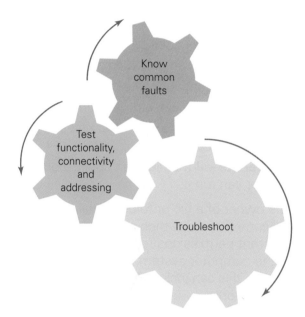

Figure 10.32 Know about common faults, test for them, troubleshoot the problems

Make the grade — P6

P6 is a practical criterion, asking you to set up and test a LAN. Sections 10.4.1 to 10.4.5, inclusive, describe the steps you need to perform and things you must think about in order to successfully achieve this. Evidencing your network set up is likely to be achieved through photographs, videos and witness statements. You could even produce a leaflet or web page which describes what you did.

The second part of P6 asks you to test the network. A test log containing details of the categories you have been testing and the actual outcomes is a good way to evidence this. Ensure you have tested some functionality, connectivity and addressing.

10.4.6 Security

You will need to apply **basic security settings** to your network as the last action in the set up (see section 10.4.2). There are many different security settings that you can apply even on a relatively basic peer-to-peer network.

Firewall configuration

Although you can install third-party firewall applications, Microsoft Windows® comes with a working firewall which is quite easy to configure.

You can access this by opening the Control Panel and selecting Network and Internet.

Figure 10.33 Windows® firewall

Firewall options are varied but common ones include:

- Turning firewall on or off. (Be warned that turning a firewall off will reduce the computer system's protection from hackers and malware.)
- Allowing particular programs to talk to the network.
- Denying particular programs from talking to the network.

Any data that is allowed through a firewall is known as an **exception**.

Log in limits

It is possible to limit the time periods in which a user can log on to a computer system, for example preventing access outside normal work hours.

File and folder permissions

When files and folders are created they have associated **permissions**.

> ### Key term
>
> **Permissions** are a form of security and they control the ways in which a user can interact with a file or folder. Permissions range from **full control** (user can do anything) to **no view access** (user cannot physically see the file or folder).

In Microsoft Windows®, permissions are accessed by right-clicking on a file or folder and choosing Properties. The Security tab will show the permissions associated with that file (or folder) for the different users of the system.

Common permissions

- **Full control** – user can do anything.
- **Read** – user can only read a file.
- **Write** – user can create new data.
- **Modify** – user can alter existing data.
- **List folder contents** – user can see files in a folder.
- **Execute** – if the file is an application, the user can run it.

The owner of a file or folder usually has full control and can then allow or deny different permissions for different users of the computer system. On a networked system this can include users logging onto the network.

Access control

> **Access control** is a security feature in most operating systems that controls which users can access its resources. In Microsoft Windows®, access control can extend to applications and access to administrative-level functions that change system settings, such as setting the system time or scheduling processing tasks.

Figure 10.34 Windows® permissions

10.4.7 Use

This is the practical part of the unit where you get to play with the network you have assembled and configured!

Clearly there are many things you can do with a working LAN but it is worth remembering that without a router or a gateway to a WAN it is very likely that you will not be able to access the internet and browse websites. Sorry!

Common tasks you can try include:

Transfer of files – files can be transferred between computers by browsing the network and simply dragging and dropping to folders where the user has write permissions (see section 10.4.6).

Setting file permissions – you can decide who can and cannot access your folders and files by changing their active permissions (see section 10.4.6).

Sharing files – in Microsoft Windows®, folders and their files can be shared with other units by using the Share functionality. Sharing is configured by right-clicking on the folder, choosing Properties and then selecting the Sharing tab (see Figure 10.35).

Figure 10.35 Folder sharing dialogue

Common options for sharing include:

- Creating a new 'share' or deleting an existing one.
- Specifying which users can access the folder.
- Setting the maximum number of simultaneous accesses.
- Setting the permissions for the folder.
- Setting a password for access to the folder.

Allocating disk space for users

Operating systems often have the ability to allow the network administrator to set disk space for different users. This is called setting a **quota**. Generally it is a facility which is more commonly associated on client/server networks, although it is possible to practise on a simple computer system (see Figure 10.36).

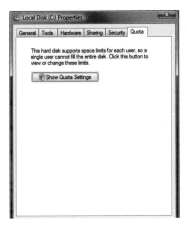

Figure 10.36 Disk quota tab

If you right-click on a hard disk drive in My Computer and select Properties, you will notice a Quota tab. Quotas are normally disabled by default but you can add a new quota for each user. This is very useful as it can prevent users wasting valuable storage with large downloaded files which are not needed (such as videos and music in a business organisation).

10.4.8 Troubleshoot

> **Key term**
>
> **Troubleshooting** means determining the nature of the problem and working out a solution.

There are two common faults that can you troubleshoot on a simple LAN: connectivity and conflicting or incorrect IP addresses.

Connectivity

The IP may be configured, the NICs may be connected to the switch and everything may look OK, but sometimes a network just will not work. How frustrating!

Network software will not work if there is no basic connectivity. In Microsoft Windows® this is usually obvious by looking at the Network icon on the System Tray or 'notification area' (see Table 10.4).

The common version of the icon you may see		What it means
	Figure 10.37 Full network connectivity	Your computer system is connected to the internet and network application clients such as web browsers should work OK!
	Figure 10.38 Limited connectivity	No internet connection, but the cables are connected OK and it would appear that the computer system is on a LAN. Note: You cannot get full connectivity unless you have a suitable gateway providing access to the internet, for example a router and external connection to an ISP (internet service provider).
	Figure 10.39 No connectivity	For a wired network (i.e. using cables) this usually indicates either: • Cable is unplugged from switch or NIC. • NIC is not working properly (its drivers may not be installed correctly). • NIC or network connection may be disabled. • IP addresses may be badly configured.

Table 10.4 Network connectivity status icon in Microsoft Windows®

Ping

A basic test that you can perform is called '**pinging**'. It may sound a little strange but it is actually a very useful utility!

Ping is a network software utility (see section 10.3.3) which will send test packets of data (containing the alphabet) from one network node to another. The receiving node should reply and the time taken for the acknowledgement can be measured (this tells us the network's **latency**).

Ping is often used as a basic test for connectivity – if ping does not work, there is obviously a problem. It is very easy to do – try Activity F.

When ping does not work ...

Ping uses the ICMP protocol (see section 10.2.3) and this can be blocked by a computer system's firewall (see section 10.4.6). You will need to check the configuration of a computer system's firewall to ensure that pings are allowed, whether they are 'incoming' or 'outgoing'.

Conflicting or incorrect IP addresses

On a LAN using the common TCP/IP protocol it is important that all computer systems are on the same network and that each computer system has a unique IP address (see Figure 10.41).

Activity F

Checking connectivity with ping

There are various ways to do this but the best way is to open a command prompt in Microsoft Windows® and use the Ping command. All you need is the target node's IP address.

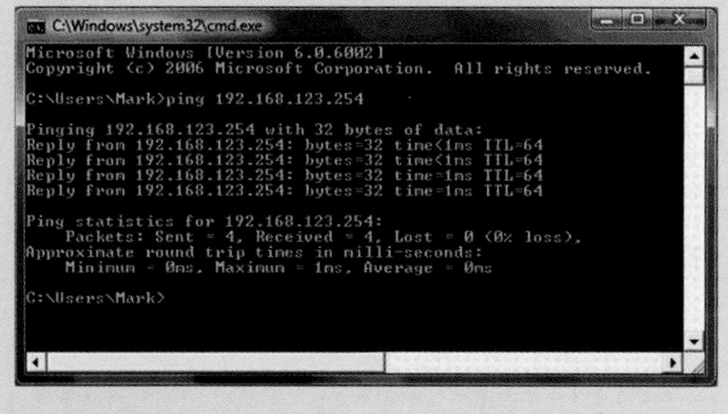

Figure 10.40 A successful ping of 192.168.123.254

If there is a connectivity problem, pinging will fail. Linux® also uses the ping command and the instruction is very similar to the Windows® version.

Try pinging another node on your network – it could be a server, another workstation or even a network printer.

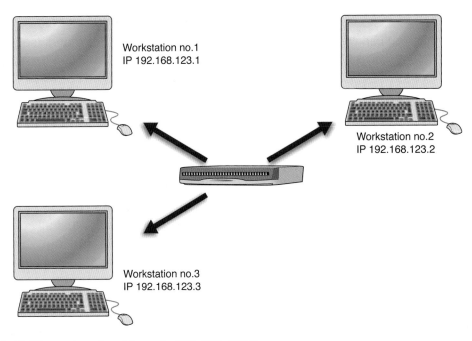

Workstation no.1
IP 192.168.123.1

Workstation no.2
IP 192.168.123.2

Workstation no.3
IP 192.168.123.3

Figure 10.41 The network address is 192.168.123.<u>0</u>

Activity **G**

Changing an IP address

IP addresses are usually either **manually set** (this is called a **static IP**) or they are **automatically leased** from a server or a router using a service called **DHCP (Domain Host Configuration Protocol)**. On a small LAN it is likely that you will set static IPs. In Microsoft Windows® this is achieved by:

1. Accessing Windows® Network connections

2. Selecting the correct NIC

3. Choosing its Property settings

4. Selecting TCP/IP (version 4)

5. Setting manual IP address and subnet mask (will be 255.255.255.0).

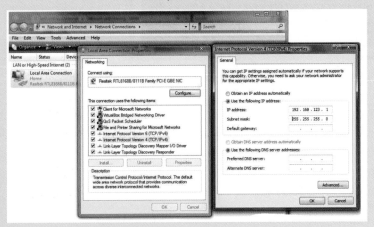

Figure 10.42 Setting the NIC's IP address manually to 192.168.123.1

Make the grade `M2`

Partly an extension of the work you have done for P3, criterion M2 asks you to suggest possible solutions to resolve connectivity problems. Apart from physically checking for good cable connections between a NIC and a switch (or hub) on a wired network, the most common solutions will involve checking for conflicting (or incorrect) IP addresses and testing for basic connectivity. Reading through the information on troubleshooting in section 10.4.8 should give you a helping hand here.

This criterion may be evidenced through a witness statement, report, wiki, presentation, podcast or viva.

Help with assessment

Your tutor will give you one or more assignments that you will complete as coursework. This could consist of:

- Presentations
- Videos and screen captures
- Witness statements and/or an evidence log
- Web pages or wikis
- Leaflets or reports
- Podcasts
- Blogs
- Posters.

You should read the guidance given for each of the criteria (shown across the unit) carefully and remember to check your work.

Achieving Success

In order to achieve each unit, you will complete a series of coursework activities. Each time you hand in work, your tutor will return this to you with a record of your achievement.

This particular unit has 11 criteria to meet: 6 Pass, 3 Merit and 2 Distinction.

For a **Pass** you must achieve **all 6** Pass criteria.

For a **Merit** you must achieve **all 6** Pass and **all 3** Merit criteria.

For a **Distinction** you must achieve **all 6** Pass, **all 3** Merit criteria **and both** Distinction criteria.

(r) Further reading

Textbooks

Donahue, G.A. *Network Warrior* (O'Reilly Media, 2007) ISBN 0596101511

Lowe, D. *Networking for Dummies (For Dummies (Computers))* (John Wiley & Sons, 2007) ISBN 0470056207

Hogan, C.J., **Chalup**, S.R. and **Limoncelli**, T. *The Practice of System and Network Administration* (Addison Wesley, 2007) ISBN 0321492668

Journal

Network World

Websites

www.networktutorials.info/index.html
www.practicallynetworked.com/

Unit 16
Database systems

Learning objectives
By the end of this unit you should:

1. Understand the principles of database systems
2. Be able to create non-relational database systems
3. Be able to use database software tools.

In order to pass this unit, the evidence you present for assessment needs to demonstrate that you can meet all of the above learning outcomes for this unit. The criteria below show the levels of achievement required to pass this unit.

To achieve a **pass** grade the evidence must show that the learner is able to:	To achieve a **merit** grade the evidence must show that, in addition to the pass criteria, the learner is able to:	To achieve a **distinction** the evidence must show that, in addition to the pass and merit criteria, the learner is able to:
P1 Explain the principles of database systems	**M1** Explain the importance of maintaining data integrity in a database system	
P2 Design a non-relational database system, including different data types	**M2** Explain the choice of fields, data types and primary key in a non-relational database system	
P3 Create a non-relational database system from a given design	**M3** Explain the need to calculate data storage requirements	
P4 Import data into a non-relational database system	**M4** Sort records in a non-relational database system	**D1** Test a non-relational database system to meet a given design
P5 Produce queries to extract meaningful data from a non-relational database system	**M5** Produce meaningful reports based on database queries	**D2** Explain the benefits of using reports
P6 Create and use data entry forms		

Continued on next page

To achieve a **pass** grade the evidence must show that the learner is able to:	To achieve a **merit** grade the evidence must show that, in addition to the pass criteria, the learner is able to:	To achieve a **distinction** the evidence must show that, in addition to the pass and merit criteria, the learner is able to:
P7 Export data from a non-relational database system		
P8 Produce user documentation for a non-relational database system		**D3** Justify improvements that could be made to a database system

Introduction

Databases really are everywhere. They are used to store information about all kinds of different things including people, stock, suppliers and customers.

This unit will help you to develop skills in using databases. You will learn how to ensure that data is correctly input to a system and you will explore the types of information you can get out of a system.

You will be assessed through coursework which could be in the form of:

- Presentations
- Databases and test plans
- Witness statements of an observed practical exercise
- Web pages and wikis
- Report/user guide or document

- Screenshots
- Verbal evaluation of your solution.

16.1 Understand the principles of database systems

This section will cover the following grading criteria: **P1** **M1**

16.1.1 Database basics

Databases are everywhere: schools and colleges, libraries, doctor's and dentist's surgeries, supermarkets, garages, florists, grocers, music and DVD stores, clothes shops, gyms, hotels, kennels, banks, building societies, hospitals, fast food outlets – and there are many more examples.

Within each of these organisations the following information could be stored: customers, sales, products, suppliers, purchases, stock, manufacturing, accounts, VAT.

These databases are organised in such a way that data can be easily entered and stored, edited, deleted and manipulated to support the activities of the organisation.

Example uses

To be able to appreciate fully why databases are better than manual alternatives, consider the following:

A small guesthouse has eight double rooms. The owners store all of their room bookings in a database and they need to make sure that the dates entered are as accurate as possible. They specifically want to make sure that the checking-out date is after the checking-in date!

In this example (Figure 16.1), the checking-out date is validated by comparing what the user inputs into the checking-out date with the checking-in date.

Figure 16.1 Validation on date

More sophisticated systems will also check that the room being allocated is not already in use!

Once a valid date has been entered, the input will be accepted and the user will be able to complete the booking.

Advantages and disadvantages

The advantages and disadvantages of computerised databases are summarised in the following scorecard.

Scorecard

Computerised databases

+ Easy to use
+ Records are easy to access and retrieve
+ Data can easily be manipulated in many different ways (for example, trends can be established, data can be viewed from different perspectives)
+ Data can be validated to ensure that it is accurate when input
+ Easy to store
− Database structures must be carefully developed to ensure that they work as efficiently as possible
− There are laws that control the use of databases
− Many people feel that simply too much information is stored about us
− The costs of technology can be prohibitive

Objects

One of the most frustrating issues with computing and IT is the new terminology that you have to learn and understand. Database technology is no different in requiring you to learn new terminology. Some of the most common terms encountered are given below.

An **object** is something that can be designed, selected and manipulated. Tables, queries, forms and reports are all examples of objects.

Database **tables** consist of rows and columns of information, where the row contains a **record** and the column becomes a record **field** (this will be explored later).

Room_bookings						
Booking_ID	Customer_Nam	Telephone_	Room_Numl	Check_in_d	Check_out_	Add New Field
3	Mr & Mrs Smith	05555 558954	6	22/11/2010	26/11/2010	
4	Helga Watzke	06666 687987	2	24/11/2010	29/11/2010	
5	Miss Johnson	06666 412434	1	21/11/2010	23/11/2010	
*	(New)					

Figure 16.2 An example of a table

A **query** is used to manipulate the data stored in the tables. This data can be sorted (for example alphabetically in **ascending**, A to Z, or **descending**, Z to A, order). The data can be filtered to show only records containing a specific word or phrase, or you can use the data to perform calculations. Being able to query the data is the main advantage that computerised databases have over data that is stored manually. The results of queries can be displayed on the screen or printed.

To enable users to use databases more easily, the data in tables is often (in fact usually) accessed through a **form** (see Figure 16.3).

Room_bookings

Room_bookings

Booking_ID:	3
Customer_Name:	Mr & Mrs Smith
Telephone_Number:	05555 558954
Room_Number:	6
Check_in_date:	22/11/2010
Check_out_date:	26/11/2010

Figure 16.3 An input form

The form changes the way that the user accesses and uses the records.

Reports are used to display the information that is stored in the database or alternatively to show the results of a query in a more business-like way. The main advantage of creating a report rather than just printing out the results of the query is that with a report, users can add headings, sub-headings, dates, page numbers and other types of formatting.

Room_bookings   22 November 2010

Booking_ID	Customer_Name	Telephone_Number	Room_Number	Check_in_date	Check_out_date
3	Mr & Mrs Smith	05555 558954	6	22/11/2010	26/11/2010
4	Helga Watzke	06666 687987	2	24/11/2010	29/11/2010
5	Miss Johnson	06666 412434	1	21/11/2010	23/11/2010

Page 1 of 1

Figure 16.4 A report

Reports will be covered in more depth later in the unit.

Data types

Just as with software development, understanding data types is an important part of being able to work successfully with databases.

Text – this data type will allow you to hold any alphanumeric data. This means that it can hold numbers, characters, combinations of numbers and characters (for example E101ITP) or symbols. The **default** (manufacturer preset) number of characters that is set to be stored in a text field is 50, although this number can be adjusted to any number between 1 and 255.

Number – you can use number fields to store whole numbers (for example 6 or 492) or numbers with a decimal part (such as 134.87). If the number is decimal, you will need to set how many numbers will be displayed after the decimal point (this will ensure that when numbers are displayed, they will be consistent).

Currency – setting a field as currency will automatically add a £ sign to the value that has been keyed in. As with number above, you will need to choose how many numbers you wish to display after the decimal point.

Date/Time – this field allows you to key in a date in most recognised formats and stores it in a specific way. The main options within this data type are:

General Date	08/04/2005 13:23:41
Long Date	8 April 2005
Medium Date	8-Apr-05
Short Date	08/04/2005
Long Time	13:23:41
Medium Time	01:23 PM
Short Time	13:23

AutoNumber – an AutoNumber is a number that the computer generates. If you use an AutoNumber in a field, each time a record is created the number will increase by 1.

LookupWizard – this is a very useful data type because you will be able to set the values that will be stored in advance and the user will simply then choose from a **list**. For example Mr, Mrs, Ms, Miss, Dr, Rev would all be possible titles for a customer.

One of the key issues with good database design and construction is choosing the right data type.

Estimating the size of a database

Depending on the database software you use, you may well be able to estimate the size of your database. The following example calculates how big the database will be:

Booking_ID	AutoCounter (4 bytes)
Customer_Name	Text of 20 characters (20 bytes)
Telephone_ Number	Text of 20 characters (20 bytes)
Room_Number	Number (4 bytes)
Check_in_date	Date (stored as text – dd/mm/yyyy is 8 bytes)
Check_out_date	Date (stored as text – dd/mm/yyyy is 8 bytes)
Maximum record size	**64 bytes**

If we used all the available space in each field (keyed in the maximum number of bytes possible), each record would take up 64 bytes of memory.

Taking this a little further, if we knew that we were going to store, say, 1,000 records, we would be able to calculate that our database would have a size of 64,000 bytes and if the database grew to 10,000 records, we would effectively be storing 640,000 bytes.

So how much storage does the data in our existing database need?

Take the following example:

3	4 bytes
Mr & Mrs Smith	14 bytes
05555 558954	12 bytes
6	4 bytes
22/11/2010	8 bytes
26/11/2010	8 bytes
Total	**50 bytes**

The above record would only need 50 bytes to store it in full.

In addition, some databases have what is called an **overhead**. This is where additional memory is used to store information about the objects as well as the data stored in the tables, such as the company logo which is used in reports, or the design of a query.

These overheads are more difficult to calculate. However, being able to estimate the size of a database can still be a useful skill.

16.1.2 Database structures

Tables

As discussed previously, **tables** are the foundation to any database. Most databases contain a number of tables that store different information. For example, one table may contain all the organisation's information on customers, another table may contain all the supplier details. It would be very unusual to combine this information to create a single table.

For this unit, however, your database will only contain one table.

Fields

The **fields** are the columns in the table. Each field has a **field heading** (basically a name, such as Customer_Name in the example above). All the data in a field will have two things in common:

- All the data in the field will be of the **same type** (for example text or number).
- All the data will be **related**. For example, all the customer names in the table shown will be keyed into and stored in the Customer_Name field. Similarly all the Booking_IDs will be stored together in the Booking_ID column (or field).

Records

A **record** is a single piece of information with all its relevant parts. For example, 4, Helga Watzke, 06666 687987, 2, 24/11/2010, 29/11/2010 **represents a single record**. Each record is stored in a **row** in the database table.

Primary key

Each record that is stored must have something completely unique about it. This is so that records that are similar can be told apart. Usually, a field is selected which will contain a unique piece of data. This is then allocated as the **primary key**.

Selecting a suitable field for this can be difficult. If, for example, we were creating a database of students, we could potentially have a number of students with the same name. The name would, therefore, **not be unique** and could not be used as a primary key.

Similarly, in a school or college where there are hundreds or thousands of students, the

date of birth would probably be the same for a number of students – so again, it would not be suitable.

As such, and as shown in the data previously, an **ID** is created, often using the AutoNumber. This will never be repeated in any record, and so this will be considered unique.

16.1.3 Data integrity

The choices you make as a database developer and user are easier if you have some very basic guidelines that you can always follow.

Given below are some suggestions which will help you make the right decisions. They will help you ensure that your database is more likely to be correct.

Data accuracy

When you create a database you will have the opportunity to include some on-screen instructions, to **prompt** the user about what needs to be keyed in. For example, you would like the user to key in their height.

Your prompt for input is as follows:

Height [   ]

What should your user input? 1.3 m? 1.3 metres? 1.3? 130 cm?

A more helpful instruction would be:

Height in metres (e.g. 1.3) [   ]

Consistency

We have already talked about the currency data table and making sure that the computer stores all the numbers in the currency field with the same number of decimal places.

Figure 16.5 shows the formatting tab that is visible when you select Currency as a data type.

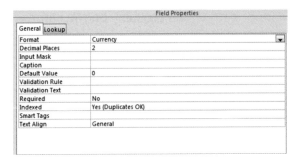

Figure 16.5 Formatting currency

Choosing '2' as the number of decimal places will make sure that all numbers are consistent when displayed. For example:

6.98

495.39

10.00

128.30

Without the formatting, the display would have looked more like this:

6.98

495.39

10

128.3

Similarly, the computer can be set up to ensure that all postal codes are stored in a consistent way, for example:

BS13 9MM

BS139MM

BS1 39MM

These are all variations of the **same** postal code.

Validation rules

Validation rules are used to limit the user in terms of what can be keyed into the field. There are a number of ways that validation rules can be applied.

The easiest way to apply validation is to use a **lookup list** (using the LookupWizard data type is one example). The user is then only able to select from a given list of options.

There is no physical keying in required and as such there is less opportunity for the user to input something incorrectly.

A second option is to give a field a specific **default value**. In this instance, the manufacturer's default of 0 can be redefined by the user. Let us say that the most common value keyed into a field is 25. If the default is set at 25, then unless it is changed, 25 will always appear in this field.

The third option is to set the **top** and **bottom expected values**. Let us say, for example, that we have a field for a person's age. Clearly a person cannot be less than 0 and he or she is unlikely to be. Similarly, keying in a value of 233 for a person would be inappropriate.

To ensure that this does not happen, you would create a validation rule such as

>=0 and <= 120

This means greater than or equal to 0 and less than or equal to 120.

Now, when the user keys in a value, the computer will automatically check to see whether the value is between these numbers. The inclusion of the = sign also means that the person can be 0 (this would be for someone who has not reached their first birthday!) or 120.

Validation rules are extremely important in ensuring **data integrity**.

16.1.4 Tables

Single (non-relational)

Most databases are what is known as **relational**. This means that there are tables of data that are linked together.

Let us look at an example. This is a simple invoicing system. To create an invoice, the database system uses information from the customer records and the stock records. This information is combined and used to create the invoice.

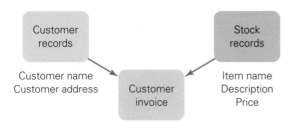

Figure 16.6 A relational database

In this relational system, the customer is entered once in the customer records and the items are entered once into the stock records. These records are then used in the invoice.

Relational databases are quite complex to set up and if you continue to study Information Technology at the next level, you will probably create a relational database like this.

In your system, however, you will not be asked to create a relational database, but a single (non-relational) table database.

To explain how it would be different let us look at the following:

Transactions					
Customer Name	Address	Item Name	Description	Price	Total
Customer Name	Address	Item Name	Description	Price	Total
Customer Name	Address	Item Name	Description	Price	Total
Customer Name	Address	Item Name	Description	Price	Total
Customer Name	Address	Item Name	Description	Price	Total
Customer Name	Address	Item Name	Description	Price	Total
Customer Name	Address	Item Name	Description	Price	Total

Figure 16.7 Non-relational database

In a non-relational database you only have one table of data. Each time there is a new sale, the customer information will have to be typed in again and again and again! Because the customer information and the item information is being typed in each time, there is a greater possibility of mistakes and consistency!

16.1.5 Database design

Table structure

A table is the basis for all modern databases. The data in the table is organised into rows and columns. The rows are the records and the columns are fields.

Each field will have the same information in it. For example, if you created a table of information about your class, it would probably look something like Table 16.1.

Name	Address	Telephone number	Date of birth
Miranda York	15 High Street	05555 165784	16/09/1994
Janice York	15 High Street	05555 165784	23/08/1995
Adam Uzokwe	2a Bramley Terrace	05555 344797	01/02/1995

Table 16.1 Sample table of information about a class

The data is organised in this way so that a user could print out, for example, all names with the relevant phone number or all names with dates of birth.

Each field has a fixed **data type**. This means that the type of data in it is decided beforehand.

In our example:

Name	would be text
Address	would be text
Telephone number	could be a number, but then you would not be able to input the first 0 – to do that it must be stored as text
Date of birth	would be a date

Each field has **properties**. These are settings that **format** or **control** the data in the field and will include the data type, any validation (checks about the data entered) or input masks (these are not covered in this text and again you would learn about these if you studied at a higher level) which are where you set an input to be handled in a particular way. This is quite common on postcodes.

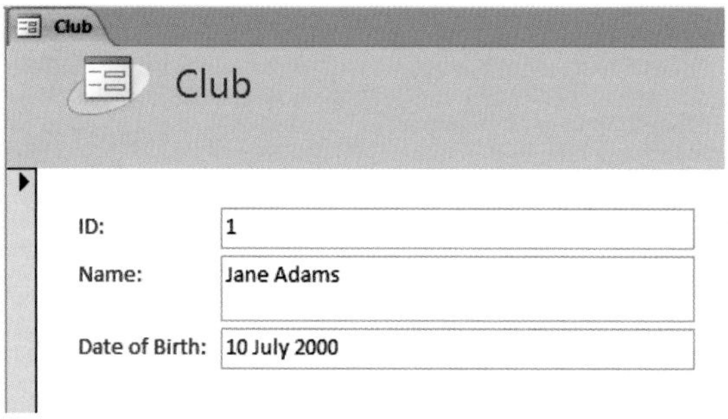

Figure 16.12 Club form

When the user keys in information, it goes into the table. Validation events can also be applied to fields to control the data that is input and the format in which the data is entered. Each record is presented to the user one at a time. You will have an opportunity to create a table, queries and forms in section 16.2.

Make the grade — P1 — M1

These two criteria are the only non-practical assessment criteria in the unit and you will probably be asked to evidence them through a presentation, poster, podcast or leaflet.

For P1 you will need to explain the principles of database systems. You should explain the advantages and disadvantages of using databases. It will help if you can relate your advantages and disadvantages to real examples of systems. You must identify and describe at least two advantages and two disadvantages.

M1 expands on P1 and you will need to explain why it is important that the data in a database has integrity (it might help if you begin by explaining what data integrity is).

16.2 Be able to create non-relational database systems

This section will cover the following grading criteria: P2 M2 M3

This section is wholly practical and to help you work with a database, it takes you through an entire scenario. We will use the club database to support this activity.

16.2.1 Table

Single (non-relational)

The first step with any database is to create a table. The table is basically a formal structure into which data is input so that it can be stored. The table needs to be designed, in other words the fields have to be named and the type of data to be stored needs to be specified along with any formatting.

16.2.2 Design

Structure diagrams

It is important to know in advance exactly how your table will be structured and the best way to record this is in a formal way. The example below shows all the important information about the table – its name, its fields, which of the fields is the primary key, the data types and any relevant properties.

In reality you would probably be given some sort of form to work with, like in the example shown in Figure 16.13.

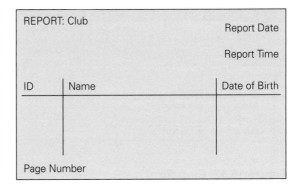

Figure 16.13 Application form

From this you would create the following structure (see Figure 16.14).

Table: Club	
* ID	AutoNumber
Name	Text, 30 characters
Date of Birth	Date/Time, Long Date

Figure 16.14 Structure

From this information the table can be created.

Screen designs (input, output)

In addition to designing the structure a developer also needs to design the screens the user will see and use – specifically the **input** screen (often a form) and the **output** screen (often a report). This design can be computer generated as in the examples below or can be hand drawn.

FORM: Club

ID

Name

Date of Birth

Figure 16.15 Form design

REPORT: Club

Report Date

Report Time

ID	Name	Date of Birth

Page Number

Figure 16.16 Report design

Once the design has been recorded, development of the database can begin.

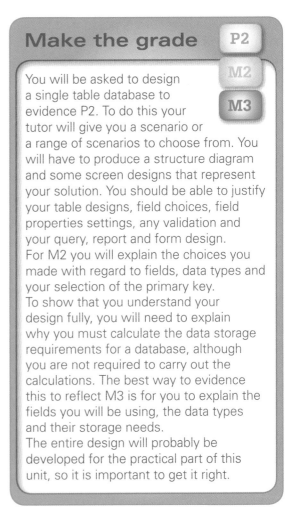

Make the grade   P2   M2   M3

You will be asked to design a single table database to evidence P2. To do this your tutor will give you a scenario or a range of scenarios to choose from. You will have to produce a structure diagram and some screen designs that represent your solution. You should be able to justify your table designs, field choices, field properties settings, any validation and your query, report and form design.

For M2 you will explain the choices you made with regard to fields, data types and your selection of the primary key.

To show that you understand your design fully, you will need to explain why you must calculate the data storage requirements for a database, although you are not required to carry out the calculations. The best way to evidence this to reflect M3 is for you to explain the fields you will be using, the data types and their storage needs.

The entire design will probably be developed for the practical part of this unit, so it is important to get it right.

16.2.3 Creating tables

This section will cover the following grading criteria:

Creating tables

When you first create a database, you will need to name it before you start. Click on the Microsoft Access 2007® icon.

Then under New Blank Database click on Blank Database and enter the File Name: Kids Club. Now click on Create.

Figure 16.17 Create

The system automatically opens the first table and creates an **ID field**.

Figure 16.18 New table

We need to add the remaining fields and change any relevant properties. We will do this in the **Design View**. To get to the Design View, click on Table1: Table underneath All Tables and then **right click** to bring up the menu.

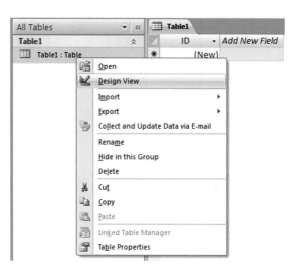

Figure 16.19 Menu for Design View

When you click on Design View, the system immediately asks you to save the table and name it. It suggests the name of Table1. Simply delete the suggested name and type in Club. Click OK.

Fields

You can now add the other fields and set their data types and properties.

Notice the little key beside the ID field (this means it is the primary key so the data in it will be unique).

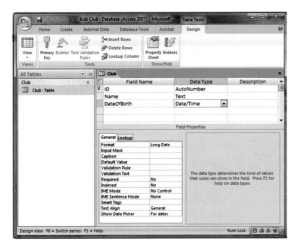

Figure 16.20 Design View

Do not forget to adjust the text field to accommodate 30 characters as that is what you said it would be in the structure.

Data types

The data types need to be set for each of the fields.

Activity C

Data types

There are four main data types: AutoNumber, Text, Numeric and Date/Time. Copy and complete the following table. Input the data type, describe it and then give some examples of that data type (for example, a text example would be A or a).

Data type	Description	Example values

Check that the data types are set correctly for the fields in your database.

Field properties

Remember that you do not only set data types, but you can also change the properties of a data type. Let us compare the field properties of two different data types – Text and Date/Time (see Figure 16.21).

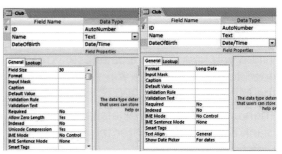

Figure 16.21 Comparing Text and Date/Time properties

Text fields are 'sized' – this is known as the field **length**.

Date fields can be **formatted**. In Figure 16.21 the format has been chosen as Long Date, so the date would look like this: 21 September 2000. As a Short Date, it would look like this: 21/09/2000.

For this example we will use a Long Date.

Giving a field a **default value** means that a pre-chosen value will always be displayed unless it is changed by the user. In Figure 16.22, the default value has been set as Now(). This means – put in today's date!

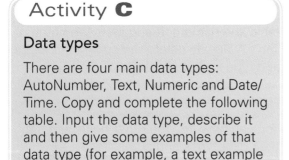

Figure 16.22 Default value

The **fieldname** should always be carefully chosen for two reasons.

- The name of the field should represent the data that is being stored in it. For example, a field named DateOfBirth should store dates of birth and a field named Addresses should store addresses! How confusing would it be if the DateOfBirth field stored the addresses and the Addresses field stored the dates of birth?
- By naming fields sensibly, creating and running queries will be much easier!

Validation

The simplest validation action is making a field **not NULL**. This forces the user to input a value, and without a value the record will not be saved and the user cannot move on!

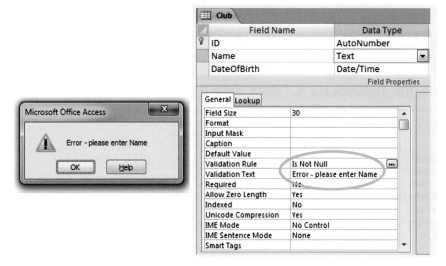

Figure 16.23 Validation

Validation can be actioned on most data types; for example it could be used on dates of birth, telephone numbers or post codes – in fact on any field that is essential to the system.

You should experiment with validation rules, but be prepared to spend time developing them as they do not always work as expected!

Modification

You must be *very* careful if you find you need to modify your database because if you make a mistake, you could lose some or all of your data.

For example, if you decided that you had made a mistake and that the text field you had created needed to be a number field, then when you change it in the Design View of your table and you attempt to switch back to the Sheet view, you will see some kind of alert (Figure 16.24).

Figure 16.24 Modification alert

This is warning you what will happen. The error messages are slightly different depending on how you try to modify the table.

It is easy, however, to add fields if you need to. In our example we are going to add a Gender field so that we can identify whether the individuals in the database are male (M) or female (F). We are also going to limit the input to M or F.

Field Name	Data Type
🔑 ID	AutoNumber
Name	Text
DateOfBirth	Date/Time
Gender (M or F)	Text ▾

General	Lookup
Field Size	2
Format	
Input Mask	
Caption	
Default Value	
Validation Rule	= "M" Or "F"
Validation Text	Please enter M or F

Figure 16.25 Adding a field

16.2.4 Naming objects

How to name

Just as it is good practice to give your fields sensible names, you should also do the same with the objects in your database like tables, forms, queries and reports.

Later in this unit we will create some forms, queries and reports so you must make sure you understand how best to name them. For example, if you remember with the Kids Club we created a single table. When naming it we called it Club and when saving we added Table. This means it is the Club Table. Similarly in the example in Figure 16.26 we have created a query on member ages, an input form for the club table and a report on members.

Naming the objects in this way makes it obvious what they are (the little icons beside each object also help!).

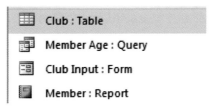

Figure 16.26 Naming

Why it is important

Giving your objects and fields sensible names means that your database will be much more organised. You will be able to find tables, queries and reports more easily. This is particularly important as your database grows and you add more tables.

Making it appropriate

Tables and forms are usually easy to name, but queries and reports can be more difficult because you are likely to have many more queries and reports than tables and forms! This can mean that at times a name for a query or report might be quite long. For example:

Members aged between 11 and 13: Query
Members 13 or older: Report

Just think carefully about your database and how you design it. This should help you avoid silly mistakes.

16.2.5 Data storage requirements

Legal requirements

Every IT professional should know and understand that there are laws that influence how and why data is stored. The main focus of these regulations is around information about people.

The **Data Protection Act 1998** replaced the original Data Protection Act from 1984. It sets out how companies collect, store and use the data that they gather as part of their day-to-day activities.

In principle, the main points of the act are:

- Data about individuals should be gathered fairly and legally.
- Individuals should be informed about the data that is being stored and how it will be used by the organisation.
- The 1998 version of the Data Protection Act now includes guidance on information held in both manual and electronic form.
- It requires that personal data must be accurate and up to date.
- It requires that any incorrect data must be correctly edited or deleted from the system.
- Data must only be kept for as long as it is needed (and then it should be deleted or destroyed).
- Organisations must protect data and keep it safe from those not authorised to access it.

The final important point of the Act also covers data that is transferred, particularly overseas. The law says that the data *must not* be transferred to a country which does not itself have legislation similar to that in the UK to protect the data.

Activity D

Data protection

Working with a partner, create an A3 poster about the Data Protection Act 1998.

Illustrate your poster by including images of at least three places where you think data is being kept about you!

Estimation

Activity E

Estimating

We have already considered how we calculate the potential size of a database in section 16.1.1.

Calculate how much storage each record in our Kids Club database will need. If we have 50 records in our database, how much storage will be used?

Discuss your answer with your teacher.

16.2.6 Testing

One of the most important aspects of developing any IT solution (hardware, software, website, network etc.) is that the solution itself is tested thoroughly to make sure it is fully working. So, in each case you will become used to creating test plans that test the solution properly.

For a database, we need to make sure that we check all of the forms, queries and reports. We will also need to test any validation in any database tables.

Essentially, we will create mini test plans to test every part of the system, one object at a time.

Test plan

To record the planned tests a test plan is completed. Each of the tests is given a **test number**, what is being tested is then explained, a **test description** then lays out how the test will be carried out (and will also record the data that will be used in the test if that is applicable). The **actual results** of the test are recorded, together with the **actions required** to fix any problems found.

TEST PLAN TEMPLATE

Test subject (e.g. database table) ....

Date of test   ....

Test Number	What is being tested	Test Description	Actual results of test	Actions required

Figure 16.27 A test plan template

Test data

A good developer will think carefully about the data that is used in the test. Here are some basic guidelines on what data should and could be used.

- **Normal data** – this is the type of data that would be expected to be input when the system is being used normally, for example a date in a date of birth field.
- **Extreme data** – this is data that is less likely to be input, for example, an age of 105. This would not be impossible, but it would be unlikely!

- **Erroneous data** – this is data that is intentionally incorrect (such as characters where numbers are expected and vice versa), to check that the system can handle these inputs.

Databases are usually tested with **dummy** (made-up) data, but eventually the developer should use real or 'live' data that is provided by the system users.

Checking data

There are various ways of **checking** that the data that has been input is accurate.

Just as with any other document created in modern software, Access® has its own **spell-checking** facilities.

Unlike Word®, however, notice that the dialogue box offers the user the opportunity to ignore a field. In this case the button reads Ignore 'Name' Field. If clicked, the names in the column will be ignored. This can be very useful.

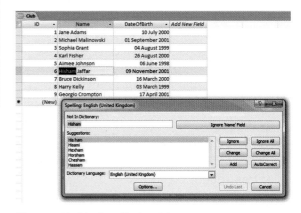

Figure 16.28 Spell checking

Other methods of checking include **sorting** the data, maybe into **alphabetical** or **chronological** (by date) order and checking it visually, comparing the display or a printout with the original source data.

The layout, titles, alignment and content of all reports and queries should be checked carefully to make sure that the information is accurate.

Query processing and output

To test a query it is likely that you will run the query and check the result manually against the original data. It is often helpful to have an annotated (marked up) print of the original data so that the query output can be compared. In the example shown in Figure 16.29 each of the records that should appear on the query result have been marked with a star.

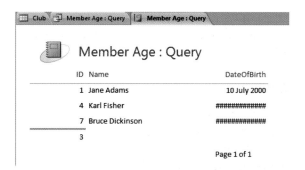

Figure 16.29 Original data

In this query example we are going to search for all records where the date of birth is:

> Between #01/01/2000# And #31/12/2000#

When the query is run (or actioned), the results appear (see Figure 16.30).

Figure 16.30 Query results

Now the two can be compared.

Report output

In this example we are going to use the member age query and simply turn it into a report. How we do this will be covered later in the unit. For the moment you should simply consider the report that the system has output.

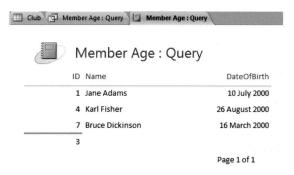

Figure 16.31 Query report with hashes

To test the output you would again need something to compare the results with and we can use the original data that we used before. However, you should see immediately that although we can see the ID numbers and names, we cannot actually read the dates of birth because some of them are displayed as hashes.

Why is this? This is simply because in the design of the report, the date of birth field has not been made wide enough! Simply dragging and dropping the left-hand side of the field will solve the problem.

Figure 16.32 Query report with dates

16.2.7 Importing data

External sources

There are only two ways of getting data into a database:

- Type it in field by field, record by record.
- Import the data from another source.

When importing data from other databases, the process will probably be relatively straightforward as the data will already be organised. It may have to be converted to the new software before it is imported, however.

The two examples we are going to explore are importing from spreadsheets and from text files.

To demonstrate the process we have created a spreadsheet that has the same fields as our database and provides an additional three records.

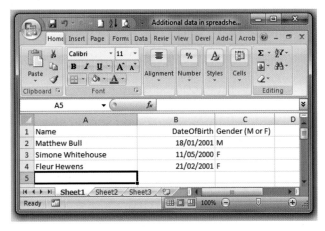

Figure 16.33 Additional data in spreadsheet form

We now open our table and click on the External Data tab and then on Excel® in the Import options.

Once the file to be imported has been identified, the user then needs to say what the system needs to do with the data: put it in a new table, add it to the end of the current records in a particular table, or create some sort of external link.

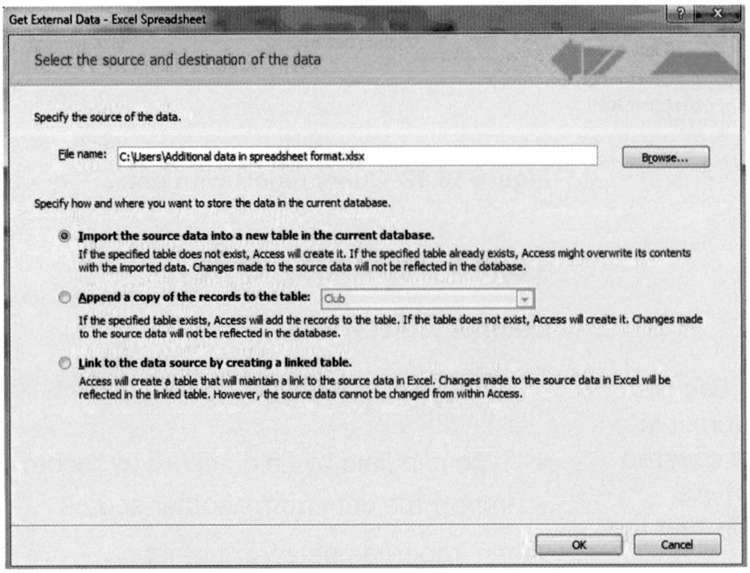

Figure 16.34 Import spreadsheet

We could try to append these spreadsheet rows to our 'Club' table but that can cause unexpected problems. In this instance we will import the source data into a new table in the current database and click OK. The system identifies immediately that our spreadsheet has more than one page and it asks us to clarify which worksheet we want to use. The data in each of the worksheets is visible if we click between them. We choose the relevant worksheet and click on Next. We now confirm whether or not the spreadsheet has row and column headings (in this instance the system has already made that decision for us so we do not change it).

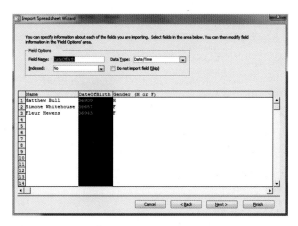

Figure 16.36 Setting fields

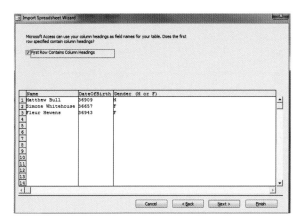

Figure 16.35 Confirm

When we click on Next the Spreadsheet Wizard gives us an opportunity to format the data types one by one. We do this by clicking into the relevant field.

When we click on Next again, the Wizard then lets us choose from three options in relation to primary keys. As the table where the data will eventually go has an AutoCounter, we do not want the Wizard to add a primary key so we choose No primary key and click Next.

On the final screen we have an option to give the imported data a suitable table name. We will choose 'Members spreadsheet' and click on Finish.

We can now open the Members spreadsheet table and copy the three records. Then we simply click on the Club table and paste.

ID	Name	DateOfBirth	Gender (M or F)
1	Jane Adams	10 July 2000	F
2	Michael Malinowski	01 September 2001	M
3	Sophia Grant	04 August 1999	F
4	Karl Fisher	26 August 2000	M
5	Aimee Johnson	06 June 1998	F
6	Hisham Jaffar	09 November 2001	M
7	Bruce Dickinson	16 March 2000	M
8	Harry Kelly	03 March 1999	M
9	Georgio Crompton	17 April 2001	M
10	Matthew Bull	18 January 2001	M
11	Simone Whitehouse	11 May 2000	F
12	Fleur Hewens	21 February 2001	F
*	(New)		

Figure 16.37 New records added

Even at this stage we can go back and add a further manual record (Figure 16.38).

11	Simone Whitehouse	11 May 2000	F
12	Fleur Hewens	21 February 2001	F
13	Sandra Roisl	01 March 1998	F

Figure 16.38 Another new record

We can then continue to import data. The second example is importing records we have created in Notepad® (as a text file). Notepad® is one of the accessories that are built into most versions of Windows®.

Figure 16.39 Additional data in text form

This time, we select the External Data tab, and then we choose Text File from the Import options.

The next dialogue box is the same as previously where you choose the source of the data and how you want the import handled (when imported into a new table). We click on Next.

This time we have slightly different dialogue boxes. In the next one that opens it is asking us questions about how the data is organised in the text file. We are using the **delimited** option, which means that each item of data is separated by a comma or a tab (in this case it is a comma).

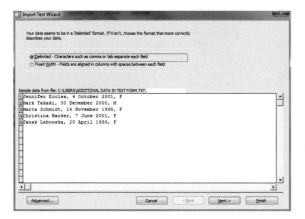

Figure 16.40 Confirm text

Then again, as previously, we go through a series of screens where we set data types etc. You *must*, in this instance, identify all fields as Text to make sure that they paste into your database correctly.

We are asked about the primary key and we select No primary key and finally we name our table 'Members text'.

Now we will need to change the data type of the Date of Birth field in our pasted table to Long date (to reflect the original table) and we can add our records to the Club table.

ID	Name	DateOfBirth	Gender (M or F)
1	Jane Adams	10 July 2000	F
2	Michael Malinowski	01 September 2001	M
3	Sophia Grant	04 August 1999	F
4	Karl Fisher	26 August 2000	M
5	Aimee Johnson	06 June 1998	F
6	Hisham Jaffar	09 November 2001	M
7	Bruce Dickinson	16 March 2000	M
8	Harry Kelly	03 March 1999	M
9	Georgio Crompton	17 April 2001	M
10	Matthew Bull	18 January 2001	M
11	Simone Whitehouse	11 May 2000	F
12	Fleur Hewens	21 February 2001	F
13	Sandra Roisl	01 March 1998	F
14	Jennifer Eccles	04 October 2001	F
15	Mark Takaki	30 December 2000	M
16	Marta Schmidt	14 November 1998	F
17	Christina Barker	07 June 2001	F
18	Janak Lebowska	20 April 1999	F

Figure 16.41 Final data

Deleting records is also easy. Simply open the table, highlight the record to be deleted and then press the Delete key. The record will be removed and you will be asked to confirm that you are sure (Figure 16.42).

![Microsoft Office Access dialog box. You are about to delete 1 record(s). If you click Yes, you won't be able to undo this Delete operation. Are you sure you want to delete these records? Yes / No buttons. Below are records: 11 Simone Whitehouse 11 May 2000 F; 12 Fleur Hewens 21 February 2001 F; 14 Jennifer Eccles 04 October 2001 F; 15 Mark Takaki 30 December 2000 M]

Figure 16.42 Deleting

Be very careful when you are deleting records that you are deleting the right ones, as there is no way of recovering deleted records once they have been erased.

16.3 Be able to use database software tools

16.3.1 Sort

The table is usually ordered by the ID (or the primary key) because that is the unique data in the database. However, you can organise or re-order the data in different ways.

Fields

To reorder a list based on dates of birth, for example, you open the table, click on the DateOfBirth field, then simply click on one of the **sorting icons** on the Home tab in the Sort & Filter options.

Figure 16.43 Sorting icons

It will reorder this list like this:

ID	Name	DateOfBirth	Gender (M or F)
5	Aimee Johnson	06 June 1998	F
16	Marta Schmidt	14 November 1998	F
8	Harry Kelly	03 March 1999	M
18	Janak Lebowska	20 April 1999	F
3	Sophia Grant	04 August 1999	F
7	Bruce Dickinson	16 March 2000	M
11	Simone Whitehouse	11 May 2000	F
1	Jane Adams	10 July 2000	F
4	Karl Fisher	26 August 2000	M
15	Mark Takaki	30 December 2000	M
10	Matthew Bull	18 January 2001	M
12	Fleur Hewens	21 February 2001	F
9	Georgio Crompton	17 April 2001	M
17	Christina Barker	07 June 2001	F
2	Michael Malinowski	01 September 2001	M
14	Jennifer Eccles	04 October 2001	F
6	Hisham Jaffar	09 November 2001	M
*	(New)		

Figure 16.44 Sorting by date of birth

Order

Data can be sorted in **ascending** order: A to Z (alphabetical) or 1 to 100 (numerical). It can be sorted in **descending** order: Z to A (alphabetical) or 100 to 1 (numerical). Dates can also be sorted in ascending or descending order.

Usually, when data is sorted, it is sorted for a reason, rather than just for the sake of it!

16.3.2 Queries

Queries **interrogate** the data in a database. This is how data is manipulated. It can be filtered based on specific criteria, sorted and then the user has a choice about what is actually displayed in the **query result**.

The query result is the output for display after a query has been executed.

Queries

Queries can be run based on a **single criterion** or **multiple criteria**, depending on what the user is trying to extract. To create a query, you can use the Query Wizard which is on the Create tab.

When creating a new query you will have to choose from four options. At this level you only need to know about Simple queries, so you will select the Simple Query Wizard.

Although the Wizard will allow you to select which table you wish to use as the basis of your query, and which fields you would like to include, it does not give you the opportunity to set any criteria. To do this, open the query in Design view after it has been created. Create a basic query using the Club table and selecting all available fields (just move all of them from the left to the right – from available to selected). Give it the name Club Query and choose the Modify the query design option (so that we can work with the criteria). Click on Finish.

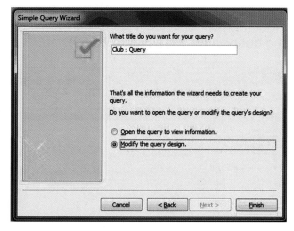

Figure 16.45 Query Wizard

Single criterion

What now follows is a series of queries that have been created to demonstrate how queries work. In the first query, we are going to filter the data to show only the male club members. To do this we simply key in M in the Gender (M or F) field, on the row marked Criteria.

Figure 16.46 Criterion

When the query is run, this is the result (Figure 16.47).

Figure 16.47 All the boys

This is known as a single criterion query as it only uses one criterion to filter the data.

Multiple criteria (AND and OR)

Alternatively, the user might wish to display all females **AND** only those who are born between two specific dates, say 1 January 2000 and 31 December 2000. The query would look like this (Figure 16.48):

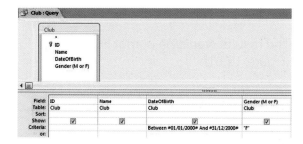

Figure 16.48 Two criteria

The results would look like this (Figure 16.49):

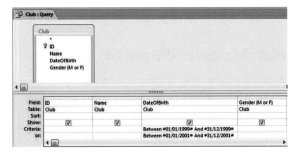

Figure 16.49 Girls born between 1 January 2000 and 31 December 2000

For a record to be included in the final results, both criteria would have had to have been met: female AND born between the given dates.

Another filter criterion is **OR**. This is where there are again two or more criteria, but only one of these needs to be met for the results to be included in the output list. Let us have a look at an example using the date. The user wants a list of all members whose dates of birth fall in two separate years. This has to be an OR, because no one can be born in two different years!

The query would look like this (Figure 16.50):

Figure 16.50 Born between two date ranges

The results would be output like this (Figure 16.51):

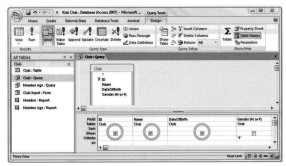

Figure 16.51 Output of the OR query

Notice that only those born in 1999 and 2001 are included in the list.

Selecting fields

In addition to being able to use criteria to filter the data, the user has a choice about which fields will actually be displayed when the query is run (see Figure 16.52).

Figure 16.52 Choosing display fields

As can be seen in Figure 16.52, on the Show row, the check boxes are all ticked apart from the box in the Gender (M or F) field. This means that when the query is run all fields will be displayed in the output, apart from Gender.

The query result now looks like this (Figure 16.53):

ID	Name	DateOfBirth
1	Jane Adams	10 July 2000
3	Sophia Grant	04 August 1999
5	Aimee Johnson	06 June 1998
11	Simone Whitehouse	11 May 2000
12	Fleur Hewens	21 February 2001
14	Jennifer Eccles	04 October 2001
16	Marta Schmidt	14 November 1998
17	Christina Barker	07 June 2001
18	Janak Lebowska	20 April 1999
*	(New)	

Club : Query

Figure 16.53 Query result on female members

Sorting

As we have seen in the examples, data in databases can be sorted by date, numbers or alphabetically to suit different needs.

Referring back to the most recent query, the data that is extracted after running a query can also be sorted by adding a sort option on the Sort row of the query (Figure 16.54):

Figure 16.54 Sort descending

The query result now looks like this (Figure 16.55):

ID	Name	DateOfBirth
14	Jennifer Eccles	04 October 2001
17	Christina Barker	07 June 2001
12	Fleur Hewens	21 February 2001
1	Jane Adams	10 July 2000
11	Simone Whitehouse	11 May 2000
3	Sophia Grant	04 August 1999
18	Janak Lebowska	20 April 1999
16	Marta Schmidt	14 November 1998
5	Aimee Johnson	06 June 1998
*	(New)	

Club : Query

Figure 16.55 Sort descending result

To get a good understanding of manipulating data, you will need lots of practice!

Improving efficiency – using shortcuts

The most commonly used shortcut in Access® is a **Lookup**. If a Lookup is used, the user does not need to input a value, but will be able to choose one from a list. This is useful as it ensures data accuracy, data consistency and it takes less time for the user to achieve the input!

The Lookup tab is situated next to the General tab on the field properties of most data types.

When the Lookup tab is selected you can see that the default is a **Text Box**. That is a box where you simply key in the text. The other options available to you are a List Box and a Combo Box. For the purposes of this exercise we are going to select a List Box.

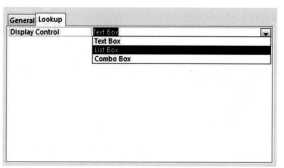

Figure 16.56 List box

The dialogue box will now change to appear like the one shown in Figure 16.57.

General Lookup	
Display Control	List Box
Row Source Type	Table/Query
Row Source	Table/Query
Bound Column	Value List
Column Count	Field List
Column Heads	No
Column Widths	
Allow Multiple Values	No
Allow Value List Edits	No
List Items Edit Form	
Show Only Row Source V	No

Figure 16.57 Setting up a value list

In the Row Source Type box we now select Value List, and again the dialogue box changes (Figure 16.58).

General	Lookup	
Display Control	List Box
Row Source Type	Value List
Row Source	M;F
Bound Column	1
Column Count	1
Column Heads	No
Column Widths	
Allow Multiple Values	No
Allow Value List Edits	No
List Items Edit Form	
Show Only Row Source V	No

Figure 16.58 Value list options

Into the Row Source box we now simply key in the values we wish to select from in the List Box, each separated by a semi colon. When the user now inputs data into the table, the list will appear as a dropdown box and the user can simply select from the options.

ID	Name	DateOfBirth	Gender (M or F)	A
1	Jane Adams	10 July 2000	F	
2	Michael Malinowski	01 September 2001	M	
3	Sophia Grant	04 August 1999	F	
4	Karl Fisher	26 August 2000	M	
5	Aimee Johnson	06 June 1998	F	
6	Hisham Jaffar	09 November 2001	M	
7	Bruce Dickinson	16 March 2000	M	
8	Harry Kelly	03 March 1999	M	
9	Georgio Crompton	17 April 2001	M	
10	Matthew Bull	18 January 2001	M	
11	Simone Whitehouse	11 May 2000	F	
12	Fleur Hewens	21 February 2001	F	
14	Jennifer Eccles	04 October 2001	F	
15	Mark Takaki	30 December 2000	M	
16	Marta Schmidt	14 November 1998	F	
17	Christina Barker	07 June 2001	F	
18	Janak Lebowska	20 April 1999		
*	(New)			

Record: 18 of 18   No Filter   Search

M
F

Figure 16.59 The list of options

Meaningful data

Data is usually manipulated and interrogated for a reason. Why, for example, might the Kids Club staff want to see a list of dates of birth in a particular month? They could produce the list to remind staff which of the children have birthdays, so that they can celebrate!

16.3.3 Reports

Benefits

The main benefits of creating reports are that they present the information in a structured and professional way. With a report you can add titles, page numbers, information about who created the report; you can change spacing, colours of fonts etc.

When working with reports you can view the report from four perspectives:

* Report View – is the on-screen version of the report.
* Print Preview – as it will appear on a printed page.
* Layout View – how it is laid out (you can adjust individual rows and columns here and check how it will look before it goes to print).
* Design View – in this view you only see the objects (headings etc.) and you cannot see the data. You can change headings and column headings in both Layout and Design View.

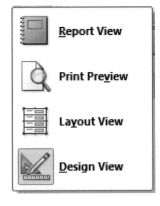

Figure 16.60 Types of view

Figure 16.61 shows a report made from the main Club table.

Figure 16.61 Membership report

Always check your reports very carefully to make sure that everything is as it should be. Sloppy reports give a sloppy impression!

Role of tables and queries

The simplest way to create a report is to use a query or table that has already been prepared. The table, for example, could already have been sorted or the query could already have filtered the records (using criteria) to display the required results.

Automatic creation – Wizards

As with tables and queries, users have a choice whether to set up reports themselves (with no help from the software) or whether to use the relevant Wizard.

Creating a report is the one aspect of database development that is significantly easier if the Wizard is used. This is because the Wizard will align the report automatically and create an appropriate layout. The user then merely needs to tweak the report, adding any required headings or labels, or moving aspects of the form around.

Layouts

When using the Wizard a number of options will be presented from which the user can choose, including the style that should be used for the report. You will also choose whether to display the report in portrait or landscape orientation.

Activity F

Orientation

Investigate the difference between portrait and landscape orientation (if you do not already know) and to show you understand the difference, explain it to another member of your class.

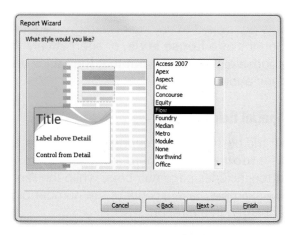

Figure 16.62 Report styles

Do not worry if you make a mistake. You can either Cancel and start again or you can follow the process to the end of the report and modify it later.

Adding

It is important to understand that reports are linked dynamically to the table or query they were created from. This means that if you delete or edit records and re-run the report, the changes in the data will be reflected.

Similarly, if the report is created from a query and the query changes (the criteria on filters or the sort order for example) the report will change accordingly.

Editing

In Report View you can also edit your report, including changing the style. To do this, click on Report View then on the Format tab, before choosing a new format from the selection available in the AutoFormat options.

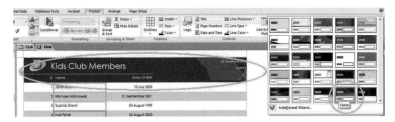

Figure 16.63 Using AutoFormat

It is possible that an organisation will adopt one of the options as a **house style**, or alternatively the user can just choose a style and layout that they think will appeal to their audience.

Special fields

At the bottom of the report you will notice what is known as a **footer** – in fact there are two of them. The page footer often includes page numbers, while the report footer will, for example, have a count of the number of records that appeared in the report.

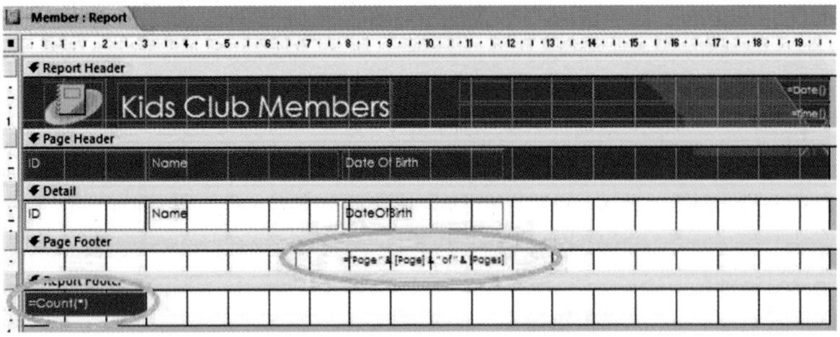

Figure 16.64 Report design view

These additional bits of data are known as **special fields**.

Look at Figure 16.65.

Figure 16.65 Report footer

The basic Access® report templates use the in-built function =NOW() to insert the date into the report automatically (see if you can find this on the Report design view image).

Multiple criteria

In a more complicated table such as one with more fields, it is possible to apply a range of criteria to a report. For example, Figure 16.66 shows some sales records.

ID	Name	Area	Total Sales
1	Arthur, Felicity	South East	£19,586.26
2	Bevan, Tom	Midlands	£18,715.67
3	Obaku, Anton	North West	£15,781.65
4	Yar, Ruth	South West	£18,987.22
5	Quinnan, Steve	South East	£13,654.54
6	Pinner, Yvonne	North East	£23,178.97
7	Khan, Ashram	Wales	£21,875.31
8	Hester, Claire	North West	£22,266.49
9	Hanson, Drew	North East	£20,004.28
10	Brooke, Melanie	South West	£19,874.66
11	Knight, Amanda	Midlands	£17,356.24
12	Thomas, Paul	Wales	£18,333.77
13	Peach, Michael	North East	£21,780.20
14	Ashwood, David	Wales	£22,437.00
15	Nakvarich, Bazyli	North West	£18,787.14
16	Chen, Jennifer	Midlands	£19,387.21

Figure 16.66 Sales data

We will now create a report where the data is organised in ascending order of geographical location and also in descending order of sales total (Figure 16.67).

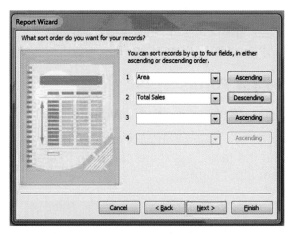

Figure 16.67 Sales Report Wizard

When the report is run, the results are now organised like this (Figure 16.68):

Figure 16.68 Report results

Notice that the records are grouped **by area and then** within each area the total sales are **in reverse** (descending) **order**.

This type of report is easy to create, more or less at the touch of a button!

As reports are quite complex, the user or database developer should formally write down what each report is designed to achieve and include it as part of the technical documentation.

16.3.4 Forms

Automatic form creation – Wizards

While we have seen data entered directly into the table, it is more common to create user input forms.

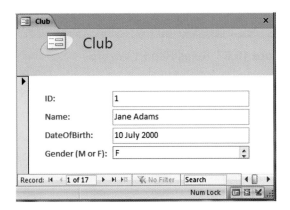

Figure 16.69 Input form

In Access 2007® you have a number of options to choose from that will help you make a form. You must begin by clicking on the Create tab, and then choosing from the Forms options (the Wizard is on the More Forms dropdown menu.

Figure 16.70 Create forms

Once created, the user can click on the Form Design to make changes to layout and style.

To use the Wizard, you simply click on it and then follow the prompts through the whole process. You will be asked, for example, which fields you want to include on the form.

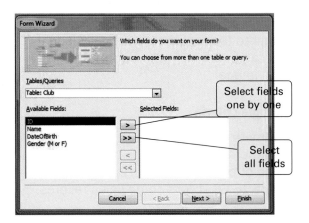

Figure 16.71 Form Wizard

You will be asked how you want to view the data, in a column or as a table. You will also be asked what sort of background you would like for your form. Finally, you will be asked to name your form.

Formatting forms

Once created, the labels on the form can be formatted. To do this you must be in Design View and you click on the Property Sheet.

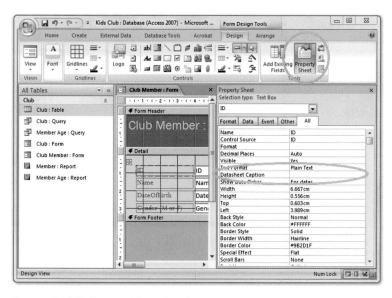

Figure 16.72 Formatting the form

Titles can be changed, **labels** (additional information about the inputs, for example) can be added and the **data entry order** (the order in which the fields are accessed) can be changed.

You might have to change the tab order if you add a field manually to your form after you have created it. To access this option, you must be in Design View and you place the cursor in the form header (or in the detail), right click and choose Tab Order.

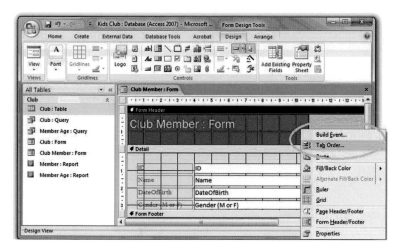

Figure 16.73 Form tab order

When the tab order option is clicked, you will be presented with a list of fields (Figure 16.74).

Figure 16.74 Selecting the order

Changing the order is easy and is described in the dialogue box.

16.3.5 Exporting data

Do not forget that the results of both queries and reports can be exported into other databases as well as into spreadsheet workbooks. This is useful because databases do not have the same functionality as spreadsheets, for example, which means that once exported you can do even more with the data, such as create charts and graphs.

To demonstrate this, we will now export the results of a query and a report into Microsoft Excel®.

Query results

Using the gender query created in the Kids Club database to extract female club members, we will now export the results to a spreadsheet. Having clicked on the relevant query, we now click on External Data and then on the Excel® icon on the Export options.

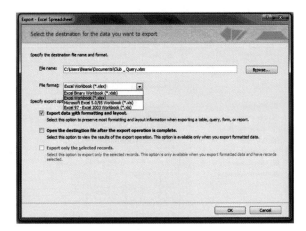

Figure 16.75 Exporting to a spreadsheet

As part of the options, you will need to name the file (and say where it should be stored), you will choose the file format (or version of Excel® you will be using the file in) and then choose from the remaining options (as they are check boxes, you can choose more than one).

Once you click OK the exported file will be available for use.

Report results

Report results can be exported as Word® or text files or as HTML documents. The process is almost identical as for the query results. In earlier versions of Microsoft Access®, the reports could also be exported to Excel®, but this is not a feature that is supported in Microsoft Access 2007®.

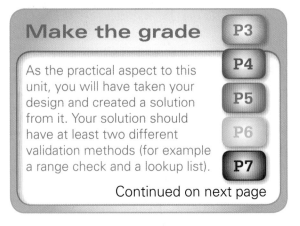

Make the grade   P3

P4

As the practical aspect to this unit, you will have taken your design and created a solution from it. Your solution should have at least two different validation methods (for example a range check and a lookup list).

P5

P6

P7

Continued on next page

Continued...
| M4 |
| M5 |
| D1 |
| D2 |

For P3, P4, P5, P6 and P7 you will have created a solution with at least two forms (based on tables or queries).

Your evidence will largely come from your electronic database file or printouts. In addition, your tutor might observe you or you might be asked to present aspects of your database supported by notes.

For M4 and M5 you must provide evidence that data has been sorted and that at least two reports have been developed that display meaningful information (including headings and good layout).

D1 will be evidenced through your testing documentation. You could complete the testing plan and support it with screen printouts of your testing activity.

The final criterion (D2) requires one further level of explanation, by explaining the benefits of creating and using reports. What benefits do they bring to a business? Give some examples.

16.3.6 User documentation

This section will cover the following grading criteria: P8 D3

User guide

Any developed software solution should have a user guide. In the past, the user guide would have been a published document of some type that had the following:

- Setting up instructions (how to install and get started)
- Instructions for using the features (using the functionality of the software)
- Troubleshooting guide (what to check if things go wrong)
- Technical information (information about the table, query, form and report design that the user might find useful if they need to change something).

Today, however, it is more usual to have an online user guide or an electronic version of a user guide on a CD.

Activity G

User guides

To make sure you always have the right support when you use software, find an online user guide for each of the software products you use and record the web address (URL) in a table like the one below.

Software	URL
Microsoft Access 2007®	http://office.microsoft.com/en-us/access-help/

Suggesting improvements to your database

The final aspect of designing and developing any solution is identifying and justifying improvements that could be made to the system.

This could be additional **functions**, adding **extra fields** to improve the information that is available once the data is manipulated, improvements to reports or queries, more **shortcuts**, better user **prompts** or anything else that you feel might make your solution better.

To do this, it is often helpful if you have been able to find someone else to use your database and to give you some feedback.

Make the grade   P8 D3

Your user guide will provide all the necessary evidence for P8, but do not forget to include both technical information (meant for database administrators) and user guidance (intended for users).

Continued on next page

Continued...

When the whole solution is finished, you will be asked to talk about your database and suggest and justify some improvements. You will need to justify a range of improvements to meet D3.

This particular unit has 16 criteria to meet: 8 Pass, 5 Merit and 3 Distinction.

For a **Pass** you must achieve **all 8** Pass criteria.

For a **Merit** you must achieve **all 8** Pass **and all 5** Merit criteria.

For a **Distinction** you must achieve **all 8** Pass, **all 5** Merit criteria **and all 3** Distinction criteria.

Activity H

Quiz

Answers to the quiz questions can be found at the back of the book.

1. Name three advantages and three disadvantages of using databases.
2. Name two of the four database objects.
3. Name the four primary data types.
4. What does validation do?
5. Which view does the user use to input data into a table (if there is no input form)?
6. What is the default field size for text (you might need to check inside your version of Access®)?
7. What does a list box do and why are they used?
8. What does a Wizard do?
9. What does a query do?
10. What is a footer? Give an example of something you might find in a footer.
11. What is landscape view?
12. What is portrait view?

Achieving Success

In order to achieve each unit, you will complete a series of coursework activities. Each time you hand in work, your tutor will return this to you with a record of your achievement.

Help with assessment

Your tutor will give you one or more assignments that you will complete as coursework. This could consist of:

- Presentations
- Databases and test plans
- Witness statements of an observed practical exercise
- Web pages
- Report/User guide or document
- Screenshots
- Verbal evaluation of your solution.

You should read the guidance given for each of the criteria (shown across the unit) carefully and remember to check your work.

Further reading

Textbooks

Heathcote, F. *Basic Access 2000–2003* (Payne-Gallway Publishers, 2004) ISBN 1904467784

Heathcote, F. *Further Access 2000–2003* (Payne-Gallway Publishers, 2004) ISBN 1904467741

Oppel, A. *Databases Demystified: A Self-teaching Guide* (McGraw-Hill Osborne, 2004) ISBN 0072253649

Websites

http://office.microsoft.com/training/training.aspx?assetid=rc061181381033

www.tutorialsforopenoffice.org/category_index/base.html

Unit 17
Website development

Learning objectives
By the end of this unit you should:

1. Know web architecture and components
2. Understand how websites can be used by organisations
3. Be able to design website components
4. Be able to create website components.

In order to pass this unit, the evidence you present for assessment needs to demonstrate that you can meet all of the above learning outcomes for this unit. The criteria below show the levels of achievement required to pass this unit.

To achieve a **pass** grade the evidence must show that the learner is able to:	To achieve a **merit** grade the evidence must show that, in addition to the pass criteria, the learner is able to:	To achieve a **distinction** the evidence must show that, in addition to the pass and merit criteria, the learner is able to:
P1 Identify the hardware and software components which enable internet and web functionality		
P2 Describe the role of web architecture in website communications		
P3 Explain the uses of websites in organisations		
P4 Design website components, considering client needs	**M1** Explain the techniques that can be used on web pages to aid user access to information	**D1** Evaluate different design features of a website
P5 Use appropriate formatting tools, styles and templates to prepare content for the website	**M2** Describe the use of interactive websites and what techniques can be used to provide interactivity	
P6 Create website components to meet client needs	**M3** Use automated features in web development software	
P7 Review website components, suggesting improvements	**M4** Refine website components based on user feedback	**D2** Explain how a created website meets the defined requirements

Introduction

The world wide web has become the world's foremost platform for communication, education, entertainment and collaborative working. It is built from a combination of hardware and software technologies which you will learn about in this unit. Website development is a skill which is becoming sought after as the web expands and more and more companies are seeing the commercial benefits of having an online presence. This unit should provide you with a basic grounding in this subject.

You will be assessed through coursework which could be in the form of:

- Presentations
- Practical sessions which may be photographed, videoed or witnessed
- Printed or electronic images
- Screen captures
- Websites and designs
- Blogs
- Podcasts.

17.1 Know web architecture and components

This section will cover the following grading criterion:

P1

17.1.1 Components

Before you start web development it is useful to know the different types of hardware and software components that work together to provide users with website content.

Hardware

Key types of hardware include: web servers, mail servers, proxy servers and routers. These will be dealt with in further detail below.

Web servers will deal with multiple requests (from different users) simultaneously. Web servers are normally protected from hackers and viruses by powerful firewalls.

Key terms

A **web server** is a computer system with a good hardware specification which is used to run a web server application (see software).

The web server receives HTTP (hypertext transfer protocol) requests for web pages and associated assets (such as images and sounds) and transmits these back to the client computer system which has asked for them.

A **mail server** is a term used to describe the hardware which receives incoming email from local network users and remote senders and also forwards outgoing email for delivery to remote networks. It uses a software application also called a mail server to do this.

A **proxy server** is often used to filter and cache requests made from web browser client systems to remote web servers. The proxy can decide to either change (or ignore) the request or quickly serve a recently 'saved' version of the requested web page rather than contacting the remote server for a 'fresh' copy.

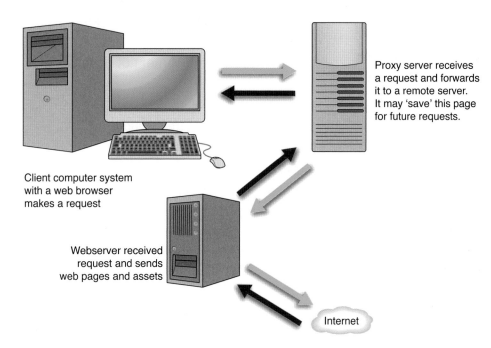

Proxy server receives a request and forwards it to a remote server. It may 'save' this page for future requests.

Client computer system with a web browser makes a request

Webserver received request and sends web pages and assets

Internet

Figure 17.1 A proxy server

Proxy servers are often used to:

* Circumvent parental/company/school/college security
* Speed up repeated web page access
* Filter and log requests made by client systems
* Block access to undesirable content, providing alternatives instead.

> ## Key term
>
> A **router** is a complex networking device, making decisions about which of several possible paths should be used to relay network data between the servers and the client computer systems. Web pages move between many different routers in their journey from web server to web browser.

Software

In addition, different types of software are required in order to provide website content. These include web server applications, web browser applications and email clients.

Key term

A **web server application** is a powerful piece of software which runs on web server hardware. Its job is to host requested web pages and assets (such as images, sounds etc.) and 'serve' them to remote computer systems which have requested them.

Popular web hosting applications include:

- Apache® HTTP server
- Microsoft® Internet Information Services (IIS)
- Oracle iPlanet® Web Server.

Key term

A **web browser application** is a client which lets the user browse the world wide web by requesting web pages and assets via a protocol called HTTP. Once the pages and assets have been received from the web server it is the browser's job to render these on screen.

There are many different web browsers and the best websites are designed to cater for those most commonly used. At the time of going to print these are the most popular web browsers world-wide:

- Microsoft® Internet Explorer (48 per cent)
- Mozilla Firefox® (31 per cent)
- Google Chrome® (13 per cent)
- Apple Safari® (5 per cent)
- Opera® (2 per cent)

There are many different **email clients** used worldwide and they all have similar basic functionality. They all, for example:

- Compose new emails
- Read incoming emails

- Manage multiple email folders
- Send read receipts
- Permit the attachment of documents to outgoing mails
- Maintain an address book for the user.

Popular email clients include:

- Microsoft Outlook®
- Mozilla Thunderbird®.

Make the grade   P1

P1 asks you to identify the hardware and software components which enable internet and web functionality. Identification usually involves listing the relevant technologies and you can find out about these by reading through section 17.1.1. Do not forget to include both software and hardware and clearly label which is which!

17.1.2 Web architecture

Web is an abbreviation of the term 'world wide web' (WWW).

Key term

The **web** is the most visual aspect of the internet. Created from millions of web pages written in HTML, these pages can contain text, images, sounds, video and hyperlinks.

The hyperlink is particularly important as it provides the 'stepping stone' to another resource – somewhere in the world – that the user might want to see.

Architecture is a way of describing how things are put together, so in terms of looking at the architecture of the WWW, we have to turn our attention to a number of different organisations and concepts.

Internet service providers (ISP)

> ### Key term
> An **internet service provider** or **ISP** is a company which provides a paying customer with access to the internet and the WWW via its own routers and network. Some ISPs also provide additional services such as website hosting and email facilities.

ISPs in the United Kingdom include:

* Talk Talk
* Virgin Media
* British Telecom (BT)
* Sky
* Orange.

Web hosting services

For further information about web hosting services see section 17.4.4, Publishing.

Domain structure

All web servers exist within a **domain** of some kind. The domain is used a bit like a house address as it helps other computer systems find it and 'post' requests to it. Just like an address, domains have a number of components – this is similar to an address having a street name, city or town name, county name and postcode.

Domains are organised into a **structure** which is set as an international standard (see Figure 17.2).

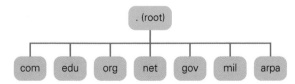

Figure 17.2 Domain structure with the original seven top level domains

The top of the domain structure is called the **root** and it is represented by a . (dot). Below the root have traditionally been seven **top level domains (TLDs)**:

* **.org** (non-profit organisations)
* **.net** (ISPs)
* **.edu** (education)
* **.gov** (government)
* **.com** (company)
* **.arpa** (ARPA)
* **.mil** (military).

> ### Key term
> **ARPA** is the US Department of Defense's Advanced Research Projects Agency. They were instrumental in the creation of ARPAnet in the late 1960s which evolved into the internet that you know today.

In 2003 seven new ones were added:

> **.aero**, **.biz**, **.coop**, **.info**, **.museum**, **.name** and **.pro**.

In addition, there are TLDs for countries such as **.uk** (for United Kingdom) and **.de** (for Deutschland, the German name for Germany).

A **fully qualified domain name (FQDN)** for a web server can therefore be written like this:

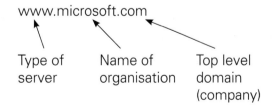

Domain name registrars

A **domain name registrar** is a company which is allowed to manage the assignment and registration of internet domain names in a particular country. In the

UK, the following companies can register .uk domain names for you:

- www.uk2.net
- www.names.co.uk

… and there are many more. Each company will have a **search facility** which will allow you to check whether a particular domain name (such as btec-first.co.uk) is available (see Figure 17.3).

Figure 17.3 Checking the availability of a domain name

17.1.3 Web functionality

Web 2.0

> **Key term**
>
> Web 2.0 is a shift in usage rather than a physical upgrade to the world wide web. Web 2.0 is a term first used by the publisher O'Reilly in 2004 and it is used to describe a collection of new approaches in how users interact with the web.

The new approaches have happened because of improvements to the underlying software which powers the web and changes in users' online habits.

The key features of Web 2.0 are based on greater interactivity, user-centred content and the development of virtual communities.

The following sites and functionality could be described as belonging to Web 2.0:

Blogs and **microblogs**, such as

- Twitter
- Wordpress
- LiveJournal
- Google Blog

Video sharing, for example

- Youtube
- Vimeo
- Hulu
- Google Video

Online photosharing, for example Flickr

Social networking sites, such as

- Facebook
- Bebo
- Myspace
- LinkedIn
- Friends Reunited

Social bookmarking, for example

- Stumbleupon
- Digg
- Del.icio.us
- Reddit

Podcasting

Key terms

Weblog, or '**blog**' for short, is a word used as both a noun and a verb. As a noun it describes the online diary of thoughts, feelings and topics of interest that a user will post to as they go about their daily life. Used as a verb, blog is the act of doing the updating, for example, 'she's blogging'.

Microblogs like Twitter limit users to 'tweets' of up to 140 characters at a time.

Bloglines (www.bloglines.com) is a news aggregator which will group together all your favourite blogs from across the world wide web (see Figure 17.4).

Figure 17.4 Bloglines

Online applications

Users are used to working alone with application software on their own computer system but applications which work on the world wide web offer easy collaboration with other people. In addition they allow users to access functions that they may not have (or want) installed on their own computer system.

Popular online applications include:

- **Gliffy** – create and share online diagrams
- **Farmville** – grow your own online farm with friends
- **Kerpoof** – create online cartoon artwork and share with friends
- **Mint** – online banking and money management
- **Google Docs and Spreadsheets** – online creation of documents and spreadsheets.

Activity A

Explore online web applications

www.go2web20.net is an online portal for online applications, offering a treasure trove of searchable and categorised online applications which are mostly free to use.

See what types of interesting online applications you can find!

Make the grade   P2

P2 asks you to describe the role of web architecture in website communications. This is essentially detailed in section 17.1.2 and your answer should include the role of the ISP, domain structure, web hosting services and domain name registrars.

17.2 Understand how websites can be used by organisations

This section will cover the following grading criterion:

Uses of websites

Broadly speaking websites fall into three basic categories:

- **Customer facing**
- **Internal use**
- **Non-profit**.

Customer facing

These types of websites are developed as a tool for generating more money for their creators by advertising their services or products.

By the early twenty-first century, most businesses have their own websites and are said to be customer facing.

These websites are generally listed in any literature that the company produces or are placed on the product itself, encouraging customers to visit.

These types of website can be used to provide:

- Marketing opportunities
- An online product catalogue
- Online shopping
- Business and contact information
- Customer support (such as downloadable user guides or product forums).

Some websites are **password protected** and require payment in order to access their content (for example music file downloads such as Apple's iTunes).

Others provide secure online shopping facilities and these sell any manner of goods, anything from holidays to houses to sweets. Online auction houses such as eBay® are also commercial websites.

Internal use

Organisations often use websites for internal purposes. These websites may contain sensitive information which is not intended to be shared outside the organisation and is accessible as part of an **intranet**.

Key term

An **intranet** is a website that can only be accessed within an organisation through its LAN (local area network) or by Virtual Private Network (VPN) for home workers. Intranets are protected from outside intrusions by security measures such as firewalls.

Other internal uses for the intranet's website content may include:

- Information repositories – storing electronic telephone directories, email addresses, company news, staff handbook etc.
- Training facilities – tutorials and information which employees can use to learn new skills as part of their continuing professional development (CPD).

Non-commercial

These types of website are created for non-profit-making reasons. Generally they continue to exist through the creator's own finance, use of third-party advertising, sponsored links or donations from generous visitors who value the resources provided.

Typical examples of non-commercial websites include:

- Personal pages – about the creator, can include an on-line diary or blog
- Advice and guidance – 'how to' pages
- Fan or review sites
- Clubs and societies
- Charities
- Educational
- Governmental (local or national).

Make the grade   P3

P3 requires you to explain the uses of websites by organisations. This will include the basic uses that commercial and non-commercial organisations make of the world wide web. Do not forget to include recent developments in web technologies, such as Web 2.0 in your answer.
Case studies are a popular approach with particular company websites being assigned to you by your teacher for examination. How do websites improve organisational efficiency? For example do they enable more effective communication between the customer and the company if a faulty product is bought? If yes, explain why this is so.

17.3 Be able to design website components

This section will cover the following grading criteria: P4 M1 M2 D1

17.3.1 Design

When it comes to designing a website, good planning and paying attention to detail are both very important considerations.

Tools

There are many different techniques available when planning a website, perhaps the most commonly used is the **storyboard**.

A storyboard is used to plan the website pictorially, showing each page as a **named thumbnail** with the **inter-page navigation** clearly shown.

Let us explore the storyboard approach through a sample case study.

Newhampton Football Club

A local football team is planning to develop a website to showcase their club history, upcoming fixtures, players and charity fund-raising events. A simple storyboard is needed to outline the website's structure.

Figure 17.5 shows a potential solution.

Figure 17.5 Storyboard for Newhampton Football Club website

After a plan has been created, and amended if necessary, it should be possible to sketch out the pages in more detail, taking information from the client to help **populate** the pages.

When sufficient detail has been collected, sample pages can be shown to the client for feedback.

Mood board

A mood board can be used to plan the visual style of the website, detailing the colour schemes, layout, sample imagery and fonts that may be used. (See http://weblog.404creative.com/wp-content/uploads/2007/02/moodboard.jpg for a good example of a mood board.)

Style

Other design considerations include the organisation's **house style**; this includes use of corporate colours, logos, popular catchphrases and marketing slogans.

The homepage of McDonald's is a good example of this: a clean minimalist design using their familiar logo and with a simple (but effective) navigation scheme.

Figure 17.6 The UK website of McDonald's

It is always useful to remember that a company's commercial website is an extension of their presence in the marketplace. The large amount of money some organisations spend on their websites is testament to just how effective they feel their website actually is in attracting new customers.

Another important design aspect, though it may seem odd, is **continuity of layout**. The better websites use a tried and tested layout with which users quickly become familiar and comfortable.

Sites with a consistent layout are generally easier to navigate and encourage people to explore since they feel reassured that they are unlikely to 'get lost' in a maze of poorly organised or bewilderingly different pages.

17.3.2 Construction features

Most web pages are constructed from a set of similar features. Let us examine a sample page; Figure 17.7 is from the BBC's online news service.

Figure 17.7 The main page of BBC news online

Let us discuss a few of the more common construction elements:

Hyperlinks

> **Key term**
>
> A hyperlink is used to connect one online resource to another. The resource may be another page, another place on the same page (bookmark), a separate image, a video, an animation or even a piece of music. Hyperlinks often link to resources on other websites.

Hyperlinks use **uniform resource locators** (**URLs**) to specify the resources they connect to across the internet. In theory, this resource could be anywhere in the world – as long as the URL is correct and the resource actually exists.

Here are some sample hyperlink destinations:

http://www.bbc.co.uk/weather/ukweather/temperature.shtml

http://www.microsoft.com/windows/default.mspx

http://www.sainsburys.co.uk/home.htm

Visited hyperlinks

Web browsers can remember a page from a previous visit and **colour code** hyperlinks like so:

Blue means **'unvisited'** – the user *has not* clicked this link before.

Purple means **'visited'** – the user *has* clicked this link before.

This is not guaranteed, however, as browsers can override these colour settings and so can individual web pages by using particular formatting in the HTML.

Frames

> ## Key term
>
> **Frames** allow the designer to split a physical browser screen into a number of different 'panes'. Each pane can show a separate (but linked) web page.

Frames have a somewhat mixed reputation – they are liked by some web designers and disliked intensely by others.

Figure 17.8 illustrates this:

Logo.html	Heading.html
Menu.html	Page1.html

When a link is selected on the left-hand menu, its associated page (such as 'page2.html') can replace page1.html in the largest frame.

Figure 17.8 Web page with four frames

A popular web page technique is to use **'hotspots'**. The first type of hotspot is concerned with areas of a web page which naturally draw the eye of the visitor. These areas (top-left and right-hand edge) are useful for placing important logos, key information or advertising.

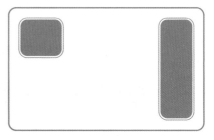

Figure 17.9 Hotspots on a web page

The second type of hotspot is concerned with **images**, particularly those that are intended to be used as an **image map**.

> ## Key term
>
> An image map is a picture which is divided up into several different areas or hotspots. When the user clicks on a hotspot, it acts as a hyperlink to a different page or resource.

Let us take a look at a working example (Figure 17.10).

Figure 17.10 A fruit bowl

We can use this image as an intuitive 'menu' system by drawing shaped hotspots on various areas to link to different pages of fruit produce.

Figure 17.11 Hotspots and their hyperlinks

In order to create an image map we have three basic choices:

- We can create an image map using a paint program and manually write the HTML code necessary (this is tricky).
- We can use a commercial **image map maker** such as Boutell's Mapedit program (http://www.boutell.com/mapedit) which is designed specifically for the job (see Figure 17.12).

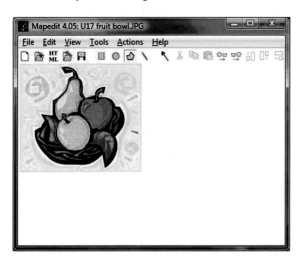

Figure 17.12 Mapedit at work, creating the hotspots

- We could use a full HTML editing suite such as Adobe®'s Dreamweaver which incorporates an image map maker.

Perhaps the simplest technique for now is to use the image map maker Mapedit. Here is the simple **HTML code** that is produced from a utility like Mapedit.

```
<img src="U17 fruit bowl.JPG"
usemap="#U17 fruit bowl" alt=""
style="border-style:none" />
<map id="U17 fruit bowl" name="U17 fruit
bowl">
<area shape="circle" alt="yellow apple"
coords="84,105,26" href="yellow apple.
html" title="yellow apple" />
<area shape="circle" alt="red apple.html"
coords="121,69,22" href="red apple.html"
title="red apple.html" />
<area shape="poly" alt="green pear"
coords="80,24,68,45,57,57,61,81,91,71,95,
55,102,51,97,43,100,31,89,21" href="green
pear.html" title="green pear" />
<area shape="default" nohref="nohref"
alt="" />
</map>
```

This code could now be inserted into a suitable page for web browser testing.

Figure 17.13 An image map with hotspots in Google Chrome®

The hotspots *do not*, of course, show up on the actual image. In Figure 17.13, the mouse cursor is hovering over the 'yellow apple' hotspot and it is showing the suitable alternative text. When clicked, the appropriate page all about yellow apples would load.

Interactive features

A clickable **email hyperlink** is a common sight on a web page. When the email link is clicked, the user's email client appears (for example Microsoft Outlook®) with the target email address pre-filled (and sometimes the subject, too).

Here is the HTML needed …

```
<a href="mailto:me@mysite.co.uk?
subject=An example">Contact us.</a>
```

… and here is the web page view (Figure 17.14).

Figure 17.14 An email hyperlink in Mozilla Firefox®

… finally the user's default email client will appear when the email link is clicked (Figure 17.15).

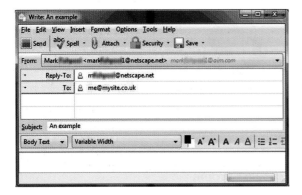

Figure 17.15 User's email client with details pre-filled

Many modern commercial websites prefer to use **form-based** email submission instead, as typically these do not rely on the user being on their own PC with their personal email software installed and running. This would allow users to send emails from computer systems in public places, such as libraries, hotels, schools or conference centres.

Make the grade P4 M1 D1

Criteria P4, M1 and D1 are all connected. P4 asks you to design website components considering a client's needs – this will require you to create storyboards and sample pages to meet the requirements laid out in a client's brief. This might be supplied by your teacher or be provided by a real-life client. M1 asks you to explain techniques that can be used on the web page to aid user access. This should focus on the construction features and interactive elements of a website (see sections 17.3.2 and 17.3.3 (below)). D1 asks you to evaluate the different design features of a website – this could be the website you will create for P6 or a pre-made website you have visited or been given to investigate by your teacher.

17.3.3 Interactivity

On a basic web page, user input is limited to the keyboard and mouse.

There are many, many different ways that you can add **interactivity** to a web page, although perhaps the most common way to achieve this is to use a **form**. A form is an HTML component that can be used to collect data from the user.

Forms use combinations of familiar interface elements such as text boxes, buttons, radio buttons, checkboxes and drop lists to collect all manner of data.

eBay's advanced search is a good example of a form (see Figure 17.16).

Figure 17.16 eBay's advanced search page

Some forms are used to process queries while others are used to permit data entry via the keyboard, for example registration screens or visitor feedback forms (see section 17.4.7). Data entered into these types of form is typically posted to databases which store the information for future use, such as customising the website appearance or functionality for your future visits.

17.3.4 Client need

When designing a website for another person or organisation it is absolutely vital to consider their needs. This is called, 'thinking about the **target audience**'.

The website should not be created as an exercise for fulfilling your own personal tastes or creative flair but as a direct reflection of what the customer actually wants.

Detailed below are some common concerns that the client may have.

Accurate and current information

- Is the information on the website correct and as up to date as possible?
- How easy will it be to maintain the website and keep the information current?

Clear navigation

- Is it obvious how to move around the website from page to page?
- Can visitors get at the information they want quickly (within two or three clicks)?
- Can the visitor easily find their way back to the home page?

Fast download speeds

- Will the website load quickly on computer systems with slower connections?
- Have images been compressed where possible?
- If not, should there be a choice in content (low- or high-graphics versions)?

Suitability of language

- Is the language grammatically sound with no spelling errors (which can detract)?
- Is the language appropriate to the expected visitor (not too technical or unprofessional)?
- Are there pages available in different languages (this is very important for multinational companies)?
- Is there language present that may anger, insult or offend?

Choice of images

- Are the images used suitable and do they match the accompanying text?
- Are the images of a suitable photographic or artistic standard?

- Are the images the right size?
- Are the images likely to anger, insult or offend (especially in the global market)?

Appropriate formatting

- How effective is the page layout?
- Are the fonts and colours appropriate (for example using corporate colours)?
- Can font size and colours be changed easily to assist accessibility for visitors with reading or cognitive difficulties?

Make the grade M2

M2 asks you describe the use of interactive websites and the techniques that can be used to provide interactivity. Most websites have interactive features which capture user input either in terms of registration, searches or user feedback. Describe the use of HTML forms to capture this type of user input and how it may tailor the website for your future visits.

17.4 Be able to create website components

This section will cover the following grading criteria:

17.4.1 Format and edit

Key term

HTML is a **hypertext mark-up language** and as such, describes the content of a page and how it is structured. It should not specify the formatting.

Common web functions

A number of web design functions are used in most web pages. Table 17.1 lists some of the most basic elements you will use.

Web design element	Description of the element
Bookmark	A bookmark is a way of allowing a user to 'jump to' particular parts of a web page. It uses the <A> tag: **<a name="top"></a>**
Hyperlinks	Hyperlinks are at the heart of any website, helping to link pages and resources together. Hyperlinks can be in the form of text or images and also use the <A> tag. Hyperlink to an **internal bookmark**: **<a href="#top">Top of Page</a>** Hyperlink to an external link: **<a href="http://www.google.co.uk">Visit Google</a>**
Graphics	Images can be incorporated into web pages. Many different file formats can be used but .JPG, .PNG and .GIF are the most efficient to use.

Table 17.1 Common web design elements (continued on next page)

Web design element	Description of the element
Fonts	Fonts can be chosen by name but in order to be displayed correctly on the end user's web browser, they have to be installed on their computer system. Most web pages simply specify font families, such as serif or sans serif.
Text formatting	Text can be formatted on a web page to change its appearance. Common formatting includes: • Changing the font • Changing the size • Changing the colour • Changing its alignment (left, centre or right)
Background	A web page can use a background colour, pattern or image. The selection of the background is important as you must ensure that it does not obscure the text in the foreground. To avoid this most websites use simple black or white backgrounds to improve readability or allow the user (via JavaScript®) the ability to select their own preferences.

Table 17.1 Continued

HTML tags

As you have seen, HTML uses a number of special **tags** to identify its different sections. Most tags have a **start tag** and an **end tag**, such as **<HTML>** and **</HTML>**, respectively.

Table 17.2 shows some basic HTML tags to get you started.

Start tag	End tag	What it means
<HTML>	</HTML>	This marks the start and end of an HTML document.
<HEAD>	</HEAD>	Start and end of an HTML document's head(er). It contains information such as its title and keywords that may be useful to search engines.
<TITLE>	</TITLE>	Placed usually within the <HEAD> and </HEAD>, every HTML document *must* have a title to identify its content. The title is the text usually displayed in the web browser's title bar when the page is loaded.
<META>	None!	**Meta tags** are used to describe the document itself rather than its content. A simple example would be: <META name="Author" content="U N Owen"> This specifies the author's name.

Table 17.2 Basic HTML tags (continued on next page)

Start tag	End tag	What it means
<BODY>	</BODY>	This represents the start and end of the document's main body. It is easiest to think of this as the central canvas of the HTML page.
<P>	</P>	Starts and ends a paragraph of text.

Table 17.2 Continued

Note that HTML is not case sensitive.

```
<html>
<head>
<title>BTEC First Diploma IT</title>
<META name="Author" content="U N
Owen">
</head>
<body>
<p>This is a test!</p>
</body>
</html>
```

You can key this short HTML document into a basic text editor (such as Microsoft Notepad®) and it should then open successfully in a suitable web browser.

File extensions

Web pages typically use either a '.htm' or '.html' extension. You need to save the file as **'mypage.html'**.

Here is our HTML web page loaded into Microsoft's Internet Explorer® (Figure 17.17).

Figure 17.17 Our quick web page; notice the browser's title bar …

17.4.2 Combining information

Information on a web page can be collected from a number of different sources.

Common sources include:

- scanner
- microphone
- digital camera (photograph or video)
- application package data (such as a spreadsheet)
- original artwork
- music or sound effects
- animations
- clip art.

For example, if we wanted to include an image of a notebook (such as 'notebook.jpg') on our web page we would need to add the appropriate tag to our HTML.

You can use the HTML <IMG> tag to insert previously created pictures.

This is how you can place images onto your web page:

```
<html>
<head>
<title>BTEC First Diploma IT</title>
<META name="Author" content="U N
Owen">
</head>
<body>
<p>This is a test!

<IMG src="notebook.jpg" alt="A
computer notebook.">

</p>
</body>
</html>
```

The **'alt'** attribute is used to supply an alternative text description of the picture. This is seen as good practice as it enables users to know what the image is if they are unable to display it on their system. Alt tags are also useful for visually impaired users as their screen reader software can read them out loud.

As you will see from Figure 17.18, the alternative description appears over the picture of the notebook when the mouse pointer hovers over it.

Figure 17.18 Our web page with an image of a notebook ('notebook.jpg') included

Fonts and text formatting

Modern web page formatting is achieved using **CSS (cascading style sheets)**, which is the preferred technique.

It is possible to keep the content of a web page in one file (the .HTML) and the formatting in another (a .CSS file). Although it is not within this book's scope to cover all forms of CSS formatting, the following example demonstrates how it works.

Here is the revised HTML ('mypage.html'). Note the new **stylesheet** link:

```
<html>
<head>
<title>BTEC First Diploma IT</title>
<meta name="Author" content="U N
Owen">
<link rel="stylesheet" href="mystyle.css">
</head>
<body>
<H2 align="center" class="style3">BTEC
First Diploma IT</H2>
<H2 align="center"><img src="notebook.
jpg" alt="A computer notebook."
align="top">
</H2>
<p align="center" class="style2"><span
class="style1">Welcome to the world of
Information Technology..! </span><H3>
</p>
</body>
</html>
```

And the connected 'mystyle.css' file:

```
.style1 {font-family: Arial, Helvetica, sans-
serif}
.style2 {color: #000000}
.style3 {
        font-family: Arial, Helvetica, sans-
        serif;
        color: #FF0000;
        font-weight: bold;
    }
```

These CSS instructions create three styles of formatting: style1, style2 and style3.

- Style 1 specifies a particular font family.
- Style 2 specifies the colour 'black'.
- Style 3 specifies a particular font family, the colour red and to use bold.

RGB (Red Green Blue) **colour codes** are discussed in more detail in Unit 23 (Computer Graphics).

Here is the resulting appearance in a web browser:

Figure 17.19 The CSS-formatted appearance of the new page

CSS can also be used to change the background colour of the page.

```
.style1 {font-family: Arial, Helvetica, sans-
serif}
.style2 {color: #FFFFFF}
.style3 {
        font-family: Arial, Helvetica, sans-serif;
        color: #FF0000;
        font-weight: bold;
        }
body {background-color: #000000}
```

Like so:

Figure 17.20 Now with a black background!

17.4.3 Checking

Once the website has been created, it is necessary to check it to see that it is **functional**.

Image size and resolution

Images have to be of good quality, especially if the website is customer facing. However large, uncompressed images can take a long time to load on slow (narrowband) connections. You may have had this irritating experience at some point during your web surfing!

It is often said that users have little patience when it comes to waiting for pages to load – if it takes too long, they will go elsewhere. For a commercial website this means losing a potential customer (and their money).

If large, high-quality images are needed, it should be possible to allow the user to preview these with either a lower-quality sample or a simple 'thumbnail'. The user can then decide whether they want to wait while a larger file downloads; this gives them more control and the web servers a reduced workload!

You must test the speed and quality of any images and ensure that all images actually load correctly.

Links not working

Internal links

Internal links are links within the same page ('anchors') or to another page within the same suite of pages. These need to be tested before publishing as non-working internal links can be very irritating and frustrating for the casual visitor.

HTML editors such as Adobe Dreamweaver® have an automated 'internal link' facility which identifies such defects.

External links

External links are typically hyperlinks to other pages, often to different web servers, which may not be available from time to time.

External links should be checked regularly to ensure that the URLs for a resource have not changed.

A number of sites place an advisory note on their site as a disclaimer to indicate that they are not responsible for the content of another site they are linking to.

All links must be tested whether they are internal or external.

Content

Check the actual content of the web pages.

- Is the content accurate and representative?
- Is the content up to date?
- Is the content appropriately presented?
- Do interactive elements such as input forms, Javascript®, Java® applets etc. work correctly? This is particularly important if the website is being built for a client, particularly as a commercial site.
- Does it use appropriate imagery, company logos etc.?
- Are the corporate colours and general colour scheme correct?
- Does the site allow for accessibility issues?
- Are the fonts used appropriate?
- Is the layout clear or cluttered and confusing?

17.4.4 Publishing

There are a number of different ways that you can publish a website.

On an intranet

Publishing web pages on an organisation's intranet is not normally difficult. If security is exceptionally relaxed in the company, it may be possible to simply 'drag and drop' the files to the appropriate web server's directory. But this is unlikely and

is a very insecure arrangement! Typically the company will employ an intranet manager to oversee publishing and routine maintenance.

The easiest option would be to send the intranet manager a CD or email attachment which includes all the necessary HTML files, graphics and any other assorted media in the form of a single archived file (such as a '.ZIP').

Since archives can retain the folder structure from the original files, when the files are 'unzipped' into an appropriate web server folder the files and their sub-folders are automatically recreated.

All that would then be necessary would be for the intranet manager to hyperlink the new pages to the existing intranet site.

On the internet

This is somewhat more difficult but there is a general order in which steps should be taken.

1. Select a **hosting company** for suitable **web space**.
2. Purchase a suitable **domain name** for your website (such as www.btec-first-it.co.uk). This can cost as little as £3 for an entire year. Obviously not all combinations are available for purchase (they may already be in use); a domain registration company will allow you to check the availability of your preferred name.

   Some hosting companies also sell domains so it is possible to purchase a complete domain name and web space package.

   If you purchase the web space and domain separately, it is necessary to request that the domain name is **re-pointed** towards your web space. Be warned, this can take time and often requires an additional fee.

3. **Upload** your website pages, graphics etc. to your web space. This usually happens via a **FTP** (**file transfer protocol**) client or a web-based interface.
4. **Register** the page with a number of **search engines**. The hosting company may help you achieve this.

Since the web space you have purchased is yours to use as you see fit (within the usage agreements stipulated by the hosting company), it is possible to perform full file and folder management; moving, copying, deleting and renaming files as required.

Figure 17.21 shows a typical online hosting page showing its different package deals.

Figure 17.21 A sample web hosting company

Activity B

Self publishing

Use a search engine to find a UK-based company which provides free web hosting.

Register and find out how to upload some of your sample web pages to it.

17.4.5 Web development software

You can develop web pages in a number of different ways. The most common techniques are detailed below.

Text editor

A basic **text editor** (such as Microsoft's Notepad®) can be used to create a simple web page by directly keying in the HTML code.

Some more advanced text editors recognise HTML files by their extension (either .HTM or .HTML) and can produce a form of 'syntax highlighting' which helps the designer read the HTML code more easily; different parts of the HTML being differently coloured.

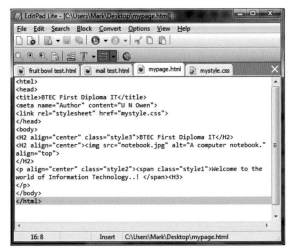

Figure 17.22 A text editor being used to create a web page

Some web designers take great pride in the fact that they have created their (quite often complex) page using such a basic tool, often placing a 'built with Notepad' message on the page itself!

Using a text editor to create a web page

- You have to know HTML syntax fairly well to get started.

- There is no HTML help.

- You have to load a separate web browser to preview your page.

+ Immediate, fast-loading tool.

+ Not very complex to use.

+ It is cheap. Text editors (such as Notepad®) often come as part of the operating system.

+ If you learn the HTML syntax this way it makes editing pages much simpler.

Specialist software and HTML editors

Specialist software for editing HTML comes in various sizes, prices and levels of complexity. Most are **WYSIWYG** ('what you see is what you get') tools that allow the designer to create the page visually. The program then 'writes' the equivalent HTML. These tools make effective use of the 'drag and drop' approach to modern software design.

More complex software also has W3C validation (for HTML standardisation), comprehensive support for JavaScript®, Java® and CSS for formatting.

Key term

International standards for web page design are set by the **W3C** (**World Wide Web Consortium**). Websites such as http://validator.w3.org/ enable the user to validate their web page's HTML to see that it meets W3C approval.

Such software packages also assist the website management process (by organising the pages into a complete interconnected site) and can upload to a host server for publishing and submit details to search engines.

Popular specialist software for website design includes:

- Adobe Dreamweaver®
- Microsoft Expression Web®
- CoffeeCup HTML Editor®
- Quanta Plus®

Specialist website design software

- Software can be expensive.

- Software can be complex to use, especially for advanced features.

- It can require a more powerful computer system in order to run.

+ Fast; WYSIWYG 'drag and drop' design means quick assembly of pages and sites.

+ You do not have to learn HTML.

+ Comprehensive help systems and samples are usually provided.

Embedded facilities

Office productivity application software such as Microsoft Word®, Microsoft Excel® and Microsoft PowerPoint® can also export their data in an HTML format, effectively creating web page content very easily.

Generally this is performed through the File-> → Save as type menu option and obviously demands very little HTML skill from you.

Adobe Flash® is another popular tool for creating web page content, especially that rich in **multimedia** (pictures, sound, music, animation or video) and requiring more advanced levels of user interaction. In order to view Flash® animations, a web browser needs a **Flash Player®** installed (these are free to download).

Figure 17.23 Adobe Flash® creating an animation

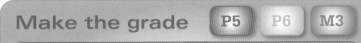

Make the grade   P5   P6   M3

These three grading criteria are connected as they all focus on the practical task of creating an interactive website to meet the needs of a client.

P5 asks you to use appropriate formatting, tools, styles and templates to prepare content for the website. This really asks you to think about the layout and appearance of the website you are going to make.

P6 asks you to create website components to meet client needs. This is the main practical part of the unit and the part that is likely to take you the most time. It should not matter how you build the website – you could use a simple text editor and brave HTML and CSS or use specialist web development software such as Adobe Dreamweaver® if you prefer. Your website should be built from the design submitted for P4.

M3 asks you to use automated features of web development software (see section 17.4.6 below). It is likely that your website may use frames, tables or templates; if this is the case simply take some screen captures of using these Wizards and document them with the website screen captures, HTML and CSS for submission. Again, this is another highly practical task.

17.4.6 Automated features

Many specialist software applications which help users create websites have automated features (often called '**wizards**') which quickly create web page elements that usually prove either laborious or tricky to do by hand.

Common examples include tables, frames and templates. These will be discussed in further detail below.

Tables

Tables are a popular component of web pages but it is time consuming to create them manually in HTML.

Adobe Dreamweaver® has a simple dialogue box which automates the process of constructing a table. By providing a few details (such as columns, rows, border thickness etc.) it will create the required HTML code.

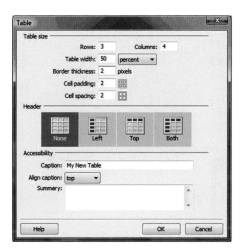

Figure 17.24 Adobe Dreamweaver® Table Wizard

Figure 17.25 shows what the table will look like.

Figure 17.25 New table

This will create the following HTML code:

```
<table width="50%" border="2"
cellspacing="2" cellpadding="2">
  <caption align="top">
  My New Table
  </caption>
  <tr>
    <td> </td>
    <td> </td>
    <td> </td>
    <td> </td>
  </tr>
  <tr>
    <td> </td>
    <td> </td>
    <td> </td>
    <td> </td>
  </tr>
  <tr>
    <td> </td>
    <td> </td>
    <td> </td>
    <td> </td>
  </tr>
</table>
```

Frames

We learnt about frames back in section 17.3.2.

Although most web designers use these sparingly, they are popular enough to merit wizards in most website specialist applications.

Adobe Dreamweaver® can divide any single web page into a number of frames and different combinations are possible (see Figure 17.26).

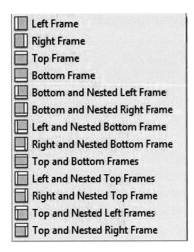

Figure 17.26 Adobe Dreamweaver® frame combinations

Templates

Templates exist for websites just as they exist for documents and presentations. Although it is possible to download free templates online, most website specialist software has a number of templates which can be chosen via a wizard.

A template usually divides a web page up into a number of different **divisions**, with each division having **placeholders** for text, images and hyperlinks. They may also have complementary colour schemes already set.

In Adobe Dreamweaver®, templates are chosen when creating a new web page.

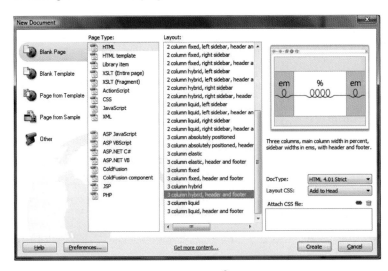

Figure 17.27 Adobe Dreamweaver® template layouts

Using a template will enable a web designer to assemble some workable web pages quickly. However, they will undoubtedly need further customisation to meet the user's needs and target the audience's expectations.

Activity C

Use wizards and automated features

In available web development software attempt to use a wizard (or equivalent) to create:

- Tables
- Templates
- Frames
- Navigation bars
- Image galleries.

17.4.7 Review

Reviewing the website is a key part of the process. Unlike the earlier checking, this is really concerned with whether the website meets the client's needs and whether the website visitors like it or not: even fully functioning websites can completely miss the point!

The key question is: 'Is the website fit **for purpose?**'

Reviewing relies on feedback – coming from both the client and the users.

Getting feedback

A simple fact: visitor opinions matter! A popular technique for gauging visitor opinion is to use **feedback forms**. These invite the visitor to express their opinions of the website; sometimes it is actually encouraged through offering some attractive incentive – a free prize draw, for example.

Common questions on a feedback form might include:

- User's email address (for mailing notices regarding future website updates)
- User's occupation (helps to discover what demographic is using the site)
- User's age
- How often they visit the site over a specific period of time
- User rating of various features (typically on a poor, OK, good, excellent scale)
- Which features they find the most (and least) useful
- How they find the site's navigation (can they quickly find what they are looking for?)
- What improvements they would like to see
- How they discovered the website (this helps with marketing and advertising).

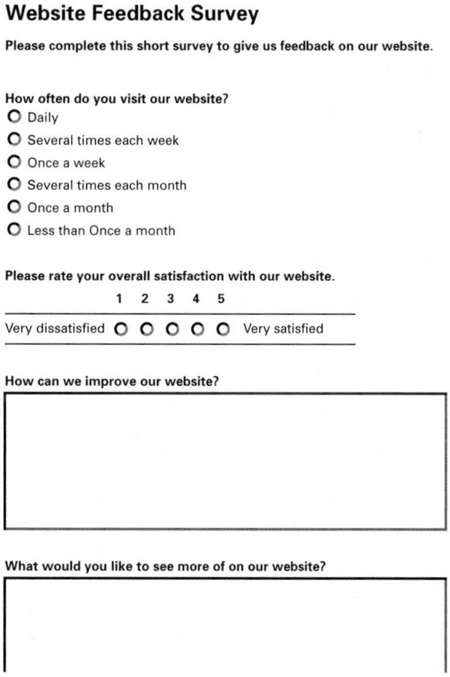

Website Feedback Survey

Please complete this short survey to give us feedback on our website.

How often do you visit our website?
- O Daily
- O Several times each week
- O Once a week
- O Several times each month
- O Once a month
- O Less than Once a month

Please rate your overall satisfaction with our website.

       1 2 3 4 5

Very dissatisfied O O O O O Very satisfied

How can we improve our website?

What would you like to see more of on our website?

Figure 17.28 A simple website feedback form

It is common to use a **simple checklist** like so:

- Is the content appropriate?
- Is there any unnecessary and/or distracting animation?
- Are there any inappropriate graphics?
- Are any of the graphics unclear or difficult to see?
- Does the web page download slowly (possibly due to large images)?
- Are there navigation problems?
- Are the fonts clear and easy to read?
- Are the background and foreground colour combinations poor?
- Does the content reflect the requirements of the client?

Page size

The web page should display comfortably on the most common desktop **resolutions** as used by most users. Currently this is **minimally 1024 × 768**.

A design decision will have been taken to either display contents absolutely (in other words fix them in size) or allow them to shrink or expand as needed.

The best way of checking this is to view the pages on a combination of different web browsers, operating systems and desktop resolutions. This will approximate the audience's diversity of hardware and software to a reasonable degree.

Special requirements

It is quite common for resources on a website to require additional software (often called **browser 'plug-ins'**) in order to experience particular files or embedded web page objects. Flash® animations, video clips, Java® applets and Adobe Acrobat® **PDFs (portable document files)** are by far the most common.

If you are using these types of objects to enhance your site, it is usually good practice (and courteous) to supply the necessary external links so that visitors can download the appropriate software if they do not already have it installed.

Improvements

As noted, visitor feedback is an important factor when determining how well a website is working and what, if any, improvements can be made. There are some basic improvements that can be considered:

- Response times – can the website respond more quickly to user needs?
- Interactivity – websites which engage the visitor tend to be visited more often.
- Clarity – websites which are not clearly laid out or are confusing to navigate often do not get repeat visits.

Activity D

Create a feedback page

Create a simple feedback page for your website where you can collect the thoughts and views of your visitors.

Make the grade   P7   M4   D2

These three grading criteria are connected as they all focus on your review of the website you have created.

P7 asks you to produce a personal review of the website components you have created suggesting any improvements that could be made.

Partly a practical task, M4 is similar to P7 except it asks you to refine website components based on user feedback. This means you have to let a user test

Continued on next page

Continued ...

your website, get their feedback and then make improvements to its design and implementation based on their comments. Document this as a three stage process: (1) original components, (2) what the user said and (3) which components you improved in response to the feedback. D2 is really an extension of both P7 and M4 as it asks you to argue that your website meets the requirements originally defined by the user. This is really a matching exercise – go back to the original requirements and prove you have created components and content which match each need. Using your user's review from M4 is also useful as it will support your judgements.

Activity E

Quiz

Answer the following quiz questions. Check your answers at the back of the book.

1. What is a web server?

2. What is a TLD?

3. What is a domain name registrar?

4. What is an intranet?

5. What is HTML?

6. Give three design considerations when creating a website.

7. Explain the purpose of the following HTML tags:

    a) <HEAD>

    b) <TITLE>

    c) <IMG>

    d) <P>

8. What software can be used to upload your website pages to your host's server?

9. Why is a form used?

10. If an image has different clickable areas, what is it called?

11. Name three automated features in specialist web development software.

12. What is the HTML technique that splits a page into a number of different 'panes'?

Achieving Success

In order to achieve each unit, you will complete a series of coursework activities. Each time you hand in work, your tutor will return this to you with a record of your achievement.

This particular unit has 13 criteria to meet: 7 Pass, 4 Merit and 2 Distinction.

For a **Pass** you must achieve **all 7** Pass criteria.

For a **Merit** you must achieve **all 7** Pass and **all 4** Merit criteria.

For a **Distinction** you must achieve **all 7** Pass, **all 4** Merit criteria **and both** Distinction criteria.

Help with assessment

Your tutor will give you one or more assignments that you will complete as coursework. This could consist of:

- Presentations
- Videos and screen captures
- Witness statements and/or an evidence log
- Websites, pages or wikis
- Leaflets or reports
- Posters.

You should read the guidance given for each of the criteria (shown across the unit) carefully and remember to check your work.

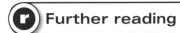 **Further reading**

Textbooks

Adobe Creative Team. *Adobe Dreamweaver CS4 Classroom in a Book* (Adobe, 2008) ISBN 0321573811

Brannan James, A. *Web Design in Simple Steps* (Prentice Hall, 2009) ISBN 0273723537

Chesire, J. *Microsoft Expression Web 3 In Depth* (QUE, 2009) ISBN 078973981X

Websites

www.excellentsite.org

www.webpagesthatsuck.com

http://www.w3schools.com/

Unit 18
Software design

Learning objectives

By the end of this unit you should be able to:

1. Know the features of programming languages
2. Know the software development process
3. Be able to design software development solutions.

In order to pass this unit, the evidence you present for assessment needs to demonstrate that you can meet all of the above learning outcomes for this unit. The criteria below show the levels of achievement required to pass this unit.

To achieve a **pass** grade the evidence must show that the learner is able to:	To achieve a **merit** grade the evidence must show that, in addition to the pass criteria, the learner is able to:	To achieve a **distinction** the evidence must show that, in addition to the pass and merit criteria, the learner is able to:
P1 Describe the characteristics of programming paradigms	**M1** Describe the features of programming languages, including how sequence, selection and iteration are used	
P2 Identify the factors influencing choice of programming language		
P3 Describe the stages of the software development life cycle		
P4 Outline a specification for a business requirement	**M2** Select and justify the programming language to be used	
P5 Design a software solution to a business requirement using appropriate design tools	**M3** Describe the data types and software structures used in a design solution	**D1** Develop algorithms to represent a design solution
P6 Review the design against the original requirement		**D2** Evaluate the design tools used

Introduction

Many businesses use commercial application software to solve their everyday processing needs. Occasionally a business cannot find an application that fits a processing need that has been identified. When this happens the business has no choice but to build a bespoke (tailor-made) solution using an appropriate programming language.

This unit is designed to give you your first taste of modern software design, encouraging you to understand user requirements and giving you the confidence to design a workable solution. Some sample worked problems have been included for you to get a more rounded idea of the software design process.

You will be assessed through coursework which could be in the form of:

- Presentations
- Practical sessions which may be photographed, videoed or witnessed

- Designs (written or graphical) such as flowcharts or storyboards
- Screen captures
- Blogs
- Podcasts.

18.1 Know the features of programming languages

This section will cover the following grading criteria: **P1** **P2** **M1**

Before we can examine different features of programming languages it is worthwhile taking a pause to explain just what a programming language actually is!

Computers only understand **binary** instructions, sequences of patterned 1s and 0s which open and close electronic circuits inside the CPU. Programming a computer in binary is often referred to as **machine code programming** or **low-level programming**. In the earliest days of computing, this was the only option!

Modern programming languages are designed to be more person-readable than binary. As such, these high-level languages require translation into their machine code equivalents so that the CPU can execute the commands.

Figure 18.1 illustrates this point.

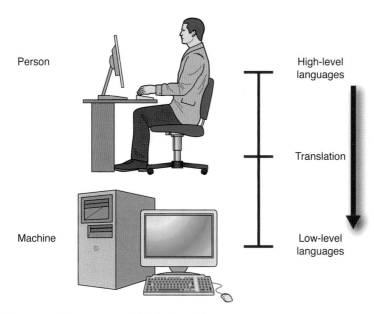

Figure 18.1 Low- and high-level languages

Programming languages – what you need to know …

Scorecard

Low-level language

+ Needs no translation before CPU can understand it, so very fast!

+ Full control over CPU

− Difficult to write

− Difficult to read

− Difficult to 'debug' (find errors and correct them)

− Is specific to the CPU being used; this means that low-level program code is not 'portable' from one type of CPU to another.

High-level language

+ Easier to learn as more like a natural language

+ Easier to debug

+ Translators are available for many different CPUs so the code can be portable

+ Modern translators (commercial compilers) are very advanced and can generate low-level program code that is as efficient as low-level code that was written 'by hand'.

The following demonstrates a comparison between high- and low-level languages:

```
cout <<"BTEC First Diploma";
```

```
10110100    00000101
10111010    00000101
00000001
11001101    00100001
11001101    00100000

01000010
01010100
01000101
01000011
00100000
01000110
01101001
01110010
01110011
01110100
00100000
01000100
01101001
01110000
01101100
01101111
01101101
01100001
00100100
```

Both programs output the phrase 'BTEC First Diploma' on a PC using an x86 compatible processor (such as a modern Intel or AMD processor).

The left-hand example is written in **C++**, a popular language developed in 1983 as an extension to an earlier language called C.

The right-hand example is machine code as shown in binary.

Although both samples of code do the same thing, the C++ code would need to be translated into the machine code before it could work.

Of course, if we had written the code in binary originally, then no such translation would need to take place.

Which would *you* prefer to learn?

Which do you think is more *commercially productive?*

18.1.1 Programming paradigms

Although it is difficult to count precisely, there are hundreds of different programming languages and they can all be categorised in a number of ways.

Key term

A **programming paradigm** is the style or approach used to problem solving. A distinct paradigm can group together many similar programming languages.

Table 18.1 shows three of the mostly widely recognised
programming paradigms, lists some example languages
and gives some of their key characteristics.

Programming paradigm	Example languages	Key characteristics
Procedural	COBOL (common business oriented language) BASIC (beginner's all-purpose symbolic instruction code) Pascal	• Often called **'imperative'** languages • Programs are written as step-by-step instructions designed to solve a problem • Programs are often **modular** (split into small modules which each do a different task) • One of the oldest forms of programming • Common terms include **variable**, **function** and **procedure** (both function and procedure are a type of module).
Object oriented	Ruby Python C++ Microsoft C#® Oracle Java®	• Form the basis of most modern programming languages • Use **classes**, which contain both **data** and **methods**, to create **objects** which interact to solve problems • Classes model the way the real world works • Common terms include **encapsulation**, **polymorphism** and **inheritance** (a way of extending existing program code).
Event driven	Microsoft Visual Basic® Microsoft Visual Basic. NET®	• A modern approach to problem solving • Common terms include **events**, **event triggers**, **event handlers**, **exception handlers** (which deal with problems that occur rather than forcing the program to crash) • Programs do not follow a fixed step-by-step approach • Often use a **main loop** which 'listens' for events ('things that happen', such as a mouse click) • Programs respond to events which trigger pre-written event handlers which 'do something' • Often used in **GUIs** (graphical user interfaces) where the order of processing that the user can choose is not fixed • Can be used to **prototype** software interfaces very quickly.

Table 18.1 Common programming paradigms

Activity A

Obtaining different programming languages

Software design does not have to be expensive!

Although costly editions of all programming languages are commercially available, there are many freely downloadable versions which you can use to help you get started on your software design career.

Shown below are some of the languages discussed in the unit and where they can be downloaded:

Procedural

BASIC   http://www.freebasic. net/index.php/download

Pascal   http://www.freepascal. org/download.var

Object oriented

Bloodshed   http://www.bloodshed.
Dev C++   net/dev/devcpp.html

Microsoft   http://www.microsoft.
Visual C#®   com/express/Downloads/
              #2010-Visual-CS

Event driven

Microsoft Visual
Basic .NET® express edition

       http://www.microsoft.
       com/express/Downloads/
       #2010-Visual-Basic

Make the grade   P1

This criterion asks you to describe the characteristics of programming paradigms.

A thorough read through section 18.1.1 should give you the information you need. Remember you will need to be able to compare the core qualities of programming paradigms, in other words, what makes them different.

You can strengthen your answer by listing some of the languages which belong to each paradigm. Table 18.1 will help you with this.

18.1.2 Features

Most programming languages in these three paradigms use similar building blocks to create solutions. The most common features include:

- Variables and constants
- Assignment statements
- Output statements
- Input statements
- Arithmetic, logical and relational operators
- Sequence
- Selection
- Iteration

We will use Microsoft's Visual C#® and Visual Basic .NET® to illustrate real programming code as we take a look at each of these.

Variables, constants and naming conventions

> ### Key term
> A **variable** is a form of **identifier**;
> a 'name' which represents a value.

In programming, a variable is used to store and retrieve data from the computer system's RAM. Every variable should have a unique (and meaningful) name.

In order to reserve enough RAM for the variable, we must select an appropriate data type (see section 18.3.3).

For example, if we want to store our user's age in a variable:

```
int iAge;
```
Microsoft Visual C#®

```
Dim iAge As Integer
```
Microsoft Visual Basic .NET®

This is called a **declaration**. This line of code essentially reserves enough RAM to store an integer (a whole number) and allows us to refer to that reserved RAM by the name we have picked: iAge.

Professional programmers often prefix the name of their variables with an initial letter which indicates the variable's data type. Choosing to do this is considered to be good practice; it is known as using a **naming convention**, this particular one is called **'Hungarian notation'**.

Even better practice would have been to add a **comment**, so:

```
int iAge;  // stores the user's age
```
Microsoft Visual C#®

```
Dim iAge As Integer  'stores user's age
```
Microsoft Visual Basic .NET®

Local and global variables

In simple terms what this means is: how **visible** is the variable? In a large program split into a number of different modules, a **global variable** would be visible to all modules whereas a **local variable** would only be visible within the module in which it was declared.

Professional programmers prefer to use local variables where possible as it tends to make programs easier to debug – any faults with the variable have to be in a particular module.

Constants

In addition to variables it is possible to create another type of identifier: a **constant**.

> ### Key term
>
> Like a variable, a **constant** is another form of identifier. Unlike a variable it cannot change its value while the programming is running.

```
const int iMAXAGE = 125; // oldest allowable age
```
Microsoft Visual C#®

```
Const iMAXAGE As Integer = 125 'oldest allowable age
```
Microsoft Visual Basic .NET®

In this example, 'iMAXAGE' is declared as a constant and given the value of 125.

In the program we will now use the constant 'iMAXAGE' whenever we want to refer to the value 125. There are two advantages of this:

- It improves the readability of the program code.
- If we want to change the maximum age we *only* have to alter the constant's declaration – *not* find every occurrence of '125' in the code.

Assignment statements

> **Key term**
>
> An **assignment statement** is used to give a variable a value.

When an assignment is performed successfully, the previous value stored in the variable is overwritten. In most languages an '=' (equals sign) is used for the **assignment operator**.

```
iAge = 16;   // set user's age
```
Microsoft Visual C#®

```
iAge = 16    'set user's age
```
Microsoft Visual Basic .NET®

If the variable is being assigned for the first time, we call this process **'initialisation'**. Some programming languages do not initialise new variables to sensible starting values (such as 0). Where this does not happen automatically, initialisation must occur to ensure that the variables are ready for use.

Output statements

All programming languages have a basic method for generating output, normally to screen.

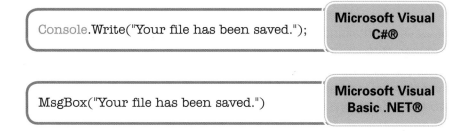

```
Console.Write("Your file has been saved.");
```
Microsoft Visual C#®

```
MsgBox("Your file has been saved.")
```
Microsoft Visual Basic .NET®

It is also possible to output the contents of a variable to screen as part of a message:

```
Console.Write("Do you still feel young at {0}?", iAge);
```
Microsoft Visual C#®

```
MsgBox("Do you still feel young at " & iAge & "?")
```
Microsoft Visual Basic .NET®

If iAge currently had the integer value 16, the associated screen output would be as given in Figures 18.2 and 18.3.

Figure 18.2 Screen output in Microsoft Visual C#®

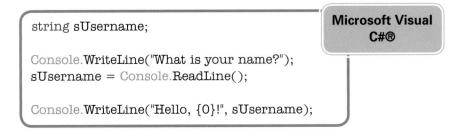

Figure 18.3 Screen output in Microsoft Visual Basic .NET®

The content (16) of the variable (iAge) is **inserted** into the correct part of the message.

Input statements

There are many different ways of obtaining input. For now we will just focus on basic keyboard input.

The following code prompts the user for a value (their name) and stores it in a variable ('sUsername'). To prove it has been successfully stored in RAM, we then output it.

```
string sUsername;

Console.WriteLine("What is your name?");
sUsername = Console.ReadLine();

Console.WriteLine("Hello, {0}!", sUsername);
```
Microsoft Visual C#®

Figure 18.4 Output in Microsoft Visual C#®

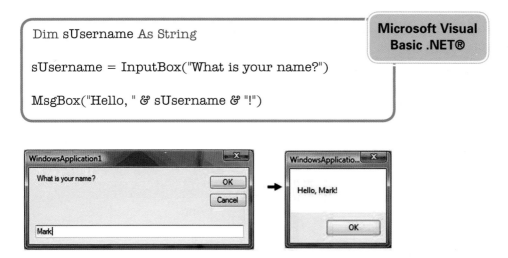

```
Dim sUsername As String

sUsername = InputBox("What is your name?")

MsgBox("Hello, " & sUsername & "!")
```

Microsoft Visual
Basic .NET®

Figure 18.5

The stored **string** (their name) is then repeated to the user, complete with a greeting.

Arithmetic operators

These are the basic elements for writing numerical calculations in a program. The number of arithmetic operators in programming languages varies greatly but there are some that are absolutely fundamental (see Table 18.2).

Arithmetic operation	Microsoft Visual Basic .NET®	Microsoft Visual C#®
Add	+	+
Subtract	-	-
Multiply	* (asterisk)	* (asterisk)
Divide	/ (forward slash)	/ (forward slash)
Modulus (obtains the remainder)	Mod	% (percentage)
Increment (increase by 1)		++
Decrement (decrease by 1)		– –

Table 18.2 Common arithmetic operators

In addition, **parentheses** (brackets) may be used to alter the natural order of operations (division, multiplication, addition and subtraction).

For example

fAverage = iNum1 + iNum2 + iNum3 / 3

fAverage = $($iNum1 + iNum2 + iNum3$)$ / 3

The second version (which forces all the addition to be performed first) is the correct one and requires the use of parentheses.

Logical operators

Most programming languages have **keywords** or **operators** to process **logical operations**. Table 18.3 lists these logical operations and their various implementations.

Logical operation	Microsoft Visual Basic .NET®	Microsoft Visual C#®
AND	And	&&
OR	Or	||
NOT	Not	!

Table 18.3 Common logical operators

Logical operators can be used to create more complex conditions. These conditions are then used to make more flexible selections and iterations.

Relational operators

Relational operators are used to make direct comparisons between values. The result of this type of comparison can only be true or false.

Table 18.4 lists these relational operations and their implementations in the two different languages.

Relational operation	Microsoft Visual Basic .NET®	Microsoft Visual C#®
Equal to (test for equality)	=	==
Not equal to (test for inequality)	<>	!=
Greater than	>	>
Less than	<	<
Greater than *or* equal to	>=	>=
Less than *or* equal to	<=	<=

Table 18.4 Relational operations

TIP

If you have trouble remembering which symbol is 'less than', think about it as a squashed 'L':

ess than

Activity **B**

Interpreting operators

How well do you understand the new operators you have read about?

Work out whether these Microsoft Visual C#® expressions evaluate to TRUE or FALSE. Look at the Answers section at the back of the book to check.

1. 10 > 5

2. 6 < 6.1

3. 'A' != 'B'

4. FALSE == FALSE   *Continued on next page*

Continued ...

5. 7 > 2 AND 5>=5

6. 3 < 10 OR 99 < 67

7. "REBEKAH" == "rebekah"

8. (10+2) >= (60/5)

Sequence

> ### Key term
> A **sequence** occurs when actions are performed one after another (in other words, step by step).

In this example the action list will always be A, B and C.

Selection

> ### Key term
> A **selection** occurs when a decision is made that determines which of two (or sometimes more) possible actions are taken.

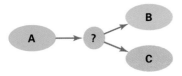

In this example, either Action B or Action C is followed, not both. This would mean that the actions list could either be: A, B or A, C.

Selections traditionally use either **if ... then ... else** or **case statements**.

```
Dim iAge As Integer
iAge = 16
If (iAge >= 18) Then
  MsgBox("In the UK, you are now a responsible adult.")
Else
  MsgBox("In the UK, you are still a minor")
End If
```

Microsoft Visual Basic .NET®

```vbnet
Dim idayofweek As Integer
idayofweek = 3

Select Case idayofweek
    Case 1 : MsgBox("It's Monday!")
    Case 2 : MsgBox("It's Tuesday!")
    Case 3 : MsgBox("It's Wednesday!")
    Case 4 : MsgBox("It's Thursday!")
    Case 5 : MsgBox("It's Friday!")
    Case 6 : MsgBox("It's Saturday!")
    Case 7 : MsgBox("It's Sunday!")
End Select
```

Microsoft Visual Basic .NET®

Iteration

> ### Key terms
>
> **Iteration** is just a fancy name for a loop, in other words something that happens repeatedly. In programming, loops generally repeat until they are told to stop; this is achieved with a **condition**.

Sometimes the decision is placed after the actions. We call this '**post-conditioning**'.

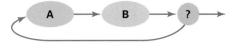

Because of this, the actions in a post-conditioned loop always work at least once. Perhaps the most common example of a post-conditioned loop is **do … while** and flavours of it exist in most programming languages. For example in C#®:

```csharp
int counter;

counter = 1;

do
{
    Console.WriteLine("Counter is currently {0}", counter);
    counter++;
} while (counter <= 10);
```

Microsoft Visual C#®

And its equivalent in Visual Basic .NET®:

Microsoft Visual Basic .NET®

```
Dim counter As Integer
counter = 1

Do
  MsgBox("Counter is currently " & counter)
  counter = counter + 1
Loop Until (counter > 10)
```

Sometimes the decision is placed before the actions. We call this **'pre-conditioning'**.

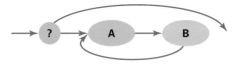

In a pre-conditioned loop, the actions **may never** be processed at all! Perhaps the most common example of a pre-conditioned loop is **while ... do** and flavours of it exist in most programming languages. For example in C#®:

Microsoft Visual C#®

```
int counter;

counter = 1;

while (counter <=10)
{
  Console.WriteLine("Counter is currently {0}", counter);
  counter++;
}
```

```
file:///C:/Users/Mark/AppDat...
Counter is currently 1
Counter is currently 2
Counter is currently 3
Counter is currently 4
Counter is currently 5
Counter is currently 6
Counter is currently 7
Counter is currently 8
Counter is currently 9
Counter is currently 10
```

Figure 18.6

And its equivalent in Visual Basic .NET®:

```
Dim counter As Integer
counter = 1

While (counter <= 10)
   MsgBox("Counter is currently " & counter)
   counter = counter + 1
End While
```

Microsoft Visual Basic .NET®

You may be wondering why we have both pre- and post-conditioned loops. The answer is simple: there are simply some occasions when one technique is more appropriate to use than the other.

Activity C

Understanding sequence, selection and iteration

In order to build a program we often need to use collections of these different constructs and may 'glue' them together to form a working solution.

Examine the following construct diagrams and work out the different combination of actions that are possible. Check your answers at the back of the book.

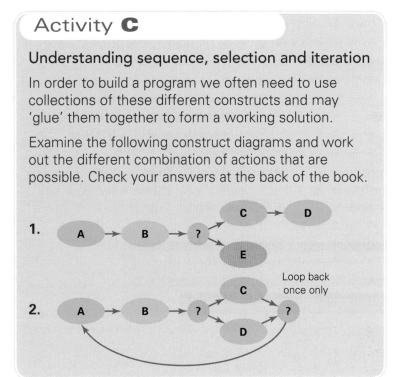

This criterion asks you to describe the features of programming languages including how sequence, selection and iteration are used.

By reading through section 18.1.2 you should be able to see that these three constructs are the building blocks of software design. In addition you should be able to explain confidently how input and output works and why variables, assignment statements and operators are vital considerations for any software design.

A good technique may be to write some sample code and show how each of these language features is used to solve a problem – proving their importance and flexibility.

18.1.3 Types of language

Over the last 50 years, there have been literally hundreds of different programming languages created. Some languages have since fallen out of favour with professional developers or been superseded; others cover very specific 'niche' markets (for example, programming vending machines). A number of languages are popular within the industry because they are fast to work with and generally produce reliable and robust (not likely to 'crash') solutions.

In addition to languages in the three paradigms discussed earlier, other types of language are available. These include visual languages, JavaScript® and markup languages.

Visual languages

This category is often misused: be careful! Visual languages are best demonstrated as using graphical development tools and to create software. The user can often create basic programs by dragging and dropping icons, logic pathways and special symbols.

Every visual component (its appearance and function) may in fact represent many thousands of lines of traditional program code in a non-visual language. A typical visual language is **VisSim** (see Figure 18.7).

Other types of languages exist, of course. Let us take a look at two more you may already be familiar with.

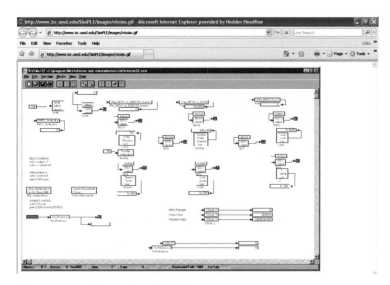

Figure 18.7 Example of VisSim

JavaScript®

Despite what some people may say, **JavaScript®** and **Java®** are *not* the same thing! Although the name is similar, JavaScript® is only distantly related to Sun's full object-oriented programming language.

JavaScript® is Netscape Communications' name for its own ECMAscript dialect.

JavaScript®'s primary purpose is to provide automation and interactivity for existing web pages. Because of this, JavaScript® is often included within the HTML page itself, although it is possible to store it separately in .JS files.

Figure 18.8 demonstrates a simple JavaScript® automation of a web page.

Figure 18.8 JavaScript® working in a web page

```html
<html>
<head>
<script = "JavaScript">

function check()
{
  var reply = confirm("Return to www.edexcel.org.uk?")
  if (reply)
  {
    window.location = "http://www.edexcel.org.uk";
  }
}
</script>
</head>
<body>
<form>
<input type="button" onclick="check()" value="Leave this page?">
</form>
</body>
</html>
```

Markup languages

Markup languages are used to **describe** the way in which text is presented to a reader. A number of markup languages are available and, while they are not programming languages in the truest sense, they do provide solutions to set problems.

HTML

Hypertext markup language (**HTML**) is currently the most popular way of creating web pages for publishing on the world wide web (WWW). The language was created by Tim Berners-Lee who now leads the **World Wide Web Consortium** (**WC3**). This organisation regularly publishes standards for web page creation to ensure that pages remain interoperable – that they 'work together' – on different computer systems.

HTML uses a series of **block tags** to indicate the start and end of structured text and web page elements (such as images, tables, bulleted lists etc.).

```
<html>
<head>
<title>BTEC First Diploma in IT</title>
<META name="Author" content="M Fishpool">
</head>
<body>
<p>Welcome to the BTEC First Diploma in IT!

<IMG src="computer.jpg" alt="Computer System">

</p>
</body>
</html>
```

The central idea of HTML is the **hyperlink**; a special link which when clicked takes the user to another resource (such as an image, a piece of music, a document or a video) which may be on the same page or on another computer system located somewhere else.

18.1.4 Choice of language

Why does a programmer choose a particular language?

If the programmer is able to choose which language to use, it may simply be a case of **familiarity** – they will simply use the language that they know best.

However, there are other important factors to take into consideration.

These include:

- **Cost** – Languages have **development costs** (incurred during production) and maintenance costs (incurred after the solution has been delivered). Some languages prove more costly than others. For example, a solution that is not that reliable will create a lot of costly maintenance over a period of time. In addition, different programming language IDEs (integrated development environment) can vary greatly in price.

- **Organisational policy** – Many organisations specify both the language and development environment to use. This is particularly true in governmental work where security is vital. A famous example of this is the programming language called Ada – it was designed specifically for use by the United States Department of Defense.

- **Availability** – Programming languages are just like any other. They have to be learned and practised for some time before a level of competency is reached. How many trained and experienced staff are available? Is the program language available for the hardware used in the organisation (in other words, is a compiler available)?

- **Reliability** – Different languages may be seen to be more reliable than others. **Mission critical systems** would not be created using a programming language whose dependability was less than 100 per cent.

- **Suitability** – It is absolutely critical that programming languages are suitable for the task at hand, particularly when taking into consideration their features and tools. For example Java®, while being very useful for web-based applications, is perhaps not so suitable for controlling real-time systems where rapid response to real-world events is crucial.

- **Expandability** – A critical part of ongoing maintenance is the ability to expand an existing solution. Some programming languages, particularly object oriented ones, are good at this.

Make the grade   P2

This criterion asks you to identify the factors influencing the choice of programming language.

It should be remembered that as many different paradigms and types of language exist, the reasons for selection may be numerous and varied. You are advised to refer to the considerations listed in 18.1.4 (below) when forming your answer but should be mindful that not all available languages fit neatly into the three paradigms. Take a look back at some of the other types discussed in section 18.1.3.

Tip – think about these languages and factors when designing your software solution (P5) as justifying your choice will be important for achieving M2.

TIP

If you have trouble remembering the factors above, think C-O-A-R-S-E.

Table 18.5 gives some advantages and disadvantages of some of the most popular programming languages.

Language	Advantages	Disadvantages
C++®	Well established Popular in industry Supports object-oriented paradigm Standardised Not limited to Microsoft Windows® operating system Efficient Some C++ compilers are free	Syntax can be difficult to learn Development can be slow Case sensitive
Visual Basic .NET®	Allows rapid development of applications Quick, visual results for the new programmer Friendly drag-and-drop development Auto-corrects case used when keying code Relies on Microsoft Windows® operating system	Generally not fast Generally not very efficient
Pascal	Encourages good programming practice Good for new programmers ISO standard Not case sensitive	Not really used in industry; better as an educational tool Lacks language features to get most out of computer system
JavaScript®	JavaScript® interpreter is present in most web browsers (it is free)	Can be unpredictable as it can vary when run under different web browsers Can be difficult to find and fix errors ('debug') Limited in scope Can stop when error is encountered Generally not fast Case sensitive

Table 18.5 Language comparison

So, which should you use?

Ultimately the choice of programming language has as much to do with the target user's expectations as the skills and knowledge of the actual software designer (you!).

At this level, any of the languages listed above represent a reasonably good trade-off between **functionality**, **ease of development** and potential **quality of** the end product.

18.2 Know the software development process

This section will cover the following grading criteria: **P3** **P4** M2

18.2.1 Software development life cycle

Developing a solution for a problem reflects a natural life cycle. New solutions are designed and implemented because a new business need has been identified.

The stages of building that new solution can be shown visually:

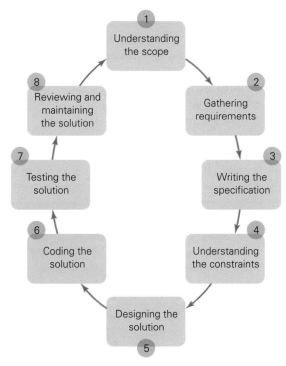

Figure 18.9 Software development life cycle

Let us examine each stage of this cycle in more detail.

Stage 1: Understanding the scope

> **Key term**
>
> **Scope** is a word used to describe what is within the boundaries of the problem. It is a definition of what is and what is not included in the business need. It will include a list of people, processes, data and information that should be considered.

The importance of the scope cannot be underestimated – bad solutions are often designed because there is poor understanding of what the user really needs.

Understanding the scope is vital in order to understand the nature of the problem.

Stage 2: Gathering requirements

Before the problem is tackled it is vital that the **functional requirements** – what is wanted from the solution by those who are affected – are clearly known.

Those affected by the problem are commonly referred to as **stakeholders**.

This will absolutely specify what the solution *does* and *does not* cover. A staggeringly high number of commercial solutions fail because these requirements are poorly researched; it is a common failure of IT projects worldwide.

Common techniques for gathering requirements include:

- observation
- interview
- questionnaire
- analysing documents and paperwork.

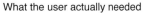

What the user actually needed   What the designer thought   What the programmer
                                       the user wanted   eventually created

Figure 18.10 Understanding the user's needs is important!

Stage 3: Writing the specification

Table 18.6 lists the elements you have to put together
before you can design a solution.

Inputs	This is simply any data that is entered into the system by its user. Every input will need to be separately identified and listed. This can take some time to investigate fully.
Outputs	These are the things required from the system, as requested by the user. In order to program the solution correctly, the designer will need to know: • What are the outputs? • How should the outputs be displayed? • When are the outputs generated?
Processing	These should be basic descriptions of the processing that is required, for example: calculate total cost, check user password is correct, print bill. These process descriptions can then be **decomposed** (broken down) into more **detailed algorithms** as part of the design phase (see section 18.3.2). **Remember** – the processing required should convert the inputs into the desired outputs.

Table 18.6 Continued on next page

Storage	Storage typically means two things: • Temporary data stored in RAM (variables) • Permanent data stored on backing storage (such as hard disk) in a data file. Identified data should include: • Any piece of data mentioned in the problem • Any calculated value needed to solve the problem • Any value which will be output. At this point it is worthwhile identifying whether the storage items are numeric, text, date or Boolean.

Table 18.6 Continued

Building a good user interface is a separate subject of its own – Human Computer Interface/Interaction (**HCI**) – getting it right is not easy!

Part of the specification should decide:

- How will the end user interact with the program?
- Will they use a mouse, keyboard or both?
- Which colours should be used?
- What types and sizes of font should be used?
- How is the screen laid out?

Forms design is an important part of this aspect.

Stage 4: Understanding the constraints

> ### Key term
>
> A **constraint** is some kind of **limiting factor**; something which could prevent you completing a task satisfactorily.

There are a number of constraints you will need to consider:

- Hardware platform – what type of computer system is to be used?
- Operating system software – availability and compatibility

- Timescale for development – is there enough time?
- Funding – how much money is available?
- Workforce – availability of trained developers, quality assurance testers etc.

Stage 5: Designing a solution

This means using a suitable **design tool** (see section 18.3.2) to build a solution based on the specification provided.

This may be paper-based or electronic depending on the design tools being used.

Modern IT solutions can be partly carried out by software tools, with programs effectively writing new solutions.

Avoid the temptation to rush ahead into the coding; many mistakes are made this way and a lot of time is needlessly wasted!

Stage 6: Coding a solution

This involves converting the design into program code. This is a job usually performed by experienced software developers.

Developers have to select the correct programming language before they start – certain design features will always fit some languages better than others (see sections 18.1.1 and 18.1.2).

It is common for software developers to work in a team. If this is the case, it is important that they are all clear about their individual responsibilities and adopt similar working practices and a consistent 'in-house' style in an effort to standardise.

Programs written in a **modular way** (broken into smaller modules such as procedures and functions) ensure reusability through shared libraries. Use of classes will also permit easy code reuse and speed up the development process.

Ideally, all developers need to have an understanding of how their modules fit into the larger solution, even if they do not know how modules which they have not written actually work.

Stage 7: Testing the solution

Good testing is very important. Two common testing methods are used: **Black Box** and **White Box**.

Black Box testing does not care about *how* the program was written (in other words, peeking inside). It only wants to see how closely a program meets its list of functional requirements: does it do what it is supposed to do?

White Box testing examines the performance of the program code, ensuring that what has been programmed is generating the right results. White Box takes much more time and usually starts after Black Box testing has been completed.

Testing is part of the **quality assurance** process in the software development life cycle.

Thorough testing guarantees that the solution should work properly and meet the identified needs of the target users. A **test plan** is used to explain the **testing strategy** being used.

Test plan

A test plan should attempt to:

- Check different **logical pathways**. For example, does the test check both halves (true and false) of a conditional statement (such as If … else) or all possible outcomes of a case statement? Have all the loops been successfully tested?

  Flowcharts are particularly good for this as the logical pathways are easy to see. The tests should touch upon all flow arrows on the diagram.

- Check **normal data**. The program needs to be tested with data that is within a sensible range; in other words, data likely to be input.

- Check **extreme data**. It should also be tested with values which, while still within a sensible range, are less likely to be input. These are the values on the extremes (both high and low). For example, an age over 115 years is not impossible, but it is extreme (about 1 in 2.1 billion people).

- Check **erroneous data**. Not all data entered into a program will be sensible. In order to ensure it is robust, **spurious data** should be tested. This typically includes values outside valid ranges and wrong types of value (such as alphabetic when a number is expected).

Collecting suitable test data is important, both in quantity and quality of spread.

The test plan structure should include:

- Test – what is being tested; which part of the program is being tested.
- Date – when the test is taking place; this is important as it may link to a particular version of the program.
- Expected result – what results we expected to get out of the program by tracing through first on paper.
- Actual result – the results generated by the computer using our supplied test data.
- Corrective action – if a problem was discovered, what was done to the program to fix it.

Many formats exist for this type of content. A **trace table** is often seen as a simple way of tabulating and comparing such results. An example of a trace table is given in Table 18.7.

The trace table allows us to record the values entered and logical pathways used when a program runs both on paper (the 'dry run') and live.

The comparison between the actual and expected results will show quickly how accurate the programmed solution is and also, given the variables involved in any particular test, where any possible problem will be found.

Screen captures are a good addition to any trace table as they reinforce the actual results of the program running.

Stage 8: Reviewing and maintaining the solution

This stage's components can be examined separately.

Review is a reflective process, looking at the solution and comparing it with the

Trace table for program 'Water Mover'

Date: 12 September 2010

Test: Calculation of water weight based on volume

#	Box H	Box W	Box L	Vol. (in cm^3) expected	Vol. (in cm^3) actual	Calculated weight expected (kg)	Calculated weight actual (kg)	Corrective action
1	10	20	30	6,000	6,000.0	$0.001 \times 6,000$ = 6 kg	6.0	None!
2	20	40	60	48,000	48,000.0	$0.001 \times 48,000 =$ 48 kg	12.0	Fix data type problem

Table 18.7

original requirements that you gathered from the target user.

The key questions you should ask are:

- Have the requirements been met?
- How well is the solution working?
- Can anything be improved?

Maintenance never stops. Programs are written to solve a problem which exists at a particular point in time. As business or personal needs change, the solution will seem less ideal.

Maintenance usually includes:

- Fixing minor errors that occur
- Making small adjustments which add extra features and functionality.

So, why is it a software development life cycle?

Good question! This is because even the best solutions eventually need replacing as the target user's needs change. When this happens it is back to Step 1 (Understanding the scope) and the whole process starts again.

Make the grade — P3 P4 M2

These criteria are linked. For P3 you will be asked to describe the stages of the software development life cycle. This is shown visually in Figure 18.9 and is detailed throughout section 18.2.1. You need to be able to remember the order of these stages and say what actions are performed in each one.

P4 asks you to outline a specification for a business requirement. This will mean producing a document that (minimally) covers the scope, inputs, outputs, processing and user interface of your planned solution. The scope should describe the essential requirements of the target user's problem and should

demonstrate that you understand (and can explain) the issues and needs in your own words. You should also be able to propose a target programming language at this point.

The business requirement you describe for P4 could be set by your teacher as part of a case study or it might be from a real-life user.

M2 should come naturally as you work on the specification, as it asks you to select and justify your choice of programming language. Head back to sections 18.1.2, 18.1.3 and 18.1.4 for help with this. In most situations you will conclude that a particular paradigm or type of language is the most suitable one to use – for this criterion you must explain why.

18.3 Be able to design software development solutions

This section will cover the following grading criteria:

P5 P6 M3 D1 D2

18.3.1 Design

Once you have gathered the necessary requirements and understand the problem, it is time to think about the design of the solution. The structure of the design can be broken down into a number of simple elements:

Functions
Does the solution need any particular functions for calculating specific values? If so, which values are to be calculated? And how is this to be performed (what is the formula)?

Procedures
Does the solution need to be broken down into separate procedures (modules)? Which modules are required? And what does each module actually do?

Objects
Is the solution lending itself to an object-oriented paradigm? If so, what are the objects required? And how do the objects interact?

Data
What data needs to be stored in the solution?
What variables are required?
What constants are required?
What data types should be used?
Are the variables global or local?

Files
Does the solution need to make use of a data file to store data more permanently? If so, which files? And what data will be stored in them?

18.3.2 Tools

There are a number of design tools available. In order to use the tool effectively, however, it has to be appropriate to the type of solution in hand.

The most common techniques are listed below. Familiarise yourself with them.

Storyboards

> **Key term**
>
> A **storyboard** is a creative way of representing a solution to a problem. It combines visual elements of forms design with events and actions to show how a solution would look and function.

Storyboards are particularly useful when developing solutions in Visual Basic .NET® or Visual C#® as they can be reproduced quickly in their Form Design View.

A storyboard is useful because it allows us to show the expected on-screen appearance of the application before it is written and plan how it will work. The actual mechanics of the solution (in other words what kinds of decisions and calculations it makes) may not actually be described at this point.

Worked activity D

Creating a storyboard

Let us create a simple storyboard for a sample problem. A target user has asked us to create a software application which will help them convert a temperature in degrees Fahrenheit to its equivalent in Celsius (and vice versa).

What we will need in terms of visual components:

- 1 × form
- 3 × labels
- 2 × text boxes
- 2 × buttons

We will also need the calculations to convert between Fahrenheit and Celsius.

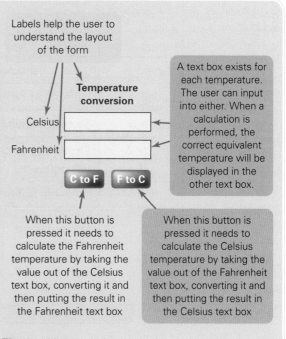

Figure 18.11

Action lists

> ### Key term
>
> An **action list** can be used to complement a storyboard but it can also be used in its own right. It usually looks like a table which lists the basic elements of the solution and what each element is responsible for.

Worked activity E

Creating an action list

Let us create a simple action list for the same temperature conversion problem. The action list must contain information for the following eight elements:

- 1 × form
- 3 × labels
- 2 × text boxes
- 2 × buttons

We will also need some variables to store the results of the calculations which convert between Fahrenheit and Celsius.

Element name	Element type	Description	Action
FrmTemp	Form	Stores the visual elements which represent the application	Can be dragged around the screen by the user
LblTemp	Label	Temperature conversion heading	None
LblCel	Label	Celsius heading	None
LblFah	Label	Fahrenheit heading	None
txtCelsius	Text box	Stores Celsius temperature	User can enter temperature
txtFahrenheit	Text box	Stores Fahrenheit temperature	User can enter temperature
btnCtoF	Button	Clickable button which will convert Celsius temperature to Fahrenheit	On click will put result of: $F = C * 9/5 + 32$ in txtFahrenheit text box
btnFtoC	Button	Clickable button which will convert Fahrenheit temperature to Celsius	On click will put result of: $C = F - 32 * 5/9$ in txtCelsius text box

Storyboards and action lists describe a solution in a pictorial and text-based format. Other tools are available which describe the actual processing involved in more detail and are often more graphical in nature.

Graphical tools

Graphical tools use a combination of special symbols and text to describe a solution. There are a number of different graphical tools available – far more than we can cover in this book! We will limit our focus to the two you might encounter: flowcharts and structure diagrams.

Flowcharts

> # Key term
> You may have seen these used in other subjects. **Flowcharts** are a familiar visual aid for describing the logical steps needed to solve a problem. Many user manuals use them to explain complex sequences of instructions.

Flowcharts use a standard set of drawn symbols. These are shown in Table 18.8.

Name	Symbol	Description
'Terminator'		An **oval** symbol which is used to **start** or **stop** the flowchart
'Decision'		A **diamond** symbol used for **making choices**, such as if … else
'Process'		A **rectangle** which is used to show an **action** or **calculation** that must be performed
'Input or output'		A **parallelogram** that can either be used to specify a **user's input** or the **desired output**
'Connector'		A **circle** that is used to **connect different sections** of a flowchart together; used particularly when it would be difficult to draw flow arrows
'Flow arrows'	↓ →	Arrowed lines used to indicate the **flow of logic** in the solution. Logic, by default, goes top-to-bottom, left-to-right

Table 18.8 Flowchart symbols

As with any design tool, the flowchart should not contain any programming language, only natural language (for example English) should be used. A limited use of general symbols is acceptable. Microsoft Word® has these symbols in its shapes library.

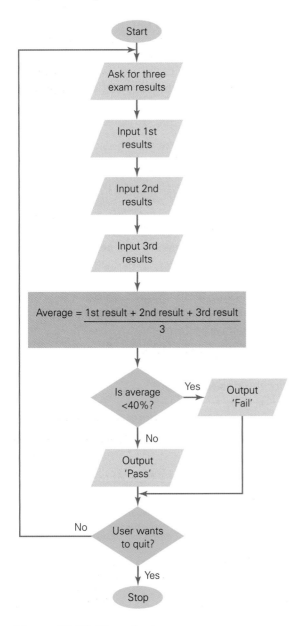

Figure 18.12 Flowchart

Worked activity F

Working with flowcharts

The flowchart in Figure 18.12 asks the user to input three exam results.

The program then averages these. If the result is less than 40 per cent, the program says 'fail'; otherwise it says 'pass'.

The program will keep repeating until the user decides to quit.

Structure diagrams

As you have seen, a flowchart is good at demonstrating the logical flow of a solution.

Unfortunately, even short solutions quickly become large and confusing, sometimes making it difficult for us to understand the underlying structure of the code (in other words, where the selections or loops actually are).

Structure diagrams use a simple system of lines and rectangles which breaks solutions down into the three basic building blocks of sequence, selection and iteration.

Sequence

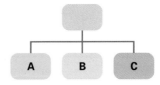

This is a sequence; first action A, then action B, followed by action C.

Selection

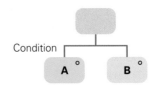

Notice the small 'O' in the top-right corner of each option box to show they are selections rather than a sequence. (Remember: O = option!)

Unlike the sequence, the selection uses a condition to perform either A or B, not both.

If the condition is true, A is performed else B is performed.

Iteration

Notice the small '*' (asterisk) symbol in the top-right corner of the lower box. This indicates that the box will occur a number of times. (Remember: * = loop!)

Iterations are shown by a pair of boxes. The 'top' box indicates a multiple, built from the 'lower' box repeating 0 or more times (as specified by the condition).

Let us examine the exam results solution again, but this time using the structure diagram design tool.

C1 user wants to quit

C2 average < 40 per cent

Reading structure diagrams

Do not worry: students often find reading these diagrams difficult at first!

The most important thing to remember is that these diagrams are read top-to-bottom, left-to-right.

In Figure 18.13 there are two conditions (we have called them 'C1' and 'C2') and these control the main iteration (C1) and the selection (C2). And do not forget: repeated elements have an asterisk and optional elements have an 'O' in the top-right corner of the box.

Algorithms

> **Key term**
>
> An **algorithm** is a set of step-by-step instructions designed to solve a problem.

Algorithms can be developed from design tools (or be used instead of them). A common way to represent an algorithm is by using **pseudo code**.

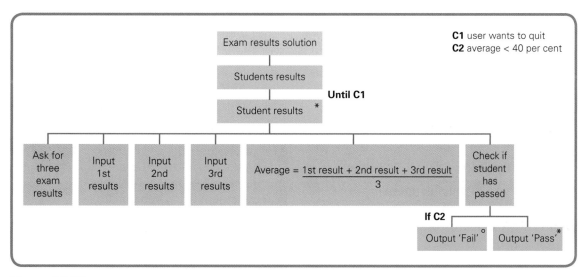

Figure 18.13

Pseudo code

> ## Key term
>
> **Pseudo code**, literally meaning 'false code' (from the Greek), is a way of writing the outline steps required in an algorithm without having to write any real programming language code – the pseudo code is written in a natural language, such as English.

For the exam results solution, the following pseudo code would be adequate:

```
Repeat
  Ask for three exam results
  Input 1st exam result
  Input 2nd exam result
  Input 3rd exam result
  Average = (1st exam result + 2nd exam result
  + 3rd exam result) / 3
  If average < 40
    Output 'fail'
  Else
    Output 'pass'
  Endif
Until user wants to quit
```

You may sometimes see pseudo code with line numbers – this is OK. What you should not see is anything specific to any particular programming language.

> ## Activity **G**
>
> ### Using a design tool to create a solution
>
> Read through the following problem.
>
> 'Doorway to Infinity' is an online retailer that sells comics. The business currently calculates order costs manually but has been investigating the possibility of having a simple software solution to do the job.

Their costs are **£2.25** per comic.

Standard postal costs are a **one-off fee of £1.50 plus 25p per comic**.

Next day delivery costs an **additional one-off fee of £3.00**.

1. Design a possible solution using a suitable design tool of your choice.
2. Now try creating the same solution using a different design tool!

> ## Activity **H**
>
> ### Convert the solution to real programming code
>
> Examine the solution you have designed. Which programming language do you think is most appropriate to use?
>
> When you have selected it, have a go at creating a working solution with that language.
>
> Produce printed listings of the program code and screen captures of your application actually running.
>
> How easy was it to get your program running successfully? And did it fulfil the original requirements?

> ## Make the grade   P5 M3 D1
>
> P5 is another critical criterion – it asks you to design the software solution to a business requirement using appropriate design tools. Some of the design tools you could use are covered in sections 18.3.1 and 18.3.2. Your teacher may prefer you to use different ones, this does not matter. *Continued on next page*

continued...
M3 asks you to describe the data types and software structures used in a design solution. A data table is a good way to demonstrate the variables and data types used (see section 18.3.3 below).

D1 asks you to develop an algorithm to represent the design solution. If you look at section 18.3.2 you will see that most design tools provide an outline solution. Creating an algorithm with pseudo code (for example), would provide a stepping stone to a fully programmed solution. Note: Although you *do not* have to create a programmed solution for D1, it is anticipated that learners may want to as it will let them demonstrate their practical skills. If attempted, this should use the same language identified in the specification for criterion M2.

18.3.3 Data types

Key term

Data types are one of the essential building blocks of software design and are used to specify the kind of values which need to be stored in the computer system's RAM.

You have already seen variables in section 18.1.1 and have been introduced briefly to their data types.

The actual names of the data types available will vary from language to language but common categories are typically found (see Figure 18.14).

Let us take a look at these in a little more detail.

Character – Sometimes abbreviated to **char**, this can store **one character**; in other words, any symbol in the computer system's character set such as alphabet, digit, punctuation, currency symbols etc. Examples include: A, &, ", @, 9, #.

A character normally needs **1 byte** of RAM storage.

String – A string is a number of characters joined together. The string can be composed of any number of valid symbols. Some languages may define a limit for the length of the string (such as 255 characters or bytes). Examples include: 'BTEC First Diploma', '01412 989922', 'Jane Smith', '#123'.

Some languages use what are called **ASCIIZ** strings, where a zero (0) value marks the end of a string, for example, B T E C 0.

Other languages place the length of the string in the first byte, for example, 4 B T E C.

Integer – Often abbreviated to **int**, an integer is a **whole number** (with no decimal part). Integers can be **positive**, **negative** or **neither** ('unsigned'). Examples include: 2814, +52, −7.

Programming languages place a limit on the size of integers. However, this usually depends on how much RAM an integer is

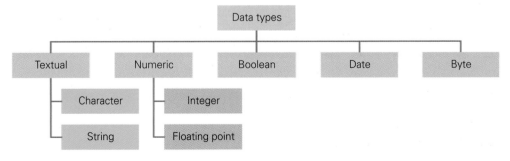

Figure 18.14 Common categories of data types

allocated and whether the integer is signed (positive or negative) or unsigned. Some languages have short or small int variables which use less RAM.

For example, for an **8 bit integer**:

Signed range (maximum and minimum)

	128	64	32	16	8	4	2	1
+127	0	1	1	1	1	1	1	1
−128	1	0	0	0	0	0	0	0

Unsigned range (maximum and minimum)

	128	64	32	16	8	4	2	1
255	1	1	1	1	1	1	1	1
0	0	0	0	0	0	0	0	0

Integer sizes in most modern programming languages are minimally 16 bit in size.

Floating point – These are 'real' numbers (numbers which have a decimal point and fractional part). Examples include: +1025.34, −117.1234, +0.4.

Floating point numbers have two main components: the **mantissa** and the **exponent**.

For example, +**1.34** E + **2** or **1.34** $\times$ **10^2**

In this example, both values equal 134.

1.34 E + 2 means move the decimal point two places to the right.

1.34 $\times$ 10^2 means multiply 1.34 $\times$ 100 (10 squared).

The mantissa represents the accuracy of the number while the exponent represents the magnitude.

In programming languages floating points come in various sizes (see Table 18.11 on the next page for an example). Larger floating point numbers offer greater magnitude and accuracy of numerical data.

Boolean – The name reflects the field of **mathematical logic** developed by nineteenth-century English mathematician **George Boole**. Boolean values are true or false, yes or no. This reflects the 0 and 1 binary values used by computer systems.

Date – Computer systems typically have a **real time clock** (**RTC**). As such, date and time processing is fairly easy. Date data types may be stored in different ways. For example:

As YYYY-MM-DD   10 July 2011 would be 2011-07-10

As DD-MM-YYYY   10 July 2011 would be 10-07-2011

Byte – A byte stores 8 bits of computer data.

Data table

Although this is a design consideration, it is timely to introduce the concept of a **data table** at this point. Fulfilling a similar function to a **data dictionary** (typically when working with databases), the data table is a simple method for documenting identifiers (such as variables and constants) and data types used in a solution.

The common convention is to draw a table with the following headings:

Data table for 'Program Name'						
Identifier name	Variable or constant	Data type	Typical value	Storage	Local or global	Description

Table 18.9 Data table

A separate row is then used for each identifier used in the solution, for example:

Identifier name	Variable or constant	Data type	Typical value	Storage	Local or global	Description
iRadius	Variable	Integer	10	4 bytes (32 bits)	Local	iRadius is specified as a whole number so I have used a standard integer

Table 18.10 Data table use

Your description can be recycled to use as the comments for each declaration if you choose.

> **TIP** (t)
>
> A data table is an efficient way of showing the variables and data types you plan to use in your solution. This is very helpful when completing work for criterion M3!

Data type	Storage	Example
Boolean	4 bytes	True or false
Byte	1 byte	0 to 255 (unsigned)
Char	2 bytes	0 to 65,535 (unsigned)
Date	8 bytes	1 January, 1 Common Era to 31 December, 9999
Decimal	12 bytes	+/−79,228,162,514,264,337,593,543,950,335 with no decimal point; +/− 7.9228162514264337593543950335 with 28 places to the right of the decimal; smallest non-zero number is +/−0.0000000000000000000000000001

Table 18.11 Example data types in Visual Basic .NET®

Data type	Storage	Example
Double	8 bytes	–1.79769313486231E308 to –4.94065645841247E–324 for negative values; 4.94065645841247E–324 to 1.79769313486232E308 for positive values
Integer	4 bytes	–2,147,483,648 to 2,147,483,647
Long	8 bytes	–9,223,372,036,854,775,808 to 9,223,372,036,854,775,807
Short	2 bytes	–32,768 to 32,767
Single	4 bytes	–3.402823E38 to –1.401298E–45 for negative values; 1.401298E–45 to 3.402823E38 for positive values
String	10 bytes + (2 * string length)	0 to two billion characters

Table 18.11 Continued

Data types in an example language

Table 18.11 shows some actual data types available in Microsoft's Visual Basic .NET® programming language.

Other programming languages may have data types with different names but they will be identical in purpose. When you start to program in a specific language, an important first step should be to familiarise yourself with the data types available.

Activity I

Data types in other programming languages

Choose another popular programming language from section 18.1.3 such as:

C++®
C#®
Java®

Investigate which data types the language would use to store the following data values:

1060   3.23   'E'   True   'Neptune'

18.3.4 Software structures

Software designs are built from a number of different structures and elements (including the variables and data types we have already seen).

Given below are some common software structures with a brief overview provided for each.

Sequence – Any collection of program statements that are performed one after the other.

Selection – A decision or conditional statement whose result lets the program execute one set of program statements or another. These form the program's logical pathways.

Iteration – A block of statements which are repeated based on some conditional statement evaluating to true.

Modules – In programming, a term used to describe different parts of a program. The implementation of a module (size, layout etc.) will vary from language to language.

Functions – A practical example of a module. Generally, functions are used to calculate a value, although some may perform actions instead. They are re-usable.

Procedures – Another practical example of a module. Procedures tend to perform actions. As with functions, these are re-usable.

Classes – Part of the object-oriented programming paradigm, a class contains both data and functions which describe a real-world 'thing'.

Objects – A concrete instance of a class, complete with its personal data.

Data abstraction – One of the key principle ideas behind the creation of classes. In data abstraction the data type is less important than the operations which can be performed on it; in a sense the data type is hidden behind a limited number of functions/methods.

Pre-defined code – Generally a term describing code which is already written and which can be used in a developer's solution (with permission). This may take the form of a **compiled module**, a **'call'** to the operating system or a **'snippet'** of ready-made code which can be inserted into their solution.

Most programs are built from combining these different elements in various patterns and quantities.

Readability

You can improve the readability of your software solution by following these simple steps:

- Always **comment** your program code sensibly.
- Always select **meaningful names** for your variables.
- Always use **indentation** to highlight the structure of your program code.
- Always try to keep solutions as **simple** as possible.
- Always use the **most appropriate** software structures.

Quality of code

The quality of code is judged through several criteria. Let us look at the most obvious ones you should consider using when making decisions about the quality of your software solutions. The following should help you remember how to check for quality:

Quality solutions are like **PEAR RUM!**

Portable – code can be recompiled for different hardware and software platforms with minimal modification.

Efficient – they calculate results and perform operations as quickly as possible.

Accurate – they produce results with an acceptable level of accuracy.

Robust – they do not crash when given bad or silly input.

Reliable – they work the same way every time they are used, with no unexpected surprises.

Usable – be intuitive for the end user to operate.

Maintainable – be easy to modify and improve (as needed).

18.3.5 Review

> ### Key term
>
> In terms of software design a review asks you to reflect on:
>
> - The solution's strengths
> - The solution's weaknesses
> - How well the program met the business requirement (and the target user's needs)
> - How it could be improved.

In order to review effectively you must compare and contrast the final product to the original requirements specification. It will require the co-operation of all the stakeholders in order to secure the necessary findings and this could take some time.

End-users of the software can be interviewed, observed or given a questionnaire to complete.

The use of **focus groups** to dig down into user viewpoint is also valuable.

In addition, it is likely that a section on further developments may be created, listing:

- An overview of corrections made (to errors)
- Improvements (to existing performance) that could be made
- Expansions (to existing functionality) that could be invested in.

Review should be an ongoing process, exploring program performance and end-user satisfaction at regular intervals. If faults are found which cannot be remedied using minor maintenance, the software development life cycle (as seen in 18.2.1) will start once more.

Make the grade   P6   D2

For P6 you will be asked to review the design against the original requirement. The review (which could be oral or written) must demonstrate how closely the solution meets the problem that was provided. You should also review the quality of the solution you have created; you will find a lot of support for this in section 18.3.4. For example, is the code efficient? Does it produce accurate results? Is it usable? D2 should form part of your P6 answer by asking you to evaluate the design tools used (leading us back to section 18.3.2) and *not* the solution. Did you use an appropriate design tool? Did it help you create a solution from which you could create good program code? How easy was the tool to use? This is a judgement

only you can make – it does not matter whether you made the right choices or the wrong choices as long as you can explain your reasoning.

Achieving Success

In order to achieve each unit, you will complete a series of coursework activities. Each time you hand in work, your tutor will return this to you with a record of your achievement.

This particular unit has 11 criteria to meet: 6 Pass, 3 Merit and 2 Distinction.

For a **Pass** you must achieve **all 6** Pass criteria.

For a **Merit** you must achieve **all 6** Pass **and all 3** Merit criteria.

For a **Distinction** you must achieve **all 6** Pass, **all 3** Merit criteria **and both** Distinction criteria.

Help with assessment

Your tutor will give you one or more assignments that you will complete as coursework. This could consist of:

- Presentations
- Videos and screen captures
- Witness statements and/or an evidence log
- Web pages or wikis
- Working programs
- Podcasts
- Blogs
- Flowcharts, structure diagrams etc.

You should read the guidance given for each of the criteria (shown across the unit) carefully and remember to check your work.

Further reading

Textbooks

Bowman, K. *Systems Analysis: A Beginner's Guide* (Palgrave Macmillan, 2003) ISBN 033398630X

Flanagan, D. *JavaScript Pocket Reference* (O'Reilly, 2002) ISBN 0596004117

Wang, W. *Visual Basic 6 for Dummies* (Hungry Minds Inc. US, 1998) ISBN 0764503707

Willis, T., Reynolds, M., Crossland, J. and Blair, R. *Beginning VB.NET* (Wrox Press Ltd, 2002) ISBN 1861007612

Websites

http://visualbasic.about.com/

www.guidetoprogramming.com/joomla153/

www.vbexplorer.com/VBExplorer/VBExplorer.asp

www.profsr.com/

Unit 23
Computer graphics

Learning objectives

By the end of this unit you should:

1. Know the hardware and software required to work with computer graphics
2. Be able to create computer graphics to meet a user need
3. Be able to use computer graphics to enhance a document.

In order to pass this unit, the evidence you present for assessment needs to demonstrate that you can meet all of the above learning outcomes for this unit. The criteria below show the levels of achievement required to pass this unit.

To achieve a **pass** grade the evidence must show that the learner is able to:	To achieve a **merit** grade the evidence must show that, in addition to the pass criteria, the learner is able to:	To achieve a **distinction** the evidence must show that, in addition to the pass and merit criteria, the learner is able to:
P1 Identify the hardware and software required to work with computer graphics	**M1** Describe the features of different graphical hardware devices	
P2 State the functions of a defined graphics software package	**M2** Describe the features of different graphics software packages	**D1** Evaluate a graphics software package on its ability to create and edit computer graphics
P3 Describe the differences between raster (bitmap) and vector graphics	**M3** Use graphics software to edit an image for a given purpose	**D2** Explain the impact that file format, compression techniques, image resolution and colour depth have on file size and image quality
P4 Use specialist hardware to acquire images for a defined purpose		
P5 Create an original graphic for a defined user need using graphics software		
P6 Use graphics to enhance a document incorporating acquired images and objects		

Introduction

Images are an important part of modern document and web page design. In order to create great images it is useful to understand how computer graphics are produced, including understanding the hardware and software required and the skills necessary to acquire and manipulate them.

This unit is designed to give the learner a basic overview of computer graphics and provide some useful tips about how best to use them.

You will be assessed through coursework which could be in the form of:

- Presentations
- Practical sessions which may be photographed, videoed or witnessed
- Printed or electronic images
- Screen captures
- Viva
- Blogs
- Podcasts.

23.1 Know the hardware and software required to work with computer graphics

This section will cover the following grading criteria:

Key terms

Graphics are visual presentations on some surface such as a paper, canvas, wall or a computer screen that are used to educate or entertain.

Pixels are picture cells or elements which make up a display by combining their 'dots' to form an image.

Resolution is a measurement denoting the size of an image by counting the number of pixels across and down, for example, 1024 × 768. Higher resolutions provide better quality images but typically require more RAM.

In order to work with graphical images we need the appropriate equipment. Some of the sample equipment that we use is described in detail in the following sections.

23.1.1 Hardware

Hardware is physical, it can be touched. Although many different types of hardware are used in a computer system, some parts are more specific to creating graphics.

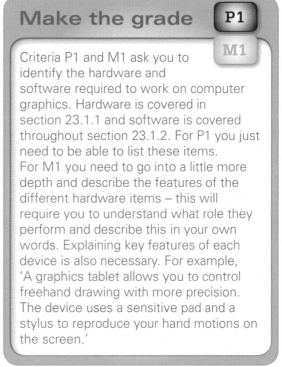

Make the grade P1 M1

Criteria P1 and M1 ask you to identify the hardware and software required to work on computer graphics. Hardware is covered in section 23.1.1 and software is covered throughout section 23.1.2. For P1 you just need to be able to list these items. For M1 you need to go into a little more depth and describe the features of the different hardware items – this will require you to understand what role they perform and describe this in your own words. Explaining key features of each device is also necessary. For example, 'A graphics tablet allows you to control freehand drawing with more precision. The device uses a sensitive pad and a stylus to reproduce your hand motions on the screen.'

Graphics or video card – a component inside a computer system that can generate video displays and output them on a computer screen.

Figure 23.1 A modern graphics card

Powerful graphics cards can be very expensive, with well-featured examples costing thousands of pounds. An entry level graphics card is around £40 with some video cards actually onboard, in other words built into the computer system's motherboard.

There are various **input devices** which can be used:

- **Mouse** – This is a hand-held device which may be **optical** or use a **mouse ball** to detect movements on a work surface, translating these to on-screen pointer movements. Many mice are now **wireless** using **infrared** (**IR**) or **radio waves** instead of cables.
- **Stylus** – This is a pen-like device with which the user can 'draw' a picture on the flat surface of a **graphics tablet** (see Figure 3.7). This picture then appears on the screen and can be manipulated using the selected graphics software.
- **Digital camera** – Once very expensive, digital cameras are now a part of everyday life and a popular feature in mobile telephones. The quality of a digital camera is often popularly determined by its **image resolution** which is measured in **megapixels**; the bigger this number, the higher the resolution, the better the picture. Digital cameras typically store their pictures on various forms of **memory card** which can be removed and read by special **card readers** attached to a computer. This is often the preferred technique as it prevents camera batteries from being drained.
- **Scanner** – A scanner is a device which converts a physical image (for example a photograph or drawing) into a digital image. Although hand-held scanners are available, the desktop scanner is the most common.

And various **output devices** which can be used:

- **Printer** – Various types of printer exist but perhaps the most popular types either use **liquid ink** (for example **inkjet**) or **toner powder** (for example **laser**). Both types of printer can print both **monochrome** (black and white) images and **colour**, depending on the model purchased. Although the price of printers has reduced markedly in the last 10 years, the price of their **consumables** (such as the printer cartridges) remains relatively expensive in comparison, although refilling them helps recycling efforts and keeps costs down.
- **Plotter** – A type of printer which uses pens to produce complex line-based drawings, typically for construction, engineering or CAD (computer aided design). Plotters tend to be either of the '**flat bed**' or '**drum**' variety.

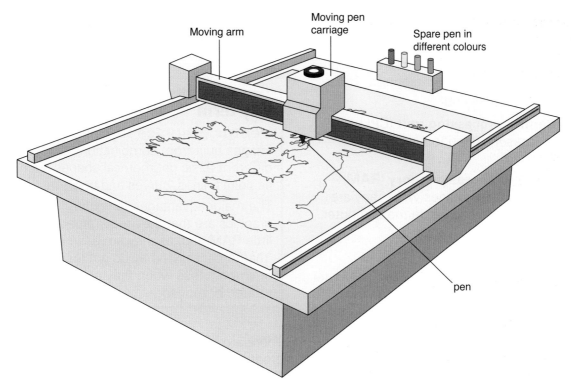

Moving arm

Moving pen carriage

Spare pen in different colours

pen

Figure 23.2 A flat bed plotter

- **Monitor** – A monitor, also called a 'screen' or VDU (visual display unit), is used to display graphical signals created by the graphics card.

There are two popular types of monitor display technology in common usage:

CRT (cathode ray tube) – An older type of technology that works by firing electron beams at a glass screen coated with a phosphorescent layer. Where the beam hits, the area of the screen 'glows' to form an image.

LCD (liquid crystal display)/TFT (thin film transistor) – This is a newer form of computer display that has rapidly taken over in popularity from CRT monitors. LCD screens work by switching on and off millions of tiny red, green and blue filtered pixels.

Scorecard

LCDs

+ Brighter display without distortion

+ Less distortion at edges of the image

+ Lower power consumption (about one-third of a comparable CRT)

+ Longer lifespan

+ Reduced flicker

+ Lower radiation emissions and electromagnetic interference

− Slower response time for screen updating

− LCDs might have a limited viewing angle

General hardware

Do not forget that other hardware elements inside the computer system are also key to processing computer graphics. These include the following:

- **Central processing unit (CPU)** or processor – used to run graphics software.
- **Random access memory (RAM)** – used to store images while they are being processed inside the computer.

File storage

RAM only stores data while the computer system is switched on. To save your graphics work over a longer period of time, we can use various types of file storage.

- **Hard disk** – A magnetic storage medium that can store gigabytes (GB) of graphical information for future use. Hard disks can be internal or external.
- **CD-ROM (compact disc-read only memory)** and **CD-R (compact disc recordable)** – Optical storage media that can store around 700 megabytes (MB) of graphical information.
- **USB (universal serial bus) flash memory** – A popular, small and very portable key-fob-sized unit that can store gigabytes of graphical information.
- **Memory cards** – Digital cameras typically store their pictures on various forms of memory card. Alternatively cameras can be connected to a computer by USB or **firewire cables**. Some also use **wireless connectivity** via **Bluetooth** or **Wi-Fi**.

23.1.2 Software

There are many different software applications for creating and manipulating computer graphics. These tend to be categorised by the type of computer image they process.

Vector graphics software

Creating vector graphics is a specialised skill.

> ### Key term
>
> **Vector graphics** are graphical images built from combinations of different basic geometrical shapes such as points, lines, curves and polygons.
>
> The major advantages to vector graphics are that they require very little RAM and, as they are described 'mathematically', they do not lose detail or smoothness when they are scaled, rotated or moved.

There are a number of commercial products which do this well, including Corel Draw®, Microsoft Visio® and Inkscape®. Visit the links given below to see what each can do.

Corel Draw®

Example: http://www.itreviews.co.uk/graphics/normal/software/s892.jpg

Information : http://www.corel.com/servlet/Satellite/gb/en/Product/1191272117978

Microsoft Visio®

Marketed as part of Microsoft's Office® suite, Visio® is a tool that allows you to create elegant diagrams (such as network diagrams, room layouts, flowcharts etc.) using vector graphics.

Example: http://www.microsoft.com/presspass/images/features/2008/02-05VisioPro_ITChart.jpg

Information: http://emea.microsoftstore.com/UK/en-GB/Microsoft/Visio-Standard-2010

Inkscape®

This application is freeware but is well-featured and easy to use. Inkscape is freely downloadable for Microsoft Windows® and Apple Mac® from: http://inkscape.org/

Dedicated raster (bitmap) software

Most computer users are familiar with bitmap graphics.

> ### Key term
>
> A **bitmap** or **raster** graphic file is one where the image consists of many smaller dots or pixels. If the image is zoomed, the separate pixels become very 'blocky' and visible (or 'pixellated').
>
> Bitmap graphics are not as efficient to use as vector images because each pixel must be physically stored. Additionally, any attempt to scale them will result in a loss of detail and quality.

Popular examples of raster software include Microsoft Paint® and the Gimp.

Microsoft Paint® comes free with Microsoft Windows®. Although it is not as fully featured as a commercial package, it can be used to make basic alterations to bitmap graphics and create simple images.

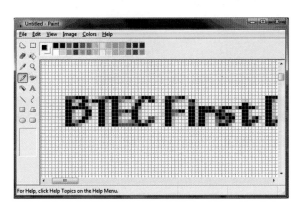

Figure 23.3 Microsoft Paint® zooms into a bitmap to show the pixels

The Gimp is the **GNU Image Manipulation Program**. It has an advanced set of features for processing bitmapped images. The Gimp is available for many operating systems including Microsoft Windows®, Linux® and Apple Max OS X®. It is a freely distributed piece of software and is available for download from: http://www.gimp.org/downloads/.

Dedicated photo-manipulation software

Some graphics software has specific features for processing photographic images. Perhaps the world's most popular photo-manipulation software is **Adobe Photoshop®**. This software is so popular, in fact, that when images are manipulated they are often said to have been 'photoshopped', although Adobe® do not apparently approve of this usage.

Figure 23.4 Adobe Photoshop® on an Apple Mac®

Common features include:

- Adjusting the colour balance
- Brightening or reducing light levels
- Reducing flash 'red eye'
- Healing of rips and abrasions
- Retouching (getting rid of 'imperfections' in the image, such as wrinkles on a person's skin).

Other popular photo manipulation software includes:

- Adobe Photoshop Elements®
- Paintshop Pro®
- Serif Photo Plus®.

Graphics facilities in other applications

Many other types of application also contain basic facilities which let the user insert and manipulate images. Microsoft Word® is a good example of this type of package as it contains a number of graphical functions.

Word®'s Insert tab can be used to:

- Add AutoShapes such as block arrows, banners, basic symbols etc.
- Draw basic geometric shapes such as lines, polygons, circles and ellipses
- Add WordArt (stylised lettering)
- Add diagrams or organisational charts
- Insert clip art or pictures
- Change colour of text, lines or how a shape is filled
- Change line width or style
- Add shadows or make AutoShapes appear in 3D.

Figure 23.5 Microsoft Word® Picture Tools tab

Word®'s Picture Tools tab can be used to:

- Change a picture from colour to greyscale, monochrome or washout (which makes it very faint, like a watermark)
- Increase and decrease the picture's contrast
- Increase and decrease the picture's brightness
- Crop the picture (trimming bits of the image that are not wanted)

- Rotate the picture
- Compress the picture so it uses less memory (and disk space)
- Change how the text wraps around or flows over the picture.

Although Word®'s image editing facilities are basic, they are convenient and useful if the user does not want to learn a complex graphics package in order to make simple changes.

Other tools

Many different applications are used to view a gallery of images.

Microsoft Windows® has a built-in tool which is called the Windows Photo Gallery. Although limited, it can perform basic zoom, rotation and photo 'fix' operations.

Figure 23.6 Windows'® Photo Gallery

Windows Explorer® can also view a folder's contents in '**thumbnail**' mode.

Popular commercial image viewers and photo gallery software include:

- ACDSee® http://www.acdsee.com/
- Google Picasa® http://picasa.google.com/
- PicaLoader® http://www.vowsoft.com/
- Irfanview® http://www.irfanview.com/

Generally image viewers have more limited editing capabilities when compared with most full graphical editing packages.

Common functionality includes:

- Image file management (copy, move, renaming)
- File format conversion (such as from vector to bitmap)
- Printing
- Resizing
- Rotating
- Slideshow presentation
- Uploading to web-based galleries
- Scanning support.

Image viewers and photo gallery applications become particularly useful when image collections become too large to manage through the operating systems' usual file manager (for example Windows Explorer®).

Many functions include '**batch**' operations where a number of files or folders can be processed in one go. A common example of this could be for file renaming, resizing or converting to a different file format.

Make the grade

P2

M2

D1

These three criteria are very closely linked and can be tackled in order. P2 asks you to state the functions of a defined graphics software package – this means pick a particular graphics software application and list what it can do. M2 extends this by asking you to describe the features of different graphics software packages – pick at least two which you can compare and contrast easily, such as Adobe Photoshop® and Inkscape®.
D1 asks you to evaluate a particular graphics software package on its ability to create and edit computer graphics. This is subjective (it is your opinion) but you

could look at third-party reviews on the world wide web to get some help. Try to explain if it is easy to use, has a good range of tools or if the menu system is too confusing! You need to make some judgements here but be prepared to explain your reasons!

23.1.3 File handling

Two important skills for any IT user working with computer graphics are to be able to **recognise** different image **file formats** and be able to **convert** between them.

Key term

File format means the way in which data is organised and structured within a file. Different file formats are used for different types of data (for example, sound is stored in a different way to a spreadsheet). An application must understand a particular file format before it can read its data.

Image files can be found in many different formats, some of these are **compressed**.

Key term

In computing, **compression** is a way of reducing something's size through a complex mathematical calculation. In order to reassemble it properly, it must be possible to **decompress** the data as well.

It is common for most files to have a **file extension** which tells both the user and the computer system what type of format the data is stored in.

Common graphical file formats that you may encounter are
shown in Table 23.1.

File extension	What is it?	File size
.BMP	A **bitmap** file format created by Microsoft® and often used by Windows®. Bitmaps are not compressed and often take a lot of memory and hard disk space. They are 'lossless' however, because every single pixel of graphics data is stored.	842 x 600 in 16.7 million colours as .BMP is 1,482 kB
.JPG or .JPEG	A file format created by the **Joint Photographic Experts Group**. JPEG files use a **compression calculation** to reduce 'similar' colour areas. Because of this, JPEGs are 'lossy' and become 'blocky' when the compression rate is set particularly high. They are particularly useful for photographs and downloading from the world wide web.	842 x 600 in 16.7 million colours as .JPG is 239 kB
.GIF	A **graphics interchange format** file. Although GIFs are lossless, they are limited to a maximum of 256 colours making them poor choices for photographs. They are, however, the preferred file format for **line-based diagrams** and **cartoons** which typically have fewer colours. **GIF87** is the original format. A later format, **GIF89A**, adds support for **animation** (commonly known as 'animated GIFs'). The GIF format is patented by Unisys.	842 x 600 in 256 colours as .GIF is 153 kB
.PNG	**Portable network graphics**. Created by the **W3C** (**World Wide Web Consortium**) as a replacement for the GIF. PNG files are lossless compressed bitmaps. PNG files are slowly becoming the preferred file format for the web, but software support is still a little patchy.	842 x 600 in 16.7 million colours as .PNG is 533 kB
.WMF	Created by Microsoft®, a **Windows® Metafile** is a graphical file format that can include vector-based images. If it is used to save a bitmap, there will be little difference in its file size to a standard .BMP file.	842 x 600 in 16.7 million colours as .WMF is 1,482 kB
.TIFF	The **tagged image file format** can store both photographs and line art. Created by the company Aldus for use in **desktop publishing** (**DTP**). TIFFs are lossless and can also store vector graphics.	842 x 600 in 16.7 million colours as .TIFF is 591 kB

Table 23.1 Common graphical file formats

Converting files

Very often it is necessary to convert a file from one format to another. Most graphics software allows you to do this with a minimum of fuss. For example, the Gimp uses a simple 'Save as' option which allows you to select the graphics file format you want to use.

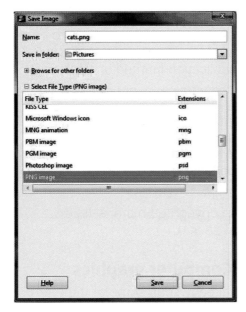

Figure 23.7 The Gimp's 'File … Save as' option

Alternative options include using websites which have online file format conversion. Have a look at the following link to see an example of one of these websites: http://www.online-utility.org/image_converter.jsp.

File management

Being organised is the key to having a searchable library of images that you can use with the minimum of effort.

Two important tips are:

- Organise images into **appropriate** folder structures as shown in Figure 23.8.
- Always use sensible, **meaningful** filenames for your images.

Moving and deleting files

All modern operating systems have facilities to move and delete files; image files work in the same way. Generally it is possible to drag-and-drop a file from folder to folder or use the cut and paste options.

Once a file has been deleted it is often placed into a '**recycling bin**' where it can be recovered if a mistake has been made. Even if the file has been removed from the recycling bin it is normally possible to recover it (with specialist software) if you act quickly!

Compression techniques

There are many ways to compress an image. Common techniques include using **compressed file formats** such as .JPG, .GIF and .PNG. An alternative is to use software utilities such as **WinZip** (www.winzip.com) or **WinRar** (www.rarlab.com) which can compress files.

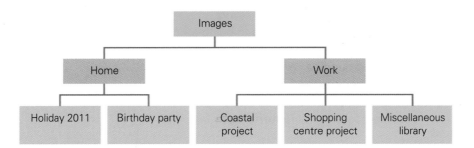

Figure 23.8 Folder structure grouping together related images

23.2 Be able to create computer graphics to meet a user need

This section will cover the following grading criteria: **P3** **P5** **D2**

23.2.1 User needs

In order to create an image it is important to understand the target audience's needs.

> **Key term**
>
> The **target audience** is a specified group or category of persons who you want the product to appeal to. This might be based on region, age, gender or economic status (the '**demographics**').

User requirements are the aspects with which the image must conform:

- Physical image size
- Colour depth (how many possible colours can be used in the image)
- Image resolution
- File size
- Appropriate content
- Realistic, cartoon or impressionistic visual style.

Constraints

Sometimes user requirements are constrained (limited in some way). This typically occurs when images have to be created within an organisation or for a specific publication (printed or electronic).

Common constraints might include:

- House style
- Colours that can be used (such as organisational corporate colour scheme only)
- File format
- Use of copyrighted material (see section 23.3.1).

23.2.2 Computer graphics

We have already seen some of the differences between bitmap and vector images. If we perform a quick comparison we can see in which instances each type is preferred (see Table 23.2).

Type of image	Advantages	Disadvantages
Bitmap	Lossless format Ideal for realistic images such as photographs	Large image size Loss of detail when scaling Have to be a rectangular shape
Vector	Efficient image size No loss of detail when scaling The image is not limited to being a rectangular shape as they have no background so can appear in front of other images Easy to convert to a bitmap through a process called **rasterising**	Images are not 100 per cent realistic – they are limited to combinations of basic geometric shapes

Table 23.2 Bitmap vs vector

Generally bitmaps are used for photographic or realistic images whereas vector images are used for scalable applications such as Adobe Flash® animations.

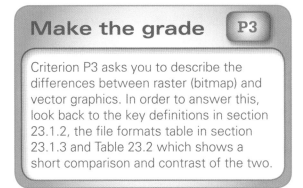

Make the grade **P3**

Criterion P3 asks you to describe the differences between raster (bitmap) and vector graphics. In order to answer this, look back to the key definitions in section 23.1.2, the file formats table in section 23.1.3 and Table 23.2 which shows a short comparison and contrast of the two.

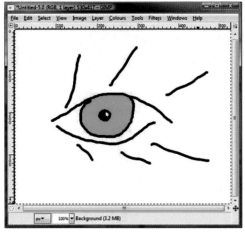

Figure 23.10 Freehand eye created with a brush

23.2.3 Tools and techniques

Sadly it is beyond the scope of this book to cover all possible graphical techniques. The following section uses the Gimp to demonstrate just a few of the different **tool types** that you may find useful.

Standard software tools

Freehand draw

Being able to use a brush, pen or pencil tool to draw freehand is a basic function in most graphics software. It is not easy as it requires a steady hand – using a graphics tablet will help!

Freehand tools can be adjusted to enable different types of drawing. Some of these options are shown in Figure 23.9 – the most common changes are made to the brush shape, size of brush, colour and softness (how fuzzy its edges are).

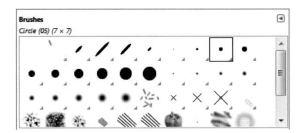

Figure 23.9 Brush types

Rotate and flip

Rotating an image is a **transformation effect**. Images can be rotated 90 degrees clockwise or anti-clockwise or be freehand rotated.

Flipping an image will create a mirror image of the graphic reflected either vertically or horizontally. These various transformations are show in Figure 23.12.

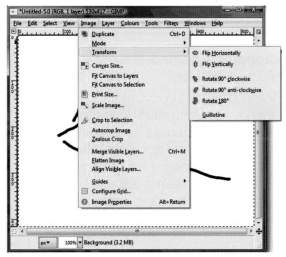

Figure 23.11 Transformation options in the Gimp

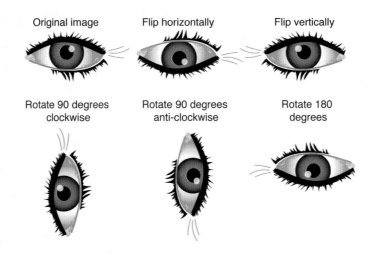

Original image   Flip horizontally   Flip vertically

Rotate 90 degrees clockwise   Rotate 90 degrees anti-clockwise   Rotate 180 degrees

Figure 23.12 Original image and five transformations

Crop

> ### Key term
>
> **Cropping** an image means to remove any part of the image which is not required. This may mean removing excess white space or removing an entire section of an image (such as a person's body when all that is required is the head).

Cropping is a standard tool found in most graphics software.

The photograph in Figure 23.13 was intended to be used to illustrate a book on Spanish history as it perfectly captured the wall of a historical old castle on the outskirts of a town. Unfortunately the photographer has managed to capture both a modern building and road signs in the picture! These could be removed by cropping them out of the picture.

Figure 23.13 Castle wall with the modern world intruding!

As with many graphics software applications, the Gimp has different types of crop tool (see Figure 23.14).

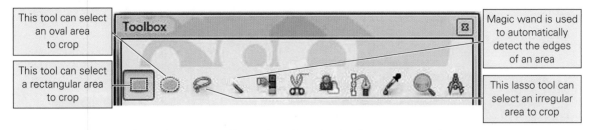

Figure 23.14 Part of the Gimp's toolbox showing the various crop tools

Select the area to crop by using a selection tool to mark the area we want to keep.

Use the Gimp's crop tool to remove the unselected area (see Figure 23.15).

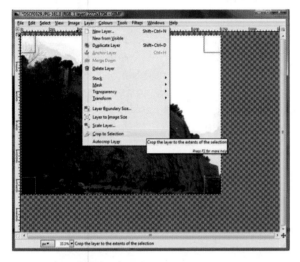

Figure 23.15 Photograph has been cropped to size

The photograph, having been cropped to remove modern objects, is now fit for purpose.

Layout grids

A **layout grid** is another common feature in graphics software. The grid acts as a visual guide which the graphic artist uses to align their designs by '**snapping**' objects to it.

The grid sizes are usually customisable (in pixels) so it is possible to be very precise. In the Gimp it is possible to access the layout grid through the View option. Click on Show Grid. The grid is shown in Figure 23.16.

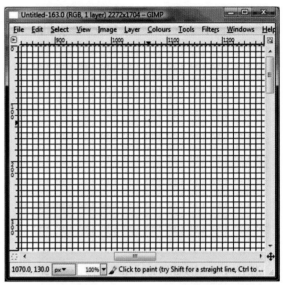

Figure 23.16 The grid is now visible

If the user has also selected the 'Snap to Grid' option, objects will automatically align to the nearest grid point.

Special effects

Most graphic software has special tools which can process the image using certain **filters** or effects to change the appearance of the graphic. A few of the most common special effects are shown in Table 23.3.

Templates

Templates are graphics which contain a mixture of fixed and editable elements. For example, if you access the following link:

http://upload.macromedia.com/exchange/photoshop/previews/Wanted.jpg

Original

Posterise

Posterise reduces the number of tones in an image to create a stark 'comic strip' effect.

Desaturate

Desaturate removes the RGB (red, green, blue) to leave a greyscale image.

Pixelate

Pixelate reduces the number of pixels in an image leaving a 'blocky' image similar to the technique used to disguise victims in crime reconstructions.

Table 23.3 Graphic special effects

you will find a Wild-West style 'Wanted' poster where all the elements are fixed apart from the actual details of the 'outlaw'. By using this template you only have to add your own photograph, names and crime details to produce your very own customised design! A quick Google®

search will link you to hundreds of freely downloadable templates that you can experiment with.

Templates are a popular way of creating customised graphics quickly and many can be downloaded for free or at a nominal cost to the digital artist.

Activity A

Using templates

A quick search online will provide many free templates for your favourite graphics software application.
Try downloading a template and customising its editable elements.

You could even attempt to create your own template, for example an ID badge, an exam certificate or a party invitation.

Key term

RGB – the red, green and blue **colour model** – is perhaps the most popular way to describe colours in most graphic software.

Each colour is represented as a combination of its red, green and blue values, with each value being between **0** (less) and **255** (more).

Simple RGB examples include:

Black 0,0,0

Red 255,0,0

Green 0,255,0

Blue 0,0,255

White 255,255,255

Shape libraries

Many graphics editing programs have libraries of pre-defined shapes which can be incorporated into a new image. Figure 23.17 contains pre-defined shapes from Paint Shop Pro®'s Picture Tube tool.

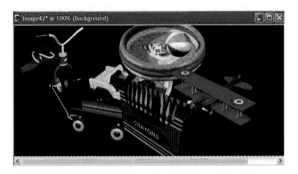

Figure 23.17 Pre-set images from Corel Paint Shop Pro®

Colour balance

Colour is a balance of **RGB** (red, green and blue) **values**.

Sometimes a digital artist will want to change the balance of these colours to fix a problem in the original image or to enhance it.

For example, the photograph in Figure 23.18 was taken of a secluded bay on a fairly overcast day. With little sunshine the sea looks particularly cold and uninviting! The local tourist board wants to make the water look more attractive in order to entice more people to visit. The graphic artist has been asked to change the colour balance of the sea.

Step 1 – The first step is to use the Gimp's **lasso tool** to select the perimeter of the bay.

Figure 23.18 Lasso tool is used to select the bay

Step 2 – The second step is to use the Gimp's **colour balance dialogue** to adjust the **RGB mix** of the bay.

Figure 23.19 Adjusting the RGB colour balance for the selected area

Figure 23.20 shows the amended image.

Figure 23.20 The secluded bay – now Tourist Board approved!

Activity B

Enhancing colour

The covers of many magazines use photographs which enhance the colour of their subjects.

Take a picture of yourself (or use an existing picture of a celebrity) and try to enhance the colour of their eyes or hair by changing the RGB balance.

Put the two images side by side to contrast them. Was it effective?

Colour change

Occasionally a graphic artist will want to replace one particular colour in an image with another – usually when a mistake has been made. Modern graphics software makes this quite easy to achieve. Let us revisit our freehand eye image from Figure 23.10 and change the colour of the iris from green to brown.

Step 1 – Using the Gimp, we access the 'Colour Exchange' menu option as seen in Figure 23.21.

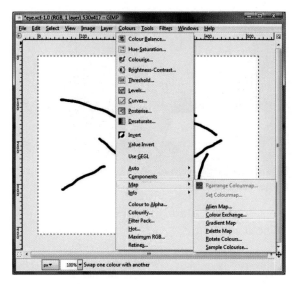

Figure 23.21 Colour exchange menu option in the Gimp

Clicking this option will display a new Colour Exchange dialogue box (see Figure 23.22).

Figure 23.22 Colour Exchange dialogue

This dialogue box allows us to select a colour in the image we want to replace (in this case, the green in the iris) and replace it with a new colour chosen from the available palette.

Step 2 – Middle click (mouse wheel) on the current colour of the iris (green).

Step 3 – Select the new colour from the available palette (blue).

Step 4 – Click OK button. If you have the 'Preview' checkbox, you will get a peek at the finished colour exchange.

Make the grade D2

D2 is a complex criterion as it asks you to explain the impact that file format, compression (sections 23.1.3 and 23.2.2), resolution and colour depth have on file size and image quality. An ideal tactic might be to create the same image and convert it to a number of different formats and colour depths to demonstrate how compression works to affect different file sizes.

Colour depth

Key term

The **colour depth** of an image is usually expressed in the number of possible colours an image can use. The higher the number of colours possible, the more realistic it will look. Higher colour depth will mean a bigger file size, so should only be used when absolutely necessary. Most graphics software applications have options to change colour depth.

Table 23.4 shows the effect on a photograph when the colour depth is altered.

A photograph in 24-bit colour (16.8 million colours – also called 'true colour'): 649 kB

The same photograph in 16-bit colour (65,536 colours – also called 'high colour'): 286 kB

The same photograph in 8-bit colour (256 colours): 218 kB.

The same photograph in 4-bit colour (16 colours): 110 kB

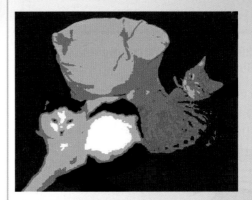

The same photograph in 1-bit colour (monochrome): 28 kB

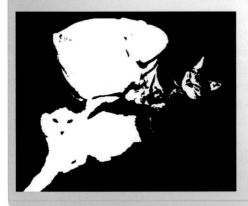

Table 23.4 Changing the colour depth

Make the grade   P5

P5 asks you to create an original graphic to a defined user need (see section 23.2.1). It is likely that your teacher or a client will give you a brief for a new image. You will need to design and create the image using an appropriate graphics software application. You should try to use many of the techniques covered throughout section 23.2.3 in order to achieve this. For submission, your work will probably be either printed or shown electronically.

23.2.4 Reviewing

The **review process** is a vital stage of undertaking any graphic design work.

Reviewing should initially be performed by the designer, ensuring that the image is checked against the following criteria:

- If the image contains text, has it been proofread for errors?
- Is the physical size of the image appropriate?
- Is the file size of the image appropriate (for example for downloading)?
- Is the resolution of the image appropriate?
- Is the graphical file format correct?
- Does the image meet the customer's requirements and expectations?

The customer will then need to approve the image and may make additional suggestions for possible modifications and improvements.

23.3 Be able to use computer graphics to enhance a document

This section will cover the following grading criteria: **P4   P6   M3**

Graphics are a great way to grab a reader's attention by enhancing the attractiveness of a document.

23.3.1 Acquired images

Key term

Acquiring – in graphical processing, the verb 'acquire' is used to describe the general act of obtaining a digital (in other words, computerised) image from another source.

Common methods of acquiring images include: screen capture (for example using Print Screen in Microsoft Windows® to 'grab' the current screen or using the Snipping tool), digital photography, scanning and downloading using a website.

Specialist hardware that might be used to acquire images includes digital cameras, mobile telephones and flatbed scanners

The following example demonstrates the process of **acquiring**, **manipulating** and **inserting** an image into a word-processed document.

Step 1: Select picture

An image is selected (Figure 23.23). It is an old photograph that will need some manipulation in order to be useful as it was not acquired very well. It is currently too dark and will need rotating and cropping before we can use it in our document.

Figure 23.23 Sample photograph

Step 2: Scanning image

The image was originally scanned using the default scanner software. Unfortunately the original photograph is no longer available and there is a problem with the image's orientation.

Figure 23.24 Scanning the original photograph

Step 3: Save scanned image

The image is saved as a suitably named .BMP (bitmap) file. Remember that saving the file as a bitmap ensures that no graphical information is lost.

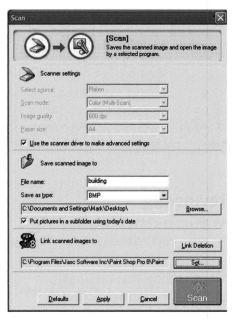

Figure 23.25 Saving the scanned image

Step 4: Plan the manipulation of the image

We need to open the image file with our graphics software – the Gimp.

In the Gimp we will need to:

- Rotate the image
- Crop the image (removing the cars at the bottom of the photograph)
- Raise the light levels on the image
- Save the file with a new name.

We will then need to insert this tweaked image into our pre-prepared document in Microsoft Word®.

Step 5: Rotate the image (see section 23.2.3)

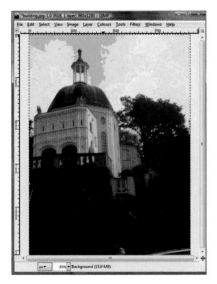

Figure 23.26 After a clockwise rotation of 90 degrees

Step 6: Crop the image (see section 23.2.3)

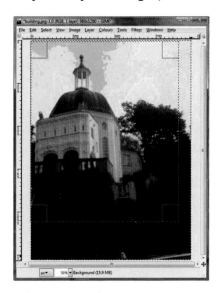

Figure 23.27 Cropping to remove the cars

Step 7: Raise the light levels on the image

This is achieved through the Colours tab followed by the selection of Brightness-Contrast (see Figure 23.28).

Figure 23.28 Adjusting the brightness and contrast

Step 8: Save the image

The manipulated image is saved as a .JPG image called 'Building edited.jpg'.

Step 9: Inserting into document

We will load our document into Microsoft Word® and use the Insert Picture button on the ribbon. We then select our picture from the available images we have previously saved. Remember to select 'Building edited.jpg'!

Step 10: Manipulating within the document

It is likely that our image will be the wrong size and in the wrong location!

But do not worry; we can resize it and move it to where we want in the document. As mentioned in section 23.1.2, most word-processing software has basic tools for performing these tasks.

Step 11: Resize image

Word® can visually resize an image without making any permanent physical changes to the actual image. This is done by clicking on the image to select it and then using the **sizing handles**. We now use the sizing handles to format the image to a more manageable size.

Figure 23.29 Sizing handles around a resized image

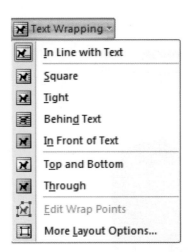

Figure 23.30 Text wrapping options in Word®

Step 12: Text wrapping

> ## Key term
>
> **Text wrapping** changes how text and other elements on the page **flow around** a graphic.

Once an image is selected, the Picture tools part of the ribbon is active and we can access the text-wrapping options by using the Format tab.

Word® has a number of text wrapping options (see Figure 23.30).

Each text-wrapping option is different. For example, 'Square' will allow text to follow around each side of the image; 'Top and Bottom' will only allow text above and below the image. You should try experimenting with them for best effect! We will be using the 'Square' option.

Step 13: Positioning

Once you have set the text-wrapping options, it is possible to click and drag your image to its intended place. Microsoft Word® also has the ability to position the image for you on the page using some pre-set layout options. We will be placing the image on the centre-right of the page.

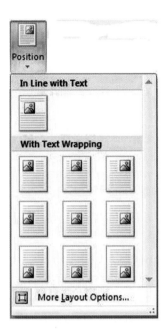

Figure 23.31 Position options for layout

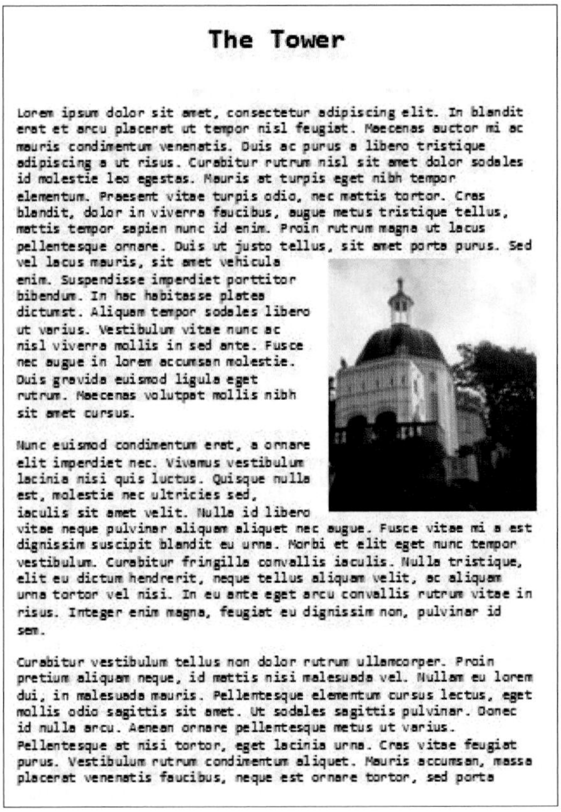

The Tower

Lorem ipsum dolor sit amet, consectetur adipiscing elit. In blandit erat et arcu placerat ut tempor nisl feugiat. Maecenas auctor mi ac mauris condimentum venenatis. Duis ac purus a libero tristique adipiscing a ut risus. Curabitur rutrum nisl sit amet dolor sodales id molestie leo egestas. Mauris at turpis eget nibh tempor elementum. Praesent vitae turpis odio, nec mattis tortor. Cras blandit, dolor in viverra faucibus, augue metus tristique tellus, mattis tempor sapien nunc id enim. Proin rutrum magna ut lacus pellentesque ornare. Duis ut justo tellus, sit amet porta purus. Sed vel lacus mauris, sit amet vehicula enim. Suspendisse imperdiet porttitor bibendum. In hac habitasse platea dictumst. Aliquam tempor sodales libero ut varius. Vestibulum vitae nunc ac nisl viverra mollis in sed ante. Fusce nec augue in lorem accumsan molestie. Duis gravida euismod ligula eget rutrum. Maecenas volutpat mollis nibh sit amet cursus.

Nunc euismod condimentum erat, a ornare elit imperdiet nec. Vivamus vestibulum lacinia nisi quis luctus. Quisque nulla est, molestie nec ultricies sed, iaculis sit amet velit. Nulla id libero vitae neque pulvinar aliquam aliquet nec augue. Fusce vitae mi a est dignissim suscipit blandit eu urna. Morbi et elit eget nunc tempor vestibulum. Curabitur fringilla convallis iaculis. Nulla tristique, elit eu dictum hendrerit, neque tellus aliquam velit, ac aliquam urna tortor vel nisi. In eu ante eget arcu convallis rutrum vitae in risus. Integer enim magna, feugiat eu dignissim non, pulvinar id sem.

Curabitur vestibulum tellus non dolor rutrum ullamcorper. Proin pretium aliquam neque, id mattis nisi malesuada vel. Nullam eu lorem dui, in malesuada mauris. Pellentesque elementum cursus lectus, eget mollis odio sagittis sit amet. Ut sodales sagittis pulvinar. Donec id nulla arcu. Aenean ornare pellentesque metus ut varius. Pellentesque at nisi tortor, eget lacinia urna. Cras vitae feugiat purus. Vestibulum rutrum condimentum aliquet. Mauris accumsan, massa placerat venenatis faucibus, neque est ornare tortor, sed porta

Figure 23.32 Image correctly positioned in the text

Make the grade P4 M3

It is likely that your teacher may link these criteria as they ask you to acquire an image (P4), edit that image for a given purpose (M3) and then enhance a document by incorporating acquired images and objects (such as clip art).

Section 23.3.1 shows an image being acquired from a scanner (though you could use a digital camera or mobile telephone) and then being edited and inserted into a Microsoft Word® document.

You will need to document a similar process. A leaflet or report might be an appropriate way to demonstrate your skills at this type of task.

Clip art library

Many types of graphics software and word-processing applications have a clip art library. These are usually **royalty-free** (with no charge to use) collections of **vector-based images** which are available in various styles and categories.

Microsoft Word®'s clip art library can be accessed from the Insert tab on the ribbon.

Modern software has clip art libraries which can searched, expanded by importing online collections and organised by the user. Once a clip art item has been inserted into a document or image, it can be manipulated like any other acquired image.

Activity C

Using clip art

Explore a word-processing or desktop publishing application to see which categories and styles of clip art are available to use.

Continued on next page

Relevant laws and guidelines

Image copyright

The **Copyright, Designs and Patents Act 1988** is the current UK copyright law and it legally covers artistic works for 70 years after the death of their creator.

The basic purpose of copyright is to give the creator some say over how their images are used by other people.

Creative works (such as pictures and images) are often called '**intellectual property**' and just as other people should not help themselves to your physical possessions, neither should they use your intellectual property without your permission.

For images, copyright covers:

- Copying an image
- Modifying an image
- Distributing an image (including electronic transmission)
- Renting or lending an image
- Public exhibition of an image.

Copyright is granted by the creator for specific uses. For example, if copyright permission is given so that an image can be exhibited, it does not extend to making a copy or altering it.

To learn more visit: http://www. copyrightservice.co.uk/.

23.3.2 Objects

The use of objects is important when creating computer graphics. You must become confident at working with the following types of graphical object:

- bitmap images (see section 23.1.2)
- clip art (see section 23.3.1)
- vector images (see section 23.1.2).

You should also be able to use other types of objects such as text, pre-defined shapes and freehand drawings (see section 23.2.3).

Activity D

Create a leaflet

Create a simple leaflet to promote the city or town where you live.

It should include basic information about the landmarks and attractions and should have attractive and well-positioned images to enhance its appearance.

Use a combination of specialist hardware to acquire the images, graphics software to edit the images and a suitable word-processing or desktop publishing application to produce the leaflet.

Review which skills you used to complete this task.

Achieving Success

In order to achieve each unit, you will complete a series of coursework activities. Each time you hand in work, your tutor will return this to you with a record of your achievement.

This particular unit has 11 criteria to meet: 6 Pass, 3 Merit and 2 Distinction.

For a **Pass** you must achieve **all 6** Pass criteria.

For a **Merit** you must achieve **all 6** Pass and all 3 Merit criteria.

For a **Distinction** you must achieve **all 6** Pass, **all 3** Merit criteria **and both** Distinction criteria.

Help with assessment

Your tutor will give you one or more assignments that you will complete as coursework. This could consist of:

- Presentations
- Videos and screen captures
- Witness statements and/or an evidence log
- Web pages or wikis
- Leaflets or reports
- Gallery slideshows
- Images
- Posters

You should read the guidance given for each of the criteria (shown across the unit) carefully and remember to check your work.

Further reading

Textbooks

Sanchez, J. *The PC Graphics Handbook: A Reference Manual on PC Graphics Hardware and Software* (CRC Press; 2003) ISBN-10: 0849316782

Walsh Macario, J. *Graphic Design Essentials: Skills, Software and Creative Solutions* (Laurence King, 2009) ISBN 1856695999

Website

http://graphicdesign.about.com/

Unit 27
Spreadsheet modelling

Learning objectives

By the end of this unit you should:

1. Know what spreadsheets are and how they can be used
2. Be able to develop spreadsheet models
3. Be able to test and document spreadsheet models.

In order to pass this unit, the evidence you present for assessment needs to demonstrate that you can meet all of the above learning outcomes for this unit. The criteria below show the levels of achievement required to pass this unit.

To achieve a **pass** grade the evidence must show that the learner is able to:	To achieve a **merit** grade the evidence must show that, in addition to the pass criteria, the learner is able to:	To achieve a **distinction** grade the evidence must show that, in addition to the pass and merit criteria, the learner is able to:
P1 Describe the uses of spreadsheet software		
P2 Explain why spreadsheets may need to be converted to alternative file formats		
P3 Develop a spreadsheet model to meet particular needs	**M1** Refine a spreadsheet model by changing rules and values	**D1** Evaluate a spreadsheet model suggesting further refinements
P4 Use simple formulae and functions to process information		**D2** Use automated features in the spreadsheet model
P5 Use data types and formatting to present information	**M2** Justify choice of tools for presenting data	
P6 Use appropriate tools to present data	**M3** Analyse and interpret data from a spreadsheet model	
P7 Test a spreadsheet to ensure that it is fit for purpose		
P8 Produce user documentation for a spreadsheet model		

Introduction

Because spreadsheets are so versatile, they are used regularly to provide information that will help managers to make decisions.

Spreadsheets allow users to store, manipulate and analyse data and then provide ways to present that data to others. They can be automated to make them more efficient and easy to use. In this unit you will create a spreadsheet model to meet a particular business need.

You will be assessed through coursework which could be in the form of:

- Presentations
- Spreadsheet models
- Witness statements of an observed practical exercise
- Web pages
- Leaflets
- Reports
- Screenshots.

27.1 Know what spreadsheets are and how they can be used

This section will cover the following grading criteria: **P1** **P2**

27.1.1 Use of spreadsheets

How do organisations use spreadsheets? Let us look at a couple of examples:

A manufacturing company that makes chocolate products could use sales information (what it sells and when) to plan its production. For example, if sales are high in December, April and September, the company could plan to make more in November, March and August.

Another example could be an organisation using spreadsheets to **forecast** future events. For example, a company that has borrowed money has to pay it back with an additional payment called interest. Interest is charged so that the lender makes a profit. The company would use the spreadsheet to forecast how much the loan will cost if interest rates change.

Presenting information

In general terms spreadsheets are used to present information in such a way that the relationships between different pieces of data can be clarified or interpreted. An example here would be the idea of sales and production. Consider the following case study.

Case study

Gadgets for U is a small production company making self-opening letter boxes. Adam Chandler, the Managing Director, is concerned that the company is slipping into overdraft with the bank. He discusses his concerns with the Sales and Production Managers who have no immediate answers, although the Sales Manager says his statistics show that sales have been steadily increasing each month over the period in question.

They speak to the Finance Manager who produces the following table of information:

Gadgets for U Financial statement			
	Sales	Costs	Profits
April 2009	£24,256.00	£13,098.24	£11,157.76
May 2009	£26,075.20	£14,080.61	£11,994.59
June 2009	£28,030.84	£15,136.65	£12,894.19
July 2009	£30,133.15	£18,381.22	£11,751.93
August 2009	£32,393.14	£19,759.82	£12,633.32
September 2009	£34,822.62	£21,241.80	£13,580.82
October 2009	£35,867.30	£21,879.06	£13,988.25
November 2009	£36,943.32	£27,707.49	£9,235.83
December 2009	£38,051.62	£28,538.72	£9,512.91
January 2010	£39,193.17	£29,394.88	£9,798.29

Table 27.1 Financial statement spreadsheet

Look at the above data – can you see anything obvious?
The Finance Manager cannot really detect anything from the table of figures either and has created the following chart which consists of known sales each month, less known costs, which gives a profit figure.

Continued on next page

Continued ...

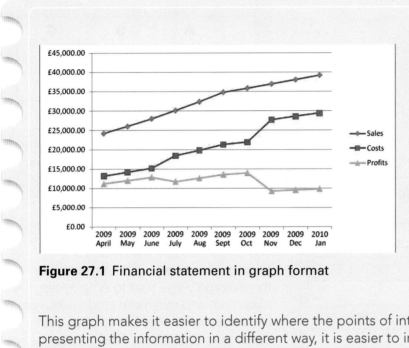

Figure 27.1 Financial statement in graph format

This graph makes it easier to identify where the points of interest are. By presenting the information in a different way, it is easier to interpret the relationships between the different sets of data. While there was a very slight fall in profits in July 2009 (even though sales were rising at that stage), there is a significant drop in profits of almost £5,000 in November 2009. Since then, profits have only risen minimally.

The Managing Director can now see that the Sales Manager is correct; sales have indeed risen steadily over the period. The sudden increase in costs in November is also visible, at the same time that profits go down. In reality, costs are made up of a number of factors and this still does not fully provide answers to the Managing Director's concerns.

It does, however, give the relevant managers an indication of where they should look for the answers. The questions they now need to address are 'Why did costs go up so dramatically in November 2009?' and 'Why have they continued to rise and not fallen again?' This will help them to understand the business and find solutions to business problems.

Calculations

Once a spreadsheet has been developed it can be used repeatedly, just by changing the relevant data. One such example would be to calculate the payroll for Gadgets for U employees.

When the spreadsheet is set up, with the names of the employees and the relevant columns to handle how many hours have been worked, basic pay rate, how much overtime, overtime pay rate, how much tax and National Insurance to deduct, the same spreadsheet could be reused each week.

Thus, the only data that would need to be **input** each time would be the number of hours worked for each employee; the **output** (the net salary) would be **processed** (calculated) automatically. This is an example of how a spreadsheet can be used to repetitively and accurately perform calculations.

Activity **A**

Wages spreadsheet

Using the Gadgets for U pay advice (below) to give you the column headings, work with a partner to design a spreadsheet that would do the actual calculations.

	A	B	C
1			
2			
3			

Create the spreadsheet and input five wages calculations to test the system.

Check your answers with a calculator.

Gadgets for U
Pay Advice

Name of Employee

Hours worked

Pay rate

Gross Pay (hours x pay rate)

Pension contribution

Tax deduction

National Insurance contribution

Net pay (gross – pension – tax – NI)

Work out where the calculations would go, and what the formulae should be. It will help if you number the rows and columns as you would in the actual spreadsheet, for example

You could also use the data in a spreadsheet to calculate statistics like the average wage paid to employees, the maximum and minimum credit taken with each supplier or the time it takes your customers to pay you. These statistics are used by managers to make decisions.

List management

Sometimes, when you are dealing with large sets of data (spreadsheets with lots of rows and columns), the spreadsheets themselves can be difficult to work with. To help with these spreadsheets there are different techniques that can be used. Here are some examples:

Data entry forms are used to make input easier. The user only sees the form and the data is put into the spreadsheet in the correct column automatically. How does the computer know which month to put the data into? It uses the month that the user has input on the form to work out which row to use.

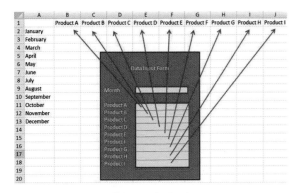

Figure 27.2 Data entry form

Drop down lists reduce the amount of input that the user has to do. Let us say that in a particular column in a spreadsheet the user *always* had to input a day of the week (excluding Saturday and Sunday). To create a list, with a spreadsheet open, you choose the cell where you want the list to appear (in this case A1), you then click on group **Data Validation** in the **Data Tools** on the **Data** ribbon. On the **Settings** tab, select **List** from the **Allow**: options. All that is now left to do is choose which bit of the spreadsheet the list is in (you can do this by clicking on the first value and dragging down onto the last value. Then click OK.

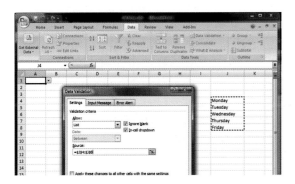

Figure 27.3 Drop down lists

When you click into the box with the drop down list, you will see the list. You can then choose from the options by clicking on it.

The data in the spreadsheet can also be **sorted** (ordered in some way) or **filtered** (where some data is removed, leaving only data in a particular range visible). This will be covered in the next section.

Freezing panes – when there are lots of rows and columns of data, it can sometimes be difficult to see the row and column headings, particularly when you move across or down to view data beyond the normal boundaries of the screen. You can solve this problem by 'fixing' or 'freezing' the row and column headings, even if the data below moves across. Let us see how this works.

In Figure 27.4 you can see all of the data in a spreadsheet.

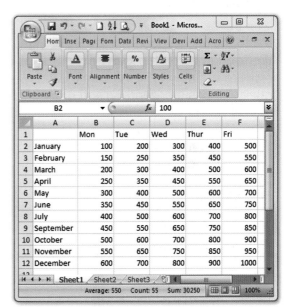

Figure 27.4 Spreadsheet data

If we reduce the size of the window so that not all of the data is visible (Figure 27.5), when we move into row 7, column E all the headings will have disappeared!

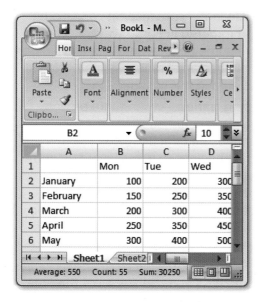

Figure 27.5

To fix the headings in place and allow the data to move, we need to click **Split** in the **Window** group on the **View** ribbon. The software will now split the whole window equally, across (horizontally) and down (vertically).

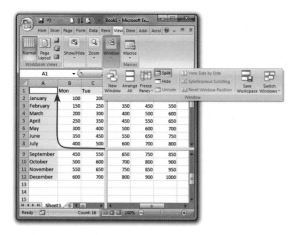

Figure 27.6 The window is now split in four

The user can now literally pick up the cross point and drag and drop it at the point where the row and column headings meet, and release the mouse.

It is now possible to reduce the size of the

available window and move down to the December Friday figures. The headings will still be visible.

Freezing panes is very useful if you are inputting data or reading it and you want to make sure you are always in the right place!

The last of the list management functions we will mention here is **Autofill**. This can be used to complete columns or rows of information automatically. This will be covered in greater detail later in this unit.

Interpreting data

To make decisions about the data in the spreadsheet it needs to be **interpreted**. Two common techniques for manipulating data are sorting and filtering. The following activity on the next page explains how this works.

You are now going to sort this data. To do this, you need to highlight the area from April 2009 to the last value at the bottom of the Profits column.

Now click on Data, then on Sort and select the options as shown in Figure 27.7. Click OK.

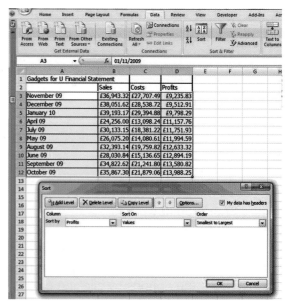

Figure 27.7

Activity B

Sorting and filtering

Create a spreadsheet using the following Gadgets for U data you saw at the beginning of this unit:

Gadgets for U financial statement	Sales	Costs	Profits
April 2009	£24,256.00	£13,098.24	£11,157.76
May 2009	£26,075.20	£14,080.61	£11,994.59
June 2009	£28,030.84	£15,136.65	£12,894.19
July 2009	£30,133.15	£18,381.22	£11,751.93
August 2009	£32,393.14	£19,759.82	£12,633.32
September 2009	£34,822.62	£21,241.80	£13,580.82
October 2009	£35,867.30	£21,879.06	£13,988.25
November 2009	£36,943.32	£27,707.49	£9,235.83
December 2009	£38,051.62	£28,538.72	£9,512.91
January 2010	£39,193.17	£29,394.88	£9,798.29

Table 27.2 Gadgets for U financial information

Can you now identify which three months made the best profit?

Using the same spreadsheet, you are now going to **filter** the data to show only those months where the costs were between £15,000 and £21,000.

Again, you will need to highlight all the rows and columns.

Now click on Filter in the **Sort & Filter** group on the **Data** ribbon. You will notice that columns B, C and D have gained list boxes. Click on the list box at the top of the Costs column. Now click on Number Filters, then on Greater Than Or Equal To.

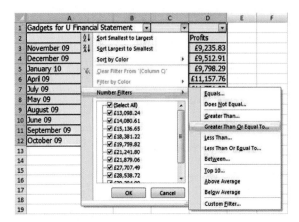

Figure 27.8

Complete the dialogue box as shown in Figure 27.9, choosing the words from the dropdown boxes and keying in the values.

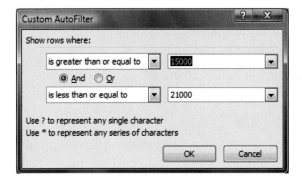

Figure 27.9

Click on OK. The list should now display as shown in Figure 27.10. If you wanted to, you could now highlight these and sort them.

	A	B	C	D
1	Gadgets for U Financial Statement			
7	July 09	£30,133.15	£18,381.22	£11,751.93
9	August 09	£32,393.14	£19,759.82	£12,633.32
10	June 09	£28,030.84	£15,136.65	£12,894.19

Figure 27.10

Nature and purpose

Manipulating data and presenting information

Spreadsheets have multiple uses. When data has been stored, it can be **manipulated** in a number of different ways.

Firstly, the data can be displayed in **rows** and **columns** as part of a **table** of information. It can also be displayed as **graphs** and **charts**. Take the following example of stock information for a skateboarding firm run by Steve Hodder (SHS). Table 27.3 shows how much stock they have, organised into the different component categories that make up a skateboard. The table also has information about the accessories that they stock. Each category is displayed as a total.

Shoes	£26,785
Trucks	£11,444
Decks	£ 9,238
Wheels	£14,516
Clothing	£38,570
Accessories	£ 4,597

Table 27.3 SHS stock information

This table tells the reader that the company has, for example, £4,597 worth of skateboarding accessories.

The same data could now be represented more visually using a **pie chart** or **bar chart** (see Figures 27.11 and 27.12, respectively).

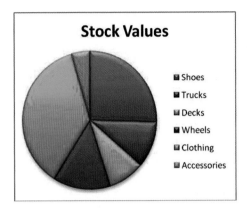

Figure 27.11 A pie chart of the SHS data

Clothing	£38,570
Shoes	£26,785
Wheels	£14,516
Trucks	£11,444
Decks	£ 9,238
Accessories	£ 4,597

Table 27.5 Data ordered by stock value

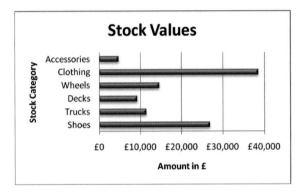

Figure 27.12 A bar chart of the same data

The original data can also be sorted into **ascending** alphabetical order by category or in **descending** order of stock value.

Accessories	£ 4,597
Clothing	£38,570
Decks	£ 9,238
Shoes	£26,785
Trucks	£11,444
Wheels	£14,516

Table 27.4 Data ordered by category

An alphabetical list by category (such as Table 27.4) might be useful if there are lots of entries in the table and the user wants to be able to find a specific category quickly.

Alternatively, the organisation might want to know how much money there is tied up in stock. In this case they would order the list in descending order of stock value (Table 27.5) and they would immediately be able to see which category accounted for the largest stock holding.

How the data stored in a spreadsheet will be viewed or presented will be decided by understanding how the information is going to be used.

When a spreadsheet file is opened as a new document, it has a set of **default options** (predefined settings which can be changed by the user), including the number of spreadsheet pages it contains.

There are three default sheets in a spreadsheet file unless the default is changed by the user. Each spreadsheet is on its own **tab** (visible at the bottom of the screen) and clicking on the tab itself will allow the user to move between the different sheets. The combined sheets are known as a **workbook**.

Terminology

In general, all spreadsheet software uses the same terminology to refer to various aspects of the working environment. The most common terms used are **row**, **column**, **field** and **cell**.

> ### Key term
>
> A **row** is a horizontal display of data (left to right). Rows are always numbered for reference purposes.
>
> A **column** is a vertical display of data (top to bottom). Columns are identified using letters of the alphabet.
>
> A **cell** is a single data entry point. This is referenced using the row and column identifiers.

When the word **field** is used in connection with spreadsheets it identifies data of the same type. If we use the earlier example of the skateboard stock, the Category column would be considered a field, as would the Totals column. The field is also usually the column heading.

Understanding what a spreadsheet cell is is important when you are learning about spreadsheets because calculations use a **cell reference**.

Look at the following example:

	A	B	C
1	2	3	

In the example, cells A1 and B1 both contain an **integer** (whole) number. In the cell referenced C1 we would like to display the answer to the calculation that adds 2 and 3 together. We know that the answer is 5! We now have three options:

a) Calculate the answer manually and key the number 5 into cell C1.

b) Put a formula into cell C1 saying = 2+3 (add 3 to 2).

c) Put a formula into cell C1 saying = A1+B1 (add the contents of cell B1 to A1).

Clearly a) is not a good option as it would be pointless using a software package and doing the hard work ourselves! So we will choose from b) or c). However, while both would work, keying in the physical values (2 and 3) would reduce the functionality of the software. This is because if you refer to the cells in the formula rather than to their actual number values, then when the value inside one of the referenced cells changes, so will the answer! So, if we have used a formula in cell C1 and we change the value in cell A1 from 2 to 5, the answer in cell C1 will automatically update to 8.

We will be working more with formulae in the next section.

User need

Spreadsheets need to be designed, paying attention to the **needs** of the user. In other words:

- The purpose of the spreadsheet
- The inputs into the spreadsheet
- Its processing requirements
- The outputs from the spreadsheet.

It is not uncommon, once a spreadsheet has been set up, for the developer to **lock all areas** that the user does not really need to access (so where the outputs are located, or the row and column headings) to prevent the user from keying into a cell accidentally, thereby overwriting what might have been a complex formula or function.

Before we really begin investigating formulae and functions, we need to make sure we understand the basic spreadsheet view.

Microsoft Excel®'s main screen looks like this:

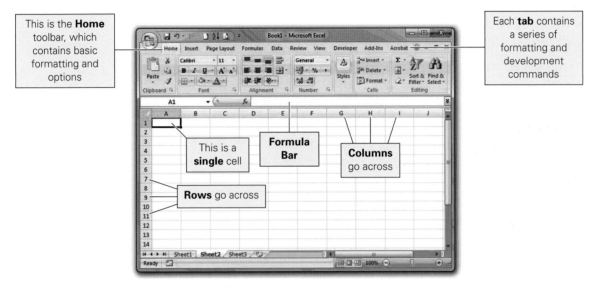

This is the **Home** toolbar, which contains basic formatting and options

Each **tab** contains a series of formatting and development commands

This is a **single** cell

Formula Bar

Columns go across

Rows go across

Figure 27.13 Microsoft Excel 2007®

Workbooks

Workbooks are individual files that contain one or more sheets.

Activity **C**

Spreadsheet terminology

You are working with a group of school children who are using spreadsheets for the first time. The teacher has asked you to create a one-page leaflet that explains all the main terms used in spreadsheets.

You can include images to illustrate the leaflet and make it more child-friendly.

Business uses

Activity D

The business uses of spreadsheets

As part of this unit we have already considered some of the business uses of spreadsheets.

You are now going to do a short interview with someone working in one of the following areas and find out how they use spreadsheets as part of their job:

Administration, Accounts, IT, Production, Marketing, Human Resources, Distribution, Education, Sales, Performing Arts, Graphic Design, Building Trades.

The person you are interviewing might not use spreadsheet software themselves (so they might not create the spreadsheet, they might simply use information in a spreadsheet).

Identify the following:

1. Whether the person is a spreadsheet creator.

2. Whether the person uses the information from spreadsheets.

3. What the spreadsheet is used for.

27.1.2 Alternative formats
Converting to other formats

There will be times when you find you have information in a spreadsheet file that you need to use in another software application. To be able to use the information in another format, you may need to convert it. How can you do this?

In Microsoft Excel 2007® (and in most versions of Microsoft Excel®) this process is very straightforward. To save in a different file format, you need to choose a different file type when saving the file. Some alternative formats are shown in Table 27.6.

Format choice	Description	Example
.xls	An Excel® spreadsheet. This is the default format applied when you save a spreadsheet in Microsoft Excel® (for versions before 2007).	
.xlsx	Microsoft Excel 2007® file format. With .xslx format the gridlines and alignment are stored in addition to the data and this is then used to organise the display.	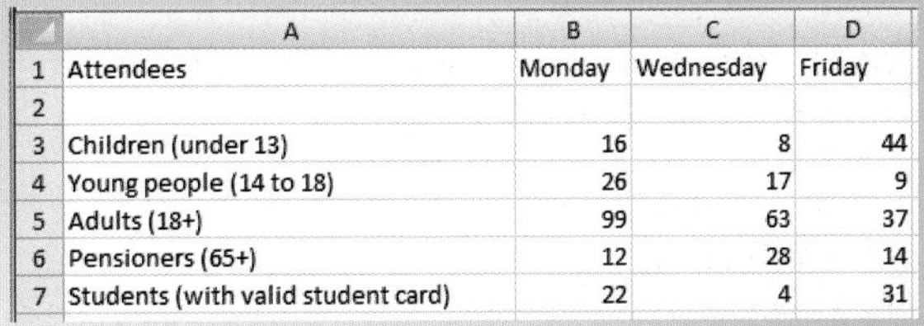 **Figure 27.14** .xlsx format
.csv	This stands for **comma separated value**. When you save a spreadsheet in this format, the contents of the cells are stored in a file and the data is separated by commas. A new line in the file indicates the beginning of a new line in the spreadsheet.	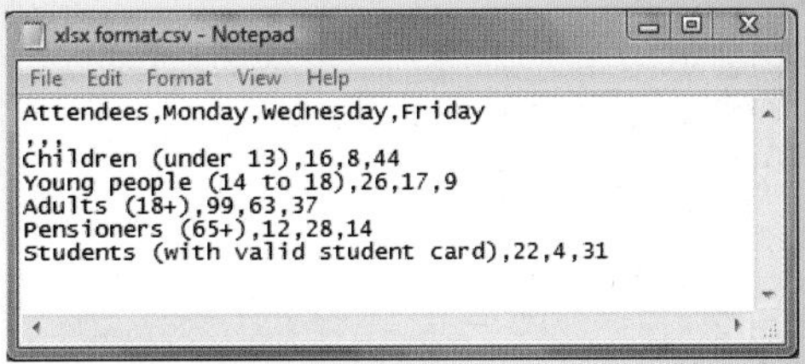 **Figure 27.15** The same file opened in Notepad® as a .csv file
.txt	This format is a simple **text file** and opens in Notepad®. Figure 27.16 shows how the content of the file looks now. In this instance, the commas are missing and an attempt has been made by the software to align the information using default tabs. A text file can be imported into most computer applications.	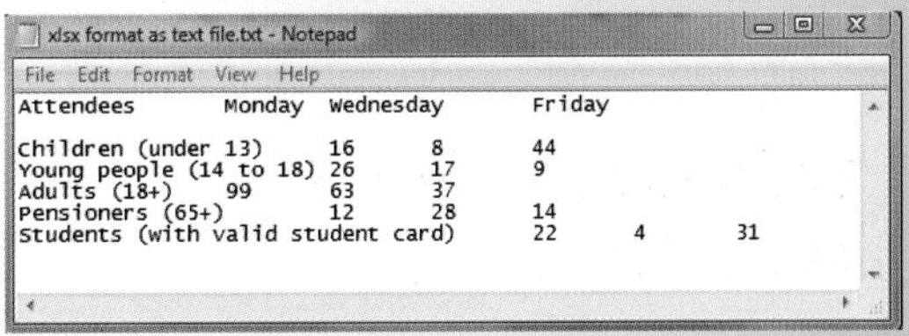 **Figure 27.16** Text file
.html	The **hypertext markup language** format option prepares the data to be opened as a web page by a web browser. This allows the data to be used as part of a website.	

Table 27.6 Alternative file formats

Activity E

Exporting data

Use the following data (that you also used in earlier activities) and create a .txt and a .csv file.

Display the contents and check that they look like the samples in Table 27.6.

Gadgets for U financial statement	Sales	Costs	Profits
April 2009	£24,256.00	£13,098.24	£11,157.76
May 2009	£26,075.20	£14,080.61	£11,994.59
June 2009	£28,030.84	£15,136.65	£12,894.19
July 2009	£30,133.15	£18,381.22	£11,751.93
August 2009	£32,393.14	£19,759.82	£12,633.32
September 2009	£34,822.62	£21,241.80	£13,580.82
October 2009	£35,867.30	£21,879.06	£13,988.25
November 2009	£36,943.32	£27,707.49	£ 9,235.83
December 2009	£38,051.62	£28,538.72	£ 9,512.91
January 2010	£39,193.17	£29,394.88	£ 9,798.29

Show your tutor the saved files in your user area or on your removable storage.

Make the grade

For P1 you will describe how spreadsheet software is used – for example to present information or carry out calculations. As you will also need to show that you understand calculations and functions, you should give some examples.
For P2 you must explain why you might want to convert spreadsheets to different file formats.

27.2 Be able to develop spreadsheet models

This section will cover the following grading criteria: **P3** **P4** **M1** **D1**

27.2.1 Spreadsheet models

Entering and editing data

When you work with a spreadsheet you will need to be able to show that you can enter and edit data. This will involve you typing data into rows and columns and being able to identify which cell a piece of data is stored in.

We suggested earlier in this unit that when you create formulae and functions you should refer to the cell where the data is stored rather than input a number value, so that the value can change without you having to change the formula or function itself.

Cell referencing

When using cell references in formulae and functions we need to decide whether we will use **absolute** or **relative referencing**. We will now consider what the difference is and how it works.

Firstly, we need to understand what happens to formulae when they are copied and pasted.

Here is an extract from a small spreadsheet:

	A	B	C	Formulae in column C
1	3	19	22	=A1 + B1
2	11	17	28	=A2 + B2
3	42	26	68	=A3 + B3
4	106	33	139	=A4 + B4

What we actually did (having keyed data into cells A1 to B4), was to key the formula = A1 + B1 into cell C1. We then copied and pasted the cells down.

As we did so the formulae adjusted themselves automatically to accommodate the changing row numbers:

Formulae in column C	
=A1 + B1	A1 to
=A2 + B2	A2 to
=A3 + B3	A3 to
=A4 + B4	A4

This is known as relative referencing because as each cell is filled, it changes automatically **relative** to the last cell position. There are times, however, when we do not want the formula to change like this.

Look at the following example:

	A	B	C	Formulae in column C
1	3	4	12	= A1 * $B$1
2	11		44	= A2 * $B$1
3	42		168	= A3 * $B$1
4	106		424	= A4 * $B$1

In the above example, cell B1 contains a value which needs to be used in every calculation. If we do not apply absolute cell referencing, as we copy and paste the cells down column C, B1 will become B2, then B3, then B4 (just as the A column references have changed).

Using the **$ (dollar) symbol** as part of the cell reference means that even when copied and pasted, that particular value will NOT change.

Why use this functionality? Why use the cell reference B1 rather than simply keying in the value 4?

Because if we had typed = A1 * 4 into cell C1 and copied it down, while the cell reference would have changed, the value would not have and had we then wanted to change the value 4 to 7 at a later date, we would have needed to change every single formula that contained the number 4. As it stands, we can simply update the value in cell B1 and every calculation that relies on it will update automatically.

Autofilling cells

Spreadsheets also contain functionality to fill cells automatically when the series to fill the cells is predictable. This is demonstrated in the examples below.

Series demonstration (variation of 1)

	A	B	C	D	E	F
1	1	2				
2					5	
3						

Figure 27.17

Spreadsheets can autofill a series of numbers. In the example shown in Figure 27.17 the numbers 1 and 2 had to be keyed into cells A1 and B1. They were then highlighted and dragged to the right. Notice the number in the small square that appeared underneath cell E2 (the last value in the sequence) – this shows what the last value will be when the mouse is released.

Series demonstration (variation of 2)

	A	B	C	D	E	F
1	1	3				
2					9	
3						

Figure 27.18

Notice in Figure 27.18 that the numbers 1 and 3 have been input, and the series will complete: 1 3 5 7 9.

The computer will automatically **predict** the values that need to be inserted.

Series demonstration (dates)

This can also be done with **predictable text**.

	A	B	C	D	E	F
1	Jan	Feb				
2					May	
3						

Figure 27.19

Again, if gaps are left between the first two values, the computer will work out the series while observing the same gaps.

This is an incredibly useful function. What the user must ensure is that both the first and second values are highlighted *before* attempting to drag across.

Activity F

Autofilling

Try using Autofill to automatically input the days of the week (remember to put in the first two days – say Sunday and Monday).

Try again, but this time display every other day (for example, Monday, Wednesday, Friday etc.).

Linking cells and the use of paste

Pasting cells is useful where the user wants the value (formula or function) from one cell to be copied to another cell. The process is simple:

- Select the cell you want to copy.
- Right click the mouse button.
- Select copy from the menu.
- Move to where you want the data to appear.
- Right click the mouse button.
- Select paste.

This action will *only* copy the value from one cell into another. Although there are many different options for pasting cell information other than the actual value in the cell (using the **Paste Special** dialogue box) such as a formula only or a cell format, for the purposes of this unit we are only going to consider the **Paste Link** functionality.

There are times when we need to paste a value that has been calculated in a spreadsheet to another part of the spreadsheet to be used in another calculation. Here is an example:

	A	B	Formula in Column B
1	John Weston Sales		
2	January	1,298	
3	February	2,597	
4	March	1,792	
5	Total sales	5,687	= SUM(B2:B4)

	A	B	Formula in Column B
9	Hamid Aberah Sales		
10	January	2,421	
11	February	1,599	
12	March	2,331	
13	Total sales	6,351	= SUM(B10:B12)

We now want to copy this data to another part of the spreadsheet so that we can give totals for our sales representatives over the three-month period.

	A	B	Formula in Column B
21	Sales for Jan–Mar 06		
22			
23	John Weston	5,687	= $B$5
24	Hamid Aberah	6,351	= $B$13
25	Total	12,038	= SUM(B23:B24)

What we have effectively done to achieve this is copy the contents of cell B5 into cell B23, and the contents of cell B13 into cell B24. We accessed the original position (cell B5 to start) and clicked to copy, but when we pasted the cell into cell B13, we did not simply paste but used the Paste Special option on the menu to activate the Paste Link.

Figure 27.20 The Paste Special dialogue box

Although we can see the value we have pasted, the underlying formula now contains the absolute cell referencing notation. This is known as **paste link**.

This is useful because if we change any of the original data for John Weston, in cells B2 to B4, or for Hamid Aberah, in cells B10 to B12, not only the totals will update automatically, but the contents of cells B23, B24 and B25 will also update accordingly.

Linking cells between different spreadsheets or workbooks

Not only can we paste link within the confines of the same spreadsheet, we can paste link into other spreadsheets in the same workbook, and even into different workbooks entirely. All that changes is the formula.

For paste linking in the same workbook the action is to copy the original cell, click on the spreadsheet where we want to paste the data, click on Paste Special and then on the Paste Link button. What you will now see is that the originating sheet reference has also been included in the formula:
=Sheet1!$B$5

If paste linking into a different workbook, the action is to copy the original cell, open the spreadsheet where you want to paste the cell, select the relevant destination cell, click on Paste Special and then on the Paste Link button.

What you will now see is that the originating file name and sheet number have been included in the formula: **=[Name of File]Sheet1!$B$5**

The paste link functionality is very useful if you need to use data created in one spreadsheet in another workbook. When you open the workbook that contains the link, the computer will automatically prompt you, reminding you that the spreadsheet contains cells linked to other spreadsheets and asking you to choose whether to update the spreadsheet or not. If you choose not to update the spreadsheet when opening it, it will still ask you next time you open the file. If you have chosen to update the file, it will all happen behind the scenes.

Combining information

As software suites such as Microsoft Office® have complete compatibility between the various applications within the product, it is extremely easy to copy and paste records from Access®, a table of data from Excel® or a chart or graph into Word®.

Using the paste functionality will merely copy whatever the original data was into the Word® file. Pasting with Paste Special and Paste Link will enable the user to create linked files that will update automatically (or at least will give the user the option to update automatically) when a file is subsequently re-opened.

File handling

Now that we are potentially going to create multiple files, which may or may not be linked, it is time to consider the basic concepts of good file management.

In order to work efficiently with a computer, you *must* learn how to manage your data. In order to manage it effectively, you *cannot* simply rely on your memory to help you remember what name you gave a file or where you saved it. What you need to do is to make some logical decisions about your files – how they are named and where they are stored.

Imagine your computer is a huge filing cabinet – poor management would be the equivalent of placing all your documents/ spreadsheets and database prints on top of the filing cabinet, without any real organisation. The filing cabinet is your storage device. Each drawer in the filing cabinet represents a different folder in which the relevant files are stored. The cabinet could be separated into different storage areas, each one named for easy identification:

- Drawer 1, for example, could contain all business documents for a specific client and be renamed SHS.
- Drawer 2 could contain documents for a second client DVD.
- Drawer 3 could contain documents for client WCP.
- Drawer 4 could contain your personal documents 'MyStuff'.

To demonstrate the concept we will now create a folder in the document library. To create a folder, you have to work in the Computer dialogue boxes. These can either be selected from the Computer icon on your desktop or from the Start Menu.

In the dialogue box you will need to hover the mouse over the **Documents** option in the **Libraries**. To create a folder you now need to right click the mouse. When the dropdown menu appears, click on **New** then on **Folder**. You can now name the folder.

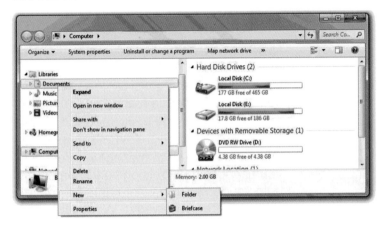

Figure 27.21 Creating a new folder

When creating and saving a file, you would then place the file inside the relevant folder. You can choose which folder you wish to save to during the saving operation in your application.

Activity G

Files and folders

Create a series of folders on your personal storage device or in your user area so that you can store your school or college work more efficiently.

27.2.2 Formulae

It might be useful at this point to explain the difference between a formula and a function.

Key term

A **formula** is where the user creates a calculation using operators (plus, minus, divide and multiply) and cell references.

There are two types of **function: user-defined** and **in-built**. In basic terms they are exactly the same – they are complex calculations that can be used in a spreadsheet many times. They are usually named: for example the SUM function totals a row or column of figures.

An **in-built function** is one which the user selects from a library inside the software. A **user-defined function** is one that the user creates. For the purposes of this unit we are only going to concern ourselves with formulae and in-built functions.

We also need to understand the difference between the cell's content and the cell's value. **Cell content** is any formula or function in the cell, whereas the **cell value** is the actual number or text (such as 26 or Hello or January).

We are now going to explore the **mathematical operators** available for use in spreadsheets before we begin to develop complex calculations.

Formulae

Add

Addition is achieved by using the **+** symbol, much as you would if using a calculator.

If we were going to use a calculator we would key in the following in this exact sequence:

6 + 2 =

This would give the answer 8.

Within the scope of a spreadsheet, however, we would insert the two numeric values into individual cells and use a formula to complete the calculation.

	A	B	C
1	6	2	

As suggested earlier, to add the two numbers together we would simply key a formula into the spreadsheet, into the cell where we want the answer displayed. In this case, that would be in cell C1.

The difference here is that we almost do the calculation backwards! The formula becomes:

=A1+B1

Or in English: cell C1 equals (or takes the value of) the contents of cell A1 with the contents of cell B1 added to it.

	A	B	C
1	6	2	=A1+B1

Having keyed the formula into the cell, it is simply a case of pressing the Enter key to execute the formula.

Let us take this further. If we wanted to add the contents of four cells displayed in a row consecutively, the formula would look something like this:

	A	B	C	D	E
1	6	2	9	3	=A1+B1+C1+D1

Had the data all been held in a single column, the formula would have been modified as follows:

	A
1	6
2	2
3	9
4	3
5	=A1+A2+A3+A4

There is a simpler way of executing this calculation which we will see later in the unit when we begin to look at in-built functions.

Subtract

Subtraction is achieved by using the - symbol. Again, it is the same symbol that we use on a calculator. To subtract 2 from 6 we need to modify the formula in the cell and replace the + symbol with a - one.

	A	B	C
1	6	2	=A1-B1

In English: cell C1 equals (or takes the value of) the contents of cell A1 less the contents of cell B1.

Divide

Divide is achieved by using the **/** symbol. This is the first of the two spreadsheet operators that are different from those used on a calculator. When using a calculator we are used to using the ÷ symbol. This, however, does not exist on a computer keyboard. The computer version is the forward slash symbol.

	A	B	C
1	6	2	=A1/B1

In English: cell C1 equals (or takes the value of) the contents of cell A1 divided by the contents of cell B1.

This calculation will place the answer 3 into cell C1.

Multiply

Multiply is achieved by using the * (or asterisk) symbol. On a calculator we would use a **x**. Just as with the previous examples, we need to replace the operator to change the nature of the calculation. For the purposes of this example we will use the same cells and the same data as seen previously:

	A	B	C
1	5	3	=A1*B1

In English: cell C1 equals (or takes the value of) the contents of cell A1 multiplied by the contents of cell B1.

The answer 15 will appear in cell C1.

These are relatively straightforward calculations and they are executed identically to the way that they would be done on a calculator.

So, how would the computer handle this: 3 + 7 – 6 / 2?

If you were using a calculator you would say: 3 plus 7 is 10 minus 6 is 4 divide by 2 is 2.

If you keyed these numbers and operators into a calculator you would work this sum out and achieve the answer of 2. The computer, however, would not! The computer would calculate the answer as 7. Why?

As stated earlier, computers only work with logic and as the computer would not necessarily understand how you would want the sum 3 + 7 – 6 / 2 handled, a way of working with numbers like this has been programmed into the computer itself. This method of handling figures is known as **BODMAS**.

BODMAS stands for:

Brackets

Over

Division

Multiplication

Addition

Subtraction

This is applied to all mathematical calculations that a computer executes, so when our computer sees the sum 3 + 7 – 6 / 2, this is how it calculates:

Are there any **brackets?**

No – move on.

Is there any **division?**

Yes – take the numbers on either side of the operator and work with them. The number **6** is divided by **2**, to give the answer **3** and this replaces the original 6/2 in the sum.

The sum now reads **3 + 7 – 3**

Is there any **multiplication?**

No – move on.

Is there any **addition?**

Yes – take the numbers on either side of the operator and work with them. The numbers **3** and **7** are added together to give **10** and this value replaces the original 3 + 7 in the sum.

The sum now reads **10 – 3**

Is there any **subtraction?**

Yes – take the numbers on either side of the operator and work with them. The number 3 is taken away from the number **10** and the answer is **7**.

So – the computer returns the number **7** as the answer.

This is clearly not what we had originally intended with our sum 3 + 7 – 6 / 2. How do we use parentheses (brackets) to force the computer to view the sum differently? Remember in the abbreviation that we learned earlier (BODMAS), brackets must be handled first.

By placing brackets in our sum the computer will have to look at it differently.

(3 + 7 − 6) / 2

Let us look at how the computer will handle this:

Are there **brackets**?

Yes – inside the brackets are the following numbers: 3 + 7 − 6

Applying the rules of BODMAS we need to do the addition bit before the subtraction.

3 + 7 is **10**

The sum now reads **10 − 6**

10 − 6 is **4**

We now replace all the numbers inside the brackets with the answer calculated above.

So (3 + 7 − 6) / 2 becomes 4 / 2

We have dealt with the brackets. Is there any **division**?

Yes – 4 / 2 – the answer is **2**.

Is there any **multiplication**?

No, there was none – the answer is still 2 – move on.

Is there any **addition**?

Yes, there was some, but as it was inside the brackets we have done it – the answer is still 2.

Is there any **subtraction**?

Yes, there was some, but as it was inside the brackets we have done it – the answer is still 2.

No more calculations? Then the answer is **2**.

Activity H

Calculations

See if you can work out the answers to these (the answers are at the back of the book, but do not cheat!). In each case work out what **the computer** would give as an answer:

1. 21 / (4 + 3)
2. 7 * 10 / 2
3. 6 * (7 + 3) − 1
4. (10 + 4) * 4
5. 10 + 4 * 4

Complex calculations

A common formula in a spreadsheet is the calculation of VAT. VAT is a **tax** that is applied by the Government to various products and services that we buy. Companies have a liability to pay any VAT they have collected on their sales to the Government, but they are allowed to claim back VAT they have paid other companies for purchases they have made. It works something like this.

VAT on sales − VAT on purchases = Liability to Government

However, if the VAT on sales is less than the VAT on purchases, then the organisation will receive a refund (money back) from the Government!

There are three VAT rates. These are currently as shown below, but they could change at any time:

- Standard rate: 20 per cent
- Reduced rate: 5 per cent
- Zero rate: 0 per cent

Which one the organisation applies to a sale is dependent on what the organisation is selling. The following are currently being charged at the reduced rate:

- Domestic fuel
- Installation of energy-saving materials
- Grant-funded installation of heating equipment or security goods or connection of gas supply
- Renovation and alteration of dwellings
- Residential conversions
- Women's sanitary products
- Children's car seats.

The list of items that are zero rated is huge, but here are some inclusions:

- Clothing and footwear for young children
- Charity advertising
- Some education and training
- Some exports
- Some aspects of finance and security.

The rules are very complex to say the least.

Either way, regardless of which rate is applied a spreadsheet developer will need to be able to calculate VAT so that it is correctly added to an invoice prior to it being sent to a customer.

Let us work with some blank CDs being sold by Diskount Video Discs (DVD):

A customer buys 10 CDs at 34 pence each.

The sub-total for the invoice would be £3.40.

VAT would then be added on top at 20 per cent of the sub-total.

This would be £3.40 * 20% – which would be 68 pence.

We would now add the £3.40 and the 68 pence and come out with a grand total of **£4.08**.

Let us apply this to a spreadsheet!

	A	B	C	D	E
1	CDs	Cost	Sub-total	VAT	Grand total
2	10	0.34	=A2*B2	=C2*20%	=C2+D2

Each of the cells here contains a single stage calculation.

Two stage calculations

Although the above is a two stage calculation (the sub-total is calculated, then the VAT, before the two are added together to form the grand total) we have created additional columns to handle each part of the calculation. A more common method of undertaking a two stage calculation could be the calculation of a gross salary (a person's wages before tax and National Insurance), where the employee earns two different rates, one for their basic hours and another rate for overtime. Let us look at the salaries of DVD employees. Commonly, overtime is paid at two rates: time and a half and double time.

This works out as follows:

Basic rate	£5.00 per hour
Rate at time and a half	£7.50 per hour
Rate at double time	£10 per hour

The differentiation in the pay rate will be dependent on what has been agreed with the manager before the hours are worked.

So, if we were calculating the gross salary (or wage) for an employee, we would calculate his basic pay, followed by his overtime, which would then be added together to give his gross wage. For the purposes of this example, we will assume that he or she works 37 hours per week at basic rate and has worked 4.75 hours at time and a half. What will happen here is that we will not create an additional column to calculate the basic salary and then the overtime, we will key all the relevant data into cells and do the entire calculation in one go.

	A	B	C	D	E
1	Basic hours	Rate	Overtime hours	Rate	Gross salary
2	37	5.00	4.75	7.50	=(A2*B2)+(C2*D2)

Notice the use of the parentheses (brackets) to help organise the calculation.

The ultimate answer in cell E2 would be £220.625, or £220.63 to two decimal places.

Compound interest

The best way to explain compound interest is to apply it. Let us imagine that you are going to invest £50 at an interest rate of 2 per cent per month.

At the end of your first month of investment, your money will have increased by 2 per cent, from £50 to £51, as £1 is 2 per cent of £50. This is added on to your original investment.

At the end of the second month you will again earn interest, but not £1 because that is 2 per cent of £50 and you now have £51.

It is easier to see this in a spreadsheet:

	A	B
1	Original investment	£50.00
2	Month 1	£51.00
3	Month 2	£52.02
4	Month 3	£53.06
5	Month 4	£54.12
6	Month 5	£55.20
7	Month 6	£56.31
8	Month 7	£57.43
9	Month 8	£58.58
10	Month 9	£59.75
11	Month 10	£60.95
12	Month 11	£62.17
13	Month 12	£63.41

The formula that would have been keyed into cell B2 would have been: =(B1*2%)+B1

The cell has been copied and pasted down the spreadsheet so that each cell offsets the cell reference by one as the copy and paste activity is executed.

In cell B3 the calculation would read =(B2*2%)+B2 and cell B4 would read =(B3*2%)+B3

Having set up this spreadsheet, it is clear to see how the original investment has grown as the compound interest gained over the 12 months is calculated.

As you can see, the formulae are now starting to get quite complex! Let us have a look at functions.

27.2.3 Functions
Statistical functions

Most spreadsheet software contains a library of functions that you can simply use. We are going to look at some of the basic functions that are available in Excel®. These include **statistical functions** and **logical functions**.

In the addition section earlier in the unit, we considered how we would add up a series of consecutive cells (we saw this demonstrated with the data held in both a row and in a column).

	A	B	C	D	E
1	6	2	9	3	**=A1+B1+C1+D1**

A series of consecutive spreadsheet cells is known as a **range** and all of the statistical functions shown in this unit use a range as part of the function structure.

Sum

The **Sum** function automatically adds together the contents of all the cells included in the range. If we take the above example, to get the total we need to add A1 + B1 + C1 + D1. Using the Sum function the formula is significantly shortened.

	A	B	C	D	E
1	6	2	9	3	**=SUM(A1:D1)**

The function literally means: E1 equals (or takes the value of) adding together all cells between A1 and D1 inclusive (including all the cells named in the range).

To use the Sum function the user has two options:

- Click the **AutoSum icon** which is located on the standard Excel® toolbar.
- Key the Sum function into the cell.

Keying a function or a formula into the cell is very straightforward. Using the AutoSum, on the other hand, requires some concentration! Firstly, the user must access cell B14 (which is where the total is meant to appear).

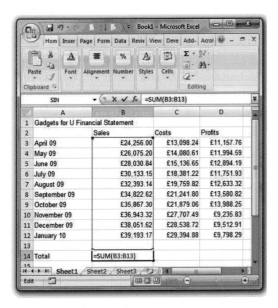

Figure 27.22 AutoSum range

When the AutoSum icon is clicked, the computer will attempt to select the range on behalf of the user. It will look for **continuous cells** above or to the left of the sum. If the selection is correct, then press the Enter key. If not, click into the start cell of the range and, holding down the left mouse button, drag down until the last cell has been covered, release the button and click Enter.

This technique for selecting a range will apply regardless of which function you use. Clicking and dragging across the range is the quickest way of identifying which cells are included in the sum.

Average

As with the Sum function, the **Average** function uses a range. However, there is no convenient icon for this. It requires the user to key it in.

The Average function takes all the cells in the range and does two things. Firstly it adds up the all the cell contents like the Sum function does. It then goes one step further. It calculates how many cells there were in the range and divides the sum by the number of cells in the range, to give the average.

Let us see how this works:

	A	B	C	D	E
1	6	2	9	3	=AVERAGE(A1:D1)

The computer adds: 6 + 2 + 9 + 3 = 20
It counts the number of cells in the range: 4
It divides 20 by 4 and returns 5
The answer 5 will appear in cell E1.

Min

The **Min** function finds the lowest (or minimum) value in the identified range.

	A	B	C	D	E
1	6	2	9	3	=MIN(A1:D1)

The computer will now search the range and find (and return) the lowest value. In this range the **lowest value** is 2.

Max

In the same way, the **Max** function finds the highest (or maximum) value in the identified range.

	A	B	C	D	E
1	6	2	9	3	=MAX(A1:D1)

Once again the computer will search the range and in this case it will find (and return) the highest value. In this range the **highest value** is 9.

Count

The **Count** function literally counts the number of **non-blank** cells in the range.

	A	B	C	D	E
1		2			=COUNT(A1:D1)

Here the computer will simply return the number 1 as there is only one cell in the identified range (the second cell B1 contains the value 2).

Countif

The **Countif** function is a little more powerful as it enables the user to count the number of cells in a range that meet a certain **criterion**.

	A	B	C	D	E
1	6	2	9	3	=COUNTIF(A1:D1,4)

To understand the function we need to take it apart:

= COUNTIF(A1:D1,4)

Function   Range   Criterion

Function – is the function's name.

Range – is the range of cells to look at (including the named cells).

Criterion – what exactly to look for.

If we apply the above function into cell E1, what will the computer return?

0! Because there is no cell that contains the value 4.

If we change the function, however, to read:

= COUNTIF(A1:D1,6)

then the computer will return the number 1, because there is one cell in the range that contains the number 6.

If we modify the data in the range, but leave the function unchanged we will now get a different answer:

	A	B	C	D	E
1	6	2	9	6	=COUNTIF(A1:D1,6)

The computer will now return the result 2.

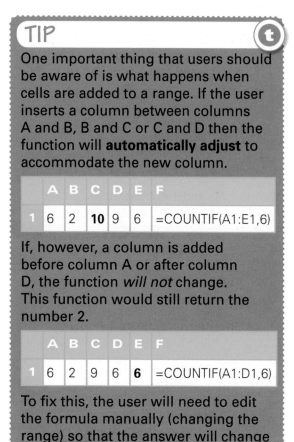

TIP

One important thing that users should be aware of is what happens when cells are added to a range. If the user inserts a column between columns A and B, B and C or C and D then the function will **automatically adjust** to accommodate the new column.

	A	B	C	D	E	F
1	6	2	**10**	9	6	=COUNTIF(A1:E1,6)

If, however, a column is added before column A or after column D, the function *will not* change. This function would still return the number 2.

	A	B	C	D	E	F
1	6	2	9	6	**6**	=COUNTIF(A1:D1,6)

To fix this, the user will need to edit the formula manually (changing the range) so that the answer will change to 3.

Logical (IF, OR, AND)

While there are many **logical** functions, for the purposes of this unit we are going to concentrate on the three most common ones: **IF**, **OR** and **AND**.

Once we start creating **logical functions** using logical operators such as IF, OR and AND, our spreadsheet becomes even more powerful.

IF

IF functions (commonly known as IF statements) are used to select one action over another; the selection is dependent on a condition. For example:

    If (it is cloudy today)
            Take an umbrella
    Else
            Enjoy the sunshine

This is similar to the If … else statements you may have encountered in Unit 18 (Software design).

All IF statements have the same structure:

    IF (condition)
            Do this if true
    Else
            Do this if false

Here is a spreadsheet example:

	A	B	C
1	3	19	=IF(A1>10,A1+B1,0)

which means in full:

    if (A1>10)
            this cell becomes A1 + B1
    else
            this cell becomes 0

Or, in English:

    If the content of cell A1 is greater than 10, return the answer obtained by adding cell A1 to cell B1, else return 0.

Looking at the data, what will the above function return?

The computer is not interested in the fact that cell B1 contains a value greater than 10 as B1 is not being checked in the condition. As such, the result that appears in cell C1 will be 0. However, if we **reverse the values** in A1 and B1

	A	B	C
1	19	3	=IF(A1>10,A1+B1,0)

then the answer will be 22 (i.e. 19 + 3) because now A1 is greater than 10.

OR

The **OR** operator allows the user to check multiple cells.

    = IF(OR(A1<20,B1>5),A1+B1,0)

In English:

    IF the cell content of A1 is less than 20 OR the cell content of B1 is greater than 5, then add the contents of cells A1 and B1 together and return the result, else return 0.

The structure is:

    IF (condition part A is true OR condition part B is true)
            Do this because one of them is true
    Else
            Do this because they are both false

Look at the following example – what will the result be?

	A	B	C
1	21	7	=IF(OR(A1<20,B1>5),A1+B1,0)

Here A1 is not less than 20 (so this will be false) but B1 is greater than 5 (so this will be true). The value 28 will be returned.

AND

The **AND** operator again allows the user to check multiple cells, but unlike the OR operator where either part of the condition can be true for the condition to return the value of true and thus execute the true part of the statement, with the AND operator *both* parts of the condition *must* be true for the true part of the statement to be executed.

= IF(AND(A1<20,B1<5),A1+B1,0)

The structure is:

IF (condition part A is true AND condition part B is true)
　　　Do this because both of them are true
Else
　　　Do this because they are both false

	A	B	C
1	10	3	=IF(AND(A1<20,B1<5),A1+B1,0)

Here A1 is indeed less than 20 (so this will be true) AND B1 is less than 5 (so this will also be true), so the computer will add the two numbers together and return the result 13.

The results of all logical functions must be checked carefully because it is very easy to make a mistake. Test these carefully as part of a testing strategy.

Finally, you should have a basic understanding of **relational operator** symbols:

>	Greater than
<	Less than
=	Equal to
>=	Greater than or equal to
<=	Less than or equal to

As we have seen, relational operators demonstrate the relationship between two values, for example 5>4, 4=4, 2<10 etc.

Activity ▮

Logical?

See if you can work out the answers to these expressions, given the following examples for X and Y. The answers are at the back of the book, so do not cheat! In each case work out what the computer would give as an answer – TRUE or FALSE?

X = 50, Y = 100

1. X > 50
2. Y <= 100
3. Y > 50 AND X < 100
4. X = 50 OR Y < 50
5. X >= 50 AND Y < 50

27.2.4 Refine

Improving efficiency

There are lots of different tools that developers can use to make spreadsheets more efficient. These include the use of **shortcuts** like **macros** to carry out repetitive tasks. For example:

If you regularly need to print a particular area from a spreadsheet and you need to make three copies, you would normally have to:

- Highlight the area
- Select it as a print area from the print menu

- Click on Print
- Change the print number
- Click OK.

With a macro, all of these activities would be **recorded** (the developer carries out the actions and the computer remembers them and turns the information into a mini computer program). The code can then be **attached** to a button so that each time the user needs to carry out the same task, he or she would simply click the button!

Macros and buttons can also be used to move between sheets in a spreadsheet to make the spreadsheet more efficient.

There is more on macros in section 27.2.6.

Formatting

Spreadsheet format

How a spreadsheet looks is important. Look at the Gadgets for U financial statement in Figure 27.23:

	A	B	C	D
1	Gadgets for U Financial Statement			
2		Sales	Costs	Profits
3	April 09	£24,256.00	£13,098.24	£11,157.76
4	May 09	£26,075.20	£14,080.61	£11,994.59
5	June 09	£28,030.84	£15,136.65	£12,894.1900
6	July 09	£30,133.15	£18,381.22	£11,751.93
7	August 09	£32,393.14	£19,760	£12,633
8	September 09	£34,822.62	£21,242	£13,581
9	October 09	£35,867.30	£21,879	£13,988
10	November 09	£36,943.32	£27,707.49	£9,235.83
11	December 09	£38,051.62	£28,538.72	£9,512.91
12	January 10	£39,193.17	£29,395	£9,798.29
13				

Figure 27.23 Gadgets for U financial statement, before formatting

Is this a good example of a spreadsheet? No – it looks like someone has thrown the information together without caring

how it looks. What about the example in Figure 27.24?

	A	B	C	D
1	Gadgets for U Financial Statement			
2				
3		Sales	Costs	Profits
4	April 09	£24,256.00	£13,098.24	£11,157.76
5	May 09	£26,075.20	£14,080.61	£11,994.59
6	June 09	£28,030.84	£15,136.65	£12,894.19
7	July 09	£30,133.15	£18,381.22	£11,751.93
8	August 09	£32,393.14	£19,759.82	£12,633.32
9	September 09	£34,822.62	£21,241.80	£13,580.82
10	October 09	£35,867.30	£21,879.06	£13,988.25
11	November 09	£36,943.32	£27,707.49	£9,235.83
12	December 09	£38,051.62	£28,538.72	£9,512.91
13	January 10	£39,193.17	£29,394.88	£9,798.29

Figure 27.24 After formatting

This is much better. It looks tidy and professional. In the next few sections you can look at the different ways of improving the formatting of a spreadsheet such as choice of fonts, use of colour or use of conditional formatting.

Fonts

Regardless of which font you choose, you should make sure that you are consistent within the spreadsheet. For example, all headings are in the same font or the main body of text is in the same font.

Fonts come in two main types:

- **Serif fonts** – fonts with embellishments
- **Sans serif fonts** – fonts without embellishments.

Here are some examples (to be able to see the difference clearly, look at the capital W in each example):

Serif fonts

Where shall we go? (Times New Roman)

𝔚𝔥𝔢𝔯𝔢 𝔰𝔥𝔞𝔩𝔩 𝔴𝔢 𝔤𝔬? (Old English Text MT)

Where shall we go? (Courier New)

Sans Serif fonts

Where shall we go? (Ariel)

Where shall we go? (Haettenschweiler)

Where shall we go? (Din)

In addition, fonts are classified as **proportional** or **non-proportional**.

A proportional font uses up a different amount of space for each character – for example, an 'I' which is tall and thin would take up much less space than an 'M'.

This font is Times New Roman (14) and it is a serif, proportional font as it uses less space for an 'I' than it does for an 'M' and it has embellishments.

```
This font is Courier New
(14) and it is a serif, non-
proportional font as it uses the
same amount of space for an 'I'
as it does for an 'M'. This font
also has embellishments.
```

Use of colour

Colours can also be used effectively in spreadsheets to improve their appearance. For example, you could colour column and row headings or you could colour specific cells to draw attention to them. You could change the colour of the font to make something stand out.

Did you know, for example, that traditionally, negative values in spreadsheets or accounting ledgers are shown in red? On a bank statement, in particular, this could be quite scary!

Conditional formatting

Conditional formatting is when something happens to change the visual appearance of a cell or range of cells when a particular condition is met. For example, if numbers are negative they could be shown in a different sized font or a different coloured font.

Microsoft Excel 2007® contains a range of conditional formatting tools that will help the user emphasise different parts of the spreadsheet. You can find this on the Home ribbon in the Styles group.

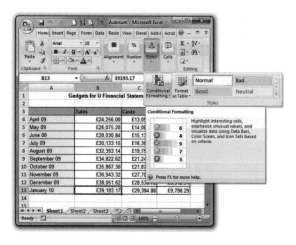

Figure 27.25 Conditional formatting

Whatever choices you make with formatting, you should always be consistent if you want your spreadsheet to look professional.

Activity J

Fonts

Working with a partner, create an A4 poster about fonts.

Illustrate your poster with examples of six different fonts. Make sure it is clear on your poster what each of the fonts are!

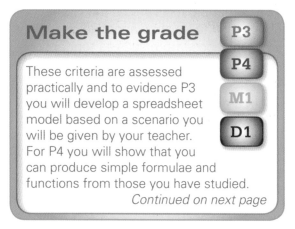

Make the grade   P3
P4
M1
D1

These criteria are assessed practically and to evidence P3 you will develop a spreadsheet model based on a scenario you will be given by your teacher. For P4 you will show that you can produce simple formulae and functions from those you have studied.

Continued on next page

Continued ...
To show that you can refine a spreadsheet and meet the needs of M1, you will adapt it and introduce refinements to improve it by making it more accurate and easier to use. Your teacher might ask you to present your changes to your class, or you could write a short report with some screen shots that show how you have made your improvements.

For D1 you must evaluate your spreadsheets and the improvements you made, also suggesting some further refinements that you might include at a later date. You do not need to make the refinements, you just need to be able to identify them and justify why you think they would be an improvement.

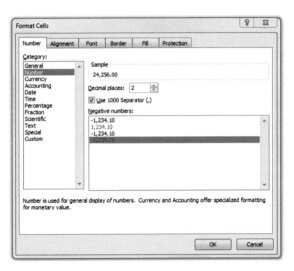

Figure 27.26 Format Cells dialogue box

27.2.5 Presenting data

This section will cover the following grading criterion:

P5

One of the most important aspects of spreadsheets is that the user needs to lay out and format the spreadsheet in a consistent and professional manner.

To format a single cell or a range of cells they first need to be highlighted, as formatting can only be applied to highlighted cells.

The formatting tools are on the Home ribbon, and there are a series of options you can choose from such as font options, alignment options, number options and styles.

There are more options available if you access the formatting dialogue box by clicking on the relevant cell and then use the right mouse button to reveal the formatting commands. You then click on Format Cells.

Appropriate data types and alignment

Explaining all the different options in their own right would be a book in itself. What follows here is an overview of formatting options and decisions.

Text

Text is exactly what you think it is. It is any characters that have been input into a cell. Text normally defaults to align to the left of the cell.

However, it can also be **centred** in a cell or **right** aligned.

Currency (or number)

Numbers can be displayed as **integers**, as **real numbers** (with decimal places) or as **currency** (again with or without decimal places).

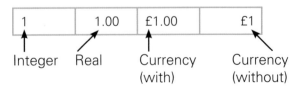

Regardless of which format is chosen, users should make sure that they apply the format consistently across the data in the range.

Dates

There are a variety of **date formats** that you can choose from (see Figure 27.27).

Figure 27.27 Date formats

The options include:

Long dates such as 21st November 2010

Short dates such as 21/11/10

You can also customise dates to use your own format.

You should be aware, however, that in the USA the month comes before the day, whereas in the UK we tend to display the day before the month.

Formatting cells

There may well be occasions when you want something in your spreadsheet to stand out. To this end there are a number of options you could choose which allow you to draw attention to a specific cell or range of cells. As with other options, the cells to be affected need to be highlighted prior to making the relevant choices.

150.00	Background colour
175.00	Font colour
203.00	Shading (with a pattern rather than a colour)
262.00	Border

Of course, you could also apply these in any combination.

Other formatting

Having made the decision to display real numbers (those with decimal points) you need to decide the number of decimal points it is appropriate to display. If we are dealing with UK currency, for example, there is no point in displaying the data to more than two decimal places as we do not have half or quarter pence; so £1.235 (one pound and twenty three and a half pence) does not have any meaning, neither does £4.8825 (four pounds and eighty eight and a quarter pence).

On the other hand, some scientific calculations might depend on a high level of **accuracy** and a number of decimal places being displayed.

To format the number of decimal places the most straightforward method is to click on the relevant icons in the Number group on the Home ribbon.

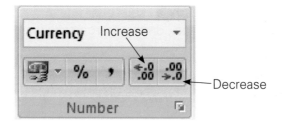

Figure 27.28 Formatting currency

All the user needs to do is to highlight the relevant numbers and then click on the increase and decrease icons as shown in Figure 27.28. One click will remove or reveal another decimal place.

Merging cells

Merging cells is where you have a single piece of information that appears over a number of columns. It is most commonly required where you want to have a heading displayed over a number of columns. In Table 27.7, the user has selected to display the heading over the first three columns.

	Gadgets for U Financial Statement		
	Sales	Costs	Profits
April 09	£24,256.00	£13,098.24	£11,157.76
May 09	£26,075.20	£14,080.61	£11,994.59
June 09	£28,030.84	£15,136.65	£12,894.19
July 09	£30,133.15	£18,381.22	£11,751.93
August 09	£32,393.14	£19,759.82	£12,633.32
September 09	£34,822.62	£21,241.80	£13,580.82
October 09	£35,867.30	£21,879.06	£13,988.25
November 09	£36,943.32	£27,707.49	£ 9,235.83
December 09	£38,051.62	£28,538.72	£ 9,512.91
January 10	£39,193.17	£29,394.88	£ 9,798.29

Table 27.7 Merging cells

To achieve this effect, simply key the title into one of the cells then highlight all cells over which the title should be displayed and click on the merge cells icon.

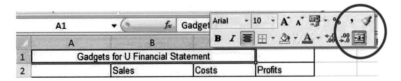

Figure 27.29 Formatting tools showing merge cells icon

Formatting charts

When you create charts and graphs, it is essential that these are correctly formatted to make sure that they are usable.

The charts given in Figure 27.30 have been produced using the following data from our fictional company SHS:

Shoes	£26,785
Trucks	£11,444
Decks	£9,238
Wheels	£14,516
Clothing	£38,570
Accessories	£4,597

In Figure 27.30, the pie chart contains a title and a legend (the legend is the panel that explains the colours). In this example, the percentages have also been added to give greater impact. The bar graph does not need a legend, but might if there were several series of data (for example Accessories 2009 compared with 2010). It has a title and it has axis labels.

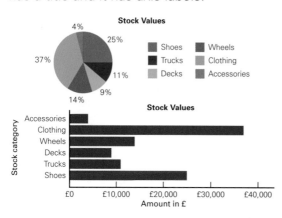

Figure 27.30 Stock values as a pie chart and a bar graph

> **TIP**
>
> On a line or bar chart there are two axes – these are known as X and Y. How do you know which is which?
>
> The X axis goes across (think of it as a cross lying at an angle) and the Y axis goes up and down.

Once a chart has been created, any aspect can be changed, including the axis on a bar or column chart, the titles and data labels (the legend can be added or removed).

In addition, the object can be moved. It can be copied and pasted into other spreadsheets or maybe even a Microsoft Word® document, and the paste link functionality still applies.

The user should always be cautions, though, when **resizing** a chart or graph as the image can be **distorted**. Making the object too small could also see some of the titles disappear and data displayed without relevant titles or labels. Also, if the image is made too large, then the writing can become blurred. The user *must* check that everything in the chart or graph is as it should be before saving or printing the image.

Chart types

It is essential that a spreadsheet developer and a spreadsheet user understand the different types of charts that are available. The most common four are listed here.

- **Pie charts** – These are generally used where you want to represent some data visually as part of a whole. The 'pie' is split into slices. The larger the slice, the more it represents of the whole. Figure 27.30 gives an example of a pie chart.
- **Column charts** – With vertical bars (upright), column charts are the most commonly used chart type. They allow users to compare columns of data visually.
- **Bar charts** – With horizontal bars (flat), bar charts are often used for comparing distances, for example. However, bar charts and column charts are actually interchangeable. Figure 27.30 gives an example of a bar chart.
- **Line graphs** – These are good for comparing trends (see Figure 27.1 near the beginning of this unit).

With any chart, users must check to ensure that the image actually means something. There is no point creating a pie chart, for example, with no title, key or legend. It will be meaningless. This is a very common error made by users in creating such charts.

Formatting sheets

In addition to users being able to format individual spreadsheet cells and columns or rows of cells, the spreadsheet itself can be formatted in a number of ways. The sheet formatting options can be accessed on the Page Layout ribbon and by selecting Print Titles (see Figure 27.31).

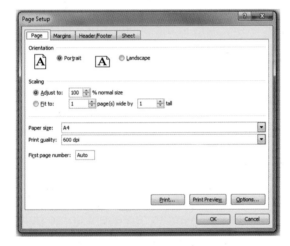

Figure 27.31 Formatting sheets

From this page, users can access the Header/Footer tab. A **header**, as you would expect, would appear at the top of the sheet and a **footer** at the bottom. Information displayed in footers often includes: name of spreadsheet author, date of creation or modification and page numbers. Headers are more likely to be used for titles.

Inserting **page breaks** is an important technique to ensure that column or row titles stay with their data. To force a page break users simply place the cursor into the cell where they want the new page to

start. Then it is simply a case of selecting Breaks from the Page Setup group on the Page Layout ribbon.

Scaling can be used to force a document to fit to a single page.

On the Page Layout ribbon, users can select to print or not print the **gridlines** on a spreadsheet. This is done by choosing the relevant option in the Sheet options group.

In order to appreciate the formatting options fully, it is best to experiment. For the purposes of this unit it is important that you have an understanding of what can be achieved.

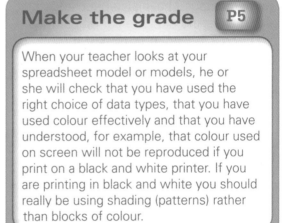

Make the grade   P5

When your teacher looks at your spreadsheet model or models, he or she will check that you have used the right choice of data types, that you have used colour effectively and that you have understood, for example, that colour used on screen will not be reproduced if you print on a black and white printer. If you are printing in black and white you should really be using shading (patterns) rather than blocks of colour.

27.2.6 Automations

This section will cover the following grading criterion: **D2**

Macros

Macros are mini programs that automate chosen actions in a spreadsheet. They can be stored within a workbook, or stored so that they can be accessed by all workbooks.

Recording a macro is a very straightforward process. You can either select the Macros button on the View ribbon or you can use the Developer ribbon that contains many of the macro functions. You can then choose to Record a new macro.

As soon as Record Macro has been selected, a dialogue box will appear. At this point you will name your macro and choose where your macro will be stored.

Figure 27.32 Setting up the macro

Once you click on OK, the macro will begin recording and every action you undertake will be logged, until you click on the Stop Recording button.

Once the recording has been stopped, you can then add a button to the spreadsheet to activate the macro. To do this you must select the Developer ribbon, click on Insert in the Controls group and then, from the Form Controls, click on the button icon.

Figure 27.33 Adding a button

Draw a button on your spreadsheet and when you release the mouse, the **Assign Macro** dialogue box will appear. Choose the macro you wish to assign.

Figure 27.34 Assigning a macro

You can also change the caption on the button to reflect what the button does (for example, Print).

Paste Link

This has already been explained in section 27.2.1. Remember, it can be very useful to link workbooks dynamically rather than trying to have all of the information in a single massive spreadsheet!

ActiveX controls and Control Toolbox

These are controls that can be downloaded, written by the developer or imported from other software applications. These controls can then be made available to different programs. It is a bit like a library of controls and tools that can be used again and again.

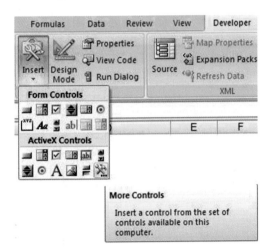

Figure 27.35 Controls

Visual Basic

Visual Basic is the programming language that is used to record automated processes in Microsoft® applications. Below is a macro that is displayed as code:

```
Sub Macro1()
Macro1 Macro
Macro recorded 20/07/2010 by Bernie
    Range("A1:A7,B3:B7").Select
    Selection.PrintOut Copies:=3,
    Collate:=True
End Sub
```

All macros start and end with Sub. When recorded, the date and the name of the developer are inserted automatically.

Once recorded and saved, the code can be easily changed. For example, amending the print range or the number of prints is achieved by changing the relevant values.

```
Sub Macro1()
Macro1 Macro
Macro recorded 20/07/2010 by Bernie
    Range("A1:A12,B3:B12").Select
    Selection.PrintOut Copies:=6,
    Collate:=True
End Sub
```

Make the grade — D2

To achieve D2 you will be expected to add automated features (i.e. more than one) to your spreadsheet model.
You could include a macro, create a link between workbooks or use some other method of automation that is supported by the application you are using.

27.2.7 Analysing and interpreting data

This section will cover the following grading criteria: P6 M2 M3

Converting spreadsheet data to charts and graphs

It has already been suggested earlier in this unit that being able to convert tables into charts and graphs is a useful way of representing data in a visually effective way. Experienced managers use both tables and charts to analyse information about their organisational performance.

Filtering and sorting lists

As discussed earlier in the unit, spreadsheets also have basic database functionality. In order to filter and sort data easily, this functionality needs to be activated.

To do this we begin by highlighting the headings, select the Data ribbon, then on the Filter button. This will activate the **AutoFilter**.

We then need to choose how we want to filter the values we want to display.

Activity K

Filtering

To understand how filtering works, it is better to actually go through the process.

Use the Gadgets for U financial statement we worked with in earlier activities.

We now need to click onto the cell containing Sales and then right click. Select Filter and then Filter by Selected Cell's Value.

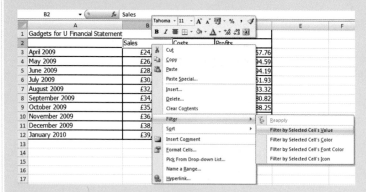

Figure 27.36

When you now click onto the icon beside the word Sales, you can make your filtering selections. You can choose to display specific values, you can sort the data and you can apply custom filters that display, for example, values between two boundaries.

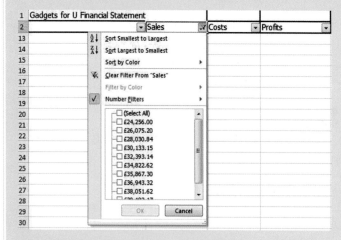

Figure 27.37

Experiment with this and see if you can display only those results that are between £30,000 and £38,000.

27.2.8 Tools

Titles in charts and graphs

The need to include titles in charts and graphs has already been discussed earlier in the unit. What we need to do now is to consider the quality of the titles.

To be appropriate and reasonable the title must:

- Be visible!
- Be accurate – without spelling mistakes
- Be consistent – use an appropriate font (size and colour) throughout
- Be representative of what the data is – the title should give the reader an immediate understanding of what the data is about. A good example would be: Gadgets for U Financial Statement (April 2009 to January 2010)

Labels

Activity **L**

Axis scales

You should choose your label on a chart's axis carefully. Again, as with the chart title, the axis label should be representative of the data. Go back through the unit and find at least two charts. Look at any labelling on the charts and consider whether the labels are representative of the data.

Did you know that you can also change the axis scale on a chart? Use the financial statement data to create this trend chart:

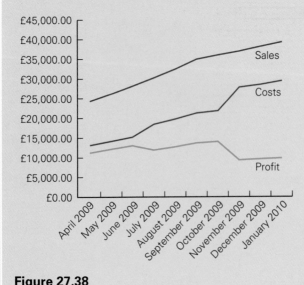

Figure 27.38

In this example, we do not really need to show the values above £40,000 because the graph does not go that high. We could also start the lower value at £5,000 rather than zero. Essentially, there is wasted space on this chart.

To change the axis, we literally click on the number values on the Y-axis and then right click and choose Format Axis to bring up the dialogue box.

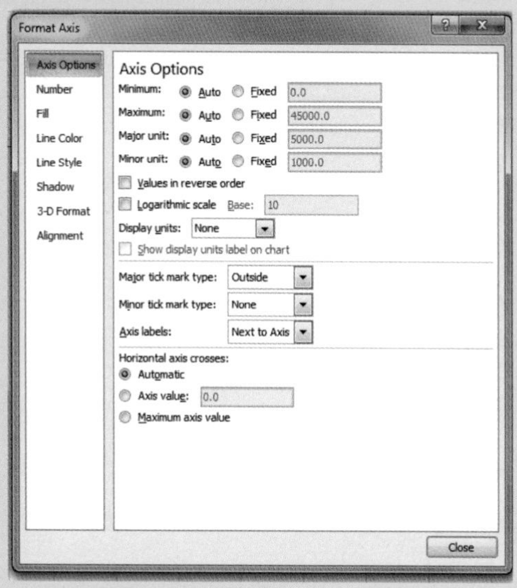

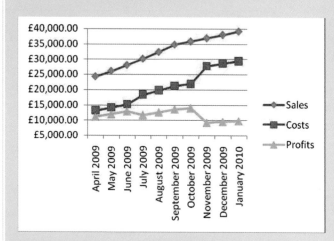

Figure 27.39 Format Axis dialogue box

In the Axis Options it shows that the minimum value is 0.0 and that the maximum is 45000.0. These values were set automatically when the chart was created. They can, however, be changed. Click on Fixed next to Minimum and Fixed next to Maximum. Set the minimum to 5000 and the maximum to 40000. This is how the graph should have changed:

Figure 27.40 Line graph with amended Y-axis

Colours

Using different colours is very effective at making data stand out – particularly where lines are close together.

You should always be careful about the colours that you use to make sure that their impact is not lost when, for example, your chart is printed on a black and white printer. In this instance it might be better to use shading and patterns.

Annotation

Sometimes, particularly with pie charts, additional annotation might be helpful to the reader.

Look again at the pie chart in Figure 27.30. In this example including the percentages is useful because of the closeness in value between the green and red wedges (trucks and decks). Having the percentages also makes it obvious that there is a lower value for decks than trucks. Would you have been able to see that clearly just looking at the chart itself if the percentages had not been displayed?

Select appropriate chart type

A competent developer will know **when** to use **which** type of chart. As we have already considered line, bar, column and pie charts, we will use this opportunity to explain about **xy (scatter) diagrams**.

An xy (scatter) diagram is a useful chart type as it allows a user to explore the relationship between two factors. For example, do ice cream sales go up in relation to the temperature? In order to test this, we will use some simple data collected over a year.

	Average temperature	Ice cream sales
January	7	150,000
February	6	125,000
March	8	146,000
April	7	175,000
May	11	201,000
June	14	224,000
July	16	245,000
August	17	260,000
September	15	240,000
October	13	213,000
November	9	170,000
December	3	224,000

Table 27.8 Data of ice cream sales over a year

The months are only included in the table to make sense of the data, but in actual fact, what we need is the temperature and the sales information.

When these are selected and applied to a scatter graph, we can see the following (Figure 27.41):

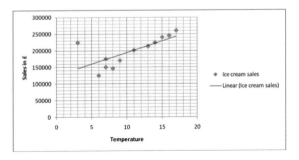

Figure 27.41 xy (scatter) diagram

Remember we are looking to see whether as the temperature goes up, the sales of ice creams go up.

The black line represents the relationship we would expect; in other words, we expect the sales to go up as temperature rises. The dots show the research and the closer they are to the line, the more we can say there is a direct relationship.

However, there is a single dot that appears to be really far away from the line. What is it about this particular dot? When we look back at the data, we can see that the sales for December are very high, when actually it is quite cold. Why is this? Because it is Christmas and many people like to buy ice cream at Christmas! This explains the anomaly!

Activity M

Chart types

Copy and complete the following grid to provide a record of the different types of chart and what they are used for.

Chart type	What it is used for

Justifying choices

When working as a developer you may well be asked regularly to explain and justify the choices you make.

When you are asked to justify your choices you should:

- Explain your choice
- Explain why you made it
- Explain why your choice was/is better than an alternative.

Make the grade   P6 M2 M3

For P6 you will create either a chart or a graph to visually represent information as defined by the user. In reality your teacher will give you some data and ask you to create the chart or graph.

To develop your work to meet M2, you will justify your reasons for choosing particular tools for presenting your data. Remember to explain why you made your particular choices rather than alternative ones.

And finally, for M3 you must show that you can interpret data from a model. You will need to manipulate the data so that you can make judgements – like, for example, putting sales information into ascending order to show which month was the lowest sales month and which was the highest. You might support this with a chart of the same information that shows the high points and low points in the sales data.

Remember you will need to make judgements and back them up with the evidence in your spreadsheet!

27.3 Be able to test and document spreadsheet models

This section will cover the following grading criteria: P7 P8

27.3.1 Test
Manual calculations

Checking calculations is a fundamental requirement for the spreadsheet developer.

It is usual to check the results of calculations from functions and formulae using an alternative method. This usually means using a calculator or mental maths to check the results. Any errors found will obviously need to be fixed.

All calculations should be tested and the test results recorded, along with any action that is required to fix the problems.

Sensible outcomes

The spreadsheet should also be thoroughly checked to make sure that the layout is appropriate and acceptable, and that the values are properly shown. For example, did you know that if a column is not wide enough then the number will not be displayed; the system will display hashes instead?

#####

This is so that no numbers can be missed because they are covered by another column!

Suitability for audience

As with all other developmental projects, spreadsheets should be evaluated to establish how well they meet user requirements.

Testing needs to be planned in advance, properly recorded and any evidence gathered. This could be in the form of screengrabs.

27.3.2 Documentation

User guide

For any developed software there is an expectation that there will be a user guide to support the program and it is no different if you are developing a spreadsheet model or a database. It needs to be clear to the user how the spreadsheet works and what he or she needs to do.

The guide will normally include a **technical specification** using traditional techniques such as diagrams, data tables, other images and text. It will also contain the

details of any formulae and functions that the spreadsheet contains.

These can easily be printed because the software allows the user to display either the numeric values or the formulae and functions.

To access this, you will need to click on the Show Formulas button in the Formula Auditing group on the Formulas ribbon.

The visual display will now change from showing only numbers, to showing numbers in cells that have nothing other than a value, and the formula or function information in any cells that contain a calculation.

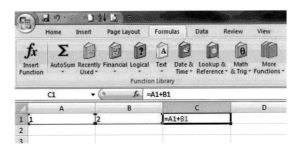

Figure 27.42 Formula view

In addition, the user guide should contain some troubleshooting advice or FAQs (frequently asked questions). For example, in the electronic Help system for Microsoft Excel 2007® there is a section called 'What happened to?' which guides a new user through the changes Microsoft® have made between the versions.

For example:

What happened to Excel® lists?

What happened to the File menu?

What happened to the Office Assistant?

This was necessary because the basic working of the application still has all the original features, but these are not in the same places as they were in the previous version where the first two menus were File and Edit!

If you find it difficult to decide what to put in the troubleshooting guide, look at the relevant section in another user guide for ideas.

Make the grade   P7   P8

P7 is complete when learners can show that they have produced and carried out a suitable test plan for a spreadsheet. It is likely that the practical evidence will contain screengrabs and an annotated test plan. For the final criterion in this unit (P8), the learners will produce spreadsheet documentation to include both a technical and a user guide for a spreadsheet model.

Activity N

Quiz

Try this quiz to test your understanding of spreadsheets. The answers are given at the back of the book.

1. What is a collection of spreadsheets in the same file called?
2. Name two different types of chart or graph.
3. What is the difference between absolute referencing and relative referencing?
4. What is a cell value?
5. Define a formula.
6. What does BODMAS stand for?
7. What is a two-stage calculation?
8. What is a data series?
9. Give an example of a data series.
10. What is a range?
11. What does the AutoSum do?
12. Name three logical functions.
13. What does paste link do?
14. What is a file path?
15. Give three examples of cell formatting.

Achieving Success

In order to achieve each unit, you will complete a series of coursework activities. Each time you hand in work, your tutor will return this to you with a record of your achievement.

This particular unit has 13 criteria to meet: 8 Pass, 3 Merit and 2 Distinction.

For a **Pass** you must achieve **all 8** Pass criteria.

For a **Merit** you must achieve **all 8** Pass **and all 3** Merit criteria.

For a **Distinction** you must achieve **all 8** Pass, **all 3** Merit criteria **and both** Distinction criteria.

Help with assessment

Your tutor will give you one or more assignments that you will complete as coursework. This could consist of:

- Posters
- Assignments
- Presentations
- Spreadsheet model(s)
- Screen shots and printouts
- Test plans and results
- Written evaluations
- Informal report(s).

You should read the guidance given for each of the criteria (shown across the unit) carefully and remember to check your work.

Further reading

Textbooks

Heathcote, P. *Successful ICT Projects in Excel* (Payne-Gallway Publishers, 2002) ISBN 1903112710

Heathcote, R. *Further Excel 2000–2003* (Payne-Gallway Publishers, 2004) ISBN 1904467768

Heathcote, R. *ICT Projects for GCSE* (Payne-Gallway Publishers, 2002) ISBN 1903112699

Websites

http://office.microsoft.com/en-us/excel/default.aspx

http://support.openoffice.org/index.html (has links to a number of Calc tutorials)

www.free-training-tutorial.com/

Unit 2

Activity D

Calculating the bill!

Item price	Quantity	Sub-total	VAT (at 20%)	Price
£18.50	10	£185.00	£37.00	£222.00
£11.90	5	£ 59.50	£11.90	£ 71.40
£ 1.95	1	£ 1.95	£ 0.39	£ 2.34
£ 2.50	2	£ 5.00	£ 1.00	£ 6.00
	Totals	£251.45	£50.29	£301.74

Unit 4

Activity L

Estimating costs

Total cost £4,310

Cost per delegate £538.75

Activity M

Estimating returns

7 canvassers

£3,255 per month

The canvassers will earn £976.50.

The marketing company will receive £651.00.

The charity will receive £1627.50.

Activity N

Breakeven

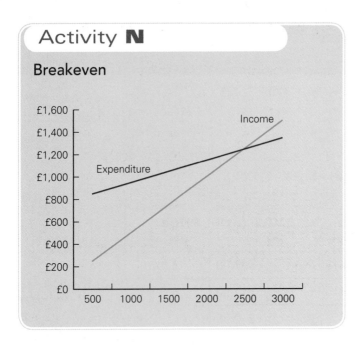

Activity O

'What if?'

Product X	
Ingredient A	3.47
Ingredient B	6.21
Ingredient C	2.22
Ingredient D	4.69
Ingredient E	6.97
Total cost for 10	23.56
Markup	23.50%
Resale value for 10	29.10
Resale price each	2.91

Product X	
Ingredient A	3.92
Ingredient B	6.21
Ingredient C	2.22
Ingredient D	6.57
Ingredient E	6.97
Total cost for 10	25.89
Markup	23.50%
Resale value for 10	31.97
Resale price each	3.20

Unit 7

Activity B

Quiz

1. Any two from: buying a replacement will be more expensive, replacements are now rare, the experience already exists to replace it (no training required).

2. Any three from: changed user requirements, better compatibility, increased capacity or speed, improved reliability or software requirements.

3. Electrostatic discharge occurs when static electricity which has built up on a surface is discharged to earth.

4. Equipment damage, loss or corruption of data and loss of service.

5. Keep components in anti-static bags and use anti-static wrist straps and mats when handling components.

6. Cross

7. Training needs, compatibility concerns, safe and lawful decommissioning for older equipment.

8. Make multiple backups of the data – especially on different media and keep in different locations!

Activity C

Slots and connectors

1. USB – Universal Series Bus, a common slot for connecting external devices e.g. mouse, keyboard, camera, scanner, printer etc.

2. PCI and PCIe – Peripheral Component Interconnect and Peripheral Component Interconnect Express, an internal slot for connecting expansion cards to a PC's motherboard.

3. SATA and IDE – Serial Advanced Technology Attachment and Integrated Drive Electronics, both interfaces for connecting hard disks.

4. DDR DIMM – Double Data Rate Dual Inline Memory Module, a type of memory slot on the motherboard.

5. AGP – Accelerated Graphics Port, an older interface on the motherboard for connecting graphics cards.

Unit 9

Activity N

End of unit crossword

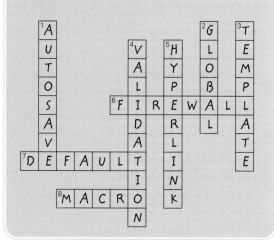

Unit 16

Activity H

Quiz

1. Any three advantages from the following:

    Easy to use
    Records are easy to access and retrieve
    Data can easily be manipulated in many different ways (for example, trends can be established, data can be viewed from different perspectives)
    Data can be validated to ensure that it is accurate
    Easy to store

    Any three disadvantages from the following:

    Database structures must be carefully developed to ensure that they work as efficiently as possible
    There are laws that control the use of databases
    Many people feel that simply too much information is stored about us
    The costs of technology can be prohibitive

2. Any two from: Table, Form, Query, Report

3. Text, Number, Currency, Date/Time

4. Validation is a process whereby the computer has been set up to check user inputs are of a particular data type, are within a given range or have a specified format.

5. Datasheet view

6. The default size is 255.

7. A list box offers a user a list of options he or she can choose from as a valid input. It reduces the potential for incorrect inputs.

8. A Wizard is a series of programmed steps that a user will go through to create an output (e.g. a table, a query or a report).

9. A query interrogates a database using criteria.

10. A footer is additional detail that is displayed at the bottom of each page of a query, form or report. Information may include page numbers, dates, author's details.

11. Landscape view has the paper with the longest edge at the top and the shortest edge down the side (the page is wide).

12. Portrait view has the paper with the shortest edge at the top and the longest edge down the side (the paper is tall).

Unit 17

Activity E

Quiz

1. A web server is a high-end server processing HTTP requests from clients to serve HTML web pages and associated assets.

2. A TLD is a top level domain; there are currently 14 of them named.

3. A domain name registrar is a company which manages the assignment and registration of internet domain names within a particular country.

4. An intranet is a website, typically belonging to a company or organisation, which is accessed through its LAN or VPN.

5. HTML is hypertext markup language – a series of tags used to define the structure and content of a web page and how one page is linked to others.

6. Any three from layout, formatting, navigation, interactivity etc.

7. a. <HEAD> defines the HEADING section of the web page

    b. <TITLE> defines the web page's title – as shown in the browser bar

    c. <IMG> defines the Image tag used to incorporate pictures in a web page

    d. <P> marks the start of a paragraph

8. FTP (file transfer protocol) client or web development software with FTP functionality.

9. To capture user input in an organised fashion, e.g. for website or customer feedback.

10. An image map with clickable hotspots.

11. Any three from tables, frames, templates, navigation bars, rollovers, image galleries etc.

12. Frames

Unit 18

Activity B

Interpreting operators

1. True
2. True
3. True
4. True
5. True
6. True
7. False
8. True

Activity C

Understanding sequence, selection and iteration

1. A, B, C, D

   A, B, E
2. A, B, C, A, B, C

   A, B, D, A, B, D

   A, B, C, A, B, D

   A, B, D, A, B, C

Unit 27

Activity H

Calculations

1. 3
2. 35
3. 59
4. 56
5. 26

Activity I

Logical?

1. **FALSE** (X is not greater than 50, it is 50!)
2. **TRUE** (Y is indeed less than or equal to 100)
3. **TRUE** (Y is greater than 50 and X is less than 100)
4. **TRUE** (While Y is not less than 50, X is equal to 50)
5. **FALSE** (X is equal to or greater than 50, but Y is not less than 50. Because both are not true, the condition must resolve as false)

Activity N

Quiz

1. A workbook

2. Any two from: pie chart, bar chart, column chart, line graph

3. With absolute referencing any cells that have been identified with a $ symbol will not change when pasted to other cells. With relative referencing, when a cell is copied and pasted the cell references change in relation to their last position.

4. The number or text in the cell

5. A formula is a sum that has been created using operators such as plus, minus, divide and multiply.

6. Brackets Over Division Multiplication Addition and Subtraction.

7. A two-stage calculation is where two different calculations are carried out at the same time in the same cell.

8. A data series is a range of values that are related to each other.

9. January, February, March or Jan, Feb, Mar or 1, 2, 3 or 1, 3, 5 (any valid series is accepted)

10. A range is a series of consecutive cells.

11. The AutoSum automatically adds up a range of cells.

12. IF, AND, OR

13. Paste link is used when a figure in a spreadsheet (taken from another area of the spreadsheet or even another spreadsheet or workbook) is pasted with update functionality.

14. A file path is the drive and folder in which a file has been stored.

15. Any from the following: background colour, font colour, shading, border.

Index

A

abuse, of IT 28–9
accessibility features 61
acquired images
  clip art library 321–2
  image copyright 322
  process 318–21
ActiveX controls 363
addressing
  DNS (domain name server) 167
  IP (internet protocol) address 167, 187–8
  MAC (media access control) address 166–7
  TCP/IP networks 166, 169–70
  testing 182
Adobe Photoshop® 303–4
advertisements 95
algorithms 173, 289–90
analysts 42
anti-static wrist straps 67, 114
applications programmers 42
assignment statements 265
AutoCorrect 148
automations, spreadsheet
  ActiveX controls 363
  cells, locking/unlocking 101
  Control toolbox 363–4
  graphs and charts 99
  macros 99–100, 362–3
  Paste Link 363
  user interface 101
  Visual Basic 364
AutoRecover 142
AutoSave 149–50
AutoSummarize 148–9

B

backing storage 59
backplane, motherboard 52, 64
bandwidth 162, 166
bar charts 361

BD (Blu-ray Disc) 51–2
binary instructions 258
BIOS (Basic Input Output System) 126
bitmap images 303, 308–9
bits 47
blogs 18–19, 160, 232, 233
bluetooth technology 163
body language 6–7
Braille software products 16–17
Broadband 27, 177
browser plug-ins 254
bus networks 165
business information
  alternatives, looking at 92
  constraints 85–6
  copyright 95
  cost effectiveness 85
  costs 92–3
  functionality 92
  investigation 79–81
  management decisions 84–5
  outcomes, expected 81–4
  performance 92
  price 92
  research 91–2, 95
  sources 93–5
business plans
  inputs 88–9
  outputs 89
  processes 89
  research 90
  timelines 89–90
business problems
  company website 87
  new product/service, launching 87–8
  system upgrades 88
  wireless office 86–7
business requirements
  business plans 88–90
  business problems 86–8
  information gathering 84–6
  information requirements 79–86

business solutions
  evaluating 105–6
  presenting 103–6
bytes 47, 292

C

C++® 278
cascading style sheets *see* CSS (cascading style sheets)
CD 51–2
CD-R (compact disc recordable) 302
CD-ROM (compact disc-read only memory) 302
cells
  autofilling 330, 340
  content *versus* value 345
  formatting 359
  linking 340–3
  locking/unlocking 101
  merging 360
  ranges 351
  referencing, absolute and relative 334, 339–40
central processing unit *see* CPU (central processing unit)
character recognition software 49
charts
  annotation 368
  colour, using 368
  formatting 360–1
  labels, and chart axes 366–7
  titles 366
  types 361–2, 368–9
classes 261
client/server networks 165, 166
clip art library 321–2
coaxial cable 174–5, 176
colour balance 313–14
colour change 314–15
colour depth 315–16
column charts 361